Wilkie Collins and Copyright

Wilkie Collins and Copyright

Artistic Ownership
in the Age of the Borderless Word

Sundeep Bisla

The Ohio State University Press

Columbus

Library of Congress Cataloging-in-Publication Data
Bisla, Sundeep, 1968–
Wilkie Collins and copyright : artistic ownership in the age of the borderless word / Sundeep Bisla.
p. cm.
Includes bibliographical references and index.
ISBN-13: 978-0-8142-1235-6 (cloth : alk. paper)
ISBN-10: 0-8142-1235-2 (cloth : alk. paper)
ISBN-13: 978-0-8142-9337-9 (cd-rom)
ISBN-10: 0-8142-9337-9 (cd-rom)
Collins, Wilkie, 1824–1889—Criticism and interpretation. 2. Intellectual property in literature.
3. Intellectual property—History—19th century. 4. Copyright—History—19th century. I. Title.
PR4497.B57 2013
823'.8—dc23

2013010878

Cover design by Laurence J. Nozik
Type set in Adobe Garamond Pro
Printed by Thomson-Shore, Inc.

∞ The paper used in this publication meets the minimum requirements of the American National
Standard for Information Sciences—Permanence of Paper for Printed Library Materials. ANSI
Z39.48–1992.

9 8 7 6 5 4 3 2 1

CONTENTS

⊶ ACKNOWLEDGMENTS ⊷

AN INTERNATIONAL Postgraduate Research Award, University Postgraduate Research Award, and Overseas Postgraduate Research Scholarship funded by the University of Sydney and the Government of Australia allowed me the time to complete the research and early drafting of this study. A semester's research leave from the City University of New York allowed me the time to complete part of the writing of it.

Many friends and colleagues encouraged me along the way. Colleagues who generously commented on parts of the work include Paula Backsheider, Judith Barbour, Nicholas Birns, Deirdre Coleman, Simon During, Penelope Ingram, Bill Maidment, Anne McCarthy, J. Hillis Miller, Ariadna Pop, Véronique Pouillard, Simon Petch, and Joseph S. Walker. I thank John Maynard for having been a friend and supporter of this project, and its author, for many years. I also thank former CUNY Chancellor Matthew Goldstein for his support. My teachers, especially Christopher Braider, David Bromwich, Jacques Derrida, Jean-François Lyotard, William Maidment, J. Hillis Miller, Thomas Richards, Mark Rose, and Alan Trachtenberg, had profound effects on the shape that this argument took. I thank the many people who responded with probing questions and comments when portions of this book were presented as talks at the University of Sydney, Columbia University, and the CUNY Graduate Center.

I thank for their assistance Eva Ksiazek and Peter McNiece of the University of Sydney's Fisher Library, as well as the staffs of Columbia's Butler Library and Diamond Law Library, the New York Public Library, Yale's Sterling Library and Goldman Law Library, Cambridge University Library, and the library of St. John's College, Cambridge.

I would also like to thank Sandy Crooms, my editor at Ohio State University Press, for her unflagging and unfailingly congenial support of this study and the anonymous reviewers of the Press for their many helpful suggestions.

I gratefully acknowledge permission to reprint material from essays originally appearing in *boundary 2, Dickens Studies Annual, Genre,* and *Victorian Literature and Culture.* This material has been extensively revised.

I thank my loving wife Caroline for her humor and help at crucial stages near the work's completion. This book is dedicated to my parents, Amarjit Singh and Raghubir Kaur Bisla. I thank them for their unshakeable confidence over the years.

PREFACE

A Spot of Ink,
More Than a Spot of Bother

"I made a private inquiry last week, Mr Superintendent," [Cuff] said. "At one end of the inquiry there was a murder, and at the other end there was a spot of ink on a tablecloth that nobody could account for. In all my experience along the dirtiest ways of this dirty little world, I have never met with such a thing as a trifle yet."

—Collins, *The Moonstone* 136

THE BEGINNING of a project of long duration—and this project, having occupied its author for over a decade, would certainly qualify as such—is often difficult to conclusively determine. Nevertheless, even now I can still clearly recall the moment I first became conscious of its subject, the author Wilkie Collins. While an undergraduate at Harvard I would occasionally come across book sales at the back entrance of the university library. These were literary housekeeping events, designed more probably to free up space on the shelves than generate revenue, in which a thrifty student rummaging through a wide variety of texts—for one reason or another being "released," as though back into the wild—might pick up something interesting for a reasonable price. It was at one of these potentially magic-filled Ivy League bazaars that I one day encountered on the surprise-laden trolley a copy of Collins's intriguingly-titled *The Evil Genius: A Domestic Story* (1886). "Here is a prize," I may well have thought to myself. The book was inscribed as a gift to the college by one "Samuel H. Scudder of Cambridge, 28 July 1886." Scudder, as I would come to learn later, had been in his time a well-known

entomologist, early editor of the journal *Science,* and at one point assistant
to Louis Agassiz, the famous nineteenth-century naturalist and professor of
zoology and geology. I bought his book—or should I say, rather, to be precise Collins's book—for the nominal price marked in at the top corner of
the inside cover, a price not significantly greater or less, but bringing with
it a more interesting backstory, than those inscribed in the other books on
the trolley. The book came back with me to my River House dorm room
for the cost of a whole half a dollar.

My new possession had such brittle pages that it was clear it would not
survive much further handling. I resolved to read it nevertheless, being careful not to do any more damage than time and the acid in the paper had
already wrought. I cannot explain why I was drawn to this particular work
among the dozens available that day. Perhaps it was the intriguing title that
captivated me, a title made even more alluring by a gradual loss in our general cultural understanding of the once common phrase describing what
might be called one's "bad angel" or "false god." I must undoubtedly also
have been attracted—capitalism having its way with me—by the low, low
price. But as enchanted as I may have been by the opportunity to buy a book
so old for so little, I was still quite aware of this copy's serious defects. Few
other books for sale that day had seemed so far along the path to giving up
the ghost, if not also as they more expansively tag it in Germany, the *geist.*
Perhaps in purchasing it I had had vague hopes that, despite its condition, it
would turn out to be one of those "finds" that make such intriguing viewing
of our modern day television antiques shows. The book turned out to be a
"find" all right, but not one of that particular type.

Back then, I was not well versed in the to-ings and fro-ings of international commerce. I had yet to learn that the purchase of nineteenth-century
English literature "on the cheap"—with no provision being made for pay-
ment to the book's foreign author—was something of an American tradition. The nominal price and the book's status as having been "released" from
(abjured by?) the "Harvard College Library" in particular and the American
Academy in general were just faint indications. The narrative contained (if
only barely) within the binding would point me toward the larger picture:
in his tale, Collins touches for a brief moment on the now nearly-forgot-
ten, century-long Anglo-American literary property war when he places the
lawyer Samuel Sarrazin into dinner conversation with Randall Linley, the
brother of the wayward husband at the center of the narrative's intrigues.
Linley's reference to the American people as "the most hospitable people in
the world" prompts a surprising reaction:

Mr. Sarrazin shook his head; he had a case of copyright in hand just then. "A people to be pitied," he said.

"Why?"

"Because their government forgets what is due to the honor of the nation."

"How?"

"In this way. The honor of a nation which confers right of property in works of art produced by its own citizens, is surely concerned in protecting from theft works of art produced by other citizens."[1] (*Evil Genius* 115)

This pointed, politically-charged reference to the copyright struggle, inserted into a book intended for an audience that would at the time have included many Americans—the scientist Samuel Scudder included—intrigued me. What kind of author was this Collins? Sarrazin's remark launched me into several years of research on the Anglo-American copyright dispute—carried out in the relatively neutral mid-way region of Australia—culminating in a PhD thesis examining Collins's major works viewed in the light of an intellectual property quarrel that, I came to understand, never stopped consuming him (as well as his good friend Dickens). For an immigrant to America, intent (much like Collins's character Professor Pesca) on being properly domesticated into my adoptive homeland, the history disclosed by this research was quite the revelation. Having emigrated from India when very young, and having been educated wholly in American schools, I was naturally, and admittedly somewhat naively, predisposed to think my new country capable of doing no wrong. I was surprised and dismayed then to read, over and over, in both English and American nineteenth-century jour-

---

1. This was a timely political intervention on Collins's part. Just prior to the serialization of *The Evil Genius,* the U.S. Congress had considered several international copyright bills, in 1882, 1883, 1884, and three times in 1885 (Solberg, "Bibliography" 788–89). This period also saw much European action on intellectual property matters, in the resolutions of, for example, the Paris Convention for the Protection of Industrial Property of 1883 and the Berne Convention for the Protection of Literary and Artistic Works of 1886. An international copyright bill between the United States and Britain would finally be passed, perhaps in some small part because of Collins's shaming influence both overtly and subtly throughout his career, only in early 1891 (Clark 149). Alas, this came a year and a half after his death in late 1889. Thus Collins could be said, so to speak, to have missed his dead-line. (We need not be too melancholy, however; not only would Collins's darker side have understood the need to honor the "breaking" ability of language, as I will be terming it in this study, but his lighter side could console itself with the fact that the Senate had introduced Senator Chase's bill on January 21, 1886—"destined to become famous, and finally, five years later to be enacted into law"—and passed it on May 9, 1888, sending it on to the House for debate [Solberg, "Copyright Law Reform" 55–56]).

nals, of the American government's iniquitous stance in relation to English authors.

But at this point I did not comprehend just how close I myself was to the controversy. For the discussion between Sarrazin and Linley, it would turn out, was a prescient comment on the very pages within which I had first met it, as I came to the surprising realization—feeling myself akin to one of Collins's many revelation-fated characters (which in a sense I was, having been following the path of a mystery Collins himself had laid down)—that I had been lured by economics (and admittedly also Collins's sensational titling) into harboring in my library a pirate American edition of the story! My bargain copy being practically given away on that fateful day outside Widener Library had been published in 1886 by M. J. Ivers & Co. of 86 Nassau Street, New York—not one of Collins's authorized American publishers[2]—as part of its "American Series," bearing a title page proudly misproclaiming Collins "The Author of 'The Lady in White.'"[3] I realized that while reading Sarrazin's complaint I had been holding in my hands a book turned against itself, so to speak. That this book's contents should have been protesting against its own particular illicit format was an irony that I found quite amusing.

But in looking at the larger context, I soon realized that this irony was in essence not an actual one; it was the commonest thing in the world for a book to be "turned against itself" (the quotation marks being this time necessary). I came to realize that, at a certain level, every one of them was. My "improper" American copy, simply in a more overt manner than usual, was bearing out the implications of the paradox being enacted in a title such as *The Evil Genius: A Domestic Story* (a title suggesting a split psyche contrasted with a more-unified-than-not domesticity). An unauthorized American copy of an authorized English original, it was overtly demonstrating something that too often remained hidden. It was bringing to the fore (and actuating) the inherent alienability of writing, an alienability that in our society was always being disguised or covered over in various ways—one being the material form of the book. Literary piracy, as opposed to "proper" publication, more readily disclosed (but not for a theoretically different reason) a struggle

---

2. Seville remarks (*Internationalisation* 299) that this company was still at this practice in January of 1891 when it issued a piracy of one of the three versions of Kipling's *The Light That Failed*.

3. This mistake could have been the actual beginning of this study, as I was undoubtedly prompted by it to wonder, somewhere below the level of consciousness, what sort of publishing environment it might have been that would have allowed for such an apparently self-mistaken error on a title page—clearly one in which the author himself was decisively alienated from certain manifestations of the finished product.

between, for want of better terms, the material and immaterial elements of the book that was constantly underway, a struggle that was always already undergirding, often only implicitly, negotiations concerning the attempted control of language.

That is, while books were manifestations of an overt physicality—indeed in some sense could not avoid seeming just that—the "writing" in them was anything but foundedly material. That writing (another term for it might be "text") was not at all as "set" (in the sense of "frozen" or "materialized") as the book-as-object would be making it out to be. The book's material "form" was thus, almost of itself, belying the radical alienability of its immaterial "content." Viewed from this perspective, the book-as-form was rendered a lie of false solidity (a lie in our own time being highlighted by the advent of our constantly refillable and erasable "E-readers" and "Tablet" computers). Thus one could say that this book that you are reading, in whatever format you currently encounter it, is essentially about the bloodless specter of the present-day E-reader haunting, nay, actively pursuing, Wilkie Collins through the nighttime streets of 1850s and 60s England. That is, in essence, a book's "immaterial side" could be actuated at any time—that book thereby being turned against "itself," against its manifest physicality—and, as a result, an author's work could be moved almost completely out of his or her control, an unhappy truth to which Collins in his life would be especially sensitive and in his narratives would be continually attesting. Thus, all books were in a sense misrepresentations, beautiful lies, evil genius-ridden entities purporting to stand as unified domesticities. In bringing out into the open the possibility for the technology of the book to be co-opted against its author's wishes, in other words, for a "domestic" story to be forcibly othered, my pirate copy had been simply highlighting the conflict taking place (often only silently) between each and every book-form in every library in the world and its text. Thus, perhaps each of these complex mechanisms, that, like *Don Juan*'s moon, "look so modest all the while," on some level, could justifiably be entitled *The Evil Genius: A Domestic Story,* and certainly, focusing more close to home, all of Collins's major novels could be entitled *A Would-be Domestic Story Plagued by an Evil Genius,* or, in other words, *Wilkie Collins and Copyright*—or, considering further, *"Wilkie Collins" and Copyright.*

The quotation marks were once more necessary because, I came to realize, this fissuring of Collins's book did not halt at its surface; the book's lack of singular identity seemed also to become, in an example of contagious textualization, Collins's characters' and even his own. This subversive contagion meshed well with Collins's deep-seated philosophy, evident throughout his career, regarding the essential provisionality of naming. In a strictly Collinsian world, all names, including the author's, would necessarily always already arrive ineffectually enclosed by quotation marks as the identities those names only half-effectually captured came to be shown to be situated at the cusp of a fundamental instability or not-at-homeness. For example, looking more closely at Collins's tale, I found it characteristic of this author that the narrative should have been unable to decide whether Sarrazin was an Englishman or a Frenchman. Calling him "a curious mixture of both," the story continued, "A British subject by birth, and a thoroughly competent and trustworthy man, Mr. Sarrazin labored under one inveterate delusion; he firmly believed that his original French nature had been completely eradicated, under the influence of our insular climate and our insular customs" (*Evil Genius* 101). The irrepressibly bifurcated nature of this character seemed a clear reference to the book's title. Here, it was evident that the would-be homogenous, domestic, insular identity/entity/"story" was in the situation of continually falling prey to its (patently unacknowledged) evil genius.

That Sarrazin should have turned out to be interested in copyright caused me then to wonder about the nature of that concept itself. After spending a good deal of time researching its history, I realized that something similar had continually been occurring in that realm as well. Though English copyright had over its history attempted to concentrate solely on the protection of monetary returns, nevertheless the French conceptions of a protection of "moral rights" and of the "*droit d'auteur*"[4]—the question of a pound of flesh, so to speak, rather than of pounds and shillings—had made themselves felt in a surprising number of English decisions and statutes. English copyright, I came to understand, had always been haunted by its own evil genius, as its "French" side periodically crossed the Channel to teach it an important lesson: that the loss of money in relation to copyright disputes was in many cases just a sign of something deeper, something more threatening at work. The fact that one's literary creation could be alienated to such an extent as to allow, and in some cases legally justify, the denial of recompense for the efforts expended in composing it was merely a signal that the author-in-language him- or herself was not at all as *unified* an entity as had originally been hoped. Sarrazin's criticism of a lack of copyright protection in the U.S. for British artists was a local effect of the more general issue signaled in the book's title. The author's always already having agreed

---

4. On moral rights and the *droit d'auteur* see Edelman, Edelman, and Brown.

to embark on a negotiation with language had rendered him or her vulnerable to an undesired alienation, had opened up the domesticity to (self-) alienation at the hands of an ill-controlled evil genius.

Discussions of linguistic repetition, wherever I encountered them, whether in eighteenth-century legal discourse, nineteenth-century fiction, or twentieth-century literary theory, all seemed to be pointing to a curious state of affairs, a state of internal division, of the sign, the text, the book, the author. I began at this point to formulate a question that while quite dauntingly large in scope nevertheless seemed to afford at least the glimmer of the hope of a solution: What was the source of this evil genius afflicting copyright, the book form, and more generally the author-in-print? This question led me (after brief macro-level forays into postcolonially-focused critique, in the form of the hypothesis of the Americans attempting to express a new-found independence and protectionism through the exploitation of language's alienability, and historical contingency—led criticism, in the form of the hypothesis of transportation and communication advances broadening the Victorian literary marketplace and making possible certain intriguingly-narratable anecdotes of serviceable conduits having been sensationally exploited) inexorably to the micro-level concept of "iterability" first introduced to me by Jacques Derrida, a philosopher/theorist whose writings continually track situations of unacknowledged internal division of the type denoted by the juxtaposition of the multiplicity inherent in an "evil [vs. good] genius" and the idealized singularity inherent in a "domestic story." (Though macro-level, or so called "historical," investigations had for a good while dominated the field in which I was conducting my investigations, it gradually became clear to me that investigations of linguistic alienability situated at such a remove from the region of actual interest would have to remain somewhat significantly empty at their theoretical center, a center of paramount concern to my particularly philosophically perspicacious subject Collins). To cite just one example from amongst the many acknowledgments by Derrida of the internal division made possible by writing's undelimitable repeatability, I would repeat his citation of a line from a letter by Rimbaud: "*Je est un autre*. I is another one" ("Justices" 228). I found this kind of thinking—both in form as well as content or rather, more properly, somewhere before and beyond the form/content distinction—to fit well with a thinking that could formulate Franklin Blake's famous, self-othering revelation in *The Moonstone*: "I had discovered Myself as the Thief" (359). My encounter with Derrida's and Collins's conception of a surprising internal division made possible by the

iterability of the mark thus led, ironically, to the creation of this "book"—
a creature of airy substance if ever there was one—that you have, in one
form or another, before you at this moment.

OF COURSE, at first glance, it seemed hardly sensible to be "going post-
structural" or "theoretical" in my interpretation of the title *The Evil Genius:
A Domestic Story,* as there were available to me perfectly adequate surface
explanations of it. Indeed, this title's interpretation seemed immediately
to be marked out by a ready, almost too ready, congeniality of two particular contexts to which my author himself seemed to be *inviting* me to
have recourse (and this in a day and age when "theory" seemed particularly
out of vogue). For instance, in the passage already cited, the Primal Scene
of domestic bliss lost, if you will, the lawyer Sarrazin alludes to Herbert
Linley's "domestic troubles"—for the man has recently separated from his
wife—just before going on to note that the United States defends "works
of art produced by its own citizens," that is, defends "domestic" productions (*Evil Genius* 115). The term "domestic" in Collins's subtitle thus could
be—indeed seemed to be crying out to be—interpreted in either marital or
nationalistic terms as opposed to those associated with a unifed psyche or
textual identity. That is, Collins's choice of title seemed to be more than adequately justified by the primary subject of the narrative—cobbled together
by an elderly and increasingly ill writer intent on making enough money,
ironically, to keep his own *two* London households running smoothly—
being a fairly unremarkable family divorce drama, notable solely as a very
early representative of the genre, as well as by the fact of the text's potentially
serving as a domestic English good, that is, a portion of the "gross domestic product" of England. Regarded from the latter perspective, the subtitle
could be understood as a type of copyright claim against the predations
of foreign would-be infringers. Clearly, one did not at all need to broach
philosophical questions related to the materiality/immateriality and subject
constitution/textuality divides to come away feeling satisfied (improperly
satisfied, that is, but satisfied nonetheless) that one had adequately plumbed
the depths of "the meaning" of Collins's title. (In the same way, simple
"space issues" appeared more than adequately to explain the American academy's off-loading of its nineteenth-century guilty conscience at its back door
sales in the early 1990s.) This dictating to his critics as to how he should
be read, and often indeed as a result was read, I came to understand, was
Collins's particular gift. It was Collins's talent to render his general readers
and critics alike either surface readers or overinterpreters, never anything in

between, and in either case manifestly his subjects.[5] In reading Collins, the continual temptation to settle for one or another of his screening interpretations was a difficult one to resist, as who would want to invite the charge of being an "overinterpreter," especially of a writer seemingly so simple in style?

But this enforced subjection, I intuited, was, like all imposed subjections, crying out to be resisted. From early on in his career, Collins had been interested in screening his intentions, usually ones dealing with textuality. He had learned from a variety of sources, particularly Poe's "The Purloined Letter," which he had imitated in the youthful and undoubtedly mockingly-titled "A Stolen Letter" (1854), that the best place to hide them was sometimes in plain sight. Collins's imitation exploited Poe's strategy of having the appearance of openness or uncoveredness, paradoxically, be itself a path to the discovery of a deeply-hidden secret. In Poe's story, it will be recalled, one of the primary signs drawing Dupin's attention to the much besought letter during his first visit to the Minister D——'s apartment is "the hyperobtrusive situation of this document, full in the view of every visiter [sic]" (Poe, Poetry 696). Similarly, in "A Stolen Letter," the unnamed narrator, an attorney, has just entered the hotel room of the unscrupulous ex-clerk Mr. Davager who is away at the moment. Our narrator is looking for the incriminating letter the disclosure of which threatens to ruin the character of the father of the fiancée of his client. At this dramatic moment, he finds the room, strangely, a mass of open accesses:

> Either Mr. Davager had ridden out with the letter about him, or he had left it in some safe hiding-place in his room. I suspected it to be in his room, for a reason that will a little astonish you—his trunk, his dressing-case, and all the drawers and cupboards were left open. I knew my customer, and I thought this extraordinary carelessness on his part rather suspicious. (*Mad Monkton* 35)

And *I* knew *my* customer. Less important than noting *what* the narrator does next—memorandum in pocketbook found, protruding thread in carpet discovered, new mocking letter (*à la* Poe) produced, and that galling doppelganger/non-doppelganger substituted for the original[6]—is remarking

---

5. The implicit equation between opium or alcohol addiction and the reading of Collins's thrilling fictions is one that is felt with good reason by commentators on his works. For example, the playwright Watts Phillips in his satirical 1865 production *The Woman in Mauve* has a character portray reading *The Woman in White* as "a sort of literary dram-drinking" that could, if unwatched, end one up in "Mental delirium tremens" (10).

6. The whole of Collins's project in his major fictions is "foreshadowed" here in these situation-alike—if not quite (at this point in his career) look-alike—texts fulfilling very different functions. The

how he has been led to the solution of the mystery. The open dressing-case, trunk, and drawers are made by Collins's narrator to work against themselves and to end up *arousing* rather than assuaging suspicion. I asked myself, "Did we have offered here a lesson in how to read the works of Wilkie Collins perhaps?" I determined thereafter never to be too quickly accepting "surface evidence" as conclusive in this author's narratives.

And, indeed, applying my newly-acquired knowledge to the interpretation of the title in question, I came to suspect that the facility of the possibility of side-stepping the "difficult" or "philosophical" level of interpretation of Collins's 1886 title had been a facility itself set in place through conscious design, my particular text's subtitle's reference to a "domestic" story having been craftily contextualized by Collins to offer his readers the "outs" of not one but two possible first-level interpretations. My own "Secret Dictate," passed on from *Robinson Crusoe* to Gabriel Betteredge in *The Moonstone* to me—and perhaps also from Daniel Defoe to Collins through both writers' interest in the ambiguous term "account" (money, narrative)[7]—kept leading me onwards. The existence of the obvious readings flagrantly offering themselves up in Collins's works I suspected to be both no accident and also far from the whole story. And indeed in reading Collins extensively I found that the doubling (occasionally tripling) up of messages was one of the more pronounced characteristics of his style (the obvious [too obvious] sexual reading of Basil's dream being the next instance I encountered). This author repeatedly "layered" his messages, obscuring subtle points underneath more obvious meanings, inserting basements at which the reader could exit should the pressures of the as-yet-only-whispered-about sub-basements grow too much for him or her to bear. This repeated Collinsian strategy caused me to be *more* rather than less supicious that something else might be going on, not just with regard to this title but also with regard to his more complex productions, the masterpieces of the 1860s.

I admit there can be no conclusive end to this type of game. The critic is simply caught in a situation of unceasing and increasing paranoia. Ironically, it was a paranoia of an entirely different order than that which was usually understood to grip the reader of this particular author's thrilling

---

narrator's letter substituting for Davager's is an early example of a new, unstained nightgown marked "Franklin Blake" substituting in *The Moonstone*—and nearly, but only nearly, making up the difference—for an old, stained one marked in the same way.

7. In *The Moonstone,* Betteredge ends his narrative, making up the first period of the story, with a quotation from Defoe that actualizes this particular pun: "May you find in these leaves of my writing, what *Robinson Crusoe* found in his experience on the desert island—namely, 'something to comfort yourselves from, and to set in the Description of Good and Evil, on the Credit Side of the Account.'—Farewell" (233).

stories. For it was the most natural thing in the world, when reading Wilkie Collins, that "master of mystery" or "father of sensation," to be worried. *I* was worried, however, not because I was continually expecting another surprising turn-about or unexpected plot twist around each and every narrative "corner," or conclusion of a serial part, but rather because I feared coming later to find myself not to have been reading Collins *closely enough.* This author gives one the distinct impression that he is there ahead of his readers, especially the professional ones, the reviewers and literary critics. One can never be sure of having completely fathomed him. Nevertheless, I am satisfied at having made in this study at least a start at having assessed Collins's profound thinking in something like the serious light I believe it deserves, through, as an initial step, my simply having avoided some of the false leads mischievously set up by this author himself to distract and mislead his readers.[8] The several puns and contradictions in the title and subtitle of this chance find on a library sales book trolley were collectively the figurative tall thread sticking up in the carpet. They were the opening clue in the unraveling of a mystery, the largest and most intricate that the remarkable mind of Wilkie Collins ever created.

Sarrazin's complaint in *The Evil Genius* had been in its purport, as I say, a revelation for me, as also had been what the simple existence of that complaint signaled, Collins's apparently very serious belief—undoubtedly encouraged by his friend Dickens—in the transformative power of fiction. I was intrigued to have discovered an author attempting to put back on proper

---

8. To say nothing of my having avoided, additionally, some of those false leads set up by my too-modish professional field, a modishness made only more severe by its having endured a formidably prolonged employment crisis. This crisis has culminated in a determined pressure over the last two decades directing the Victorian field's members towards acquiescing to a practice of subsisting upon fundamentally sterile, pre-contextualized virtuoso performances in "archive-diving" in place of true literary analyses that might be built upon in some productive way by future critics. The marked sterility of these critiques is contributed to by a less than forthright temporal-structural arrangement or particular sequential conjuring trick, noted first by the admirable critic Joel Fineman, that lies at the basis of many New Historical interpretations. Gallagher and Greenblatt summarize Fineman's critique thus: "There is an obvious problem with this procedure: one chose an anecdote—out of the hundreds of thousands of possibilities—because it 'sounded like' a passage in Marlowe or Shakespeare, and then achieved a spurious effect of surprise and confirmation when it turned out to sound like Marlowe or Shakespeare" (47). These critics then go on to attempt, to my mind unsuccessfully, to argue Fineman's criticism away by contending that an individual New Historicist's goal of "reanimating" the past can be accomplished through a sort of expression of good faith on that critic's part: "The histories one wanted to pursue through the anecdote might, therefore, be called 'counterhistories,' which it would be all the more exhilarating to launch if their destinations were as yet undetermined and their trajectories lay athwart the best traveled routes" (52). Fineman's point remains sound that too often the destinations of these critiques are *pre*-determined—as opposed to "undetermined"— and that those predeterminations are subsequently covered over in order to produce the pleasing (and marketable) effect of critical/readerly surprise.

moral course a select part of his readership—striving through his fiction to shame the many American readers who would have been, he well knew, waiting to read his English product and not pay him for that privilege. My book's spine read simply "Collins/The Evil Genius." This seemingly-innocent juxtaposition began at this point to take on a new dimension of significance for me. Here was someone willing to alienate half his audience with a sermon they might not wish to hear, someone obviously with a healthy scope of perspective as well as a healthy self-regard. In short, here was an author to be closely studied. I then proposed to myself a hypothesis called up by the simple existence of Sarrazin's complaint: if the elderly Collins could have been voicing an anti-infringement protest in this particular "Domestic Story" of 1886, might it not be possible that he had accomplished something similar in the books written during his earlier, major phase—say, for instance, in his famous *The Woman in White* in which a "lady" is substituted for a "woman" (as she had been again by the inattentive American pirate publisher on the title page of my illicit copy)?[9] Could possibly that "strange family story" (*Woman in White,* ed. Sutherland 7) from 1860 about two look-alike relatives similarly be "A Domestic Story" protesting against the eventual production of look-alike books? And, going further, could its characters' allusions to "copy-book morality" and "copy-book morals" (235–36) be intended to imply something more than simple children's moral maxims, indeed, be calling for more morality in the transatlantic book trade? These questions then naturally led on to others . . .

The temptation to conclude this testamentary Preface in the testamentary style of one of Collins's witness-like characters being impossible to resist, I do hereby most solemnly state: that these are the circumstances giving rise to the project that grew into the book you have before you, Oh Gentle Reader, I faithfully and sincerely attest. (Of course such a declaration would be, in a Collins novel, accompanied by the following unvoiced—and all the more significant for being so—caveat: trust or not my word—or, more to the point, my knowledge and control of my word—as you will.)

Sundeep Bisla, New York City, 2013

---

9. In 1873 in *The New Magdalen,* Collins similarly used the strategy of mistaking, or passing off, a "woman" (Mercy Merrick) for a "lady" (Grace Roseberry) to protest against a particular social ill, in this instance his society's prejudice against fallen women.

1

Introduction

Wilkie Collins, Theorist of Iterability

But this thought of iterability, if it troubles all exclusion or simple
opposition, should not capitulate to confusion, to vague approximations, to indistinction.

— Derrida, *Limited* 128

SIGNS OF IT are everywhere—the author's relationship to the text is not
a comfortably controlled one. Whole disciplines have been founded on
this obvious proposition—certain strains of literary criticism and theory
being not the least among these—as well as on its denial. The history of
literary criticism is littered with battles fought along these lines, with Emp-
sons inevitably coming to contest the complacency of Richardses, Derridas
to contest that of Austins. Because literary idealization, wherever and in
whatever form it is encountered, will necessarily be constructing its castles
on an ethereal basis of repeatable-and-thus-falsifiable linguistic markers, it
must necessarily remain fundamentally unstable. Not surprisingly, then, the
would-be fixative conceptualizations in literary culture—of copyright and
artistic ownership, of a seemingly-singular authorial or personal identity
and/or intention, of the conventions set up to safeguard determinate meaning, among other ostensibly incontestable forms of idealized constraint—
inevitably end up in conflict with the "borderlessness" of the word.

This study will be considering the ways in which this particular conflict
between idealization or would-be deterministic limitation and kinetic muta-

1

bility manifests itself in the major fictions of the Victorian writer Wilkie Collins. These fictions are constantly alternating between two schemes of reference, represented, on the one hand, by a system of one-to-one correspondence between signifier and signified and, on the other, by one of one-to-many correspondences. Indeed, the various surprising twists of plot in Collins's narratives, more often than not, come at their basis to disclose that a given, seemingly-uncomplicated narrative written in the soothingly unfussy style of this perpetually cagey author that had seemed all along to be pledging fidelity to the former system actually had all along been pledging it to the latter. (In this respect, Collins's readers are continually forced to relive, it would seem, the hotel scene from *Basil.*) To offer one example, among the many possibilities available, of this alternation between referential systems, I would cite the point in *The Moonstone* when that master reader Sergeant Cuff—more than once cautioned by Lady Verinder that "circumstances have misled [him]" (171 and 173)—is finally definitively proved wrong when "plain long cloth" turns out not *solely* to mean, not *both automatically and completely* to correspond with, a plain servant's nightgown. The fact that Collins's fictions are to be found to be shifting between these two systems of correspondence is itself not surprising since all good, and even some merely passable, writers play with the transparent communication/polyvalent communication dyad. However, *the systematic manner* in which Collins's major fictions wholly transition over from one to the other system (a transformation offering a salutary lesson for the modern-day literary critic) is deserving of careful study, and, consequently, it, as well as the ways in which Collins deals with the implications of the manifestly illogical workings of language in general, will be the subject of this book.

Settling and Breaking

And indeed those workings *are* patently illogical, at least if logic is understood necessarily to be leading toward something that looks like "progress." The contrasting elements located at the heart of linguistic repeatability inevitably throw a wrench into this system, inevitably thwart any type of progress that had been on the point of getting underway. The source of the conflict is, to cite a phrase coined by Jacques Derrida in his seminal essay "Signature Event Context," the "iterability of the mark" (12). Language's undelimitable repeatability allows for the continual founding, or refounding, of linguistic entities and, in the same breath, for their continual unfounding, not to mention *con*founding. Emphasizing the first half of this dyad, the literary critic J. Hillis Miller defines linguistic iterability as "the possibility for every mark to be repeated and *still to function as a meaningful mark* in new contexts that are cut off entirely from the original context" (*Speech Acts* 78; emphasis added). In contrast, placing the stress solidly on iterability's capacity to escape constraint, Derrida contends, "a written sign carries with it a force that breaks with its context, that is, with the collectivity of presences organizing the moment of its inscription. This breaking force [*force de rupture*] is not an accidental predicate but the very structure of the written text" ("Signature Event Context" 9). A whirligig of effects—iterability's serving alternately as a means for language, both oral and written, to settle into place within contexts or for it to break out of them—comes to be delineated for this concept caught by Miller and Derrida at different moments along its sine wave of oscillations.[1] The iterable mark is thus disclosed, like the active butterfly, to live a life of constant resting and fluttering, fluttering and resting.

Both of these theorists consider, in essence, iterability's effects with regard to the system of linguistic reference, a system that is not so distinctly Apollonian versus Dionysian as it is often made out to seem. The system of would-be transparent communication—one-to-one correspondence between a word and its meaning giving the impression of settling—is itself merely *a special case* of the system of polyvalence—one-to-many correspondences giving the impression of breaking—and, on the other hand, the system of polyvalence is the necessary (hidden) precondition for a successful system of seemingly-transparent communication. In something resembling the yin/yang dyad, the "one" here constitutes a part of the "many" and the potential for the "many" the basis—"the general space of . . . possibility" (Derrida, "Signature Event Context" 19)—for the "one." Contending that the "play," or "broaching" aspect, made possible by the "many" situation is necessary for the actualization of the idealized "one," Derrida writes,

---

1. I will be adopting here the terms "settling function" and "breaking function" to describe the two idealized poles of iterability. These labels are derived from Derrida's early use of the terms "sedimentation"/"de-sedimentation" (*Edmund Husserl's* 36, 40n27; *Speech* 107; *Grammatology* 10; *Writing* 31, 207, and 390n3; and *Margins* 157, 214) and "*brisure*," or "hinge," a term signifying simultaneously "joint" and "break" (*Grammatology* 65). See Derrida writing in *Of Grammatology* of "the breaking of immediacy" (234) and asking, "Does a modern linguistics, a science of signification breaking the unity of the word and breaking with its alleged irreducibility, still have anything to do with 'language'?" (21). The important sentence connecting de-sedimentation with deconstruction from early on in *Of Grammatology* is also worth quoting: "[Arche-writing] inaugurates the destruction, not the demolition but the de-sedimentation, the de-construction, of all significations that have their source in that of the logos" (10).

> [I]terability makes possible idealization—and thus, a certain identity in repetition that is independent of the multiplicity of factual events—while at the same time limiting the idealization it makes possible: *broaching* and *breaching* it at once [elle l'*entame*]. . . . [E]ven in the ideal case . . . there must already be a certain element of play, a certain remove, a certain degree of independence with regard to the origin, to production, or to intention in all of its "vital," "simple" "actuality" or "determinateness," etc. (*Limited* 61 and 64)

Derrida's own particular labels for what I am calling here the breaking and settling functions are altering and identificatory iterability. He notes later in the same work that each type both makes possible and limits the other:

> [I]t must be shown why, for what reasons (which are structural, and not empirical or accidental) . . . idealization finds its limit. This limit is neither external nor internal; it is not simply negative since it renders possible the very idealization that it at the same time limits. Such is the strange alogical logic of what I call "iterability." . . . Let us not forget that "iterability" does not signify simply . . . repeatability of the same, but rather alterability of this same idealized in the singularity of the event, for instance, in this or that speech act. . . . There is no idealization without *(identificatory) iterability;* but for the same reason, for reasons of *(altering) iterability,* there is no idealization that keeps itself pure, safe from all contamination. The concept of iterability is this singular concept that renders possible the silhouette of ideality, and hence of the concept, and hence of all distinction, of all conceptual opposition. But it is also the concept that, *at the same time,* [emphasis Derrida's] with the same stroke marks the limit of idealization and of conceptualization. (119; emphasis added)

Each entity provides the "rudder" for the other in the respective journeys both are constantly launched on towards their own self-undermining, towards their eventual transformation into their counterpart. This whirligig embracing necessarily-limited idealization and anti-idealization leads, on the one hand, to transparent communication's "one" losing its privilege and authors losing along with it theirs as original sources and individual controllers of meaning as "altering iterability" inevitably comes into effect and, on the other hand, to "the many" losing its uncoordinated nature as it inevitably comes to be directed by "identificatory iterability." The two systems of reference, transparent and polyvalent, as well as the two functions through which they manifest themselves, settling and breaking, rather than being disjoint, are disclosed actually to be articulated, albeit by a whisker.

The Two Potential Errors

More than one thinker has been seduced into making one or the other of the complementary mistakes invited by the complex nature of iterability: (1) coming to believe in the conclusive disarticulation of one function from the other or (2) coming to accept the possibility of one function's potential completely to erase the other. However, the inherent connection between the two functions will not allow to stand the theories and systems that those thinkers then would be attempting to "construct" upon these fundamentally erroneous suppositions.

The tenuousness of the connection between the two functions can tend to disappear, as tenuousnesses will, and the cursory observer can be left with the impression that the functions are binary opposites. This perspective is understandable, as the natures of the functions and the language used to describe them are apt to belie those natures' inherent connection. The *impressions* of identificatory iterability and altering iterability, of settling and breaking, those manifestly mutually exclusive labels, are actually the limit-reifying end-products of the "operationality," so to speak, of these two markedly-different-seeming-but-actually-related systems of correspondence between signifier and signified. The attempt at faithfully describing this situation can lead thinkers, as it has just my own inquiry, into formulations bordering on the tortuous if not also the self-contradictory. For example, Pheng Cheah summarizes Derrida's position on iterability thus:

> Why is it that any present being always overflows itself and intimates an absolute alterity? Derrida's point is that in order to be present, any being must persist in time. This means that the form of the thing—that which makes it actual—must be identifiable as the same throughout all possible repetitions. But this iterability implies that any presence is in its very constitution always riven by a radical alterity that makes it impossible even as it makes it possible. By definition, this alterity cannot be a form of presence. Because it both gives and destabilizes presence, it subjects presence to a strict law of radical contamination. (146)

This situation cannot be helped. When one wishes, as does Cheah, to represent iterability correctly, there is no other path besides a complicated one.

The nature of the entity in question necessitates that one describe it as leading to *both* mutual exclusivity ("makes it impossible even as it makes it possible") *and* articulation ("radical contamination"). The tendency to fall into self-contradictory formulations—far from being (with a few exceptions of course) a wish by theorists to be adopting a protective or self-empowering cloak of obscurity—is brought about by the fragility of the connection between the two functions. The side denoted "the settling function" gives the impression of the "complete repetition"—as paradoxical as that may sound—of an utterance and its immediate original context, while "the breaking function" gives the impression of a more or less complete "breaking out" of the original context surrounding that utterance. This situation leaves many thinkers with the impression that the relationship between the two functions is one of a mutually exclusive "paradox."

This circumstance of a tenuous connection the description of which is constantly poised on the point of announcing that connection's denial can easily, unless carefully watched, lead to misunderstanding. Indeed, the language used to describe the two functions can itself potentially work towards the goal of misrepresentation. The strong contrast between the two functions naturally invites one to find them to be in a relation of paradox. But the critics' application of that term is actually an improper "solidification" of the functions' (pseudo-)disarticulation. There is no actual mutual exclusivity at work in the conflict ("contradiction" being too strong a word) between Miller's and Derrida's positions. An insistence on paradoxy would be to discount the important connection between the two, a connection permitting them to possibly flow and transform into each other (in Cheah's term "contaminate" one another).

A new concept has to be formulated to appropriately describe this situation, something that both is and is not a paradox at one and the same time. Thus, borrowing the concept of limit or continuum from mathematics, I offer here the concept of a "paradox of degree" as a possible practical description. This novel construction will stand in contrast to the standard form of paradox, the "paradox of kind," if you like. Theoretically speaking, only paradoxes of kind should be labeled with that term as only they possess the absolute distinctness seemingly demanded by the term ("I am a liar," for instance, admitting solely of two mutually exclusive interpretations). However, since the paradox of kind would automatically be denying the inherent connection between the two sides of iterability, it is inadequate to the task of describing this particular situation appropriately. While the terms to be used here, "settling" and "breaking," certainly imply the mutual exclusivity required by the standard form, those functions, are in the case of iterability, applicable only figuratively (similar to the manner in which the infinite series 0.999 . . . comes to be equated with 1.00) and are actually in a relation of difference of degree.

Here in this study this anomalous concept of the paradox of degree that I am proposing, while technically a violation in terminology, will operate as a useful tool. Particularly amenable to describing the markedly strange operations of language, it will serve in what follows as a conceptual map for tracking the investigations into linguistic stasis and change carried out not only by Collins but also a variety of other linguistically-oriented thinkers and for demonstrating how far, in comparison to those thinkers, Collins was able to progress in his investigations. Thus, in short, in this study the two functions comprising the iterability of the mark will be understood to be not so much "opposed" as "in conflict" with one another, their relationship of paradox of degree leaving open, all the while, the possibility of the one coming to "contaminate" the region of the other.

SHOULD thinkers in the area of iterability somehow avoid being taken in by the potential pitfall of a too-reifying or disarticulative definition of the particular "paradox" characterizing iterability, they still have another to avoid: the tempting desire to facilely erase one or the other of the functions so as to be fitting in with Enlightenment orthodoxy, an orthodoxy under which we still often labor today. Paradox in general (the distinction between degree and kind being left out of consideration for the moment) is itself an alien way of thinking in our modern, reason-governed world.[2] (And the

2. Rosalie Colie, in *Paradoxia Epidemica,* her exemplary study of paradox throughout the Renaissance, ascribes the decline of paradox in the 1700s to the advent of an Enlightenment preference for "progress": "we are invited to consider either Epimenides is a liar or that he isn't—our puzzlement, our paralysis comes from the fact that we are not permitted a third alternative. In twentieth-century 'real' life, after all, Epimenides' statement seems both obvious and trivial. . . . No wonder Galileo, Locke, and Spinoza turned away from paradoxy and, because we are willy-nilly educated by Enlightenment values, no wonder paradoxy is so difficult for us to 'read.' We are trained to expect 'development' in argument and in art" (517–18). Excluding the realm of quantum physics, paradox remains trivial (and in the case of Oscar Wilde nearly criminal) throughout the nineteenth century and the first half of the twentieth and only regains legitimacy, to a very limited degree, with the advent of poststructuralist literary theory (to the degree that that itself ever attains legitimacy in the face of the entrenched, age-old resistance to paradox, continuing in certain sectors in our own day, that then comes to lend its weight to the formidable present-day "resistance to theory"). Derrida (along with his precursors Hegel, Freud, and Empson) is to be commended for having brought this style of thinking back into currency in literary debate because it allows for demarcating issues, such as the true nature of iterability, to which Enlightenment-influenced thinking would otherwise have remained insensitive. There are several points in Derrida's work at which he attempts to relegitimize paradox at the expense of progressive logic. For instance, he writes, "As a philosophy, empiricism is

paradoxical nature of the concept of a "paradox of degree" is even further afield from logic.) Naturally, then, thinkers are tempted to move the situation completely out of this arena. Not surprisingly, iterability, especially over the last few centuries, has been prone to being misrepresented upon its entry into the (Enlightenment logic–dominated) realms of discourse and thinking. That is, more often than not, it has been represented as something half-alien to itself, as the improper privileging of one or the other of its two functions (a privileging bordering on univocity) has continually been set in operation to render it a more "comfortable" conception for our logic-governed and, perhaps more to the point, "progress"-governed world.

Naturally, it is the settling-function-privileging outlook that corresponds best with this quest for progress. This outlook allows for the formulation of systems of conclusive intention-determination,[3] systems that are constantly thereafter being found out to be lacking in solid foundations. This lack is the result of the formularizers' incorrectly having assumed the settling function to be capable of fully eclipsing the breaking function. They are lured toward this mistake by the requirements of Enlightenment-influenced "tradition," "history," and the general understanding of singular-seeming terms such as "meaning" and "intention." Everyday communication situations, unlike chapters in Collins's major novels (or in, say, William Empson's

---

still dominated by a logic I deem it necessary to deconstruct. Doubtless the concept of iterability is not a concept like the others (nor is *différance,* nor trace, nor supplement, nor parergon, etc.). That it might belong *without* belonging to the class of concepts of which it must render an accounting, to the theoretical space that it organizes in a (as I often say) 'quasi'-transcendental manner, is doubtless a proposition that can appear paradoxical, even contradictory in the eyes of common sense or of a rigid classical logic. It is perhaps unthinkable in the logic of such good sense. It supposes that something happens *by* or *to* set theory: that a term might belong *without* belonging to a set. It is of this too that we are speaking when we say 'margin' or 'parasite'" (*Limited* 127). Similarly, a few years earlier he had commented that a "Grammatology" "would no longer have the form of *logic* but that of *grammatics*" (*Grammatology* 28). I am largely in agreement with Barbara Johnson when she remarks, "The incompatibility between deconstruction and its conservative detractors is an incompatibility of logics. While traditionalists say that a thing cannot be both A and not-A, deconstructors open up ways in which A is necessarily but unpredictably already different from A" (*World* 13–14). I would simply point out that, viewed from my rubric, iterabilitists accept paradoxical "solutions" as viable ones, without needing to have recourse to the authority of any sort of overtly termed "logic." As we will see, Collins's effort, particularly in *The Moonstone,* was *strategically and structurally* to manipulate the deconstructive situation as outlined by Johnson here until that "unpredictability" was brought under control. For more on Renaissance paradox, see Geraldine, Malloch, H. K. Miller, and M. Wiley.

3. The quintessence of the settling perspective might be Knapp and Michaels' doubly view-truncating contention that the (single) intention is the (single) meaning: "The meaning of a text is simply identical to the author's intended meaning. . . . The mistake made by theorists has been to imagine the possibility or desirability of moving from one term (the author's intended meaning) to the second term (the text's meaning), when actually the two terms are the same. One can neither succeed nor fail in deriving one term from the other, since to have one is already to have them both" (724–25).

literary criticism), are not continually punctuated by moments in which people marvel at the various possible signifier–signified pairings that had been standing in the way of clear understanding (recall Lydia Gwilt's astonishment upon learning of the existence of two Allan Armadales: "Marry which of the two I might, my name would of course be the same" [*Armadale* 441]). Normally, people just "get on with" the business of communicating. However, despite these speakers', writers', thinkers', and authors' best efforts at willed ignorance, the conflicts do and will be arising. Collins felt this potential for misunderstanding deeply, especially its implications for his characters and for himself. He understood that the author, necessarily enmeshed in and intimately engaged with language, is condemned by the conflict between the two functions to establish *and* lose control—of texts, of contexts, of intentions, of meanings, and even of his or her textual identity. Each of these entities or situations is vulnerable to the possibility of having improperly brought to the fore either side of a bifurcated nature resulting from the bifurcated nature of the iterability founding it, or, more precisely, founding the language founding it. That is, Collins understood that one or the other of the conflicting sides of iterability can *appear* to be ascendent at different instances in different contexts but that this ascendancy—far from being a lasting and/or complete one—is actually illusory and fundamentally transitory.[4]

These moments of imbalance between the settling and breaking functions, though evanescent and unstable, are of actual and significant consequence. Not only do they allow for, when settling is ascendant, the establishment of the more overt—what are often erroneously considered the sum total—of the effects of language, but they also, on the other hand, when breaking is, call forth many of the potential alienations always threatening to erode the author–work relation, to say nothing of the author–self relation. As Derrida notes,

> Through the possibility of repeating every mark as the same [iterability] makes way for an idealization that seems to deliver the full presence of ideal objects . . . but this repeatability itself ensures that the full presence of a singularity thus repeated comports in itself the reference to something else, thus rending the full presence that it nevertheless announces. (*Limited* 129)

---

4. See Maynard's *Literary Intention* for a good overview of recent debates regarding authorial intention, a major point of contention in the settling/breaking debates. Several of the disagreements he describes can be ascribed, I believe, to a mistaking of either the settling or the breaking function for the complete picture.

In other words, each function has the potential for seemingly-completely (note the "seemingly" here) subverting the other, for delivering full presence or rending it, or, to put the situation once more in Derridean terms, "iterability is at once that which tends to attain plenitude and that which bars access to it" (129). While the settling function of iterability is the source of the founding of the, so to speak, "identity" of linguistic units (sometimes taking the form of what is specifically understood as "meaning" and more generally as effectivity in the ideological or crudely "historical" realms) and of their authors, the breaking function, on the other hand, is the source of that "something else" referred to by Derrida that would continually be undermining the would-be singularity and purity of the pure presence (an illusory pure presence, not surprisingly) that had made possible those foundings in the first place.

Though a chimera, the specter of the complete erasure of the breaking by the settling function nevertheless deserves to be taken seriously. That illusion makes things happen in the material world, while at the same time remaining vulnerable to having at any time its fundamentally illusory nature exposed. The result of this state of affairs is a world composed of adventitiously "stable" textual events, events that are grounded by furtive, provisional happenings that can themselves at any time be unseated. That is, the "bases of construction," as we might term them, stemming from the settling function, such as the unified authorial identity—the grounding for artistic ownership—and the unified authorial intention, must always necessarily remain at some fundamental level vulnerable to the possibility of destabilization at the hands of the breaking function. This truth is the source of much of the disturbance, even when economic concerns are left out of the reckoning, posed by the related specters of literary piracy and plagiarism for the author throughout recorded history.

Both of the functions comprising iterability have to be honored or else there comes into being an artificially-imposed, imbalanced framework tempting one to understand only one particular function or the other to actually be in existence. This is a lesson explicitly demonstrated by the gradual shift in philosophy in what I will here be calling Collins's "philosophico-textual unified novel series" or "long–novel project." In the fictions written during the peak of his powers, the 1850s and 60s, Collins conducted ever-more-foundational experiments into the nature of iterability, experiments that led him to more and more interesting and profound insights. It was this large-scale project to which the Victorian reading public, on some level, was responding, I believe, when it made his masterpieces of the 1860s such

successful bestsellers.[5] It will be my contention here that the works *Basil;
A Story of Modern Life* (1852), *Hide and Seek* (1854), "A Stolen Letter"
(1854), "A Rogue's Life" (1856), *The Dead Secret* (1857), *The Woman in
White* (1860), *No Name* (1862), *Armadale* (1866), and *The Moonstone: A
Romance* (1868) represent a single series composed of diverse fictions. Total-
ing a number of pages on the order of Proust's *À la recherche du temps
perdu,* these nominally-individualized works nevertheless form a single unit
exploring various aspects of what is essentially one issue, the iterability of
the mark.[6] Over the course of his project, Collins shifts from the situation
of overweighting the settling function (the standard Enlightenment standpoint) to that of acknowledging and even strategically manipulating the
breaking, all the while still honoring the effects of settling. Thus, he moves
from an imbalanced to a balanced perspective. In this sense his journey
is similar to that currently being taken not only by a particular strain of
twentieth-century philosophy deriving from the work of Derrida but also
by the study of Print Culture as well.[7]

---

5. John Sutherland holds that while *The Woman in White* may not have been the best-selling
English novel of the century "it is quite likely that it was the best-seller of the decade [the 1860s]" (*Is
Heathcliff a Murderer?* 117).

6. It is thematically consistent that this author who was always expressing skepticism in his narratives towards the efficacy of naming should be found to have ignored as well the propriety of individual titles and continued a particular endeavor across differing fictional "incarnations" or individual
works. As noted in the Preface, some of the aspects seen in the Major Phase are also evident in the later
works, the post-*Moonstone* productions. However, as it is only in the former that a concentrated and
sustained inquiry into the effects of iterability is carried out, it is only the pre-intellectual-breakdown
works with which this study will be primarily interested. Beginning with 1870's excessively-didactic
Man and Wife, we see a precipitous fall in the quality of Collins's fictions. Peters writes, "Though
Wilkie lived for another twenty-one years [after 1869] and wrote fourteen more full-length novels, as
well as shorter fiction and plays, none of his work, interesting though much of it is, ever reached the
standard of his novels of the 1860s" (312). Earlier she had written of the two households and families
that Collins kept from 1870 onwards (298–301). The economic stress of supporting two domestic
ensembles probably compelled him to write and publish too quickly which undoubtedly contributed
to the precipitous decline in the complexity of his later fictions. Hayter considers Collins's decline to
have been the result of his opium use: "The most obvious damage to his literary achievement which
the opium habit inflicted was its impairment of the power of sustained concentration needed for his
tightly-constructed plots which were his greatest excellence. His later novels do not hold together like
the best work of the 1860s. He worked as hard as ever at his novels, but the result was second-rate"
(270). It is also plausible that Dickens's death in 1870 contributed in some form. Several essays on
Collins's little-read later fictions are collected in Mangham's collection, *Wilkie Collins: Interdisciplinary
Essays* (see especially those by Beller, Mangham, Cox, Caleb, Depledge, Longmuir, Parker, and Allan).
See also the essays by Nayder and Law in Bachman and Cox, *Reality's Dark Light;* those by Leavy,
O'Fallon, and Wiesenthal in Smith and Terry, *Wilkie Collins to the Forefront;* and Talairach-Vielmas,
Wilkie Collins 93–202.

7. It should be pointed out that Derrida claimed merely to be describing a movement already
underway rather than originating a new one: "By a slow movement whose necessity is hardly percep-

While over the course of the past few decades the "history of the book" has become a fashionable topic of inquiry,[8] it must stand as a mere footnote to the much longer "history of iterability," and Print Culture must itself remain supplementary to, surprisingly, "Re-Print Culture."[9] Book history, given its label's excessive weighting on the side of materiality/settling, should be expected in the future either to be superceded or continually forced, from the inside, so to speak, to acknowledge (somewhat in the way that I have attempted in my Preface) the breaking side that its name would be implicitly attempting to ignore. This necessary acknowledgment might take the form of more and more strident calls for "theory" to be brought into analyses of the history of the book or for the field to acknowledge points where the book visibly fails in its materializing mission. Our present age's growing interest in "Tablets" and "E-Readers" can only have a salutary effect on this blindspot of book history.[10] This moment of downloadable and continually replaceable content clearly exposes the book for what it is: a technological form attempting to reify in certain ways the settling function's

---

tible, everything that for at least some twenty centuries tended toward and finally succeeded in being gathered under the name of language is beginning to let itself be transferred to, or at least summarized under, the name of writing. . . . The advent of writing is the advent of this play; today such a play is coming into its own, effacing the limit starting from which one had thought to regulate the circulation of signs" (*Grammatology* 6–7).

   8. Book history is a robust field. Considering just the studies of major transatlantic nineteenth-century authors in relation to the history of the book and/or copyright law, one would need to cite Sutherland, *Victorian Novelists* (1976); Patten, *Charles Dickens* (1978); Darnton, "What Is the History of Books?" (1982); Darnton, "First Steps" (1986); Welsh, *Copyright to Copperfield* (1987); Sutherland, "Publishing History" (1988); Dooley, *Author and Printer* (1992); Shillingsburg, *Pegasus in Harness* (1992); Sutherland, *Victorian Fiction* (1995); Whalen, *Edgar Allan Poe* (1999); McGill, *American Literature* (2002); Saint-Amour, *The Copywrights* (2003); Price, *The Anthology* (2003); Pettitt, *Patent Inventions* (2004); Hack, *Material Interests* (2005); Macfarlane, *Original Copy* (2007); and Alexander, *Copyright Law* (2010).

   9. See Johns, arguing a marginally different point, but nevertheless also implicitly making mine, that in the eighteenth century "Knowledge . . . spread through chain reactions of reappropriations, generally unauthorized and often denounced. . . . Enlightenment traveled atop a cascade of reprints. No piracy, we might say, no Enlightenment" (*Piracy* 50).

   10. The fact that Amazon, upon learning that it no longer had the right to distribute, had no trouble in 2009 deleting George Orwell's *Animal Farm* and *1984* from the Kindle devices of purchasers, well after the actual purchase date, shows how significant the immateriality of textuality has become in this new age. A *New York Times* reporter comments, "Retailers of physical goods cannot, of course, force their way into a customer's home to take back a purchase, no matter how bootlegged it turns out to be. Yet Amazon appears to maintain a unique tether to the digital content it sells for the Kindle" (Stone B1). In this article, the reporter makes much of the similarity between Amazon's practice and Big Brother's policy in *1984* of incinerating bad press by sending it down the "memory hole" (B1). There seems no theoretical impediment (except for the evanescence and capriciousness of the breaking function) to the possibility of some future Shakespeare taking her already-published output back and away with her upon her death.

effects and at the same time to improperly denigrate or ignore the existence of the breaking function. Of course, that function being ubiquitous, this endeavor can never be completely successful. The book has throughout its history failed in its attempts at complete materialization and will continue to fail along specific paths and circuits characteristic to it, in contrast to the ways in which manuscript copying by scribes or internet self-publication in their own ways fail.[11] It is with good reason that the author when "going into print" fears having at some level his or her literary identity unseated by the fissuring made possible by the breaking function, whether at the level of ownership, authority, unified intention, or clarity of communication. That is to say, despite all of its conspicuously flaunted materiality, the book (and therefore its "history") has never been able—as Collins knew only too well—to stave off the breaking function completely.[12]

---

11. For discussions of the problems modern intellectual property law is having in dealing with new technologies, see J. Boyle, *Shamans, Software, and Spleens* (1997) and "Politics of Intellectual Property" (1997); Lessig, *Code* (1999); Litman, *Digital Copyright* (2001); Vaidhyanathan, *Copyrights and Copywrongs* (2001); Lessig, *Future of Ideas* (2001); Goldstein, *Copyright's Highway* (2003); Vaidhyanathan, *Anarchist* (2004); Lessig, *Free Culture* (2004); Gillespie, *Wired Shut* (2007); Patry, *Moral Panics* (2009); Johns, *Piracy* (2009); Hyde, *Common as Air* (2010); J. Boyle, *Public Domain* (2010), and Patry, *How to Fix Copyright* (2012).

12. One significant problem with recent studies in the history of the book is that their authors—perhaps out of an inability to conceive of the "immaterial book" (the "entity," one hardly worthy of that name, today being continually downloaded to and deleted from our E-readers), or out of an implicit acceptance of the "intellectual property" outlook so prevalent in legal and cultural discourse in England, an outlook equating "the rights of an author in his intellectual product . . . with the property in corporeal things" (Kase 8), or simply out of a pragmatic, currently fashionable disinterest in theoretical matters—end up uncritically connecting the iterable with the non-iterable, that is, end up collapsing textuality with materiality. For example, see Hack, who in conceiving his inquiry according to a currently-fashionable bias—"My approach is historical and critical rather than theoretical"—cavalierly brings together four concepts within the provenance of one word: "this study seeks to keep distinct the four primary, contemporary referents of *materiality*—economic, physical, linguistic, and corporeal—while at the same time keeping them all in play, precisely in order to keep open the question of their relationship to one another" (1–2). The element needing more special handling than Hack gives to it is the "linguistic" (as well as "economic" insofar as that refers to copyright and intellectual property). The "linguistic" brings in a very real potential for an *im*materiality that is, by definition, not characteristic of corporeal entities. Hack understands his un-(anti-?)theoretical standpoint to be characteristic of the way the Victorians themselves approached their texts: "attention to these 'material' aspects of writing does not by itself constitute reading against the grain: on the contrary, such attention corresponds to the Victorians' own, which anticipates and solicits it" (2). However, the English citizens (and certainly American publishers) of the nineteenth century, like people everywhere and at all times, were well aware (for example, through their common vulnerability to literary piracy) of the potential for the practical applicability of the theoretical issues related to language, of the real-world effects of iterability. My study's interest in iterability's breaking function, as opposed to simply its settling one, necessitates that "textuality" be rendered fundamentally different from any singular and singularizable "materiality."

Derrida and Austin

But the fraught processes through which books attempt to come to terms with a fundamentally bifurcated textuality are not the only interactions through which to glimpse signs of this type of struggle. One might also look to the history of philosophical and literary critical thought around the world, specifically as it relates to the questions of meaning and of being's relation to language. Many a thinker in these areas has been tempted to defend the illusion of one function's conclusive extinguishment of the other. Consider for example the critic George Steiner commenting on the struggle in literary criticism between, to use his terms, "non-reading" and "common sense":

> It is this provisional subjectivity, this persistent need for reconsideration and amendment, which does give a certain legitimacy to the deconstructionalist project. No external ruling, be it the trope of divine revelation, be it the author's express dictum, can guarantee interpretation. Nor can consensus, itself always partial or temporary, across "canonic" and general literacy. . . .
> It is logically conceivable that the text before us signifies *nothing,* that it purposes or enacts non-sense. It is just possible that the author seeks to ironize his work into playful ghostliness. But the assumptions underlying this non-reading, this dissemination into the void, are themselves arbitrary and rooted substantively in the language in which they are expressed (deconstructionists and post-modernists pour out prolix treatises). I have, throughout my work, most explicitly in *Real Presences* (1989), proposed the contrary wager: on the relations, however opaque, of word to world, on intentionalities, however difficult to unravel, in texts, in works of art, soliciting recognition. Here, as so often in our muddled being, the vital grain, the life-pattern is that of common sense. (23)

Steiner here means an Enlightenment-influenced and logic-controlled (i.e., anti-paradoxical) "common sense." What critics like Steiner choose not to understand is that the defense of one or the other function is, of course, doomed to eventual failure. However, the interim can be extensive—allowing for the founding of whole fields of inquiry, including schools of reading, criticism, and philosophy (under such labels as, on the one hand, "enlightenment thinking,"[13] "analytic philosophy," "ordinary language philoso-

---

13. See Horkheimer and Adorno writing, "For the Enlightenment, only what can be encompassed by unity has the status of an existent or an event" (4). One strategy facilitating the occlusion of the breaking by the settling function is the almost imperceptible collapse of the former's subver-

phy," and, currently, even "tradition," and, on the other, "postmodernism," "deconstruction," and "formalism")—before the improperly slighted function has a chance to reassert its claims. To such an extent has the possible subdual of one half of the dyad of iterability—an apparently very seductive lure—established itself as a "tried and true" conceptual strategy that the belief in the conclusive excisability, or at least delimitability, of one function and/or unimpeachable ascendency of the other is for many thinkers, unless exceptionally perspicacious as well as courageous, impossible to resist. Time and again they succumb to this temptation, only to have their belief in the specific ordering of the world they have ascribed to, and implicitly founded their philosophy on, eventually overthrown.

Particular examples abound in the history of philosophy and literary criticism of the two possible complementary errors. We might look at representative manifestations allowing them to stand as general models for the two possible arenas of error. Taking first the less common error: offering a clear means for "de-sedimenting" one's identity, school, or local interpretation, the lure of allowing the breaking function to eclipse the settling could be described as a founding principle of Eastern, specifically Chinese, thought. The China scholar William Alford points out that the West's devotion to the settling function was not a path that it was absolutely necessary for it to have pursued:

> Given the extent to which "interaction with the past is one of the distinctive modes of intellectual and imaginative endeavor in traditional Chinese culture," the replication of particular concrete manifestations of such an endeavor by persons other than those who first gave them form never carried, in the words of the distinguished art historian and curator Wen Fong, the "dark connotations . . . it does in the West." Nor, as was often the case in the West, was such use accepted grudgingly and then only because it served as a vehicle through which apprentices . . . developed their techni-

---

sions with those random ones always available at the hands of simple improper or irresponsible recontextualization, i.e., simple "bad interpretation." Umberto Eco attempts, too abruptly, to gather together all of these types of subversion (both legitimate and chaotic) into a single, complete package and to denigrate them all under the label "overinterpretation." In defending this construction, Eco offers examples of interpretations that exceed what he labels a certain "textual economy" and describes these as "paranoiac interpretations" in oppositon to "sane interpretations" (*Interpretation and Overinterpretation* 48). He writes, "I think . . . we can accept a sort of Popperian principle according to which if there are no rules that help to ascertain which interpretations are the 'best' ones, there is at least a rule for ascertaining which ones are 'bad'" (52). Culler, approvingly citing Booth's concept of "overstanding" and the apparently undirected systematicity of Barthes in *S/Z*, argues that what Eco calls "overinterpretation" is actually a "state of wonder at the play of texts and interpretation" that should be encouraged rather than censured (*Literary* 182).

cal expertise, demonstrated erudition, or even endorsed particular values, although each of these phenomena also existed in imperial China. On the contrary, in the Chinese context, such use was at once *both more affirmative and more essential*. It evidenced the user's comprehension of and devotion to *the core of civilization itself,* while offering individuals the possibility of demonstrating originality within the context of those forms and so distinguishing their present from the past. (28–29; emphasis added)

Chinese practice here shows that culture to be more accepting of the breaking function than is in general the West. This acceptance hints that the breaking function actually will not be denied. Thus, it is not surprising that in Western culture the unstable theoretical eclipsings and occlusions carried out on behalf of "foundational certitude" should be continually exposed for what they are by philosophers and thinkers coming later in a type of game of obfuscation-and-disclosure that long ago should have been transcended.

To offer, on the other hand, an example of an allegiance to the idea of a solely efficacious settling function—one that I will touch on again later, in a different context—I would turn to the philosopher J. L. Austin's attempt at (and failure in) conclusively defending his "performative utterances" from what he describes as "parasitic" language usages such as parody or improper citation (all in one way or another examples of the breaking function making itself felt). In his lecture series published as *How to Do Things with Words,* Austin, envisioning the dream of the complete elimination of the breaking function and then building on that dream, posits the existence of a set of tightly-controlled utterances that would be allowing one, for example, to successfully christen a ship, contract a marriage, make a bet, etc. These "performative speech acts" in which the words are actually able to do what they say, albeit through a serious degree of dependence on a pre-determined context, or reliance on "appropriate circumstances," are acts simultaneously calling for and justifying, whether explicitly or implicitly, the foundational stabilizations characteristic of the settling function. Austin's mistake is the result of his implicit assumption that settling can conclusively erase breaking. Derrida will demonstrate (as does also, as we will see below, Collins in the opening of *No Name*) the fundamental dependence of "clear" (which is precisely *not* to say "simple," as it involves the intermediary steps of (1) willed ignorance and (2) a forgetting of that willing) communication on the existence of those other, "parodistic," correspondences and, by implication, the fundamental connection between the two functions.

Austin posits an idealized world in which the settling function will have conclusively triumphed over the breaking:

Speaking generally, it is always necessary that the *circumstances* in which the words are uttered should be in some way, or ways, *appropriate,* and it is very commonly necessary that either the speaker himself or other persons should *also* peform certain *other* actions, whether "physical" or "mental" actions or even acts of uttering further words. Thus, for naming the ship, it is essential that I should be the person appointed to name her, for (Christian) marrying, it is essential that I should not be already married with a wife living, sane and undivorced, and so on: for a bet to have been made, it is generally necessary for the offer of the bet to have been accepted by a taker (who must have done something, such as to say "Done"), and it is hardly a gift if I *say* "I give it you" but never hand it over. (*How to Do Things* 8–9)

Austin's performatives are only possible because the settling function through a constant effectivity and constant availability—emphasized here at the implicit expense of an unacknowledged, and perilously ignored, breaking function—makes possible the illusion of its having completely subdued or eliminated its unruly counterpart. A great degree of complacency with regard to the possibility of the complete triumph of settling (and complete exclusion of breaking) is evident in a statement such as "Our performative utterances, felicitous or not, are to be understood as issued in ordinary circumstances" (22). Austin's idealized conception of complete and total state control here, of his "ordinary circumstances" successfully having been imposed and easily upheld, signals his having wholly bought into the dream of conclusive exclusion.

He has only, however, set himself up for a return of the repressed, a return that occurs (besides hesitantly and incompletely in his own text: "in some ways there is danger of our initial and tentative distinction between constative and performative utterances breaking down" [*How to Do Things* 54]) in the form of Derrida's publication, several years after Austin's death, of an essay—one might be tempted to call it "groundbreaking" were not the disclosure of the undeniability of the breaking function as old as the hills—entitled "Signature Event Context." In that critique, Derrida discloses that Austin's repeated failure to stabilize his distinction between performative speech acts and "constative utterances," statements that merely report things, is the result of Austin's having ignored the subversions always being put forward by the breaking function, that function allowing utterances to unauthorizedly slip across the would-be impermeable border created by Austin's distinction. The possibility existing for each and every one of the protocols or conventions ("ordinary circumstances") to have been, to some extent or other, parodied (repeated with the insertion of varying degrees of a break from "ordinariness") beforehand, the breaking function allows no grounding to remain firm, no "ordinariness" to remain such. Derrida patiently examines several instances of Austin's attempt at dismissing the undismissable, at dismissing what Derrida describes as "a general iterability [actually the breaking aspect of iterability, the mere existence of] which constitutes a violation of the allegedly rigorous purity of every event of discourse or every *speech act*" ("Signature Event Context" 18). The "purity" of Austin's performative speech acts in their attempt at settling into place within their singular contexts and "ordinary circumstances" is a purity implicitly based on the dream of settling erasing breaking. As such, it is a "purity" not worthy of the name. It is a purity that must remain fundamentally impure, as it must always remain vulnerable to the charge of having attempted to deny the very possible potential—as must all systems premised on the possibility of the settling function's erasure of its other—of the return of the excluded function and (the consciousness of) its effects.

Negotiating one's way past the tradition of overweighting the settling function to the detriment of the breaking function is a difficult endeavor. Clearly, any thinker wishing to deal properly with the paradoxical workings of the iterability of the mark would need to be possessed of a personality characterized by a good deal of open-mindedness and an uncommon degree of comfort with rebelliousness. This thinker would have to be willing at certain moments to work against "tradition"—a difficult position to adopt. We have seen Jacques Derrida to be one such thinker. But, not surprisingly—the workings of iterability having remained constant throughout time—there were others before him. This book will be dealing with the investigations carried out in this area—taking the form this time of inviting Victorian fictions rather than complicated twentieth-century philosophical critiques—by another thinker of this type.

VIEWING the placement and re-placement of texts through the grid of two conflicted-but-not-contrasting functions has many effects. For one thing, in the intentional realm, the transparent passage of "meaning" from author to reader is disclosed to be a mirage—or more precisely only half the story—as we find iterability to be resulting in both the founding and unsettling of literary understanding and intention at one and the same time. Understanding and intention are, in other words, disclosed to be always already subject to the peculiar "logic" of iterability. Derrida describes the breaking side of this logic well when he observes that iterability leads to the person using language being necessarily absented—insofar as he would wish to "be" his linguistically manifested "intentions"—from the instrument he would wish to believe himself to be controlling. Summarizing his main points in the discussion after his initial oral presentation of "Signature Event Context" in 1971, Derrida comments,

> I don't think a mark can be constituted without its being able to be cited. Therefore, the entire graphematic structure is connected to citationality, to the possibility of being repeated. And since a mark is repeatable, this means that it no longer needs me to continue to have its effects. Insofar as I make use of an instrument that bears within itself its repeatability, I am absented from what I use. And it's necessary to take account of this absence. (Derrida and Ricoeur 154)

According to Derrida, the repeatability of language operates through a series of simultaneous steps—the paradox inherent in a "simultaneity" of discrete "steps" being only one of many legitimate paradoxes being invited by the paradox of degree associated with the manifestly "quirky" operations of iterability—to bring about an absenting of the subject without that subject's full volition. In short, the iterability of language allows the subject to be "the subject" and, at the same time, renders such a fulfillment of identity impossible.

Collins's interactions with the dyad formed by the settling/breaking functions were not of either of the usual varieties, were not the scientist's or philosopher's radical fear and abhorrence of the latter function or the literary artist's (think Shakespeare or Dickens) desire to constantly seek out (either pell-mell or focused on two or three general themes) situations of breaking as a means of surprising the reader (and sometimes the artist him- or herself) with new combinations and novel associations. Collins's strategy when embarking on his project was to *systematically transition* over the course of the 1850s and 60s across this dyad, from settling to breaking—from, to put it crudely, literature viewed as a precise science to literature viewed as an art. (His meticulously controlled transition in his dealings with the dyad was the result of Collins's striking self-awareness, an awareness probably stemming from the distance from himself and his usual perspective afforded by his excessive opium use.[14] Opium intoxication probably allowed

---

14. It is interesting that at the same time that Collins's use of opium increased to habitual proportions, from the composition stage of *The Woman in White* onwards—"Although Wilkie had almost certainly been an occasional opium user for years . . . it was at this time that Beard prescribed laudanum regularly as a palliative" (Peters 240)—so did his interest in the breaking function of iterability, until, of course, the unexplained, remarkable crash of his intellect after the publication of *The Moonstone*.

him to look back on his "good" or "proper" self's allegiance to the settling function and then to counteract it with villains drawn from the breaking side.) As a result, his major phase offers one of the best sites in literary history for watching in operation both sides of the dyad and for demarcating the spectrum of effects made possible by the markedly varied operations of the iterability of language.

I choose to focus on this particular novelist because his dealings with linguistic repetition are uncommonly sustained and insightful and, most significantly, because those dealings exhibit an astonishing degree of open-mindedness to *both* sides of the workings of the iterability of the mark. A close analysis of Collins's works of this period allows one to see the potential held out both by, on the one side, a pure allegiance to the settling function and, on the other, a resistance to allowing the breaking side to fall into an indiscriminate jumble of transparent and/or polyvalent communications. Collins maintains a remarkably controlled and organized trajectory from the beginning to the end of his project[15] as he progressively comes to move beyond literary stasis and to acknowledge more and more the inherent complicatedness arising from linguistic repetition. In pursuing this goal, he brings into being one of the profoundest intellectual inquiries ever attempted into the iterability of the word. Thus, here I will be not just investigating Collins's explorations into the realm of the workings of linguistic iterability but also—it being high time that such a project was attempted—endeavoring to raise the status of this writer's achievement to a level more philosophically weighty than that accessed by the much-repeated labels of "father of the sensation novel," "master of mystery," or, even, "protégé of Charles Dickens."[16]

Collins's Unusual Candidness in Thinking

Collins is more resilient and forthright than most thinkers as he comes at a certain point in his career to the realization that he has been improperly,

---

15. Dickens made a radical misjudgment in nicknaming Collins "the Genius of Disorder," in contrast to his own label of "the Genius of Order," as Collins's thinking—whatever may have been the state of other aspects of his life—was anything but disordered (See *Letters of Dickens* 8:161).

16. See Brantlinger in *The Reading Lesson* remarking, "*The Woman in White* (1860) was and continues to be regarded as setting the pattern for the 'sensation mania'" (17). For critics holding a similar opinion, see Braddon in Rance 121; Cvetkovich 24; Kendrick 19; Pykett, "Collins" 50; Sutherland, "Wilkie Collins" 243; and Wynne 4. For critics labeling Collins a master of mystery, see Peterson and Page 137. For critics emphasizing Dickens's influence on Collins, see, among several others, Burney 178 and Trodd 80.

over the course of the 1850s, overweighting one function (the settling) and underweighting the other (the breaking). This is in itself a very difficult point to reach in one's intellectual progress. It involves a good degree of candidness about one's practices. Indeed, the trajectory of Collins's intellectual development could be said to prove Paul de Man wrong when, in writing about Hegel, he contends, "It is . . . true that he does not exactly tell the story of a threatening paradox at the core of his system against which his thought has to develop a defense in whose service the aesthetic . . . is being mobilized. No one could be expected to be *that* candid about his uncertainties" (*Aesthetic Ideology* 191). However, this type of candidness—easier to entertain, admittedly, for the novelist than the philosopher or literary critic—is not the full extent of Collins's exemplary openness to the bifurcated nature of the iterability of the mark. Collins not only acknowledges his difficulties but continues forward past that acknowledgment. He not only over the course of the 1860s comprehends the source (the always-threatening breaking function) of his earlier "uncertainties" but then also accepts and *even embraces it*, going on to explore the implications of that acceptance (at first centering his investigations on the effects had by the breaking function at the level of publication and then at the level of composition). As a result, Collins offers us an unparalleled case of a Victorian author struggling with both sides of the contradictory grounding of language.

It is the complementary movements, from settling to breaking, from breaking to settling, that open up spaces of possibility for interesting escapings and coincidings to occur. It was these spaces that a century and a half ago entranced Collins to such a degree that he chose to work out what could and could not be accomplished by and within them in the novels written at the peak of his powers. Over the course of pursuing this project, Collins found, for one thing, that those spaces allowed him the opportunity of creating series upon series of startling effects, effects that earned him, whether rightly or wrongly, the label of "the father of the sensation novel." It is important, however, not to allow this rather constricted and local result—too quickly singled out by the critics from amongst the panoply available—of Collins's admirably intrepid venturings into the strange region of iterability to lessen the significant depth and breadth of his actual achievement.

It will be my contention here that while writing the fictions of his major phase Collins made the breaking and settling functions of the iterability of the mark his central topic of concern. All the while that he was seemingly solely concerned, say, with the metaphorical representation of the text as land (*Basil*) or as vulnerable female (*The Woman in White*), with parodic repetition's disclosure of the implicit bad-faith denial of illusion at the heart of realist fiction (*No Name*), with the author's loss of "substance" (as "creator rather than "disseminator") even before being taken up by the publication process (*Armadale*), or with the drug-induced splitting effects occasionally fundamentally unseating the seemingly-unified personal identity (*The Moonstone*), Collins was attempting to come to terms with the fact that the linguistic element in which he had immersed himself could either lift him up or drown him—or perform both operations simultaneously. He was coming to accept the somewhat uncomfortable fact that, in a sense, the would-be unified "domesticity" of the author's psyche established by the settling function could be fissured by a struggle that was always already taking place between the apparently-opposed good angel and evil genius of the two functions of iterability.

The apparently dual nature of the iterability of the mark allowed for the transformation of the simple and single into the complex and double, and back again. This movement captivated Collins. Indeed, so much so that Catherine Peters feels called upon to open her insightful biography with a discussion of precisely this issue, his fascination with doubles, on her way to (rather deflatingly) concluding that this interest indicated he "felt some uncertainty about his own identity" (2). Similarly Taylor writes, "Collins's novels continually conjure with identity. The self is a screen on which others' perceptions are projected and enacted; a collection of physical signs whose meaning is uncertain; a subjectivity struggling to gain coherence" (*Secret Theatre* 63–64), and Kucich contends that "Dreams, suppressed desires, doubles, and premonitions regularly haunt the subjective solidity of Collins's characters" (*Power* 95). I will be arguing here, however, that the excessive interest in doubles in Collins's fictions is not so much a manifestation of a psychological anxiety as it is that of a professional, textual one, that is, that the doubling is not that of the psyche (in the sense of the unconscious or subconscious doubling the conscious) but rather of the page. Collins was intrigued by both the possibility of overcoming iterability's breaking function and the possibility of its overcoming the singularities of his characters, texts, readers, and even himself. His perspective shuttling back and forth between the contradictory effects of iterability (with his villains generally exploiting the breaking function while his heroes and heroines generally exploit the settling), Collins was an author particularly attuned to the strange and complex movement of language.

In what follows, it may seem at times as if I had, to revise one of Holmes's better lines in *The Sign of the Four*, worked the fifth postulate of Euclid (or Derrida) into a love-story or an elopement, that is, as if I had unfairly discounted the various overtly referential aspects of Collins's texts and thereby improperly reduced the "romance," in all senses, in books like *The Moonstone,* explicitly subtitled so, to "mere" textuality or flattened semantics. However, I feel this "reduction" in the case of Collins's major fictions to be justified. Indeed, I would argue, it actually turns out to be, when the case is looked into closely enough, not a reduction at all, as the "romance" in Collins's unified novel series is often itself fundamentally *formed out of* the materials provided by not real-world elopements and love stories per se but the paradoxical workings of textuality.

In other words, Collins's romance is fashioned not from a foundation in representing "truth as it is in nature" in all its variety but in representing a small, near-magical linguistic aspect of it. His stories of this period grow out of the profoundly exotic nature of the working of textual repetition. Unlike the majority of his novelist contemporaries, and unlike himself during his later "mission fiction" period, Collins in his unified novel series comes not only to value language's transhistorical, formal, mechanical workings over its contingent and particular, extralinguistically-oriented, referential and representational ones but also wholeheartedly to accept the conflict at the basis of those workings. The incidents from "real life" that interest him are invariably ones in which iterability is breaking through into the material world, so much so that I believe he does not actually *see* the real world any longer at all. That is, "the world" as Collins perceives it is simply the world of the manuscript page (the object most usually lying in front of this professional author) transposed, *with increasing vitality,* back onto our "real world." Coincident with his acknowledgment of an allegiance to a thoroughly textualized world, are his re-creations of facsimiles of standard mid-Victorian fictions apparently operating according to a standard mode of fictional reference. That is, passing himself off—admittedly sometimes with a grand lack of success (see the increasingly critical reviews from 1862 onwards in Page 111 ff.)—throughout his project as a standard Victorian novelist intent on representing the truth of the life of his culture, Collins throughout his unified novel series is actually representing a facsimile world that has been textualized from the ground up. He creates a literary career out of writing and selling stories of near–flesh and blood characters acting according to not real life urgings but rather the formal workings of language. Collins, by creating out of textual elements an image of our own world, content out of what is usually solely empty form, thereby will move himself into a realm that might be described as, if not quite wholly his own amongst those who might be termed "theorists of iterability," then certainly his own amongst his Victorian novelist contemporaries.

The Showdown at the Tombstone

Nowhere, of course, in Collins's philosophico-textual unified novel series will one find the terms "iterability," "settling function," or "breaking function" being employed, but the effects of these concepts are nevertheless felt everywhere within it. This study will be describing Collins's execution of a transition between the two functions. Naturally, then, the cusp in this trajectory is of great interest and deserves a degree of preliminary focus. We might look at the point at which Collins comes first to allow the ascendency of the settling function to be seriously contested by the breaking function, a difficult stage for a creator[17]—someone whose role would necessarily be predicated to a significant extent on honoring the settling function—to reach. I believe we find such a moment in *The Woman in White,* a work published in 1860, near the midpoint of Collins's multi-novel project. In that work, the two contrasting functions (each championed by one of the sets of contrasting good and bad characters) directly contend for predominance, leaving up in the air until the very end of this thrilling narrative the question of which of the functions is ultimately to triumph.

The Woman in White has always been considered remarkable, the source of that remarkability most often being ascribed to one particular scene, that of Count Fosco's stealing Marian Halcombe's diary and inscribing his own narrative within it. The reader is understandably shocked at that moment to find one of the patently "bad" characters seizing the power of narration from one of the patently "good" ones. The complete transitions in narration startlingly represented by this scene and by Fosco's exchanging narrative control with Walter Hartright when his own concluding statement is effectively bookended by Hartright's final narrative are signs that our author, having come to acknowledge the connection between the two functions, also acknowledges their possibility of overturning one another—unlike in *Basil* where he appears to believe that the breaking function can safely be ignored.

This type of radical self-critique and adjustment, exemplified in the *Basil–The Woman in White* transition, is, as we have seen, a difficult standpoint for a thinker schooled in the Western Enlightenment tradition to reach, and perhaps only a character as charming as Fosco could have tempted his creator into attempting it. Magdalen Vanstone under the influence of desperate circumstances, Lydia Gwilt before her short-lived reclamation, and Franklin

---

17. Here I mean a standard Victorian author-creator, someone whose role is predicated on settling real-world, non-iterable objects into the signifier slots usually assigned them.

Blake under the influence of opium are all the descendants of Fosco. Replaying the dynamic of Milton's character Satan purportedly winning over to his party the author of *Paradise Lost,* Collins's grandiloquent creation in *The Woman in White* seduces him into moving beyond the limitations of Western "philosophical protectionism," as we might term it, as he comes to seriously entertain his "criminal side." Commenting on this influence late in his career, Collins would remark of Fosco, "His character grew on me,—a great danger to a novelist" (Yates 591). Collins was not the only conquest made by Fosco. Marian Halcombe when she first meets this mysterious, imposing figure comments, "I can only repeat that I do assuredly feel, even on this short acquaintance, a strange, half-willing, half-unwilling liking to the Count. He seems to have established over me the same sort of ascendancy which he has evidently gained over Sir Percival."[18] It was with good reason that Margaret Oliphant in her famous review of the novel was prompted to write, "The sympathies of the reader on whom the 'Woman in White' lays her spell, are, it is impossible to deny, devoted to the arch-villain of the story" ("Sensation Novels" 566). Oliphant headily continued,

> [T]here is no resisting the charm of his good-nature, his wit, his foibles, his personal individuality. To put such a man so diabolically in the wrong seems a mistake somehow. . . . No villain of the century, so far as we are aware, comes within a hundred miles of him. . . . The reader shares in the unwilling liking to which, at his first appearance, he beguiles Marian Halcombe; but the reader, notwithstanding the fullest proof of Fosco's villany, does not give him up, and take to hating him, as Marian does. . . . He is intended to be an impersonation of evil, a representative of every diabolical wile: but Fosco is not detestable; on the contrary, he is more interesting, and seizes on our sympathies more warmly than any other character in the book. (566–67)

This preternaturally-seductive character, and strong advocate for the breaking function (his attraction being partly due to his ability to disclose what must always have been waiting in the wings—of the story and of the reader's and author's consciousnesses—i.e., that constantly slighted but nevertheless present function), in seducing readers, characters, and creator alike is able to lead his creator to overcoming centuries of philosophical and narrative tradition. Having once seriously acknowledged the breaking function,

---

18. *Woman in White,* ed. Sutherland 226. In this chapter, all further references to this work, unless otherwise noted, will be to this edition and will be cited parenthetically.

Collins will continue down this path and *extend* this practice (through coming to further understand its implications) of honoring breaking in his next three novels. I will consider in depth in Chapter 3 below the implications of the diary-reading scene. Here, however, I wish to look at a slightly more subdued moment of contention between the two functions coming a bit later in the narrative.

Volume Two of the three-volume edition of *The Woman in White* is meant (as explicitly set down by Collins in the original manuscript [*Woman in White* 691]) to sensationally end with a scene signaling that in this work he has reached a certain intellectual threshold in his project's development. "The tombstone scene," as we might term it, offers us, appropriately enough, a showdown. It is a moment when the settling and breaking functions fight it out for ascendency. This encounter is the first (the dream in *Basil* being concerned, as we will see, with the slightly different issue of the status of the literary artist) of various other crucial encounters—often dealing with failures of naming, of textual label or name not matching up with material body—between the functions in Collins's major fictions: such as Magdalen "Vanstone" learning her parents were not really married in *No Name;* Lydia Gwilt realizing that her marriage to the poor Ozias Midwinter under his real name, Allan Armadale, will afford her the opportunity of pretending to be the rich Allan Armadale's widow; and Franklin Blake encountering his own name on the nightgown in *The Moonstone.* It represents a moment of contention between the body (and the settled materialization it represents) and the text (specifically that text's breaking aspects leading, in the case of this particular narrative, to a loss of social identity) and encapsulates the complex interactions that can, as a result of iterability, eventuate from such a meeting.

The scene, as it begins, has our hero Walter Hartright noticing two women approaching him as he stands beside the tombstone of his lost love, a tombstone honoring "the Memory of Laura, Lady Glyde." One of the approaching women is clearly Marian Halcombe. The other is mysteriously veiled:

> The woman with the veiled face moved away from her companion, and came towards me slowly. Left by herself, standing by herself, Marian Halcombe spoke. It was the voice that I remembered—the voice not changed, like the frightened eyes and wasted face. . . .
>
> The woman came on; slowly and silently came on. I looked at her—at her, and at none other, from that moment.

[Marian's] voice that was praying for me, faltered and sank low—then rose on a sudden, and called affrightedly, called despairingly to me to come away.

But the veiled woman had possession of me, body and soul. She stopped on one side of the grave. We stood face to face with the tombstone between us. She was close to the inscription on the side of the pedestal. *Her gown touched the black letters.*

The voice came nearer, and rose and rose more passionately still. "Hide your face! don't look at her! Oh, for God's sake spare him!————"

The woman lifted her veil.

> "Sacred
> to the Memory of
> Laura,
> Lady Glyde—"[19]

Laura, Lady Glyde, was standing by the inscription, and was looking at me over the grave. (*Woman in White* 419; emphasis added)

Shockingly, Hartright encounters Laura Fairlie over what is supposed to be her grave, the text itself here just failing, because of a significant blank line, to reenact the scene's all-important encounter between the textuality of the inscription and the "physicality" of the apparent original of "Laura." There are resonances in this scene with Basil's dream of fair and dark women pulling him in opposite directions (a scene considered in detail in Chapter 2), especially in an acknowledgment such as "the veiled woman had possession of me, body and soul," as well as foreshadowing—in Laura's seemingly impossible encounter with her own name—of Franklin Blake's self-encounter on the beach in *The Moonstone*. We are also reminded in the

---

19. The blank lines surrounding the tombstone inscription—paradoxical signs (lines that both are and are not lines of "writing") of both settling and breaking, of both inscription and de-inscription (akin to Collins's later paradoxical titling of *No Name,* a title that is not a title)—exist in the initial *All the Year Round* printing (19 May 1860) as well as in some modern editions of the story (see for example the Sucksmith edition reproducing the original's sensational varied typefaces, 378). They, along with the central plot turn of a *blank* space in a marriage register *signifying* forgery, work to emphasize Collins's interest in the process through which sometimes something can come of nothing, here exemplified in the particular situation of meaning coming from a lack of signs. Collins was intrigued by the way in which contextualization could render a *blank* an effective speech-*act*. See Zigarovich for a suggestive connection between epitaph writing (what she describes as a writing after death) and the signifying effected by the blank in the register.

phrase "her gown touched the black letters" of Walter Hartright's encountering of Anne Catherick on Hampstead Heath ("every drop of blood in
my body was brought to a stop by the touch of a hand laid lightly and
suddenly on my shoulder" [*Woman in White* 20]). Following on from the
way in that scene, as Oliphant has it, sensation is manifestly communicated
from one character to another by touch—"The reader's nerves are affected
like the hero's" ("Sensation Novels" 572)—here one entity would similarly
seem to infect the other.

The tombstone scene demonstrates Collins's artistry, his genius, in choosing situations that exemplify exactly the paradoxes in which he is most
interested. The question here simply becomes: *in which direction* is this infec-
tion traveling? Is the body reifying the letters (as the breaking function is
trumped by settling once more in Western thought) or are the letters disar-
ticulating the body and the identity founded on it (as the breaking function
comes to infect materiality)? The answer to this question holds the key to
indicating the direction in which the conclusion of this constantly-alternat-
ing story is finally headed. The fundamental subject-object ambiguity in this
encounter between body and text disrupts any simple symbolization in the
standard sense that might have been on its way to crystallizing. Materiality
and textuality, those equally valid, but not mutually exclusive, interpretations, are in seemingly irresolvable conflict here. Laura's gown is made to
touch, as Hartright has said earlier, "the hard, clear, cruel black letters which
told the story of her life and death" (*Woman in White* 417),[20] to touch the
letters testifying falsely to her death. The contagion could be traveling from
the letters to the body (consolidating the loss of identity aimed at by the
villains' earlier manipulations of the breaking function) *or* from the body to
the letters (undoing the breaking effect through the influence of a solidifying
body, that body being, in some sense, not just a particular character's body
but also the *author's* body, the anchor of the author–work tie being repeatedly defended throughout this narrative's lobbying against literary piracy, a
topic to be touched on in detail in Chapter 3). It could be exemplifying a
giving in to the falsity of inscription (a giving in to the breaking function,
here expressed in the form of textual re-inscribability) or to the "truth" of
corporeality (the settling function). Put simply, the relevant question is, who
wins? Is it to be Fosco's or the good characters' standpoint that ultimately
wrests control of this text? In which direction is Collins to be understood
to be tending at this point in his project? . . .

---

20. The "Narrative of the Tombstone" thus comes to stand in here for the whole of the narrative,
only in reverse, as the larger text of course tells the story of Laura's death and life.

A DAB HAND at handling mystery, my subject for instance, would no doubt order the disclosive process differently (i.e., "make 'em wait" appropriately), but I feel it, already, to be high time to relieve my readers of their suspense: the narrative action of *The Woman in White,* in concluding with the reestablishment of Laura Fairlie in her original position, as well as with the death of Fosco, would seem strongly—if perhaps not quite conclusively[21]—to suggest that the settling function eventually must win out, customary order here being restored and the philosophical tradition of settling-eclipsing-breaking being upheld—at least at this point in Collins's career.

Of course, the "closeness," so to speak, of this present victory hints at future losses waiting in the wings. T. S. Eliot in an article entitled "Wilkie Collins and Dickens" famously labels Collins a "master" of the art of melodrama, and likens him to Dickens and Charles Reade in their more shocking narrative moments (*Selected Essays* 381). But I would argue that Collins's melodrama—like his sensationalism—originates from a more theoretical and textual source than that of many of the other writers to whom H. L. Mansel's accusation of "preaching to the nerves" in his 1863 review of 24 sensation novels (including *No Name*) might more fittingly have applied (481). Caught up in this conflict between functions, the narrative of *The Woman in White* comes to generate what look like melodramatic effects from what is actually a conflict stemming from the paradox of degree situated at the heart of iterability. That is, the melodramatic interest in this story is generated by its repeatedly approaching the danger zone of allowing the breaking function to triumph before it breathlessly pulls back from fully opening the door to an alienation (initially of the text and eventually of the self) that would seem to threaten to become uncontrollable. What Eliot understood as a "mastery" of melodrama was actually—though he would no doubt have declined to phrase it in this way—a situation of an author gradually transitioning (and occasionally resisting that change) in allegiance between the two functions of iterability.

---

21. While I am in my analysis taking the narrative "at its word," so to speak, I would note that critics have recently been prompted to query this type of trusting standpoint. They have questioned whether it really is Laura who is liberated from the asylum (Ablow 158n1 and Dever 123n3) and whether Fosco actually dies at the end of the novel (Hutter, "Fosco Lives!"). While I confess myself to be intrigued by both propositions, especially by Hutter's suggestive interpretation of the story viewed in the light of Fosco's famous boat-house assertion that "foolish criminals . . . are discovered, and wise criminals . . . escape" (*Woman in White* 236), I believe both interpretations to be taking things too far. At this point in Collins's career "propriety" is still on the side of the settling function, on the side of Marian when she describes the Count's opinions as "glib cynicism" (240). Only after this novel will Collins come to respect the need to honor *both* functions equally.

The Woman in White's hypnotic appeal is largely the result of the very real fear that the villains, those profiteers of breaking, might indeed end up *getting away with it.* Thus, it comes as no surprise that the story's intial two volumes should be devoted to the breaking function. In those volumes, the villains Percival Glyde and Count Fosco make use of the danger posed by the breaking function to threaten not just the identities of fellow characters but also, by implication, the author's identity and the integral "identity" of his work. Crucial to the success of the villains' plot is the strategy of exploiting the vulnerability to the breaking function of the markers of Laura's identity. As a result, what we end up with in the exchange of women in the narrative is a crime of false "printing." The nurses at the asylum tell the newly (re)captured patient to "Look at your own name on your own clothes, and don't worry us all any more about being Lady Glyde. . . . Do look at your clothes now! There it is, in good marking-ink; and there you will find it on all your old things, which we have kept in the house—Anne Catherick, as plain as print!" (*Woman in White* 436). Since it is effectively the labels on the garments in which the Count causes Laura to be dressed that bring about the transformation in identities—linguistic "characters" equaling character (a favorite Collinsian structural "pun"), as the nurses peremptorily testify—the Count's crime of the theft of identity, like his theft earlier of Marian's diary (as we will see in Chapter 3), is at its basis a textual crime, a crime clearly exploiting the breaking function of linguistic iterability.

However, as noted, in this one of Collins's works it will be Walter Hartright's mission of redemption that will triumph in the end over the perils of that function. The lifting of the veil, in both a literal and figurative sense, and the removal of her false clothes will push Laura toward embodiment and reestablishment within her proper social position. Walter will insist on, among other things, the erasure of the inscription and the counteraction of the inscription's potential disembodiment of his beloved:

> She has been cast out as a stranger from the house in which she was born—a lie which records her death has been written on her mother's tomb—and there are two men, alive and unpunished, who are responsible for it. That house shall open again to receive her, in the presence of every soul who followed the false funeral to the grave; that lie shall be publicly erased from the tombstone, by the authority of the head of the family; and those two men shall answer for their crime to ME, though the justice that sits in tribunals is powerless to pursue them. (*Woman in White* 454)

Hartright at the conclusion of the story will invite the villagers present at the public re-introduction of Laura to watch as the inscription is struck off the marble, albeit only after he has the previous day made a copy of it as one of the many "testimonies" he has been collecting (633–35). As he maneuvers to bring his Eurydice back to life, after a transformative trip to Central America, Hartright will also be undoing the terrors of American book piracy, a practice manifestly exploiting the breaking function, and similarly beyond the reach of judicial tribunals. Here Collins, respectful of the desires that had originally motivated his copyright allegory, will draw back from that function as a strong discourse of honorability, in the form of Hartright's sense of mission, comes into effect to teach us a lesson that we so richly deserve, if, that is, we have been supporting that mid-Victorian system of illicit literary piracy across the Atlantic. In the restoration of Laura Fairlie to her former position in society, Collins puts forward the belief— still viable with him at this time in his career, perhaps due to the influence of his more Pollyanna-ish friend Dickens—that breaking can eventually be controlled through the expenditure of enough effort on the part of restorative agents such as the characters Marian Halcombe and Walter Hartright. As they come to reconnect Laura Fairlie's body with the social identity it had become disarticulated from, the "good" characters in this narrative fulfill the role of an ultimately triumphant settling function.

In this sense, Collins is at this point in his career still adhering to the standard party line. Only in his next three productions will he be allowing the breaking function truly to have an equal status with the settling, as the former comes to menace even the author's identity, at the level of authorial intention. But before Collins, somewhat like Wordsworth climbing Snowdon, can reach this stage in his ascent out of the valley of automatic settling, he will need to move past a particular false obstacle or metaphorical cloud bank that had preoccupied, as we will see in the next section, thinkers a century before him, the illusory "barrier" of the act of publication.

The Breaking Function and the Voluntary Act of Publication

Collins's major fictions, our present-day culture's dematerialization of the book, and Derrida's philosophical critiques are excellent places to watch in operation the conflict between textual control and the loss of it. They are not, however, the only cultural moments at which to find iterability's inherent tension making itself felt. Iterability having come into being along with language, that is, at its creation, and having been in operation ever since, it would be reasonable to expect—despite (or perhaps especially because of) the ill fit between its nature and the usual patternings of logic—moments in intellectual history of this tension's "showing through," moments in various legal, literary, and cultural contexts of the revelation of specific, irresolvable conflicts directly themselves arising from the conflict located at the heart of iterability. In other words, it would be reasonable to expect over its long history—a history coincident with the concept of "history" itself—that the conflicted grounding of iterability should not always have been successfully overlaid with a convincing degree of "reasonableness," a preferred suppressive strategy in the composition of intellectual histories.

One particularly interesting cultural moment at which to find surfacing language's fundamental tension, I would argue, is that remarkable era—situated, it should be emphasized, lest we improperly begin feeling ourselves to be especially novelly-situated, a good deal prior to our recent post-structuralist age—of spirited legal discussions in England establishing the modern understanding of copyright. The literary property debates of the late eighteenth century at one significant point call on the judges and legislators involved to consider whether or not the publication of a book has resulted in that book's copyright *also* being sold along with the physical copy. When Justice Joseph Yates, choosing to dissent in *Millar v. Taylor* (1769) from the majority opinion of the Court of King's Bench, argues that it has, he conclusively exposes the disarticulation between the fixed nature of language and his age's contemporary copyright ideology. What is most remarkable is that Yates seems genuine in his belief that selling a particular copy of a book is equivalent to selling its copyright. At that time, in both England and on the Continent, this type of contention was not so "easy" an issue to dismiss as it might seem to us today. Thoroughly steeped in the modern conception of the operation of copyright as we are, we would find it hard to justify the argument that the author's voluntary acquiescence to the process of publication is also an abrogation or renunciation of the copyright, for we clearly understand the sale of books to distinctly *not* be the granting of the right also to reprint and sell their contents—even though in various contexts we do not always honor that understanding.[22]

---

22. See William Alford's discussion of the history of the operation of intellectual property in China in his *To Steal a Book Is an Elegant Offense: Intellectual Property Law in Chinese Civilization*. For the exploitation of the alienability of iterable traces in a different context, see the more significant twenty-first century music and movie peer-to-peer sharing cases: the 9th Circuit's decision in *A&M Records, Inc. v. Napster, Inc.* (2001); the Supreme Court's decision in *Metro-Goldwyn-Mayer Studios,*

But, as Yates's dissent serves as one prominent means of bringing home, this ease of understanding has not always been the case. The arguments, opinions, and decisions offered in the landmark cases of *Tonson v. Collins* (1762) (no relation to Wilkie), *Millar v. Taylor,* and *Donaldson v. Becket* (1774), the most significant English judicial decisions on copyright in the eighteenth century, manifest a marked difference of opinion with regard to this issue. In this section I will be proposing that the conflicted foundation of the iterability of language is the impetus for that difference (a difference expressed contemporaneously also in a variety of Continental countries and, as already mentioned, in the contrast between Chinese and Western perspectives on intellectual property). That is, it will be my contention that from the moment in *Millar* when Justice Yates states that "[e]very purchaser of a book is the owner of it: and, as such, he has a right to make what use of it he pleases" (234) the debate has begun (or, more appropriately, re-erupted—Yates had argued similarly in *Tonson* while acting in that instance as counsel for the defendant) as to what level of significance should be accorded to the breaking function in the legal construction of copyright, over and against language's manifestly acknowledged settling function.

Yates's primary contention in his opinion in *Millar* is that, by publishing, the author has conceded, undone, or undermined whatever undefined elements had been setting off the work as his or her sole property. Yates attempts to map out schematically at a certain point in his remarks what seems to him to be the fundamental conflict:

> It is by legal actions that other men must judge and direct their conduct: and if such actions plainly import the work being made common; much more if it be a necessary consequence of the act, "that the work is actually thrown open by it"; no private transaction or secretly reserved claim of the author can ever control that necessary consequence. Individuals have no power, (whatever they may wish or intend), to alter the fixed constitution of

Inc. v. Grokster, Ltd. (2005); and the Australian Federal Court's decision on Kazaa in *Universal Music Australia Pty Ltd. v. Sharman License Holdings Ltd.* (2005). Despite valiant efforts of ideology-inculcation on the part of governments, the social opprobrium currently accorded the act of illegally downloading songs or movies is still felt to be significantly different from that accorded the act of stealing a material object such as a computer or car. To offer merely one example, among many, of attempted copyright ideology inculcation, one might note the commercials advertising an "I"-Rating, for Illegal Downloading, included at the start of modern DVD rentals. In those commercials, copying or downloading movies is equated with stealing a car, a handbag, a television set, and a physical DVD from a store. The simple existence of these morality lessons indicates the difficulty copyright ideology has had over the last two centuries in gaining a foothold in the popular psyche. The continual failure in the establishment of the ideology that the theft of iterable items is as significant as the theft of non-iterable ones is a sign of the breaking function of iterability making itself felt again and again.

things: a man can't retain what he parts with. If the author will voluntarily let the bird fly, his property is gone; and it will be in vain for him to say "he meant to retain" what is absolutely flown and gone.[23] (*Millar v. Taylor* 234)

Rather than turning a blind eye to breaking, as had been the common tendency in Yates's intellectual and legal culture, this particular judge pays respect to the marked strangeness of what he understands to be the "fixed constitution of things." Having accepted the reality of breaking, Yates finds himself called on as a matter of conscience—the report framing it as such: "sitting in his judicial capacity . . . he thought himself bound both in this and in every cause, to declare [his opinion] frankly and firmly" (*Millar v. Taylor* 229)—to acknowledge the existence of a particular disconnection between the writer and his words.[24]

However, Yates's standpoint is fundamentally conflicted. His thinking is situated at the cusp of a seemingly-irresolvable paradox, one that he attempts to avoid through temporal manipulation. He clearly senses that breaking is present, but he is also well aware that settling is occurring. Allowing for the existence of that latter function, he remarks, "An author is fully possessed of his ideas, when they arise in his mind: and therefore from the time these ideas occur to him; or from the time he writes them down, they are his property" (*Millar v. Taylor* 231). Similarly, William Blackstone, the famous legal commentator and counsel opposing Yates in *Tonson* in 1762, had remarked when refuting a contention made in an earlier hearing by Yates's predecessor, "Notwithstanding . . . Mr. Thurlow's assertion, I must maintain, that 'a literary composition, as it lies in the author's mind, before it is substantiated by reducing it into writing,' *has* the essential requisites to make it the subject of property" (180–81; emphasis added). Both sides having acknowledged

---

23. Yates's reasoning would be energetically criticized by Collins's good friend Charles Reade in 1875. Reade would characterize Yates as having practically single-handedly invented the breaking function of iterability: "Justice Yates . . . founded a school of copyright sophists, reasoning *à priori* against a four-peaked mountain of evidence. He furnished the whole artillery of falsehood, the romantic and alluring phrases 'a gift to the public,' &c., the equivoques, and confusions of ideas, among which the very landmarks of truth are lost to unguarded men. Since it is this British pettifogger who, in the great Republic, stands between us and the truth—between us and law—between us and morality—between us and humanity—between us and the eighth commandment of God the Father—between us and the golden rule of God the Son, Judge Yates becomes, like Satan, quite an important equivocator, and I must undeceive mankind about Judge Yates and his fitness to rule the Anglo-Saxon mind" (Reade, "The Rights" 172).

24. Yates had not been without some pressure to reconsider his position before putting it on record. Rose notes that Yates's dissent from the other three judges on the Court of King's Bench came as "the first instance of a final difference of opinion" in that court since Mansfield had taken on the chief justice role thirteen years prior: "[N]either Mansfield nor his brethren could move Yates from the anti-common-law position he had taken before the bar in *Tonson v. Collins*" (*Authors* 79).

settling to exist from the beginning (perhaps even technically before it), the task becomes to determine when—or whether—that settling comes to be eroded. His era representing the apex of the Enlightenment in England, Yates understandably finds it difficult to "go backwards," to the Renaissance mind-set that had welcomed paradox, and to allow incompatibles to exist side by side.[25] Such a move would unquestionably seem a regression. He has no other choice, then, but to understand the two functions to be existing at two separate points in time. Thus, he posits the existence, somewhere in between composition and mass dissemination of a special moment where settling turns into breaking, where the author's ownership turns into alienation, and he aligns this moment with, or collapses it into, the "moment" of publication.

For Yates, the event of the author's having agreed to go into print comes to stand as the (illusory) Rubicon between the two functions. In *Tonson* he remarks, "I allow, that the author has a property in his sentiments *till he publishes them*. . . . [F]rom the moment of publication, they are thrown into a state of universal communion" (185; emphasis added). Yates refuses to allow the two functions to be in direct conflict, his "till he publishes them" operating as a magically transformative transition point. Yates leaves out of consideration completely iterability's possible effects on the pre-publication text. This is a mistake. A thinker only partially open to the implications of the situation he is analyzing, he ends up focusing on the relatively insignificant moment of the author's having agreed to a general publication of his work rather than on the much more interesting one of the author's earlier having agreed to manifest himself through "an instrument that bears within itself its repeatability," which repeatability then renders the author "absented from what [he] use[s]" (Derrida and Ricoeur 154). The moment Yates should have been focusing on was that of the author's prior concession of having agreed to appear in language, a devil's bargain if ever there was one. This would be the moment the thinkers coming after him, Collins

---

25. Yates's colleague Justice Aston, citing William Wollaston's *The Religion of Nature Delineated* in his opinion in *Millar v. Taylor*, not only upholds reason but denigrates paradox at the same time: "I think fit (however abstract they may seem) to consider certain great truths and sound propositions; which we, as rational beings; we, to whom reason is the great law of our nature; are laid under the obligation of being governed by; and which are most ably illustrated by the learned author of the religion of nature delineated; that is to say—'That moral good and evil are coincident with right and wrong': for, *that can not be good, which is wrong; nor that evil, which is right.* 'That right reason is the great law of nature; by which, our Acts are to be adjudged; and according to their conformity to this, or deflection from it, are to be called lawful, or unlawful; good, or bad.' 'That whatever will bear to be tried by that reason, is right; and that which is condemned by it, is wrong.' 'That to act according to right reason, and to act according to truth, are in effect the same thing" (*Millar v. Taylor* 213; emphasis added).

particularly in *The Moonstone* and Derrida throughout his career, would make their primary object of inquiry—after a couple of false starts along the way in Collins's case (particularly in *The Woman in White*'s interest in the perils of publication).

In Yates's day the significant points of concern are left improperly disarticulated by the debaters on both sides. Settling and breaking are evident at every stage of the English legal debate. They are simply never allowed to coalesce into the paradox (admittedly, a paradox of degree rather than of kind) that Collins and Derrida would later be so keen to emphasize. Yates in 1762, while a counselor in *Tonson,* was already arguing for proper respect needing to be paid to the radically alienating effects of publication and to publication's removal of the distinguishing "indicia" separating the author's unpublished copy from the purchaser's copy, such distinguishing indicia being necessary, he maintained, for establishing something as a piece of "property": "How is an author to be distinguished? . . . The act of publication has thrown down all distinction, and made the work common to every body; like land thrown into the highway, it is become a gift to the public" (*Tonson v. Collins* 185). Blackstone, serving as opposing counsel, forcefully countered this critique:

> It is asserted, that the bare act of publication renders the performance common to all mankind: it was asserted; but the proof of that position, if given, totally escaped my observation. He [Counselor Yates] allows, that to constitute an abandonment, there must be plain tokens of a voluntary dereliction: in the present instance, it is so far from a dereliction, that the very act of publication shews an intention to continue the use of it, for the purpose of profit, so long as the author can. (188)

The non-cooperative nature of the adversarial Westminster legal system was bound to push the paradox of degree relationship between the functions of iterability into the form of an illusory paradox of kind.[26] And so it did here, as the act of publication came to be viewed simultaneously in the mutually-exclusive forms of a dereliction of ownership and an assertion of it. The complete contrast between Yates's and Blackstone's positions maps out the boundaries of the dispute, a conflict that should have been simultaneous and focused on origins but that ended up being fought around the markedly provisional focal point of the moment of publication.[27] This "conceptual

---

26. For a critique of the adversarial system see Fox 123–26.

27. The illusion of publication's being the seminal moment of alienation continues to entrance thinkers even up to the present day. In an intriguing analysis Susan Eilenberg elaborates on the im-

extension," as we might term it, had been in part, as I have mentioned, the result of the Enlightenment's turn away from paradox, a turn the effects of which we still see ourselves as they come to provide the impetus, for instance, for many of the celebratory pronouncements of and/or hopeful calls for the death of literary theory today.

The Failed Gambits of Speech and the Unpublished Manuscript

The debate regarding the possible effects of publication was carried on also in contemporary Continental contexts. The comparison being instructive, we might briefly look, before considering the other judges' reaction to Yates's opinion in *Millar,* at what is occurring at the time in Prussia and Germany. In the course of that particular dispute, the philosopher Immanuel Kant is prompted to defend the author's post-publication control of his or her discourse.[28] An example of the type of standpoint that Kant is contesting can be found in a quotation from a German article of 1783 by Christian Sigmund Krause:

> "But the ideas, the content! that which actually constitutes a book! which only the author can sell or communicate!"—Once expressed, it is impossible for it to remain the author's property. . . . It is precisely for the purpose of using the ideas that most people buy books—pepper dealers, fishwives, and the like, and literary pirates excepted. . . . Over and over again it comes back to the same question: I can read the contents of a book, learn, abridge, expand, teach, and translate it, write about it, laugh over it, find fault with

plications of the conflation of the author with his or her text. Noting that the chapter on identity incorporated by John Locke into the second edition of his *Essay Concerning Human Understanding* in 1694 generated a century of debate over such issues as the conception of the integral, single identity and the nature of insanity, she contends, "At the same time that the nation was worrying about the nature of intellectual property, it was also worrying about the nature of identity: the two debates, I suspect, . . . reflected one another. . . . A writer gives the reader custody of the children of his brain. The reader is entitled—for how can he be stopped?—to adopt and raise them as his own, regardless of how the author might wish them to be raised. Thus the author, by the fact of publication, loses control over something he had regarded as his. The question I would like to raise is whether he loses control of *himself.* Is publication—is allowing another access to one's thoughts—an implicit alienation or forfeiture of identity?" (Eilenberg, "Copyright's Rhetoric" 11 and 20–21). I believe that Eilenberg's analysis is hampered by its tradition-honoring focus on the moment of publication, a focus her argument seems nevertheless to wish—one that remains unfulfilled—to move its way beyond through its shift from a focus on the author's losing control of some *thing,* say his labor or his figurative "children," once regarded as his to his losing control of *himself,* of his identity.

28. See Kawohl for a discussion of the historical background to this debate.

it, deride it, use it poorly or well—in short, do with it whatever I will. But
the one thing I should be prohibited from doing is copying or reprinting
it? . . . A published book is a secret divulged. . . . Would it not be just as
ludicrous for a professor to demand that his students refrain from using
some new proposition he had taught them as for him to demand the same
of book dealers with regard to a new book? No, no, it is too obvious that
the concept of intellectual property is useless. My property must be exclusively mine; I must be able to dispose of it and retrieve it unconditionally.
Let someone explain to me how that is possible in the present case. Just let
someone try taking back the ideas he has originated once they have been
communicated so that they are, as before, nowhere to be found. All the
money in the world could not make that possible.[29]

In 1785 Kant publishes in Berlin an essay entitled "On the Unlawfulness of
Reprinting" laying out clear reasoning as to why in his view the right to print
a book should stay with the author and his or her authorized publisher and
not automatically transfer to the purchaser of an individual copy. He writes,

The author and the owner of a copy can both say with equal right of the
copy: it is my book!—but in different senses. The former is regarding the
book as a written work or speech, whereas the latter sees in it simply the
mute instrument for the delivery of the speech to him, or to the public—ie,
he regards it as a copy. This right of the author is, however, not a right to
the object, that is, to the copy; . . . rather, it is an innate right, invested in
his own person, entitling him to prevent anyone else from presenting him
as speaking to the public without his consent—a consent which cannot be
taken for granted by any means, since he has already conceded it to someone [to his publisher].[30] ("Unlawfulness" 416n)

---

29. Krause, "Über den Büchernachdruck," *Deutsches Museum* 1 (January–June 1783): 415–17;
qtd. in Woodmansee, "Genius" 443–44.

30. In 1797 in his better-known *The Metaphysics of Morals* Kant reiterates this thinking in a
section entitled "Unauthorized Publishing of Books Is Forbidden as a Matter of Right": "A *writing* is
not an immediate sign of a *concept* . . . It is rather a *discourse* to the public; that is, the author *speaks*
publicly through the publisher. . . . [T]he *publisher* speaks . . . in the name of the author. . . . Now it
is true that an unauthorized publisher also speaks, by an edition on his own initiative, in the name of
the author, but he does so without having been given a mandate by the author (*gerit se mandatarium
absque mandato*). He therefore commits the crime of stealing the profits from the publisher who was
appointed by the author (who is therefore the only legitimate one), profits the legitimate publisher
could and would have derived from the use of his right (*furtum usus*). So *unauthorized publishing of
books is forbidden as a matter of right.* Why does unauthorized publishing, which strikes one even at
first glance as unjust, still have an appearance of being rightful? Because *on the one hand* a book is a
corporeal *artifact* (*opus mechanicum*) that can be reproduced (by someone in legitimate possession of

In his essay Kant "solves," so to speak, the problem by distinguishing between the author's exertion (*opera*)[31] and the work itself (*opus*) and argues that what has been sold to the authorized publisher is not a piece of "intellectual property" (as had and would often thereafter be held in English legal judgments) but rather "the right to speak" to the public in the author's name: "A book is the instrument for delivering a speech to the public. . . . From this follows the essential point that it is not a thing which is thereby delivered, but an act (*opera*), namely a speech, and, what is more, literally. By calling it a mute instrument I distinguish it from those means there are for communicating a speech through sound" ("Unlawfulness" 407*n*). The ownership of this paradoxical "silent speech" derives from its being a manifestation of the author's personality or will. In essence, Kant is attempting to connect the book to the author (one presumably fully in control of his or her intentions) as closely as he believes the situation of literary composition warrants. Kant considers phonocentrism to hold the key to the solution of the dilemma. For him, a direct result of speech being, or at least seeming, a more intimate form of expression than mere writing is the consequence of the *opera* (the act) being closer, and presumably less alienable, than the *opus* (the thing). The right of speaking for oneself is, according to Kant, "a personal positive right" (411), "an innate right, invested in his own person" (416*n*),[32] that is essentially the author's right to dispose of as he or she wishes—"the author's ownership to his thoughts . . . remains his in spite of any reprinting" (403)—and not something that should (or even can?) be alienated. Justice Aston, sounding very much like modern-day defenders of the settling function, contends something similar in *Millar v. Taylor* when he bases his argument on the non-alienability of the author-proprietor's "intention": "[I]s there no difference betwixt selling the property in the work, and only one of the copies? . . . The proprietor's consent is not to be carried beyond *his manifest intent*. Would not such a construction extend the partial disposition of the true owner beyond his plain intent and meaning?" (222; emphasis added).[33] For Aston, the alienation at the hands of breaking

---

it), so that there is a *right to a thing* with regard to it. *On the other hand* a book is also a mere *discourse* of the publisher to the public, which the publisher may repeat publicly without having a mandate from the author to do so (*praestatio operare*), and this is a *right against a person*. The error consists in mistaking one of these rights for the other" (*Metaphysics* 71–72).

31. In the sense of an intellectual effort or speech-act, and not in the sense of the plural of *opus*.

32. Fichte will endorse this line of argument in 1793 (472).

33. Throughout this discussion I will be equating the author's "intention" to keep to himself the ownership of the published manuscript with his "intention" to convey "a particular meaning" in his writing. Both of these are the same with respect to their vulnerability to the breaking function of iterability.

"manifestly" not being desired by the author, it should simply cease to exist. Kant, being not so dismissive, but nevertheless no more efficacious, moves the issue of the author's intention to keep control into the contractual, business realm: the reprinter, essentially, is guilty of "conduct[ing] someone else's business in that person's name and yet against his will" ("Unlawfulness" 404).

Clearly, Kant's strategy of emphasizing a close author–work connection is not very different from that that had been adopted by the English judges defending the author's proprietary right (settling) against publication's alienating effects (breaking). However, in place of Kant's conceptualization of an author-as-speaker who is (presumably) automatically tied to his speech, the latter, in their turn, had offered as their preferred grounding for the author's control of the copyright in the *published book* the author's seemingly-incontestable right to the ownership of the *unpublished manuscript,* a difference that can be crudely schematized as a personality-basis/ labor-basis distinction for the grounding of literary ownership.[34] For example, in opposition to Yates's view of a radical post-publication alienation, the other judges in *Millar v. Taylor* emphasize the widely-acknowledged (almost sacrosanct) inherent pre-publication connection between the author and the manuscript, the author's "creation." This connection is most forcefully

---

34. The Prussian/German context found the personality to be the foundation of the ownership of the literary creation. In England it came to be generally understood that the ownership of a literary work resided in the labor the author had "mixed" with it. This divergence in theoretical basis for the property then led to the creation of two differing conceptions of authorship, one viewing the author as primarily a creator and the other viewing the author as primarily a disseminator. (This distinction, often operating in the background of opposing copyright arguments with each figuratively "haunting" the opposing side, has ever since plagued English and American copyright law, making it one of the most unpredictable of legal fields). The former system, the author-as-creator perspective, came to defend the author's "moral rights" (called in France "*le droit moral*") and the latter, the author-as-disseminator perspective, came to defend the perspective of literary property viewed as a vendible product that deserved protection because of the effort that had gone into its production. The former perspective stressed the settling aspects of iterability, while the latter stressed alienation and the breaking function. However, it should be noted that the Kantian or Hegelian (personality) and Lockean (labor) views of the grounding for the ownership of literary property interanimate and influence each other much more than is usually acknowledged by copyright historians, as noted in an intriguing study by Brown, who, writing of American scholars, comments that they largely have an "idealist framework" having "achieved a near-consensus, attributing differences to national variations on Enlightenment themes, in which Scottish, English and American thought more closely embraced the author as an individual in the market, whereas French thinking emphasized personal genius as resulting from a social process of Enlightenment and thus conceived literary property law as an encouragement for writers to serve the public good" (232–33). Extending his call for more nuance in copyright histories, Brown notes that the concepts of "*droit d'auteur,*" "*droits d'auteur,*" and "*propriété littéraire*" changed valence in significant and important ways after the Revolution (230–35). Then of course there is the interanimation in the other direction to be considered: for Locke's influence on France, see Hutchinson.

voiced by Chief Justice Mansfield: "It has all along been expressly admitted, 'that, by the common law, an author is intitled to the copy [copyright] of his work until it has been once printed and published by his authority'" (*Millar v. Taylor* 251).[35] Mansfield here relies on the settling function of iterability—or whatever that element is that is seemingly more automatically evident in the connection between author and manuscript than author and published book—to help him defend the author's tie to the published work (not realizing the question-begging nature of his own logic here). The fundamental proposition on which Mansfield's analysis is based, that the settling function is conclusively sealed off—and thus protected—from the breaking function, allows for the breeding of monsters.

However, both Kant and the judges neglect to adequately address what it is that might be coming in between, might be coming to disrupt their chosen seemingly-hermetically-sealed connections between the author and his will/speech or unpublished manuscript. Both parties ignore the fundamental question that their analyses would seem to be posing: how can an emanation of the will possibly come to be alienated?[36] Mansfield does not seem to see the contradiction in his extrapolating his argument of a *consistent* tie extending from undeniably-owned manuscript to unstably-owned

35. The acknowledgment of the unpublished manuscript as the incontestable property of the author having been of particular use to him, Mansfield paid that issue a great deal of attention in his decisions. In holding over *Tonson v. Collins* for a second hearing *en banc,* he delineated as the first of the two types of Chancery cases that he desired the justices and counsel to look into in the interim those cases "where there hath been no printing or publication at all. The Statute of Queen Anne seems *evidently* to distinguish this from other cases" (173; emphasis added). It is difficult to pinpoint exactly to what section of the Statute Mansfield refers as there is no mention of the ownership of manuscripts in that document. Provision II of the Act (An Act for the Encouragement of Learning 8 Anne c. 19 [1709]), dictating proper registry of the title of the manuscript in the Stationer's Register as necessary to a claim to the Statute's protections, is vague in its use of the important term "secured," that clause being evidently designed to make "some provision . . . whereby the property in every such book, as is intended by this act to be *secured* to [secured to?] the proprietor or proprietors thereof, may be ascertained" (rpt. in Patry, *Copyright Law* 3:1462; emphasis added). One is prompted to wonder whether it is a property *already* in the person that is being defended here or a property that is first being, say, "*vested*" in the person and then defended. Mark Rose writes, "The act, however, is inconsistent: although 'vesting' is used in the title, 'securing' is employed in the preamble to the second section. . . . Later in the century the proponents of perpetual copyright would seize on this inconsistency and argue that the use of 'securing' in the body of the act had more force than the use of 'vesting' in the title" (*Authors* 46n11). The issue of the reversion of copyright to the author if he or she should still be living at the end of the first fourteen year term, referred to in Provision XI of the Statute, suggests perhaps more forcefully than anything else in the document the strong proprietary tie between author and manuscript upon which Mansfield's statement relies. But this is all beside the point as both of these arguments would have been difficult to make, and they do not at all seem consonant with Mansfield's peremptory and summary tone in his use of the word "evidently" in his assertion.

36. Collins will consider this situation when in *No Name* he has Michael Vanstone ignore the clear intention expressed in his brother Andrew's no longer effective will.

published book, the latter being a situation that clearly is continually failing and continually requiring stronger and stronger rhetorical (even ideological) assertions behind it to keep it propped up, with, at one point, Mansfield going so far as to peremptorily declare that the author by publishing his literary work "does not mean to make it common: and if the law says 'he ought to have the copy after publication,' it is a several property, easily protected, ascertained, and secured" (*Millar v. Taylor* 253). Literary property, subject as it is to the breaking function of iterability, as Yates—let alone Collins and Derrida—knows only too well, can never be easily "secured," and certainly should not be characterized by a reasonable observer as such. In the same way, Kant, that famously thorough thinker, does not touch on the question of how it comes about that a personal positive right—also a manifestation of the "will," so to speak that is so closely allied to the "self" as to almost *be* that entity—can ever possibly through book piracy be "alienated"—properly or improperly being beside the point. Not surprisingly, I find this paradox (Kant's conceptualization of an extension of the will that nevertheless requires defense from alienation) to be evidence of iterability's conflicted nature showing through in his thinking.

These issues were left unexplored by the eighteenth-century commentators. However, I believe Collins, writing in the more "progressive" nineteenth century—a century less beholding to a simplistic Enlightenment understanding of anti-paradoxical progress—to be moving toward their elucidation in his unified novel series. He seems to sense—perhaps having been motivated by the dissatisfaction remaining after his earlier attempts to ignore or eliminate the breaking function in *Basil* and *The Woman in White*—the presence of a paradox of degree needing to be dealt with. At a certain point in his project (most likely during the formulation and early composition stage of *No Name*), Collins intuited that in actual fact, the one-to-one and the one-to-many systems of literary reference are not in strict opposition. There always exists the possibility for the singular situation to turn into polyvalence (*No Name*) and for polyvalence to turn into singularity through structural manipulation (*The Moonstone*). The possibility always exists for the two arenas to communicate with one another. Such communicability is inherent in the nature of the paradox of degree characterizing iterability. Therefore, alienation in the literary realm is always possible and is—because the paradox-of-kind illusion continually re-seduces—always surprising. A sort of constant "Et tu, Brute?" situation is set up by the workings of language that Collins would be happy to sensationally exploit, as we will see, in his last three masterpieces.

The Disruption Prior to Publication

The debaters in the 1700s, Kant included, fail to formulate truly fundamental critiques and simply move on from the significant questions. Much of this lack of theoretical force is the result of the red herring of publication improperly drawing away these thinkers' attention. Following Mansfield's lead, Alexander Wedderburn, counsel for Becket in *Donaldson v. Becket*, in an address delivered before the House of Lords, uncomplicatedly offers the author's ownership of the manuscript as post-publication justification of ownership:

> as it had been admitted on all hands, that an author had an interest or property in his own manuscript previous to publication; he desired to know, who could have a greater claim to it afterwards. It was an author's dominion over his ideas that gave him his property in his manuscript originally, and nothing but a transfer of that dominion or right of disposal could take it away. It was absurd to imagine, that either a sale, a loan, or a gift of a book, carried with it an implied right of multiplying copies . . . it could not be conceived, that when five shillings were paid for a book, the seller meant to transfer a right of gaining one hundred pounds: every man must feel to the contrary, and confess the absurdity of such an argument. ("Arguments of Counsel" 124)

Completely given over to the hegemony of settling, both Wedderburn and Mansfield see in the unpublished manuscript a safe, physical manifestation of the solid tie between the author and the work. Once the pre-publication right is granted, that is, once the issue of initial settling is itself seemingly settled, the substantive question becomes, what effect, if any, does publication have on that ownership? The answer, as the judges arguing against Yates are quick to point out, has to be none, given that *there is no difference*, from a theoretical perspective, between a text's pre- and post-publication manifestations. And in that last contention they are completely on the side of truth (as well as completely at odds with themselves, that is, with their initial project of justifying a connection—unpublished manuscript/published book—that would, apparently, seem to have needed no justification).

Yates correctly senses the existence of the breaking function, and the need to acknowledge its post-publication effects, but, no more than a postmodernist theorist in embryo, he pulls back from describing the unpublished manuscript *also* as somewhat out of the author's control. He cannot

envision alienation, specifically the lack of a unified intention, to be existing in the immediate, unpublished iterable utterance. Thus, he is forced
into a position of self-contradiction upon his conceding that that private
manuscript focused on so persistently by his opponents incontestably *is*
the author's property (all the better to set up the contrast that he wishes to
exploit with regard to the conclusively-alienating post-publication stage).
Acceding to the contention that a limited lending of the manuscript can
take place without the eventuation of any undue effect on the author's right,
Yates remarks,

> If the author had not published his work at all, but only lent it to a particu-
> lar person, he might have injoined that particular person, "that he should
> only peruse it"; because, *in that case, the author's copy is his own;* and the
> party to whom it is lent contracts to observe the conditions of the loan:
> but when the author makes a general publication of his work, he throws it
> open to all mankind. (*Millar v. Taylor* 234; emphasis added)

Yates had also proposed this distinction seven years earlier in *Tonson v.
Collins.* Pouncing on it in that instance, Blackstone had contended that if
a right of ownership was allowed in the case of unpublished manuscripts,
it necessarily had also to be allowed in the case of the books printed from
those manuscripts: "Printing is no other than an art of speedily transcribing.
What therefore holds with respect to manuscripts is equally true of printing"
(*Tonson v. Collins* 181). Hitting on the same vein, Mansfield in 1769 asks,
"Does a transfer of paper upon which it is printed, necessarily transfer the
copy [i.e. copyright], more than the transfer of paper upon which the book
is written?" (*Millar v. Taylor* 253). Mansfield is suggesting, through his eminently sensible question, that if there is such a right before publication there
should be one after it also, the distinction between the two states being in
his eyes untenable (dismissing at one go both all future postmodern schools
of thought viewing the pre-publication text as not fully in the author's control as well as all schools of thought viewing copyright as fundamentally a
publisher's right).

   Given that printing and transcribing by hand both actuate iterability to
the same extent (see Blackstone's sensible equation above: "Printing is no
other than an art of speedily transcribing"), Mansfield is on a theoretical
level correct to dismiss the distinction between the manuscript and book,
but the conclusion he should be drawing from this dismissal, I would argue,
is not that the author's ownership bleeds over into the domain of post-
publication but that the *lack* of it extends back into the pre-publication

stage. Mansfield should be concluding not only that there is no inherent perpetual authorial proprietary right in the published text but also that there is not one—or more precisely not the degree of conclusive "control" implied by such a right—in the *unpublished manuscript.* In other words, contagious alienation rather than contagious reification should be the direction in which this debate moves. However, the time not having been propitious for such "poststructuralist" conceptualizations, the majority of the judges in *Millar v. Taylor,* like Walter Hartright in the Tombstone Scene, would dedicate themselves to restoring proper order to what had in their opinion become a seemingly-unruly (and patently unreasonable) discussion.

The debate over literary property at this time never reaches the foundational level of its actual object of inquiry, coming, as it does, to be sidetracked by an excessive interest in the moment of publication, as opposed to that of composition, as well as by the question of what should and should not be the proper grounding (statute? labor?[37] personality?[38]) for

---

37. See Rose writing in *Authors and Owners* that the promulgation of the representation of the author as proprietor in the three major literary property cases "was dependent on the classical liberal discourse of property as represented, most famously, by John Locke's notion of the origins of property in acts of appropriation from the general state of nature" (5). In these cases the author's ownership of the manuscript was often justified by the labor that he had "mixed" with it in the process of its creation. This justification proceeded from Locke's conception of the individual's right to his own person, as outlined in his *Two Treatises of Government:* "[E]very man has a property in his own person. . . . The labour of his body and the work of his hands, we may say, are properly his. Whatsoever then he removes out of the state that nature hath provided and left it in, he hath mixed his labour with, and joined to it something that is his own, and thereby makes it his property. It being by him removed from the common state nature hath placed it in, it hath by his labour something annexed to it that excludes the common right of other men" (287–88). This view of labor as the basis for literary ownership was put forward in the debates first by William Blackstone who cited Locke in his argument during the rehearing of *Tonson v. Collins* in 1762 as a means of rendering ownership of ideas as solid as ownership of land: "Locke on Government, part 2, c. 5, same right of occupancy in ideas, as in a field, a tree, or a stone" (*Tonson v. Collins* 180). (Yates was the counsel arguing against Blackstone in that hearing.) Blackstone contended, "it would be unjust, to make him a sharer in the reward, who has been no sharer in the labour" (180). He similarly collapsed material and immaterial property when he argued, "Property may with equal reason be acquired by mental, as by bodily labour" (180). Indeed, the analogy between texts and tangible objects would come full circle as in his famous *Commentaries on the Laws of England* (1765–69) Blackstone would be making the literary work exemplary of (once solely tangible) "occupancy": "There is still another species of property, which, being grounded on labour and invention, is more properly reducible to the head of occupancy than any other; since the right of occupancy itself is supposed by Mr Locke, and many others, to be founded on the personal labour of the occupant. And this is the right which an author may be supposed to have in his own original literary compositions: so that no other person without his leave may publish or make profit of his copies" (2:405). However, the paradoxical nature of iterability shows that such an "occupancy" is very unstable (or, more precisely, it is an occupancy manifesting a paradox of degree between its effects of stability and instability).

38. The debate in England, though finding the ownership of the work often to be based on the author's labor, also occasionally follows a foundation-in-personality line. For example, Justice Aston

the "property" inherent in a literary composition. To be fair, it is difficult to picture the English judges in 1769 formulating the concept of "iterability" and seriously grappling with its conflicted workings (or even the philosophers publishing in Berlin around the same time. Far from considering the effects of iterability's conflicted character, let alone the issue of publication's screening of the actual moment of loss of control, the House of Lords ends the English discussion in 1774 on practical political grounds, extinguishing in *Donaldson v. Becket*—as a means of undoing the London booksellers' literary "monopolies"—the author's perpetual copyright over the published work. Deciding in Yates's favor—at least to the extent that *perpetual* copyright is denied—but without any real acknowledgment of even his inchoate philosophical complications, the Lords allow politics to

---

in *Millar v. Taylor* suggests that the right to keep the manuscript back from publication stems from the author's role as originator: "there is a material difference in favour of this sort of property, from that gained by occupancy. . . . For, *this is originally the author's:* and, therefore, unless rendered common by his own act and full consent, it ought still to remain his" (221; emphasis added). Later, he implies again that the work is consonant with the author's identity: "I do not know, nor can I comprehend any property more emphatically a man's own, nay, more incapable of being mistaken, than his literary works" (224). In *Tonson v. Collins* (1762), Counselor Yates allows for a personality basis when he remarks of the situation in which a printer might print a private manuscript without the consent of the author, "The piratical printer is here guilty of a double wrong:—in publishing private manuscripts without the leave of the owner; and in anticipating the profits of the first publication, to which, I acknowledge that the author is entitled" (187). Yates's split here in the piratical printer's "double wrong" of violating the right of the owner *and* of enjoying the profits of first publication suggests that the ownership of the manuscript is not based solely on the labor of the author since it is not based solely on the profits arising from that labor. That ownership must therefore be based also on something else. While Yates's later comments in the debates indicate that he did not acknowledge the text to be a fundamental manifestation of the author's personality or identity, nevertheless, he seems here to be alluding to a strong inherent proprietary tie between author and manuscript. Indeed, he seems almost to be proposing a type of right to privacy for the unpublished author in his significant use of the word "private" in the phrase "publishing private manuscripts without the leave of the owner." These types of allusions to some basis besides labor for the author's claim can be found not only in the judicial opinions but also in private discussions held at the time. For instance, James Boswell, that quintessential disseminator of another person's *bon mots,* tells us that at a dinner on 8 May 1773 Samuel Johnson discoursed on the subject of literary property: "There seems (said he), to be in authours a stronger right of property than that by occupancy; a metaphysical right, a right, as it were, of creation, which should from its nature be perpetual; but the consent of nations is against it, and indeed reason and the interests of learning are against it; for were it to be perpetual, no book, however useful, could be universally diffused amongst mankind, should the proprietor take it into his head to restrain its circulation. . . . For the general good of the world, therefore, whatever valuable work has once been created by an authour, and issued out by him, should be understood as no longer in his power, but as belonging to the publick; at the same time the authour is entitled to an adequate reward. This he should have by the exclusive right to his work for a considerable number of years" (2:259). Johnson's metaphysical right of creation coincides well with the conception of a literary property founded on the viewing of the work as an emanation of the author's personality. The stark contrast between this pre-publication metaphysical right of creation and Yates's post-publication "gift to the public" (*Tonson v. Collins* 188) marks out the boundaries of the dispute.

trump philosophy, deciding that the Statute of Anne had back in 1710 extinguished any common-law perpetual right.[39] The world not being ready for postmodern "illogic" in the late 1700s, England will have to wait for the publication of Collins's *The Moonstone,* if not also Derrida's "Signature Event Context," among other "postmodern" and "poststructuralist" works, before it can come to be situated in a position from which it can possibly properly grapple with linguistic iterability.

FROM Derrida's perspective, the unpublished manuscript, like the published one, is vulnerable to alienation, as is even, *pace* Kant, ownership based on books viewed as "speeches" to the public or simply ownership based on books seen as manifestations of the author's personality. Iterability allows alienation-inviting copies (even only evanescent, mental ones) to be created uncontrollably *from the absolute beginning.* That proliferation of copies then results in a proliferation of meanings as the same words appearing in different contexts are inevitably going to come to mean different things. Derrida writes,

> [B]y virtue of its essential iterability, a written syntagma can always be detached from the chain in which it is inserted or given without causing it to lose all possibility of functioning, if not all possibility of "communicating," precisely. One can perhaps come to recognize other possibilities in it by inscribing it or *grafting* it onto other chains. No context can entirely enclose it. Nor any code, the code here being both the possibility and impossibility of writing, of its essential iterability (repetition/alterity). . . .

---

39. Rose writes, "the House of Lords had long been antipathetic to the London booksellers' monopolies, and the outcome in *Donaldson v. Becket* was consistent with the House's previous treatment of copyright questions. But on what basis did the peers make their determination? What understanding of the nature of copyright did they adopt? Were they persuaded that there never was a common-law right? Or did they believe that there was but that it ended with publication? Or that it was taken away by the statute? . . . Some peers may have voted on the basis of legal theory, but many others, I suspect, were less concerned with the basis than with the result. Thus the peers gave an answer to the literary-property question, but they did not provide a rationale. . . . [W]hat the House of Lords did in *Donaldson v. Becket* was finally no more than to declare by authority that copyright henceforth would be limited in term" (*Authors* 102–3). Indeed, the roles and rights of the author have never been clearly elucidated, at a theoretical level, in legal discourse. A look at the debates held in England in the eighteenth-century continuing down to our own day through cases such as the 9th Circuit's decision in *A&M Records v. Napster* (2001) and the Supreme Court's decisions in the cases of *Eldred v. Ashcroft* (2003) and *MGM Studios v. Grokster* (2005) shows a repeated evasion of the complicated territory of the question of "the author" for the more readily traversable practical terrains of economics and politics (certainly the situation in the eighteenth-century cases), manifesting themselves, for instance, in questions of adequate creators' incentives or the proper duration of corporate monopolies.

> Every sign, linguistic or nonlinguistic, spoken or written . . . can be *cited,*
> put between quotation marks; *in so doing it can break with every given con-*
> *text, engendering an infinity of new contexts in a manner which is absolutely*
> *illimitable* [italics added]. This does not imply that the mark is valid outside
> of a context, but on the contrary that there are only contexts without any
> center or absolute anchoring [*ancrage*]. This citationality, this duplication or
> duplicity, this iterability of the mark is neither an accident nor an anomaly,
> it is that (normal/abnormal) without which a mark could not even have a
> function called "normal." ("Signature Event Context" 9 and 12)

Iterability, an aspect founding to an equal extent both writing and speech,
being the actual topic in question, these two contexts are, not surprisingly, indistinct for Derrida—"Every sign . . . spoken or written . . . can be
cited." The stark difference between Derrida's thinking and that of the late
eighteenth century legal theorists indicates a certain progress (a "progress"
undoubtedly both heart-warming and intensely aggravating at the same time
for the Enlightenment-influenced scholar in us all) having been made over
the last two centuries with regard to the struggle for intellectual dominion
between sequential logic and (Renaissance) paradox.

The situation in the eighteenth century is one of the undeniable hegemony of the former over the latter. In 1762, Blackstone argues that the
author, while being substituted for by words in as many as a hundred different contexts, retains, apparently, all of the force of his original intention:

> Consider writing, 1st, as an assistant to the memory; 2dly, as a means of
> conveying sentiment to distant times and places. In neither of these lights
> does the writer relinquish his title of making profits by his works; except
> that, when he has once written and published, he gives up the exclusive
> privilege of reciting to the ear; since, by parting with his manuscript, he
> has constituted a substitute in his stead, which speaks perpetually to the
> eyes of every reader. But, though he has given out one or a hundred cop-
> ies, has constituted one or a hundred substitutes to speak for him, yet no
> man has a right to multiply those copies, to make a thousand substitutes
> instead of one; especially, if any gain is to arise from such multiplication.
> (*Tonson v. Collins* 181)

According to Blackstone, who, as a means of avoiding paradox and maintaining logical progress, clearly sees one-to-one correspondences as far as the
horizon (both in space and time), the manuscript speaks exactly what the
author intends, as do the hundred subsequent copies of it, regardless of the

contexts in which they may end up. On the other hand, for Derrida there is, in a sense, full-scale "publication," with all its attendant corruptions and disruptions, *as soon as* there is formulation in language, whether that formulation takes place on paper or merely cloudily in the mind. There is no getting away, even at the most fundamental levels of identity constitution, from this alienation of intention. Operating in their inexorable, machine-like manner, linguistic iterability's effects are always there, before any volition can get underway on behalf of the multiple possible subsequent voluntary acts of relinquishment.[40]

The Relentless Pursuit of Breaking in Collins's Major Phase

The initial proliferation of copies commencing from the moment a repeatable trace or mark is created, iterability has the potential not only for absenting one from one's text but also from *oneself* (or, perhaps more properly, one's *self*). Insofar as one thinks in language, that is, insofar as one's consciousness is based in recitable and recontextualizable traces, "one" is absented from "the self," (or, better, "the" self). To the extent that it relies on language as the means of expressing, and perhaps founding, itself, "the identity" thus becomes manifold or split. It is no longer homogenous. Late in his essay when he turns his critique toward the lack of self-presence characterizing the writing of the signature, Derrida can be seen to be moving toward these propositions, that is, toward a critique of the notion of the singular, unified consciousness. He writes, "By no means do I draw the conclusion that there is no relative specificity of effects of consciousness, or of effects of speech. . . . It is simply that those effects do not exclude what is generally opposed to them, term by term; on the contrary, they presuppose it, in an asymmetrical way, as the general space of their possibility" ("Signature Event Context" 19). As an indication of the fundamental nature of this lack of unity, Derrida has earlier called iterability the "structural unconsciousness" of language (18). He notes that that most adamant testimony to the presence of consciousness, the signature, is necessarily also split by iterability: "to be readable, a signature must have a repeatable, iterable, imitable form; it must be able to be detached from the present and singular intention of its production. It is this sameness which, *by corrupting its identity and*

---

40. Derrida often comments on the "mechanistic" aspects of iterability. See, for example, his *Archive Fever; Grammatology* 79; "Psyche" 20; *Paper Machine;* and "Typewriter Ribbon."

singularity, divides [the signature's] seal" (20; emphasis added).[41] Similarly, in a response to a question about this passage he comments,

> Austin and along with him common sense . . . see the signature as the written equivalent to the source event of discourse. [It's believed that] when a signature is affixed somewhere, the origin of discourse, of written discourse in this case, is in some way stapled, marked, identifiable, and in some sense, event-like, absolutely singular. . . . [But] [t]here is no pure signature event, no pure signature. Like every event of discourse or of writing, a signature is in itself dubitable, imitable, and, therefore, falsifiable. And a theory of the signature that does not take account of this falsifiability can in no way render an account of what can be the so-called authentic effect of the signature. (Derrida and Ricoeur 142–43)

It is not just the signature's, but rather also the identity's, singularity that is here being contested and shown to be eminently corruptible through counterfeiting.

This thinking is mirrored in Collins's *The Moonstone,* particularly in the already-remarked paradox of self-alienation that characterizes Franklin Blake's famous self-realization, "I had discovered Myself as the Thief" (359). (The possible continuation here of "the Thief [of the Moonstone/ *The Moonstone*]" puts me in mind of Derrida's line, "We must be several in order to write" ["Freud" 226]). However, Collins does not move immediately from general publication (writing to be read by others), and the difficulties attendant upon that act, to internal discourse ("talking to oneself," in a sense) and its particular difficulties. He comes only gradually to dismantle the system (we will be following the gradations in this dismantling in the chapters to come) by undoing the standard view of the workings of linguistic iterability and communication. In *Basil,* he seems to consider breaking to be avoidable, attempting to tie rhetorically Basil's

---

41. The author's "intention" in giving "consent" to a particular publisher to bring out his/her work is of central concern in the preamble to the Statute of Anne's second provision: "And whereas many persons may through ignorance offend against this Act, unless some provision be made whereby the property in every such book, as is intended by this Act to be secured to the proprietor or proprietors thereof, may be ascertained, as likewise the consent of such proprietor or proprietors for the printing or reprinting of such book or books may from time to time be known . . . nothing in this Act contained shall be construed to extend to subject any bookseller . . . to the . . . penalties therein mentioned, for or by reason of the printing or reprinting of any book or books without such consent . . . unless the title to the copy of such book or books hereafter published shall, before such publication, be entered in the register-book of the company of Stationers, in such manner as hath been usual" (rpt. in Patry, *Copyright Law* 3:1462). The printer's entry of the title of the book in the Stationers Register thus becomes effectively the sign of the author's "consent"—effectively the author's signature on the contract—to allow that particular printer to publish his work.

manuscript to land in order to defend against that more disquieting function's disturbances. In *The Woman in White,* having Laura Fairlie's body's
difficulties in matching up with her largely textual identity stand in for the
vulnerable author–work tie, Collins acknowledges, but ultimately denies,
the possible threat posed by the breaking function to the ownership of (or
copyright in) the literary work. Then, having gone over to breaking, in *No
Name* he shows the system of would-be one-to-one correspondence to be
an unfairly privileged subcategory of the one-to-many correspondences of
his particular variety of sensation fiction, that latter system, in the form of
citation, apparently always available (and always waiting) to alienate the
will from the deed. In *Armadale* he revises the positions he had adopted
in *Basil* and *The Woman in White,* this time delegitimizing the solidity of
the published text and internalizing the threat of alienation inherent in the
process of publication. Thus, by the time he comes to write *The Moonstone,*
his thought has no final place of refuge in subterfuge and must finally con-
front head-on the threat posed by the breaking function to the integrity of
the supposedly unified authorial psyche and the supposedly unified intentions emanating from it. By the end of his unified novel series Collins will
have come to teach himself that one's iterable traces do and do not mean
what one had intended them to mean—one's intention to keep control
of one's published text is and is not going to be effective—and as a result
one ends up being and not being oneself. The writer in a sense ends up, as
a result of iterability, working both for and against him- or herself at the
same time. The only way to insert a gap into the operations of iterability
in order to allow purchase on and manipulation of its elements (what Yates
had unsuccessfully attempted and what we will see Collins succeeding at) is
to utilize the author-as-creator/author-as-disseminator distinction that had
been lying dormant at the basis of copyright. This will be Collins's strategy in his culminating, masterful avoidance, in his last major work, of the
seemingly-unavoidable trap of self-alienation at the hands of iterability.

THE TEMPTATION to construct a historical narrative of influence is strong
here, especially given the current fashionability of New Historical inquiry.[42]
However, that modishness notwithstanding, I believe that history in this
situation is trumped by theory, and not vice versa.[43] In other words, while

---

42. See the beginning of Chapter 3 for a discussion of this fashionability.

43. Similarly, Marxist "materialism" is trumped by Hegelian idealism. As a direct result of its
particularly materialistic bearings, Marxist critique, in one of its primary failings, must continually
fail to assess iterability correctly.

the legal discourse of the late 1700s could be understood to have directly "informed" the understanding of copyright for the legal culture of the era in which Collins is writing, that is, while the Yates–Mansfield debate could be seen to suggest a possible historical "source" for Collins's conflicted understanding of what it means to be the author and "owner" of his works in mid-nineteenth century England, that is not the direction in which this inquiry will be traveling.

Given that iterability is a timeless component of the trace-making faculty and that its workings violate "logic," it must come as no surprise that its difficulties should be surfacing every now and again at particular historical moments and be influencing significant historical constructs (constructs that then can sometimes come to be retroactively turned back on those workings, obscuring iterability through having screened it with the historical processes of which it itself was the cause rather than the effect). It is unnecessary in this case to enlist such time-bound or time-associated elements as those that gather themselves together (invariably too vaguely) under the umbrella term "historical influence." That is, the connection between the different historical moments of Yates and Collins, I am arguing, is more adventitious than causal. What might look like a series of "motivated," historical-influence-related eruptions of considerations of iterability over the course of intellectual history turn out simply to be structurally connected, as opposed to causally-connected, instances of the theoretical underpinnings of language making themselves felt every now and again, until they are (always unstably) brought under control, usually through peremptory, "common sensical" dismissal. Iterability's theoretical conflict being prone to surface on occasion, it should come as no surprise that Collins and Yates should both feel the need to honor—in their own particular ways, depending on the intellectual openness of themselves, their eras, and their societies—the conflict at the heart of the linguistic medium.

Collins's multi-volume unified novel series is a progressive seventeen-year-long exploration by one of the most precise of Victorian authors into the various ways in which the seemingly-inextricably-intertwined establishment and erosion of textual control can each be sustained and/or counteracted through rhetorical and strategic manipulations. His major fictions when looked at as a whole are seen to transition from manifesting a respect for a solidity of representation (the solid connection between signifier and signified, as well as its direct corollary the strong author–work tie) to coming, invariably shockingly, to acknowledge the breaking function of iterability. As they move along this trajectory, they write themselves past the simplistic "legal" standpoint, a perspective outlined in an interview by Derrida:

So I can say, "Well, the one who said 'I do' is someone in me but there is another one and another one and another one and I'm more than one." And what can you object to this? But the legal system implies that [when] . . . the legal subject . . . says "yes," it's "yes," there is no other one saying "no." . . . [L]anguage is such that we say something else. We always say something other than what we say. . . . If you close this possibility then there is no language anymore, there is no language. So, to have the possibility of the authentic, sincere and full meaning of what one says, the possibility of the failure, or of the lie, or of something else, must remain open. That's the structure of language. ("Following Theory" 43–44)

Collins's shadowy potential doppelganger always waiting in the wings in his dramatic narratives represents the shadow-like semi-presence—the "other one" always haunting the would-be unified "one"—exemplified in Derrida's remarks here. That semi-presence is described well by the concept of "hauntology," mentioned in his *Specters of Marx,* a concept lying at the basis of the identity composed of iterable markers. This term is intended to denote a mix of "haunting" and "ontology" (Derrida, *Specters* 50–51). The always available possibility for an unexpected Woman in White potentially to be stealing away *our* individual identities—through, for example, real-world piracies stealing away our publications' essences (or at least profits)—thus "haunts" us all continually and forever.

PART ONE

The Fictions of Settling

2

The Manuscript as Writer's Estate in *Basil*

THE LAW, full of respect for the merchant's cargo, for the écus acquired through work that is physical in some way or other, and often by dint of vile actions, the law protects landed property, it protects the house of the proletarian who has toiled and sweated—but it confiscates the work [*ouvrage*] of the poet who has been thinking.

—Balzac, "Letter to Authors" 64

Championing Settling

The main contention of this chapter—that in *Basil* (1852) Collins attempts to equate the author's manuscript with land—is not an earth-shaking proposition, to say the least. However, this equation becomes much more suggestive when it is placed within the broader contexts of Collins's own and his intellectual culture's development. Viewed from, for example, the position from which this study has set out, it becomes an instance of our author's trusting in the complete ascendancy of the settling function, as well as in ideological or rhetorical manipulation's power to keep that ascendancy in place. As Collins continues his investigations into iterability in the subsequent novels in his project, we will see him come to question that early trust.

That Collins's project should begin with an attempt at the rhetorical conflation of the author–work tie with the landowner–land relation—signaled, among other things, by our delirious author-diarist protagonist Basil losing control of his manuscript in tandem with the villain Mannion losing his handhold on the slippery coastal cliffrocks at Land's End—is not surprising.

His literary hero Balzac[1] had attempted the same conflation—via a rhetorical shaming—in his "Letter to Authors" of 1834 in the passage cited in the
epigraph above.

It is understandable that the twenty-eight-year-old Collins, when beginning his career, should have been tempted to adopt a strategy that so many
thinkers preceding him had (and so many following him would), that of
equating materiality with textuality and thereby attempting to sweep under
the rug the troublesome breaking function. He was, however, setting himself up—in this attempt to, so to speak, create land from rhetoric—as the
target of a potential De Manian–style deconstruction whereby mere rhetoric is found not to be up to the task that it has been set. Remarkably, it
would be Collins himself who would implicitly make this critique (a type of
self-correction of which very few thinkers have proven themselves capable)
through his move away from this initial naïve standpoint in the rest of the
works making up his unified long–novel project. Looking closely at this early
narrative, we see Collins establishing the base level from which he will begin
distinguishing himself from the majority of thinkers who would be profess-
ing solely a belief in the existence of the settling function of the iterability
of the mark.

In *Basil* Collins attempts to explore rhetoric's and ideological manipulation's potential for creating and controlling property at the same time
that he, in support of this effort, allegorizes the literary artist's transition
from upper-class, chosen vessel of the muse to industrious working man
laboring in the service of making his own fortune and way in the world,
a transformation seen also in, as we will see later in this chapter, contemporary Parliamentary debates over the extension of copyright. Collins here
does not seem at this point prepared to acknowledge that iterability's two
conflicting functions would be rendering it too evanescent a concept to
allow for the establishment of literary property—the foundation on which
he will be building his figurative "land" in *Basil*—as anything more definite
than an ideological construct. Collins refuses to acknowledge that writing's
breaking function, an aspect that must necessarily always accompany the
settling function, could possibly also "infect" that property that settling had
come to establish, setting a strict limit on the stability (and control of) the
literary work (as will happen with regard to the destiny of pirated copies
of *The Woman in White*) if not also similarly limiting the personality of the
author using language (as will happen in the narrative of *The Moonstone*).

---

1. See Collins's long, laudatory study of Balzac written for *Household Words* in 1859 ("Portrait").
Balzac, Fenimore Cooper, and Walter Scott were Collins's "three 'Kings of Fiction'" (Peters 377).

Here in this early work, the discourses of self-eroding property-based and personality-based authorship are left largely out of play. They will have to wait to be taken up in the later masterpieces. In those works, Collins will be willing, in a way that he was not yet in *Basil*, to explore the disintegrational or corrosive implications of the conjunction of the author's identity with language.[2]

The Comfortable Deniability of the Paradox of Iterability

The breaking function can be either ignored or considered more controllable and/or less disturbing than it actually is (admittedly itself a type of ignoring). These strategies for denigrating breaking are time-honored intellectual practices, methods of allowing Enlightenment-influenced thinkers to avoid the realm of paradox and to remain safe "at home" in that of logic. The implicit, often unacknowledged, hope is that logic will be enough to adequately deal with the challenge posed by iterability. However, the two functions being equally powerful, the efficacy of these practices cannot hold up for very long. Nevertheless, the thinkers continually will be trying.

One preferred strategy is for thinkers to "talk past" the issues in dispute, to miss (the existence of) the significant point of contention. This strategy often manifests itself in the dream of "reconciling" the two functions, that is, in other words, effectively discursively neglecting breaking, a strategy that has been attempted quite often both before and after the nineteenth century. For one instance of this attempt at rhetorical reconciliation we might look to Catherine Gallagher's *Nobody's Story* in which that critic holds that

> Behind the descriptions of proudly poor, dispossessed, and thereby dignified authors stood a background of beliefs about authorial property rights. What, after all, would be so pathetic about Charlotte Lennox's labor being "chiefly gainful to others" if there was no presumption that she had some "natural" right to profit from her productions? (155)

---

2. I am perhaps overstating the case here in characterizing Collins to be completely ignoring the breaking function. Even at this early stage he seems to feel a certain iniquity to be associated with textuality's ability to break out of control, having his villain Mannion serve in his early career as a translator-plagiarist, that is, as "a hack-author of the lowest degree . . . plagiarising from dead authors, to supply the raw material for bookmongering by more accomplished bookmongers" (*Basil*, Goldman ed. 231–32). This text reproduces Collins's revised edition of 1862. The other edition used in this chapter is the 1852 London edition, *Basil* (London: Bentley, 1852) in 3 vols. All further references to *Basil* in this chapter will be to the Goldman edition, unless otherwise noted as "1852 edition."

Here we are presented with a conception akin to the settling function in this "'natural' right." This conception is then rhetorically reconciled with its opposing function:

> The rhetoric of dispossession and dignity [settling] *relied on* the rather new idea that authors had some legally recognized vendable property [breaking] that served as the basis of their livelihood. . . . Both the idea that authors should be their own people and the idea that they are the original owners of their copyrights [settling] indicate that their new dignity, the insistence on their worth and the unfairness of their lot was *intertwined* at mid-century *with* their characterization as dispossessed proprietors [breaking]. (155–57; emphasis added)

Gallagher here is attempting to persuasively resolve the tension by tying to a particular time period the transhistorical breaking function. She is endeavoring to pass off as intimately connected a clearly time-bound ability by women to gain a livelihood by writing and a clearly eternal dispossessability of breaking-function-vulnerable writers, regardless of gender. More significantly, she mixes the two functions and their effects indiscriminately and employs rhetoric implying such mixing to be acceptable. However, far from "relying on" each other, the two functions, as we will see, have constantly remained in conflict, a truth of which Collins at this early stage of his project was himself most adamantly in denial.

In a more recent manifestation of this attempt at impossible reconciliation, Mark Rose, delivering a lecture at UCLA Law School, outlines two "incompatible" metaphors—viewing books as children and viewing books as real estate—that have been utilized by our culture throughout history to depict the author–work relation. He argues that the "fit" of the metaphors, both between themselves and with regard to the circumstances of copyright, is not a good one:

> [T]he paternity and real estate metaphors are in some respects incompatible. The former represents copyright as something distinctive and personal, an extension of the author's self in the form of a child. The latter represents copyright as objective and impersonal, a mere commodity like any other. The difficulty is that the unconscious of copyright is a mixed metaphor. ("Copyright" 9)

The literary work is shown to be a schizophrenic entity: an intrinsic emanation of the author's self and, at the same time, an always-already-alienated

commercial commodity. This "mixed metaphor," Rose argues, is dangerous, because it leads to situations such as the assimilation of "even mundane commodities to the privileged language of creativity" (10) and to the
establishment of "the problematic notion that children might be treated
as commodities" (12). In past judicial opinions, Rose notes, circus posters
have been compared to Rembrandt paintings and surrogacy disputes have
been decided along mentally-conceptual rather than biologically-conceptual
lines.[3] He asks how we are to reconcile these two clashing systems of metaphor and negotiate the schizophrenia crystallizing around "the notion that
copyright is grounded in personhood *and* the need for a property law to
regulate trade in vendible works" (9; emphasis added). He believes a resolution of the tension between creativity and commerce to be in fact possible:
"A persuasive solution to the problems our metaphors pose will be one that
does not simply reject the old tropes but finds new ways to understand
them" (15). In essence, the solution lies in the realm of what Rose calls
"rhetoric": "From the point of view of copyright's metaphors, this is not so
much a logical problem as it is a rhetorical problem. That is, *the issue is not
truth so much as persuasion. . . .* The solution should . . . have roots in the
metaphorical patterns that already exist in the discourse of copyright" (10;
emphasis added). The vagueness of the characteristics of Rose's desired solution here is a sign that quite possibly no such rhetorical solution per se exists.

I hold that the tension noted by Rose signals not so much a "rhetorical
problem," the improper application of metaphors, say, as it does a *foundational* conflict underlying the attempted control of the paradoxical workings
of language. Beginning from a simple investigation of an "incompatibility"
between metaphorical representations, Rose's analysis touches on a fundamental linguistic problem. Unfortunately, he turns back and away from
his object of inquiry and seeks for a logical "solution" (this term signifying
Rose's continuing allegiance to logic in general) to his conundrum. Rein-
venting Hegel's *aufhebung,* Rose's analysis, like Gallagher's above, seeks to
logically resolve what it finds to be a troubling instance of paradox. It should
come as a warning to those following in Rose's wake that the demand for
inexorable "progress" (of the standard, i.e., non-deconstructive, type) attach-
ing to Enlightenment logic should hold such sway as to leave him feeling
prompted by the stark *difference* in the common metaphorical characteriza-
tions of the *same* thing to propose strategies for *uniting* the two metaphors,
for, in his terms, "solving" the problem.

I contend that there is no "solution" per se, at least no logic-based,

---

3. See Rose's "Mothers and Authors" for an elaboration of the latter.

progress-valorizing one. The nature of iterability being fundamentally paradoxical, there is no means of halting the continual bifurcation in its many
manifestations. Instead of seeking to unite the two entities Rose should
simply have been asking why the same thing, iterability, should be found to
be manifesting itself in such disparate ways, as land (representing breaking
for Rose, but representing settling for, as we will see, the young Collins)
or as children (representing settling for Rose). He should have been asking
why these conflicting metaphors characterizing the control of language as
simultaneously facile and impossible would continually be surfacing. No
top-down manipulation can or will remain effective for very long. Wishing for this type of solution—in Rose's case in of all places Southern California—is akin to attempting to cement-over the San Andreas Fault. It is
like treating as a mere surface-level rift a profound theoretical one. Lectur-
ing in this same region of shifting ground, Derrida remarks, "we are used
to theoretical earthquakes here" ("Some Statements" 68), and, at least in
this case, he is correct: in essence, iterability will continually be offering
"theoretical earthquakes" that themselves will continually be undoing any
"progress" that temporarily might have been made through "surface-level"
rhetorical manipulations of copyright discourse.[4] The belief that "copyright

---

4. Reconciling the two states being impossible through the simple application of persuasive
rhetoric or logic, Rose's metaphors will always remain incompatible. Not surprisingly, we see the tension continually re-arising over the history of copyright decisions and legislation. That is, despite the
explicit testimony of several statutes, copyright remains unable conclusively to stay *either* solely concerned with providing a motor for advancement through monetary incentive or, on the other hand,
protecting the author's personality. The author's relation to the market continually threatens any sort
of close identification of the author with the text, and of the text with the author. The most significant
disruption of the close author–work bond—what I am calling the author-as-creator construct—has
been the author-as-disseminator construct, the need for the work to go out on the market, to move
from private to public. This particular need has, in our ever-more market-driven age, continually
threatened to take control of the entire scene. But it has nevertheless been consistently hampered in
this quest. The former construct—the idea of copyright's foundation in the personhood of the author
providing the basis for ownership of the work—has persisted. For example, Rose points out that in
1991 in a "landmark decision" the Supreme Court "reasserted the importance of creativity to copyright doctrine" ("Copyright" 10). In that particular case, *Feist v. Rural Telephone* (1991), it was decided
that the "spark of creativity," or minimal-degree "originality," trumps the monetary protection/incen-
tive motive for copyright (345–49). The court held, "originality is not a stringent standard; it does
not require that facts be presented in an innovative or surprising way. It is equally true, however, that
the selection and arrangement of facts cannot be so mechanical or routine as to require no creativity
whatsoever . . . creativity rewards originality, not effort" (362–64). Just when the death of the author
would seem on the verge of having been officially declared, "the author" qua creator rises again.
Something strange is at work, and the source of that strangeness—as Collins would come to learn,
indeed to teach himself during his major phase—is situated at the foundational level of the workings
of language. Similarly, the adjustments that copyright has undergone over its history have moved it in
both directions, sometimes simultaneously. To provide one example: the progressive disarticulation of
the work from the author's vitality in the lengthening of copyright's duration beyond death has been

is grounded in personhood," a common rhetorical manifestation of the set-tling function, is one that *must,* as a result of the peculiar workings of linguistic repetition, continually come into conflict with the "need for a property law to regulate trade in vendible works," a common rhetorical manifestation of the breaking function (Rose, "Copyright" 9).

Collins and Rose, a nineteenth-century author and a twenty-first-century copyright historian, are both attuned to the same difficulty, the incompatibility continually making itself felt with regard to the control of linguistic emanations and productions. And both have a similar goal: to undo that difficulty or at least somehow reduce the discomfort caused by it. Collins's strategy will be different from Rose's. Over the course of writ-ing the five fictions discussed in detail in this study, one or two standing out as amongst the most enduring masterpieces in English literature, Col-lins will come to realize that the mixed metaphors of copyright had not come into existence through the play of everyday rhetorical negotiations and surface-level metaphorical patternings and as such those negotiations and patternings were not the location of the possible solution to the rift. Collins's major fictions will contest the efficacy of any purely rhetorical solu-tions to the dilemma of authorship. I will be arguing here that, in his major phase, Collins moves beyond simple discursive-level manipulation to radi-cal recontextualization/refiguration of context. That is, Collins's recognition of the fundamental incompatibility between creation and dissemination is contemporaneous with (both the cause and effect of) his shiftings from capitulation (in *Basil*'s unquestioning adherence to the metaphor of manu-script seen as a type of land) to attempted manipulation (in *The Woman in White*'s unsuccessful, relatively novel metaphorization of the text as helpless young female) to, finally, wholesale recontextualization of the metaphors within radically altered systems (the sensation and mystery novel forms in the novels *No Name, Armadale,* and *The Moonstone*). Collins will come to realize that the fundamental incompatibility is not to be resolved by any-thing less than a radical reimagining of the existing systems in play. Over the course of pursuing his long–novel project, Collins will come to understand that the incompatible metaphors had arisen from, and were pointing back to, a deeper rupture, a rupture stemming from the conflict inherent in the peculiar functioning of language. Quite simply, they revealed the founda-tional struggle always already being brought into being, to speak metaphori-cally, from far, far below the surface, by the iterability of language.

---

a movement testifying to *both* copyright's personality- and monetary-basis, depending on whether it was at the time primarily benefiting authors or the publishers and corporations to whom the former had, more often than not, signed over their rights.

Basil and the Literary Artist

It is with good reason that John Sutherland remarks in a classic study that
"The generally accepted starting point for sensational fiction is 1859 and
the serial publication of Wilkie Collins's *The Woman in White*" ("Wilkie Collins" 243). Ever since Margaret Oliphant named and defined the genre—seeing it as a sort of real-life romance[5]—in the process of reviewing Collins's *The
Woman in White*,[6] this perspective on Collins has been generally accepted:

> Mr. Wilkie Collins is not the first man who has produced a sensation novel.
> By fierce expedients of crime and violence, by *diablerie* of divers kinds, and
> by the wild devices of a romance which smiled at probabilities, the thing has
> been done before now. . . . [But] [a]mid all these predecessors in the field,
> Mr. Wilkie Collins takes up an entirely original position. Not so much as
> a single occult agency is employed in the structure of his tale. ("Sensation
> Novels" 565–66)

While Oliphant's delineation of a novel filled with improbable, but not
supernatural, circumstance serves as a good description of all the novels I
will be discussing in this book, a description as all-encompassing as this (the
same could be said of the productions of Ann Radcliffe for instance) has the
potential for obscuring crucial distinctions. I do not find Collins's major
fictions to be in the same set as the works produced during the 1860s by
Mary Elizabeth Braddon, Sheridan Le Fanu, and Ellen Wood. We can see
Collins's divergence from the trend that he would soon be, ironically, *founding* to be evident from the beginning, actually even before the beginning, of
that genre, in his narrative of 1852 *Basil; A Story of Modern Life*. Collins's
interest in what I will here be considering a "linguistic sensationalism" leads
him, before the genre has even properly begun, to deeper insights than will
be available to the other sensationalists attempting to follow him in what
they understand his project to be (the subversion of conventional mores or
the championing of possibility over probability—necessary steps but mere
opening gambits in his larger, more elaborate chess game). I emphasize Collins's difference because, unfortunately, the after-the-fact miscategorization

---

5. Walter C. Phillips similarly defines sensationalism as "romance for the populace" (38).

6. Though Oliphant also considered in her review Dickens's *Great Expectations,* Dickens's reviewers and critics never came generally to view him as a simple sensationalist. Fortunately, Collins
criticism has recently been expanding its perspective. Good recent discussions by Lillian Nayder (*Unequal Partners*), Graham Law ("Professional Writer"), and William Baker et al. (Introduction) have
reassessed Collins's relation to the literary market.

of Collins as a sensationalist, in coming to obscure the more interesting aspects of this one of his works, has often served to misdirect the criticism of the works written in *Basil*'s wake.

Twentieth-century critics have almost invariably been prompted to consider *Basil* a sensation novel *avant la lettre*: Ronald R. Thomas calls it "the first novel that Collins wrote in the sensation *mode*" ("Wilkie Collins" 497; emphasis added); Catherine Peters holds that "*Basil*, rather than *The Woman in White*, has a strong claim to be considered the first sensation novel" (118); Tamar Heller writes that "[b]y the 1860s, critics would find a name for works like *Basil*: the sensation novel" (59); and Dorothy Goldman, viewing the work from a similarly retrospective vantage point, describes *Basil* as Collins's first "characteristic" novel and as, paradoxically, "springing from" his later more famous works *The Woman in White* and *The Moonstone* (Collins, *Basil* vii).[7] All these critics have a point. This story is not without its novelty. That novelty, particularly the narrative's shocking forthrightness, enlivened by up-to-date references to London omnibuses and newly-macadamized streets, is made by Collins, however, itself to work in the service of a very old style of thinking (text as land, the settling function as the sole one).

I will here be attempting to take a fresh look at this early one of Collins's drama-filled narratives, attempting to glimpse beyond the entrancing level of its purported "sensationalism" in order to notice its more formalistic aspects, specifically its negotiations with the materiality of the letter and the roots of language, in an effort to see what following the less travelled critical path might allow us to find. While viewing *Basil* as a proto-"sensation novel," that is, as a novel preparing the way for that trend of later fictions that would "graf[t] a progressive approach to the Victorian bêtes of sex and violence onto the primitive and even childish formulas of stage melodrama" (Winifred Hughes 5), undoubtedly opens up many avenues for discussion, it unfortunately closes off many others called up by this particular work and by the masterpieces of Collins's major period. Broadening the interpretation of the first dream had by the main character in that narrative cannot help but have interesting ramifications for our later examinations of Collins's more firmly established "sensation novels." My consideration

---

7. The critics are so intent on having Collins be part of this genre movement that they sign him up before it has come into being. Continuing this trend of reading *Basil* as an early sensation novel is the prominent treatment given to the first edition's provocative letter of dedication in the studies of sensation fiction by Walter C. Phillips (12–13 and 136–37) and Winifred Hughes (17). Indeed Phillips claims, "No single utterance" of the three novelists he treats in depth, Dickens, Reade, and Collins, "is perhaps more significant of their joint aims and preferences than that which Collins prefixed to *Basil*" (12). Kent calls the letter of dedication "a sensationalist manifesto" (264).

of Collins's relations to textuality in his unified novel series begins here, with a rereading and recontextualization of what might be considered the first "sensation scene" in the first "sensation" novel written by Collins: the first dream experienced by his hero Basil in the novel of the same name. I choose this scene as my primary point of entry into Collins's major fictions because much depends on one's not accepting the lures—especially the initial ones—continually held out by this author so skilled at manipulating the red herring and so reluctant throughout his career to crassly expose his designs. Collins was a master of the screening process and lifting this initial one of his screens will, I hope, provide a new means of assessing the rest of the fictions of his major period. As one comes readily to understand when analyzing Collins's elaborately plotted fictions, if there comes an instant when all the surface signs appear to be pointing in one direction, say, toward something as comfortably stereotypical (indeed so stereotypical as to appear anachronistically proto-Freudian) as an amorous young man's dream leaving us with, seemingly, an archetypal example of sensation-as-sexuality, that is probably the moment to begin looking in another direction, say, in that of sensation-as-textuality. Recall the sexually-suggestive red herring to be placed two years later in "A Stolen Letter," "all the drawers . . . were left open." Like the artfully-wise lawyer in that story, we need always to keep in mind what kind of customer we are dealing with in reading Wilkie Collins.

BASIL is usually read from a psycho-sexually sensationalistic perspective. This is understandable. Suspiciously all too understandable. I must admit that the narrative does indeed at first glance make for a most luridly shocking story. It is a fictional autobiography written and narrated by an eponymous and pseudonymous author-hero. Basil is the second son in a family of great station in England tracing its lineage back before the Norman conquest. As his father is immensely proud of his position among the English gentry, Basil is sure that a marriage with the beautiful Margaret Sherwin, a girl he has seen one day on an omnibus and then tempestuously dreamt of, will never be approved of as she is the daughter of a mere linen-draper. Therefore, he is willing to allow himself to be directed by Margaret's father when Mr. Sherwin suggests a secret marriage that should only be consummated a year to the day after the official ceremony has taken place. Sherwin proposes this plan so that Basil might have time to break the news to his father and because Margaret, at seventeen, seems to him a year too young to be truly married. Basil regrets the agreement immediately, but nevertheless feels honor-bound to keep his word.

Early in Basil's year of endurance, Sherwin's managing-man, Robert Mannion, returns from a business trip to France. Mannion is a former son of the aristocracy who, as a result of a past family disgrace, has plummeted in station, making his way down through the social ranks via a series of occupations, including having served a stint as a plagiarist of stories by dead authors. Mannion bears a secret enmity towards Basil's family, for it happens that Basil's father had instigated Mannion's fall by bearing witness against Mannion's father in the latter's prosecution for the forgery of a bill of credit. To this mortal grudge has been added a further one against Basil himself, as Mannion had himself been planning an elopement with the then-willing Margaret before the expeditious wedding to Basil had taken place. Mannion resolves to exact revenge for both the present affront and that one in the past through the bringing off of a surreptitious sexual assignation with Margaret the night before the year is to be complete, the night before she is to become Basil's wife "in fact, as well as in name" (82). (It is implied that Mannion has a secret future objective in carrying out this plan, but whether or not this design is the eventual fathering of the heir or heirs of Basil's line is left ambiguous.)

Happening upon the furtive couple leaving early from an aunt's party, Basil follows them unremarked to a hotel. There, having bribed the house boy, he listens through the wall of an adjoining room—the readers being kept at a suitable distance by the narration at this point—to the infamous wrong being done to him. Transformed by his rage, he then awaits the illicit lovers outside the hotel. When Mannion emerges first, Basil, in a fashion quite uncharacteristic of his usually gentle manner, proceeds to man-handle him, blinding him in one eye and deeply scarring his face. After this short burst of self-alienating rage, Basil reassumes his usual character and falls into a swoon. Thereafter, the secret of Basil's marriage is disclosed to his father and as well as being disinherited Basil is, literally, torn from the family, that is, from the family scrap-book. After Margaret dies of typhus, Mannion, in a rage over his disfigurement and Margaret's death, pursues Basil to the end of England. In Cornwall, where Basil has been hiding on the outskirts of a small fishing village while writing the history of the foregoing events, Mannion finds him and pursues him out to the cliffs at Land's End. There, while Basil climbs along a dangerous cliff-face to safety, the less careful Mannion falls to his death. Once again, the sympathetic Basil falls into a swoon, in this instance almost dying, recovering only through the timely intercession of his younger sister Clara and older brother Ralph.

Presented with such a narrative, one could well be excused for choosing to notice solely its psycho-sexual aspects. But while in the case of this particular work and, indeed, throughout Collins's career, the sexual aspects of his sensationalism are very much in evidence, and never lost on the critics, just as significant are the textual elements of that "sensationalism." This new context does not justify the use of that word without quotation marks, a *textual* sensationalism being a contradiction in terms. Of course, the tendency in the criticism to overlook that textuality is easily explained. The critics here are subject to their own predispositions, especially the generic ones that they themselves have pre-established. Since the titillation caused by the sexual and violent aspects of Collins's stories is for most of them manifestly "the point" of the "sensation fiction" label applied to his later fictions and retroactively to this one, they are from the beginning—indeed from before the beginning—immured in a cage of their own making. It becomes ever more difficult to see beyond this cage once Freudian perspectives are embraced by literary criticism in the mid-twentieth century. Thus, the critics coming after Collins, that attentive student of human nature, unfortunately position themselves at precisely the point where he would have wanted them to be. They place themselves at the mercy of an author adept at the magic trick—a fooling of themselves in which they are more than half-willing participants—that would be most likely to mystify them, the trick of exploiting what we might call the "Freudian mindset" so as to facilitate better the delivery of his veiled ideological messages below the level of conscious resistance. In hopes of avoiding being similarly hypnotized by the sexual Collins, this study will be firmly latching itself onto an image of a Collins who has here embarked on an initial attempt at representing the reification of the text as land as a means of both reinforcing the always threatened author–work relation and sedimenting the (fundamentally unstable) stable-text ideal.[8]

Basil's Dream

All of this begins, as any good prefiguring of the psychoanalytic encounter might be expected to, with a dream. As Basil's dream commences, he finds himself standing on a wide plain bordered on either side by woods and hills. Approaching him is a dark, seductive woman:

> I stood on a wide plain. On one side, it was bounded by thick woods, whose dark secret depths looked unfathomable to the eye: on the other, by hills,

---

8. The fact that the particular screen that Collins lands upon should come in the particular form of the sexual awakening of a young man will have to remain a question to be dealt with by future critics.

ever rising higher and higher yet, until they were lost in bright, beautifully white clouds, gleaming in refulgent sunlight. . . . As I still stood on the plain and looked around, I saw a woman coming towards me from the wood. Her stature was tall; her black hair flowed about her unconfined; her robe was of the dun hue of the vapour and mist which hung above the trees, and fell to her feet in dark thick folds. She came on towards me swiftly and softly, passing over the ground like cloud-shadows over the ripe corn-field or the calm water. . . . And now I could see her face plainly. Her eyes were lustrous and fascinating, as the eyes of a serpent—large, dark and soft, as the eyes of a wild doe. Her lips were parted with a languid smile; and she drew back the long hair, which lay over her cheeks, her neck, her bosom, while I was gazing on her. (*Basil* 45)

This scene is rendered in very suggestive terms, indeed, to the point almost of absurdity. Approaching Basil from either of two strongly-contrasted regions bordering a type of symbolic plain are two strongly-contrasted women: the scandalous, dark figure described here, representing his dark-haired beloved Margaret, and an innocent, fair woman, representing his fair-haired sister Clara. Each figure attempts in her own particular manner to lure Basil to her region and away from that of the other, the narrative at this moment going so far as to say that they vie for his soul. This scene is the point when Basil—situated uncannily like Walter Hartright on Hampstead Heath at the beginning of *The Woman in White,* before, as D. A. Miller has it, the woman's touch on the shoulder will have awakened his (and a general male reader's) repressed nervousness (148–56)—chooses the life of the sensuous, and very sensual, body over the chaste life of the mind and the higher thoughts of the intellect. Basil allows himself to be dragged a short way toward the woods by the dark woman before, having felt something at his back, he turns:

Then, I felt as if a light were shining on me from the other side. I turned to look, and there was the woman from the hills beckoning me away to ascend with her towards the bright clouds above. Her arm, as she held it forth, shone fair, even against the fair hills; and from her outstretched hand came long thin rays of trembling light, which penetrated to where I stood, cooling and calming wherever they touched me. (*Basil* 46)

The fair woman's penetrative "thin rays of trembling light" represent a type of inspiration or lightning—in French *éclair,* suggesting further that she is a figure for his sister Clara. This inspiration from "on high" suggests a connection between the hill she is standing on and the classical Mountain of the Muses. These subliminal literary antecedents having no useful effect on the young author Basil, however, our hero instead decides to go with the dark woman of the heated sensations:

> I felt the rays of light that had touched me from the beckoning hand, depart; and yet once more I looked towards the woman from the hills. She was ascending again towards the bright clouds, and ever and anon she stopped and turned round, wringing her hands and letting her head droop, as if in bitter grief. . . . [N]ow the woman, from the woods clasped me more closely than before, pressing her warm lips on mine. . . . I was drawn along in the arms of the dark woman, with my blood burning and my breath failing me, until we entered the secret recesses that lay amid the unfathomable depths of trees. There, she encircled me in the folds of her dusky robe, and laid her cheek close to mine, and murmured a mysterious music in my ear, amid the midnight silence and darkness of all around us. And I had no thought of returning to the plain again; for I had forgotten the woman from the fair hills, and had given myself up, heart, and soul, and body, to the woman from the dark woods. (46–47)

Very little effort is required to see sexuality in this dream. And, indeed, in her interesting psychological study of Collins's works *In the Secret Theatre of Home: Wilkie Collins, Sensation Narrative, and Nineteenth-Century Psychology,* Jenny Bourne Taylor finds just that. That is, she finds the dream to be thematizing Basil's ambivalently experienced sexual corruption: "The dream itself is both the explicit expression of sexual desire and a moralized comment on it. . . . Basil dreams of a landscape that is both a symbolic female body and an iconic moral hierarchy" (85). Taylor characterizes Basil's allowing himself to be dragged along into the depths of the woods by the dark woman as his having gone over "into sexual engulfment and spiritual defilement" (85). Taylor here would seem to be on firm ground in her interpretation.

However, it would be less than justified, given the narrative's other manifestly non-sexual concerns, to become overly-fixated by the sexual elements in the scene. It is important to also notice the scene's textual elements, elements that assert themselves less apparently, and therefore perhaps more significantly in the case of this author who throughout his career would make a practice of planting "secret recesses" within his narrative architecture. This conjunction between writing and sex is not atypical for Collins, who was, as mentioned earlier, soon to become, whether willing or no, a major figure in the sensation fiction movement, a genre that relied on cullings from the various Victorian storehouses recounting scandalous sexual vagaries and violent crimes. The startling scene of Count Fosco's stealing and inscribing his own words within Marian Halcombe's diary in *The Woman in White,* a theft and act of writing that many critics—falling for Collins's trap—are prompted to describe as a figurative "rape" of Marian (see for example D. A. Miller 164 and Tromp 85), is perhaps the most famous scene in Collins's work in which text and sex conjoin for this Victorian author so interested in the market-performance of his occasionally fairly lurid stories. I am arguing, however, that we need to look again at Basil's dream and to focus this time not on the sexual aspects but on the textual ones. The "secret recesses that lay amid the unfathomable depths of trees" of Basil's dream, when considered to be representing the inner depths of the pages of the book at the same time that they represent the scene of a sexual encounter, are a concise encapsulation of the twin foci of Collins's subsequent major fictions.

Reconsidering the dream with a more textual focus, I find it to be anticipating Gissing's *New Grub Street,* a representation of the Victorian literary artist in transition from high-class amanuensis to industrious working man, from the man concerned with inspiration coming from a "higher" source to the one colored by the inks he works in. Initially Basil is situated on a "wide plain" bounded on one side by hills and clouds and on the other by a thick wood. This bounded plain shares affinities, I would argue, with that famous textual meadow mentioned early on in Sheridan's *The School for Scandal* when Sir Benjamin Backbite describes the formatting of certain books of the time to be such as to leave us with "a neat rivulet of text . . . murmur[ing] through a meadow of margin."[9] He is referring of course to the printing of poetry in the eighteenth century, but in Collins's case it is possible to see this same type of metaphor at work, only in a character slightly altered to take account of the format of nineteenth-century prose fiction. Though we might, along with Taylor, consider the image of the disordered wood to be symbolic of the female pubis, the terms used to describe the dark woman's approach suggest another image. The woods are connected with a specifically man-made order, that of a field of wheat—here called, as was the practice at the time, "corn"—ranging itself out within the boundaries of a meadow or field of margin, somewhat like, to bring things home, the text on the page, or screen, you are currently reading.

---

9. *The School for Scandal* I.i. (Sheridan 216). Sheridan seems to have been a significant influence on Collins. In the boat-house conversation in *The Woman in White* Collins has Count Fosco refer to another line from *The School for Scandal:* "I go—and leave my character behind me," and in the "First Scene" of *No Name* Magdalen Vanstone makes her debut in a private production of *The Rivals.*

Indeed, the scene sketches less a topography than a *typ*-ography. As the dark woman comes toward Basil she passes over the ground "like cloud-shadows [passing] over the ripe corn-field. . . . " This seemingly unimportant detail will show up again when Walter Hartright, in imitation of Chaucer, opens his narration in *The Woman in White* with the following bucolic rev-erie: "It was the last day of July. The long hot summer was drawing to a close; and we, the weary pilgrims of the London pavement, were beginning to think of the cloud-shadows on the corn-fields, and the autumn breezes on the sea-shore" (ed. Sutherland 6). Though slight, the phrase has significant implications. We are left by this analogy in *Basil* with an image suggesting less a natural profusion of disordered wood than a field covered by entities arranged in rows or furrows, like the lines on a page—a veritable wheat-field of text. The once-disordered wood thus is rendered in terms suggestive of the lines ranged, or planted, by a writer in the midst of his literary labors across a page of manuscript. Rather than viewing the scene as a movement across an anatomical landscape, we should instead see Basil to be—indeed perhaps *especially* in light of the scene's overt sexual suggestiveness—choos-ing to become one with his manuscript, both the "historical romance" (*Basil* 25) he had been writing at the time of his having the dream as well as the autobiographical text—his oft-mentioned "manuscript"—he will be writing later when he recounts that dream. Basil's move away from the detached realm of inspired artist as he makes his way beyond the range of the light-ning thrown by the woman of the hills and walks off the marginal meadow and into the writing on the page, the wood, launches him on a project aimed at his becoming one with the writing that he pens on page after page, thereby more directly, more physically, participating in the creation of that work. Thus *Basil* puts into practice that relatively new conception, one that the contemporary copyright debates were helping to form, of the literary artist as laborer.[10] This transformation mimics Basil's change in class status in the narrative as he adjusts to his disinheritance by his father and his removal from the family home. As he goes off into the "secret recesses" with his "blood burning and [his] breath failing [him]" (46) he is certainly not going off to "soar above the Aonian mount, while [he] pursues things unattempted yet in prose or rhyme" but, rather, dedicating himself to the

---

10. Peters suggests that Collins differed from the other young men working at *Household Words* in the early 1850s. As opposed to that contingent described by G. A. Sala as "about the idlest young dogs that squandered away their time on the pavements of Paris and London. *We would not work,*" Collins was "already a professional . . . a prolific journalist, prepared, like Dickens, to take infinite pains over the slightest article" (Peters 98).

difficult, and sweaty, proposition of fashioning legacies out of ink, paper, and the characters sown on page after page of text. Sex here thus turns out, as it so often does in Collins's work, to have been serving as a means of hiding simply text.

This screening is not as strange as it may at first sound. Collins was a particularly private author, one who preferred to keep his motivations and maneuverings submerged. Interpretations finding sex and sexually charged matters in Collins's fictions play directly into his hands by obscuring analysis of the textual (as well as other) aspects of those fictions. These particular types of interpretation rushing to take center stage in the literary critical realm, as they are so often prone to do (sex sells, in academia as well), then make it difficult simply to discern, let alone champion, the textual elements. References to sex in Collins's works are quite pervasive and they are so often taken simply as such that one feels almost heretical taking them to be something—indeed anything—else, especially references to something as mundane as text. Thus, the argument that Collins's sensationalism was of a peculiarly linguistic form is a difficult one to make. Nevertheless, that is precisely the contention I will be putting forward here. Indeed, it should not be surprising to be reading Collins's fictions "against the grain." More the king of screeners than he was even of inventors (as the title of Catherine Peters's biography describes him), Collins was in a class by himself when it came to veiling his intentions.

To provide an example that I believe to be representative of much of Collins's dealings with sex: in *The Woman in White* we are told that Sir Percival Glyde, one of the two villains in the narrative, had at one point in the past taken to "mixing" his "ink" in Mrs. Jane Anne Catherick's "pot" during secret meetings between the two: "He was some time getting the ink the right colour (mixing it over and over again in pots and bottles of mine)" (ed. Sutherland 544). Though the circumstances would seem to insist on our giving in to the sexual or "Freudian" interpretation—as does Mr. Catherick: "You must know as well as I do what the notion was which my husband took into his head, when he found me and my fine-gentleman acquaintance meeting each other privately, and talking secrets together" (545)—to fall automatically into this perspective is also to fall into the pre-set trap of our fantastically cagey author. The truth of the matter, by Mrs. Catherick's own admission (if we are to believe her testimony), is that the two of them were *actually* interested in textuality rather than sexuality. In an attempt to save her character, she begs Sir Percival to make a vindicating avowal attesting to that fact:

"Do me justice—clear my character of a stain on it which you know I don't deserve. . . . [O]nly tell [my husband], on your word of honour as a gentleman, that he is wrong, and that I am not to blame in the way he thinks I am. Do me that justice, at least, after all I have done for you." He flatly refused, in so many words. He told me, plainly, that it was his interest to let my husband and all my neighbours believe the falsehood—because, *as long as they did so, they were quite certain never to suspect the truth.* I had a spirit of my own; and I told him they should know the truth from my lips. His reply was short, and to the point. If I spoke, I was a lost woman, as certainly as he was a lost man. (545; emphasis added)

Our narrator Walter Hartright will remain skeptical of Mrs. Catherick's sexual innocence in this matter until he learns the fundamental lesson of all of Collins's major fictions: that sometimes the sexual reading can be screening the textual one. He considers that "the clue to discovery" of Glyde's guilty secret resides "in those stolen meetings, in those familiar whisperings between the clerk's wife and 'the gentleman in mourning'":

Was it possible that appearances, in this case, had pointed one way, while the truth lay, all the while, unsuspected, in another direction? Could Mrs Catherick's assertion that she was the victim of a dreadful mistake, by any possibility be true? Or, assuming it to be false, could the conclusion which associated Percival with her guilt, have been founded in some inconceivable error? *Had Sir Percival, by any chance, courted the suspicion that was wrong, for the sake of diverting from himself some other suspicion that was right?* Here, if I could find it—here was the approach to the Secret, hidden deep under the surface of the apparently unpromising story which I had just heard. (482; emphasis added)

If this trick could be played on Hartright and the villagers of Welmingham in the narrative of *The Woman in White,* why could it not also have been played by Collins on his readers and even perhaps on those future professional readers of his, the literary critics? Could some of Collins's critics have been taking too seriously the sexually-charged misdirections put forward by an author continually described, misleadingly, and only in later times, it must be remembered, as the "father of the sensation novel"?

It is clear enough that Percival Glyde would rather be thought a libertine than have the much more damaging truth, that his birth is illegitimate, be circulated. *His* motivation for screening is clear. However, Collins's is not so readily apparent. Given the overtly moralizing nature of what has come to be known as his "mission fiction" of the 1870s and 80s, Collins would not seem to have been an author who usually shied away from proclaiming his allegiances. However, in the next chapter I will be arguing that the negative example set by Dickens's lack of success over the course of his calamitous 1842 trip to the United States had had a chilling effect on Collins. During his trip, Dickens had made several ill-reviewed speeches criticizing the Americans for their lack of morality with regard to rendering up to British authors their due.[11] His complete lack of success disheartened him and he may well have advised Collins that a direct approach would meet with little success.

As we saw with the excess of reference available in the word "domestic" (national, material, familial, psychical, or textual) in the title *The Evil Genius: A Domestic Story,* Collins enjoyed screening his deeper intentions behind more easily seen-through surface readings. Thus, I would argue that our author is most secret when he looks to be most *open,* admittedly leaving the critic in a terribly uncertain situation. (Where is this game to stop?) In this study, I will be attempting to show that Collins realized that if one could create a diversion by, say, distracting the viewer with something he or she might already be predisposed to be interested in seeing, say, sexual intrigue, then one's hidden agenda would be able to pass all the more unremarked. This is, admittedly, a dangerous game for an author to play and one which Collins excelled at at times undoubtedly—note his current, generally-accepted status as a mere constructor of puzzles—to his own detriment. His consummate artistry in screening his deeper-seated intentions has undoubtedly been a major cause of his works' inability to generate significant later academic and cultural interest. Dickens's sister-in-law Georgina Hogarth, writing to a friend in 1873, described Collins as habitually being more than a bit pleased with his own cleverness: "[H]e has many fine qualities but he has an unusual amount of conceit and self-satisfaction—and I do not think any one can think Wilkie Collins a greater man than Wilkie Collins thinks himself" (Hogarth). A direct result of Collins's seamless yet formidable meta-sophistication, paradoxically, has been the impressive durability—for more than a century after his death—of his literary-critical categorization as little more than an author of undemanding sensation novels filled with uncomplicated episodes of sex and violence. This practice of continually "pulling one over" on his readers may have backfired on Collins. Sometimes, an author can be too clever for his own literary-critical good. For example, it is to Collins's credit—and loss—to

---

11. See Welsh, *Copyright* 29–42 for a good discussion of Dickens's efforts.

have predicted that his preferred type of sexual screening would keep the readers mesmerized long before the advent of Freudian psychoanalytic literary criticism would come along with its particular variety of obsessions to effectively seal the tomb, rendering his secrets nearly unassailable for a generation or more of literary critics.

For Collins at the early stage of his career when he was composing *Basil,* that is, before the constrictive "sensationalist" label had yet been applied, the sexual and violent aspects of his fictions were not ends in themselves. The significance of this particular example of Collins's "sensationalism"—as will be seen to also surprisingly hold true of his other more famous attempts at sensation in the masterpieces of the 1860s—was the deployment of a certain "textual ideology" along with and behind the provocative veil of the sex and violence. Therefore, it is unfortunate that the mesmerizing sexual overtones of Basil's first dream have obscured more textually-oriented interpretations of it. Having undoubtedly been influenced by D. A. Miller's well-known discussion of closeting in Collins, Dorothy Goldman, editor of the Oxford edition of *Basil,* is prompted to confidently state that despite Collins's later denials the book unquestionably is "a shocking analysis of psychosexual behaviour and [Collins] knew it" (*Basil* xxii). However, I will be arguing here that the implications of the story as a whole and of this dream scene in particular offer less an insight into Collins's psyche (unless it is an insight into his constant need to screen his intentions) than they do an insight into his attitude toward the heavily-debated contemporary issue of authorial property rights, an issue that then will serve as Collins's entry point into questions regarding the theoretical groundings of language.

Debating Authorial Handiwork and Legacies

Encapsulating the quintessential Collinsian sexual/textual moment, Basil's dream offers a means of processing not only that character's daytime sighting of an attractive girl on an omnibus but also contemporary Victorian debates about the nature of literary artistry. From 1837 to 1842 England's House of Commons debated the issue of the proper length of time that ought to be allowed to the duration of the author's proprietary legacy in his or her work. At issue was the balancing of authors' heirs' rights and the interests of the public. This debate marked a singular moment when the understanding of the author transitioned from that of artist inspired from "on high" to worker in a market economy. These contemporary issues all would come to be symbolically represented in Basil's dream and the rest of the narrative of that book Collins would write in 1852 and so suggestively title, in its first edition, *Basil: A Story of Modern Life*.

However, during the times of the actual copyright debates themselves, Collins most probably cared little about the issue of literary copyright and its extension. He was thirteen years old and off experiencing the wonders of Italy when the debates over copyright began. He was eighteen and apprenticed to a tea merchant at the time they ended. During his teenage years, then—unless he was prompted by paternal influence coupled with the fact that he was the elder son of a famous painter[12]—it is unlikely that Collins would have been contemporaneously following the discussion. Nevertheless, the issues brought into focus by the debates in Parliament were to pervade the literary culture and market that Collins would shortly be attempting, unsuccessfully, to enter. His repeated failures to find a publisher for his manuscript *Iolani; or, Tahiti as It Was,* a text written in 1844 but published only in 1999, came a mere two years after the bill's passage. The issues explored in the parliamentary debates over copyright, it is my contention, informed the young Collins's understanding of the nature of literary authorship, helping to shape his conception not only of his relation to his present and future works but also his relation to his chosen profession in general.

The last session of the House of Commons to sit before the death of William IV transitioned into the accession of Victoria to the dominium of England and its colonies was presented with the proposal for a significant extension of the duration of the term of copyright. Thomas Noon Talfourd, Sergeant-at-Law and member for the district of Reading, brought forward a private member's bill proposing the establishment of a term so much in excess of the previously established duration of copyright that it occasioned more than a little debate. While the bill was altered in various minor ways in order to make it more palatable (i.e., no longer covering art works and no longer possessing a retroactive effect), throughout the course of the several attempts presided over by Talfourd to see it passed one thing remained constant—its provision for the extension of the duration of the term of copyright from the then-current twenty-eight years calculated from the year of publication (or until the death of the author, whichever turned

---

12. Collins's father, the eminent painter William Collins, would have been interested in the first introduction of Talfourd's bill as in that incarnation its provisions also extended to cover the arts of painting and design as well as literature. See *Sessional Papers* 1837 (380) I.573–85. This manifestation of the bill also included a clause that would have established a process for granting international copyright to authors residing outside England but, as Catherine Seville points out, this "clause was dropped after pressure from the government, which regarded international copyright as a matter of public policy, and an unsuitable subject for back-bench legislation" (*Literary Copyright Reform* 238).

out to be later) to sixty years after the death of the author. Talfourd's bill, as a result of its stipulation for an extensive and conclusively posthumous term for the existence of copyright, would have established copyright as a principle connected less to the body of the writer and more to literary statute.[13] Indeed, Talfourd held, his seemingly-radical revision was in actuality fairly conservative, since it went only a partial way toward re-establishing copyright in its proper relation to the author; for he believed that the individual author had been denied a rightful *perpetual* copyright in the debates held the century before. While the term as it had stood between 1814 and 1837 had certainly in many cases lasted fifteen, twenty, even twenty-five years beyond the date of the author's death, depending on how soon after publication the inevitable had occurred, the argument was continually put forward by Talfourd and his supporters as one of the necessity, and indeed responsibility, of showing proper sympathy for the bereaved family. It was argued that it was more than hard-hearted for the law to be constructed in such a manner as to allow the earnings from copyright to be spirited away from the author's family just at the moment when the death of the family patriarch and bread-winner had rendered them decidedly dispossessed in another way.

Although authors have never been exclusively male, the debate was framed in those terms. In large part, of course, this generalizing to the masculine may have been merely a linguistic commonplace. A common way of speaking that, depending on the speaker and the context, may or may not have been meant to be all-inclusive. Nevertheless, certain of the debaters' lines of argument or appeals to conscience and mercy required the figure of a patriarch to make much sense to themselves and to the populace at large. The opponents of the bill never challenged the assumption, presumably content to argue from the standpoint of author-as-patriarch because it aided them in solidifying their portrait of the author as unfair "monopolist." The proponents of Talfourd's proposal, for their part, actively perpetuated

---

13. William Wordsworth, writing to Viscount Mahon on 11 April 1842 of Sir Robert Peel's amendment to the final bill allowing that copyright should last seven years after the death of the author, states, "The result is lamentably short. . . . One point however is gained and that a very important one. The *principle* of postobit remuneration will be established. . . . Seven years are indeed only a beggarly allowance; why did not Sir R. propose at least *nine?* and then there would have been a year for each of the Nine Muses, Urania included!!!" (*Letters* 7:323). Wordsworth's reference to the "principle" of postobit copyright remuneration is an acknowledgment that the 1814 change in copyright duration to twenty-eight years after the year of publication had, in many cases, created a situation of a *practical* manifestation of posthumous remuneration. The issue of the change from remuneration for the living author to de facto posthumous remuneration after the 1814 change deserves further inquiry (especially in relation to life-after-death narratives such as *Frankenstein* 1818). Unfortunately, that investigation cannot be attempted here.

the assumption because a masculine construction of the author harmonized with their appeals to the image of an ailing male head of the family expiring (in more ways than one), his near-destitute relatives gathered at the bedside, and taking with him the springs of not only literary genius but also, more importantly, profit. A masculine author also served better than did a female or nonspecifically sexed one another related aspect of the proponents' argument, the proposed viewing of copyright as a posthumous legacy . A masculine conception aided their attempts at establishing the status of the author's copyright as property that might be handed down, as was other property upon the death of the patriarch, from father to child.[14]

Talfourd's proposed extension of copyright incited considerable debate among the members of the House. Four and a half years of acrimonious parliamentary intriguing and obstruction ensued once the anti-copyright forces—made up mainly of those publishers involved in reprinting works originally published between 1750 and 1810—had had a chance to rally themselves against this threat to their livelihood.[15] From late 1837 until early 1842 the House of Commons kept the issue shuttling back and forth between various stages of introduction, short deferral or long, and re-introduction. In the face of setback after setback, Talfourd exhibited remarkable fortitude. It was all the more unfortunate, then, that a version of the bill was made law only after he had been replaced in the House by the general election of 1841. Talfourd lost his seat immediately after his bill had suffered an especially disheartening defeat just on the point of being passed

---

14. This conception of the author's copyright devolved from the debates of the previous century. See Swartz, "Patrimony." Swartz's project in that essay is "to ask why eighteenth-century advocates of author's copyright insistently represent the author as a Father who must be allowed the right to endow his children with a decent patrimony. Here the effort to clarify (and regulate) the legal and economic standing of the author can be seen to depend on a rhetoric of paternal obligations: unless the author-as-Father could claim an exclusive property in his work, it was frequently argued, his children would be denied a patrimony" (31). Swartz focuses especially on the 1769 case of *Millar v. Taylor,* which "remains a landmark case because it signals the historic moment when copyright ceases to be thought of as a form of legal protection against 'piracy,' and becomes something more akin to modern copyright which embraces all of the author's property interests in his work" (33). The majority of the four justices of the Court of King's Bench in that case considered the author to have a common-law perpetual right in his property and they buttressed this opinion by deploying a rhetoric that elided literary property with other forms of legacy. Justice Willes stated, "He who engages in a laborious work (such, for instance, as Johnson's Dictionary,) which may employ his whole life, will do it with more spirit, if, besides his own glory, he thinks it may be a provision for his family" (*Millar v. Taylor* 218; in Swartz, "Patrimony" 37); and Lord Mansfield in his decision stated, "The property of the copy . . . may . . . go down from generation to generation, and possibly continue for ever," (*Millar v. Taylor* 251; in Swartz, "Patrimony" 37).

15. See Seville, *Literary Copyright Reform*; Feather; and Woodmansee, "Cultural Work" for thorough summaries of Talfourd's travails. For a discussion of the rhetorical strategies adopted by both parties in the debate, see Vanden Bossche.

through as the result of the unforeseen, and somewhat incomprehensible, entry into that debate of that famous man of letters and member for Edinburgh, Thomas Babington Macaulay—arguing for the other side. Macaulay made an especially impassioned and persuasive speech to the members that effectively killed the bill for that session. A major strand of his argument was the contention that "Copyright is monopoly, and produces all the effects which the general voice of mankind attributes to monopoly" (Macaulay 8:198). Subsequent debates would disclose that Macaulay had found objectionable not the spirit of the bill itself but rather simply the length of the proposed term, and as Talfourd had made the immoderate proclamation that he "despised" any half-hearted support, Macaulay had concluded that he could do nothing else but oppose the bill *in toto.* Obviously, along with Talfourd's extraordinary stamina came also a rigidity of principle that, fatally, would not allow him to compromise on unwinnable points, most particularly on the posthumous sixty-year term that he was seeking. Viscount Mahon, one of the more stalwart supporters of Talfourd's bill throughout that member's many trials, took up the baton after the election and after a year or so, through adroit political maneuvering, had brought about the passage of a bill in March of 1842 extending the term of copyright to 42 years after the year of publication, or the life of the author plus seven years, whichever turned out to be longer. Mahon's "victory" was welcomed by authors as a benefit to the profession throughout England. Not the least grateful of these, eventually, would be the aged Wilkie Collins who throughout his life would keep strict control over most of his copyrights, selling them only a few months before his death in 1889 for as much as he could obtain for the short time left on their duration.[16]

The proponents in the House of Commons specifically emphasized the need to adequately compensate the author for the pains undertaken in creating his text. Talfourd felt he had a legitimate reason for seeking extension of the term of copyright because he believed, as did many others,[17] that the House of Lords's decision in the case of *Donaldson v. Becket* in 1774 had unfairly stripped British authors of a perpetual right enjoyed hitherto, replacing it with a meager fourteen years, renewable for another fourteen

16. Clarke 5. See also Dickens's letter to Collins of 27 January 1870 (a time when both were ailing, and perhaps also quarreling) in which the former somewhat grudgingly writes, "At your request, I can have no hesitation in stating for your satisfaction that the Copyright in any of your novels tales and articles which have appeared in the periodicals 'Household Words' and 'All the Year Round' was never purchased by the proprietors of those Periodicals" (*Letters* 12:472).

17. See for example the argument of the Chancellor of the Exchequer upon his introduction of the bill into the House of Lords for confirmation on May 26, 1842 (*Hansard Parliamentary Debates,* vol. 63, cols. 777–87).

should the author still be living. This drastic shortening of the term—in fact a serious reconceptualization of the concept of copyright as Mark Rose and others have shown[18]—had come about as a result of two crucial issues having been decided about the Statute of Anne of 1710: (1) that it had been passed with the *intention* of limiting the perpetual right, and (2) that it had effectively overridden any perpetual right the author might wish to claim at common law.

Thus it is not surprising that Talfourd presented himself as championing the cause of a group the members of which had in the past been deprived of a substantial right, the right to endow their heirs or assigns with a legacy that would have lasted forever. In the first introduction of the bill into the House, Talfourd places the issue solidly within the framework of a generational succession to proprietorship, of the handing-down from father to child of the landed estate,[19] by using the concept of inheritance to suggest a tie between what had been lost in the earlier decision of 1774, and that portion that might be partially restored in his day and age by the passage of his bill:

> Although I see no reason why authors should not be restored to that *inheritance* which, under the name of protection and encouragement, has been taken from them . . . I propose still to treat [the issue] on the principle of compromise, and to rest satisfied with a fairer adjustment of the difference than the last act of Parliament affords. I shall propose . . . that the term of property in all works of learning, genius, and art, to be produced hereafter, or in which the statutable copyright subsists, shall be extended to sixty years, to be computed from the death of the author; which will at least enable him, while providing for the instruction and delight of distant ages, to contemplate that *he shall leave in his works themselves some legacy* to those for whom a nearer, if not a higher duty, requires him to provide. (Talfourd 8; emphasis added)

Talfourd employs terms that equate the author's attachment to literary "property" with the proprietary attachment to land. Specifically, he attempts to transfer to the former connection the latter's ability to pass from one person to another upon the death of the current proprietor—as would occur with an estate in fee—by transforming the past loss in *Donaldson v. Becket,* that

---

18. See Rose, *Authors.* See also Birrell, Patterson, and Saunders for discussions of the changes wrought upon copyright in Britain prior to 1842.

19. Talfourd comments, "the Statute of Anne substituted a short term in copyright for an estate in fee, and the rights of authors were delivered up to the mercy of succeeding Parliaments!" (4).

denied "inheritance," into the "legacy" proposed by his bill. In 1834 Balzac had decried the lack of a posthumous legacy for French literary property in similar terms: "Mankind has perpetuated fortunes for the eldest sons of great families, for the youngest children of bankers; it has stipulated the heredi-tariness of [property earned by] sweat; but it has disinherited the brains and vigils of writers" (65).

Talfourd realizes the need to situate copyright in terms highlighting its role as a solid form of property (the uncomfortable fit between "copyright" and "solid property" evincing the degree of ideological bridge-building required here). However, it was precisely this elision that had so disturbed Justice Yates in *Millar v. Taylor* in 1769. According to Rose, Yates was well aware of the elision surfacing in the opinions in that case, an elision that Yates took it on himself to question:

> Joseph Yates . . . was probably the most penetrating legal thinker on the anti-common-law side of the question, and he understood quite clearly what was happening. The fallacy in the assertion that a literary composi-tion could be regarded as property equivalent to an estate lay, he said, in "the equivocal use of the word 'property'; which sometimes denotes the right of the person; (as when we say, 'such a one has this estate, or that piece of goods';) sometimes, the object itself." Yates insisted on maintain-ing the distinction between a personal right and an object of property. He did not deny that a personal right might be incorporeal, but he did deny that anything incorporeal could be treated as property in the same sense as a house or land.[20]

---

20. Rose, "Author as Proprietor" 65. Yates's words are from *Millar v. Taylor* 233. See Balzac attempting in 1834 the same elision in his implicit equation between "white paper" and the marks subsequently made on that paper: "Our country, which attends with scrupulous care to machines, to wheat harvests, to the silk and cotton industry, has no ears, has no eyes, has no hands when it comes to dealing with its intellectual treasures. . . . Listen, then. If, say, a merchant sends a bale of cotton from Le Havre to St Petersburg and some beggar sneaks up to it on a small boat and lays hands on it, that beggar will be hanged. In order to secure the free passage in every country of each such bale of cotton, of sugar, *of white paper,* of wine, the whole of Europe has created a common law right. Her ships, her cannons, her sailors, all her forces are at the orders of this bale of cargo. If a merchant ship is boarded by pirates, a general alarm is raised: all these forces are mobilized, and the pirates are soon caught and executed. Up until now it has only been poetry which has shed tears for the fate of a man for whom, if his play falls through at the theatre, the booing of the audience is like a rope hanging from a beam. But what about a book, then? Oh! a book is treated just like a pirate would be treated. Everyone rushes to get at a book: it is avidly sought after, it is carried off in its swaddling-clothes, when it is still in proof-sheets; it is already counterfeited even before it has been made. The pirate can use his genius to try to escape execution, but the genius with which a book is marked only serves to make it easily discovered by its executioners. Germany, Italy, England, France extend their greedy hands towards the book, for, since this malversation [*sic*] is universal, France has been forced to imitate the other

Half a century later the elision that had so disturbed Yates would again be surfacing—actually the time-honored strategy of denigrating breaking emerging once more—this time in Parliament, once again deployed in defense of the author's natural proprietary right over his creation.

In 1774, in the House of Lords's consideration of the question of literary property in the famous case of *Donaldson v. Becket*—effectively the appeal, and overturning, of *Millar v. Taylor*—it had not been taken for granted that authors wanted or even in fact possessed a monetary property in their works; for after all, as Lord Camden argued, did not true authors write out of a general desire for glory or praise, manifestly disdaining any base monetary motive?

> Glory is the reward of science, and those who deserve it scorn all meaner views. . . . It was not for gain, that Bacon, Newton, Milton, Locke, instructed and delighted the world; it would be unworthy such men to traffic with a dirty bookseller for so much a sheet of letter-press. ("The Speeches of the Lords" in *Cases of the Appellants* 54)

This issue broached by Lord Camden was to become one of the most heated points of contention in the debates over Talfourd's bill sixty years later. Arguments in the spirit of Camden's, that authors wrote for glory rather than money, were both reviled by defenders of the bill asking how authors were to "live on air" and praised by their opponents who, ignoring the different system of remuneration most pervasive in the era of Bacon and Milton, the patronage system, countered that authors had been happy to write even before copyright had existed.

Lord Mahon, at that time merely a supporter of Talfourd's side of the argument rather than its leader, is reported as having spoken quite effectively—and in terms that will resonate with our reading of Collins's narrative—on behalf of the bill on February 19, 1840:

> [The author] should be supplied with the natural motive and natural reward for exertion; namely, that *the harvest of his toil should hereafter be reaped by his children.* It had been argued that the love of fame was sufficient motive, and that the attainment of fame was sufficient reward. He (Lord Mahon) did not deny the power of that motive, or the brilliancy of that reward. But would ask, did they apply that rule to other cases? . . . Why . . . with

---

countries as well. Thus, common law is suspended throughout Europe for the difficult product of intelligence" (66–67; emphasis added).

writers alone, attempt to dissever the two gifts of fame and fortune? Why, then, should literary men, and literary men only, be confined to the empty honours of celebrity? He asked for authors only this—*give them what is their own*—*give them what their own brains have conceived, and their own right hands have written*—give them by legal enactment what they already hold by every moral right.[21] (*Hansard Parliamentary Debates,* vol. 52, cols. 408–9; emphasis added)

Mahon here draws a connection—a not at all uncommon one in the days before computer voice-dictation—between writing and the work of the hands, a connection highlighting, that is, the role the author plays in the production of the book. The close proximity between this reference to the production of the hands and the earlier reference to the author's "harvest" suggests an image of the author as farmer or tiller of the soil, as laborer. Once again connecting text and land, late in the copyright debates Mahon refers to Backbite's line mentioned earlier to characterize the shift in printing from the late 1700s to the mid-1800s: "The demand for splendid books has ceased. . . . Before the beginning of the present century, Mr. Sheridan remarked that the manner in which the poetical works of that period were printed made them look 'like a rivulet of text meandering through a meadow of margin'; but year by year cheaper editions are published."[22] Mahon's rhetorical rendering of the author's labor as a metaphoric tilling of the land in these two cases, as the "harvest" that his children should later come properly to reap, puts back into effect a latent connection at the heart of the etymology of the word "character." Etymologists of English note that "character" not only signifies one's personality and/or a letter, as in A, B, C, etc., but also derives from the Greek for the act of cutting furrows in or plowing the soil.[23] Mahon's rhetoric here asks us to see the author as a laborer sowing seeds, or making furrows across a page, so that that author and his family might later eat, rather than to see him as a type of high-class,

---

21. Balzac also connected writing with harvests: "[France] looks on without shame as the descendants of Corneille, all of them poor, gather round the statue of Corneille, which has created wealth in all the barns of this country, which brings forth harvests that no patch of bad weather can threaten, which over the centuries will continue to make rich actors, booksellers, paper manufacturers, bookbinders, and scholarly commentators" (64).

22. 6 April 1842; *Hansard Parliamentary Debates,* vol. 61, col. 1358.

23. Rowland Jones notes that "character" and "letter" both possess an etymological tie to land: "by character is meant a real representation of nature, and by letter a call or sound upon nature; litera being from al-tir, a call upon the land, and character from ac-ar-tir, action upon the land" (entry for "Character" in Jones). Klein suggests "character" derives from the Hebrew *harash* for "he engraved, plowed" and the Akkadian *erushu* for "to till the ground" (127).

intellectual dabbler in the arts or amanuensis of God who has neither need nor right to profit by his literary works, an image on which Lord Camden, implicitly through the reference to Milton, would seem to be reliant. We are here offered by Mahon an early example of an image that would later in the century be taken up whole-heartedly by several diverse groups interested in strengthening the author–work tie: the image of the author as working-man.[24]

Mahon's strategy of rhetorically equating literary creations with land had an effect. The reaction in *Blackwood's* to the passage of his Act emphasized precisely this connection. After remarking that "it is a disgrace to British legislation . . . that copyright should ever have been the subject of a question" and acknowledging that "we have no doubt that the time will come, when this very circumstance will be quoted as evidence of the barbarism of the nineteenth century," the noted lawyer and historian Archibald Alison asks,

> why is the labour of the philosopher to be less valued and protected than the labour of the peasant? If a fellow with a spade in his hand shuts out the sea from half a dozen acres, he may transmit them to his remotest generation. . . . If one great object of every man of virtue and feeling is to leave his family at least above the privations which belong to poverty, why is the attainment of an object so laudable and so important even to the community, to be prohibited to the intellectual part of mankind, while it is fully given to the more drudging and unintelligent? (634–35)

Alison's commentary concludes with an avowal of confidence in the future: "However, all these anomalies will be rectified in time. The brains of a man will be as much protected as his boots; and robbery will be no more sanctioned in the instance of a new Iliad, or a new Paradise Lost, than in that of the good-will of a cobbler's stall, or the fee-simple of a potato field" (635–36). Here the oft-cited example in the literary critical debates of Milton's apparently exploitative contract for the sale of *Paradise Lost* for £5 (as well

---

24. One such group was the young men surrounding Dickens. It is appropriate that Talfourd should have been the dedicatee, when it appeared in volume form, of *The Pickwick Papers* (1837), that early work by that author who would do so much to popularize the image of the Victorian author as laborer. In praising Talfourd for his efforts to secure to authors and "their descendants a permanent interest in the copyright of their works," Dickens writes, "many a widowed mother and orphan child, who would otherwise reap nothing from the fame of departed genius but its too frequent legacy of poverty and suffering, will bear, in their altered condition, higher testimony to the value of your labours than the most lavish encomiums from lip or pen could ever afford" (*Pickwick Papers* 39).

as the purportedly resultant penury of his granddaughter) is reinflected to a different use.[25] Indeed, the provisions in the new Act and their establishment of a model for future Acts would make certain that, if anything, the authorial Paradise would some day be Found.

A decade after these particular rhetorical battles had been concluded, what Collins would gain by his re-conflation, in his turn, of the right to the ownership of literary property with the right to the ownership of land would be the solid claim, as proprietor, to the possession of his writings, those writings having now become, at least metaphorically, as sacrosanct as landed property. Collins brings about this conflation by adopting and perpetuating an ideology that works toward the reification of the object of literary property, "solidifying" that incorporeal and inherently disseminable entity in the more stable shape of a symbolic landscape. Thus the proprietary right to literary property regains its own lost inheritance, perpetuity, by being implicitly tied to the perpetual right characteristic of the ownership of land. Collins, by centering his narrative's concerns on the issues of authorship and landed inheritance—conjoined in the self-actuating figure of the always already bereft second son who chooses to write—lobbies his readers toward seeing literary "property" to be, no doubt to Justice Yates's undying consternation, not just a right but also a thing.

My purpose in producing these quotations from Parliament is not to propose that Talfourd and Mahon are playing etymological games. Indeed, foremost on their agendas must simply have been the swaying of the rest of the members of the House of Commons through the purport of their speeches, as opposed to through clever word-play (although Talfourd did have a penchant for interspersing lines from Wordsworth's poetry and prose throughout his discourse in deference to that behind-the-scenes proponent of the bill).[26] However, it *is* my contention that Collins in *Basil* is—as will be seen in the next section—playing etymological games and doing so for a purpose very similar to the purpose motivating the speeches of the parliamentarians. In *Basil* Collins depicts both an image of the high-class dabbler in fiction, the effete son of the upper classes, being transformed by certain sensational circumstances into a strong-armed ruffian—a type of condensed mapping of the evolution of the English literary artist from inspired aris-

---

25. See Lindenbaum on "Milton's Contract," and Macaulay commenting that "[a]s often as this bill has been under discussion, the fate of Milton's granddaughter has been brought forward by the advocates of monopoly. My honorable and learned friend [Talfourd] has repeatedly told the story with great eloquence and effect" (8:203).

26. See Swartz, "Wordsworth" for examples of Talfourd's Word(sworth)-play. For Wordsworth's interest in the bill, see Wordsworth, *Letters,* vols. 6 and 7 *passim*; Erickson; Noyes; Ward; and Zall.

tocrat to anonymous but industrious garret dweller[27]—and an instance of the chaste artist inspired from "on high" becoming a terrestrial, as well as sexual, sower of seeds. This description brings to mind a specific contemporary literary character who exemplifies these same qualities and undergoes these same transformations, the sexual/textual disseminator Nemo (Captain James Hawdon) of *Bleak House* (serialized March 1852–September 1853), a book whose early part-publications influenced the construction of *Basil.* Catherine Peters notes that Collins spent the summer of 1852 with the Dickens household at Dover:

> Dickens' orderly and self-disciplined routine, combined with his apparently inexhaustible energy, set an example Wilkie tried to live up to. "Our life here is as healthy and happy as life can be—work in the morning—long walks—sea bathing—early hours—famous meals—merry evenings—make up the various fuel with which we feed the fire of life." But he found "The sea air acts on me as if it was all distilled from laudanum," and after one of Dickens' famous fifteen-mile walks he was too sleepy even to write a letter. . . . Dickens was writing *Bleak House,* and reading the latest chapters to the household before they were published. . . . Wilkie, fired by his example, finished his novel on 15 September. (113)

Here Collins, under the strong guiding hand of Dickens, transforms from the privileged son of a famous English painter to the working man able and willing to put forth the physical and mental effort necessary to support himself and his household. These transformations—both the one effected in life by the example set by Dickens and the one exemplified in the narrative by Basil's turn to the dark woman in the dream—of the literary artist from effete, inspired dabbler to active, energetic working-man serve in Collins's mind, at least at this time, to solidly stamp the artist's copyright on his work and concomitantly to establish that work as an object of property. In Parliament, what Talfourd and Mahon were trying to do through their use of analogies that would implicitly link copyright with more solid forms of property, such as harvests and landed legacies, was to solidify an image of the author as proprietor. It is no mere coincidence that a decade later

---

27. This undertext of the author-protagonist's transforming in class position explains Collins's apparent overturning of the normal Gothic conventions, noted by Pykett: "*Basil* is an early example of the way in which Collins's modernization of Gothic reverses some of its key terms, including those of class. Whereas traditional Gothic habitually puts its middle- or upper-class heroine at the mercy of a sinister ecclesiastical or aristocratic power, Collins's modern Gothic entraps its upper-class male protagonist in a secular lower-middle-class world" (*Wilkie Collins* 114).

Collins would be putting into play a similar conception, for all three of these figures, Talfourd, Mahon, and Collins, were participating in a cultural transformation through which the relationship between the author-proprietor and his work was being consistently strengthened and the nature of the literary work increasingly "solidified" through the active promotion of settling and the tacit denigration of breaking, all in an attempt to render the literary ownership of the work an inviolable right of property.

Playing with Words and Etymologies

Having situated Basil's dream within the particular context of the contemporary copyright extension debates, we can now look at the rest of the narrative, scrutinizing it with an interest especially as to its references to textuality. The first feature to be noted about the remainder of Collins's quite sensational story is, surprisingly, a rather mundane aspect of its narrative composition: the play with etymologies. Etymological play was a constant throughout Collins's career. To give one example not unrelated to the narrative of *Basil*: on the day of reckoning for the villain of the novel written immediately after *Basil*, *Hide and Seek* (1854), Mat Grice reveals the hidden, nefarious character of the seemingly model-citizen Mr. Zachary Thorpe, the elder, by inscribing one more name at the bottom of an address "eulogizing his character" (*Hide* 402). This testimonial—described as "beautifully written on the fairest white paper" (405)—has been presented that day to Thorpe by the religious society of which he has been a member for many years:

> [Mat] handed the paper to Mr. Thorpe, bearing inscribed on it the name of MARY GRICE.
>   Read that name, said Mat.
>   Mr. Thorpe looked at the characters traced by the pencil. His face changed instantly—he sank down into the chair—one faint cry burst from his lips—then he was silent.
>   Low, stifled, momentary as it was, that cry proclaimed him to be the man. He was self-denounced by it even before he cowered down, shuddering in the chair, with both his hands pressed convulsively over his face. (408)

The "characters traced by the pencil" of Mat Grice are not just the M-A-R-Y, etc., of his sister's name but of course also reveal Thorpe's well-hidden and scandalous *character.* The man who Thorpe is revealed to be is that Arthur Carr who twenty-three years before had seduced and abandoned the pregnant, unmarried Mary who, having fled from her home in shame, later died during child-birth. This scene, as well as the rest of the narrative, plays with the double meaning of the word "character,"[28] a word that of course can refer to both handwriting (lettering) and personality.

This tie between character and characters is also apparent in the earlier narrative of *Basil,* the association being brought out perhaps most forcefully in the scene in which Basil's father, horrified by his marriage and by Margaret's subsequent actions, expels him from the family by tearing Basil's page from a familial record book:

> Here, then, if I still acknowledge you to be my son . . . must be written such a record of dishonour and degradation as has never yet defiled a single page of this book—here, the foul stain of your marriage, and its consequences, must be admitted to spread over all that is pure before it, and to taint to the last whatever comes after. This shall not be. . . . I know you now, only as an enemy to me and to my house. . . . In this record your place is destroyed—and destroyed for ever. Would to God I could tear the past from my memory, as I tear the leaf from this book! (*Basil* 203)

Character quite literally equals handwriting, or copy-book characters, in this family scrap-book containing pages headed "sometimes by copies of the Baron's effigy on his tombstone" (201). Here Basil's father expresses, both through the fact of having a book that represents his family and in the act of tearing Basil out of it, a desire for the collapsing of two levels, his "real" (for us the narratorial) and his literal. The past and the future of the family are a text from which one can easily tear things and people.

However, "character" is not the only word to have its etymology troped upon in the narrative of *Basil.* The other significant etymological manipulation in the book occurs with the word "manuscript." This word combines the Latin for hand, *manus,* with the Latin for writing, *scribere.* Of course, having suggested this etymology, I must distinguish it from that other root for words beginning with M-A-N: the Old High German for quite simply "man" as in *human* or *Norman,* meaning man from Normandy or Northman, a genealogy that, if we do not remember it, as both Mr. Sherwin and Basil seem not to in trusting Robert Mannion in his relationship with Margaret,

---

28. As does also *The Woman in White,* in which at the climax of the narrative Count Fosco flees London leaving Walter Hartright with his written confession, that is—reinflecting Fosco's line from Sheridan referred to in an earlier footnote—in which he goes, leaving his character(s) behind him.

places us at the mercy of the evil villain of the story. Sherwin, whose "managing man" (bringing together both options) Mannion is, would appear to read our villain's name simply along the *manus,* Latin rather than German, line of descent. Mannion is simply an extension of himself, his right-hand man: "I can tell you there's not a house of business in London has such a managing man as he is: he's my factotum—my right hand, in short; and my left too, for the matter of that" (*Basil* 115).

Robert Mannion is no one's right hand, and no one's left either; he's all man, as his illicit actions will come to prove—in stark contrast it would appear to the preciously-named Basil. At one point late in the story, Margaret, caught up in her Typhus-induced delirium, believing she is speaking to Mannion but really speaking to Basil, says,

> You know I like you, because I *must* like you; because I can't help it. It's no use saying hush: I tell you he can't hear us, and can't see us. He can see nothing; you make a fool of him, and I make a fool of him. . . . Why didn't you come back from France in time, and stop it all? Why did you let me marry him? A nice wife I've been to him, and a nice husband he has been to me—a husband who waits a year! Ha! ha! he calls himself a man, doesn't he? A husband who waits a year! (*Basil* 294)

Mannion's manliness was emphasized to an even greater extent in the sentence originally following "I can't help it" in the first edition: "*You* are a man; a strong, daring, conquering man: he's a——" (*Basil,* 1852 edition, 2:177). (This sentence was excised by Collins when he revised the text in 1862, undoubtedly out of deference to the respect owed to mid-Victorian propriety by a now very successful author.) The almost unlimited access to his young daughter Sherwin allows Mannion, including after-dinner teaching sessions under the fairly unobservant eye of her mother, would seem to imply that he feels that the forty-year-old Mannion must have lost all his "manly" urges years ago. This is a miscalculation of the same order as that one made in *Hide and Seek* when Joshua Grice failed to exert the strict control over his daughter Mary urged on him by his sister Joanna: "Next to his blind trust in his daughter, because he was fond of her, was his blind trust in this stranger, because the gentleman's manners were so quiet and kind, and because he sent us presents of expensive flowers to plant in our garden" (*Hide* 272). The reprehensible Carr was of course in that instance sowing seeds—as he would be doing again later, only then with fatal repercussions. Mr. Grice's mistake ended up costing him his daughter's life. Mr. Sherwin's miscalculation will similarly end up costing him his daughter, and this time we will have not a bereaved brother revamping the villain's testimonial or "character," but a bereaved husband-in-waiting revamping the villain's character, or face, outside the hotel of assignation.

Appended to the autobiographical manuscript that Basil will have completed before we reach the end of the book is a letter written by our narrator eight years after most of the action in the story has concluded. The letter is addressed by Basil to his friend Dr. Bernard, telling of the former's reconciliation with his father and of that father's recent death. In the letter Basil grants Bernard permission to publish his "manuscript." The following passage from the letter discloses not only the fictionality of all the names appearing in the story but also implicitly refers to the etymology of that word:

> While my father lived, I could not suffer a manuscript in which he was represented . . . as separating himself in the bitterest hostility from his own son, to be made public property. . . . Still I am not answering your question:—Am I now willing to permit the publication of my narrative, provided all names and places mentioned in it remained concealed, and I am known to no one but yourself, Ralph, and Clara, as the writer of my own story? I reply that I *am* willing. In a few days, you will receive the manuscript by a safe hand.[29] (*Basil* 338–39)

While "Basil," "Clara," and "Mannion" are disclosed here to be not "real" names, this second-order fictionality does nothing to disturb their underlying allegorical import, indeed, instead only heightening it. We might see not only the reference to "a safe hand" to be suggesting the *manus* root of "manuscript" but the rather redundant stress that Basil lays on the fact that he has written an autobiography, that he is "the writer of [his] *own* story," to be punningly asserting the tie between him and the possession and ownership of his writing. This remark is deployed to contrast with the earlier reference to the manuscript becoming upon publication a type of "public property."

Though it had been Basil who in the early dream had gone off with the dark woman to the secret recesses among the trees, in the story Mannion is the one who actually enjoys Margaret's favors. As a result, Basil, perhaps not a lover but certainly when enraged a writer and fighter both, "mark[s]" (*Basil* 275) Mannion, writing on his face by hurling him down on the road-

---

29. Collins repeats this reference later in his career when he has Ozias Midwinter present the written description of Allan Armadale's dream to the Manx doctor Mr. Hawbury: "'I beg your pardon,' he said, as he offered the doctor the manuscript with his own hand" (*Armadale* 140).

stones of the newly macadamized street. Mannion's face—described earlier by Basil as "a sealed book" (117)—having been mutilated and an eye put out, his character is deformed. This alteration is analogically represented afterwards by the "irregular" characters (194) exhibited in the handwriting of the threatening letter Mannion writes to Basil from his hospital bed. This deformation, the result of the two having gone *mano-a-mano*, is characterized by Mannion as the product of Basil's labors. He asks at Margaret's funeral, "Do you know me for Robert Mannion? . . . Do you know the work of your own hands, now you see it?" (303). The passage that precedes this question, besides markedly confirming the critic Tamar Heller's assertions of an influence stemming from *Frankenstein* (60), reminds us that Mannion's face has become the bad manuscript that haunts its author everywhere and forever:

> The first sight of that appalling face, with its ghastly discolouration of sickness, its hideous deformity of feature, its fierce and changeless malignity of expression glaring full on me in the piercing noonday sunshine . . . struck me speechless where I stood, and has never left me since. I must not, I dare not, describe that frightful sight; though it now rises before my imagination, vivid in its horror as on the first day when I saw it—though it moves hither and thither before me fearfully, while I write; though it lowers at my window, *a noisome shadow on the radiant prospect of earth, and sea, and sky, whenever I look up from the page I am now writing towards the beauties of my cottage view.*
>
> "Do you know me for Robert Mannion?" he repeated. "Do you know the work of your own hands, now you see it?" (302–3; emphasis added)

Basil's manuscript is everywhere. Even a turn to the prospect, to the landscape around him, would seem not to afford an escape from the sight of the work of his hands. Here the etymological root of Mannion's name would seem to have changed character along with the change in his face since "Man"nion's one-time manly face has become Basil's "hand"iwork, while, at the same time, through an associative bridging involving the terms "character" and "manuscript," the landscape around Basil would seem to have become conflated with his manuscript. In order for this equation between land and manuscript to work on us effectively, however, we must first be successfully indoctrinated into what I am calling "copyright ideology," the idea that texts themselves might be possessed and bequeathed in the same way that other forms of property were in Collins's time.

Textual Repossessions

Highlighting the emphasis on textuality that will pervade the entirety of Collins's *oeuvre,* both *Basil* and our eponymous hero's manuscript that largely makes up that narrative jointly begin with the question "What am I now about to write?" In answer, the subsequent lines are characterized by our narrator as his family legacy. Basil launches this history of his sadly mis-directed affections in the hope that it will have good effects on the succeeding generations of his family:

> I hope that, one day, [my narrative] may be put to some warning use. I am now about to relate the story of an error. . . . [M]y plain and true record will show that this error was not committed altogether without excuse. When these pages are found after my death, they will perhaps be calmly read and gently judged, as *relics solemnized by the atoning shadows of the grave.* Then, the hard sentence against me may be repented of; *the children of the next generation of our house* may be taught to speak charitably of my memory, and may often, of their own accord, think of me kindly in the thoughtful watches of the night. (*Basil* 1; emphasis added)

Basil is here handing down the lessons learned as a result of the mistakes made in his early life and characterizing the narrative in which they are recounted as a provision for his descendants to profit by, albeit, in this case, only spiritually. Nevertheless, we are not far here from the rhetoric of patrimony, referred to earlier, employed by the Victorian parliamentarians in their prolonged fight to extend the duration of copyright.

It is not surprising that the legacy of a second son should be at issue here as the concept of "congenital" dispossession—especially of the author at the hands of language—will be a central aspect of Collins's major narratives, especially of *The Moonstone.* In *Basil* we see early stirrings of this type of thinking as the author is analogized, by way of the examples of the main characters Mannion and Basil, to an aristocrat who has always already fallen in station. Mannion's fall, the result of his father's transgression, is described as at one point having led to his working as a "hack-author of the lowest degree" (*Basil* 231). In Basil's case we have someone who also, albeit in this case as a result of birth order, has to encounter and acknowledge an inherent inadequacy. Even before the beginning of the narrative Basil has been laboring through writing to regain a "lost" class position; later in Collins's career the author-figure will be working toward regaining control of a lost text or fugitive meanings. The author for Collins is in a sense always a second son. Unlike the situation in other Collins novels, most notably *No Name* (1862), this time it is not so much a matter of inheriting or not inheriting money but of, quite simply, inheriting or not inheriting land. If one is not going to inherit it, one has to create it for oneself.[30] This is what Basil, however improbably, does, by creating a manuscript. Thus he reinvokes, in the converse direction, the Victorian parliamentarians' analogy between texts and land, an analogy most clearly encapsulated in Lord Mahon's suggestion that authors had been deprived of their legacies and had their proper "harvests" taken away from them and their children. Basil is constantly preoccupied with creating the landed inheritance that his position as a second son has always already denied him. Collins will reinterpret this situation in *The Moonstone*. It is a short step from this dispossession due to birth order and that dispossession resulting from the author's agreement to contract with the vagaries of the breaking function of iterability.

There is another benefit to be derived from Basil's literary labors, this time in the psychological realm. The narrative of *Basil* implies that a certain solidity of character is a natural offshoot or product of the act of writing, for, as the manuscript pages pile up, Basil's personality comes itself to be more and more unified. The fact that Basil has been estranged from his father and thrown out of home and family, in other words, multiply dispossessed, exhibits its effects through Basil's inability as a narrator to be quite, as Jenny Bourne Taylor puts it, "self-possessed." Taylor's reading finds the trauma of Basil's having been disowned to be expressing itself thereafter in something akin to a split-personality disorder.[31] This fragmentation in Basil's personality shows up in the various narratorial stances he adopts during the

---

30. Tamar Heller, in her exceptional study *Dead Secrets: Wilkie Collins and the Female Gothic*, contends that Basil takes up writing as a profession in response to his father's dispossession of him (69). This interpretation, however, does not account for the fact that Basil has been writing all along, even *before* being officially and sensationally disinherited. Specifically, he has been writing a "historical romance" (along the lines, one gets the impression, of Collins's first published novel *Antonina; or the Fall of Rome*), for which he has been away doing research in Italy before the narrative-time of *Basil* begins. Indeed, the part of the inheritance most dear to Basil is that one that as a second son, unless he had taken up murder as a profession, he was never going to have had anyway. The significance for Basil of this congenital dispossession is made clear when our hero explicitly states that upon his return home from college "it was thought necessary, as I was a younger son and could inherit none of the landed property of the family, except in the case of my brother's dying without children, that I should belong to a profession" (*Basil* 4). That dispossession by birth order—the symbolic significance of this order only growing when we note that it is the opposite of Collins's own real-life situation—is again made explicitly evident in the meditations on Ralph's undeserving but favored position in Part I, Chapter IV.

31. Taylor's efforts in her chapter on *Basil* are dedicated to disclosing the various ways in which "the narrative voice" in the book "fractures" (*Secret Theatre* 74).

course of his telling of the story. At first he is a naive Basil. Then, after the disclosure of his "half-wife" Margaret's adultery, he appears as a knowledge-able—and fallen—Basil. Both of these Basils, however, have been all along contained within, impersonated by, a third Basil, that one hiding from the vindictive, disfigured Mannion in Cornwall while writing the manuscript of his autobiography. This last persona renders that one of naiveté taken up in the first pages of the book quite the departure from the actual situation of the fully recovered narrator. So, for Taylor, Basil is undoing, through this gradual recovery from his narratorial self-estrangements, the psychological effects of his disinheritance and his removal from the family. He is, through a form of, it would seem, the "writing cure," working toward the goal of "repossession" on various levels.

I would emphasize one movement toward "repossession" that Taylor does not explicitly mention—that movement toward the repossession of the auto-biographical text itself by its purported author, and owner, as a direct result of the solidification of that author's personality. For my study, it is quite significant that the moment when Basil's narration catches up with him, the moment when he becomes once more self-possessed, is also the moment when he highlights both the manuscript/work-of-the-hands connection and his own role in the creation of the text:

> October 19th.—My retrospect is finished. I have traced the history of my errors and misfortunes, of the wrong I have done and the punishment I have suffered for it, from the past to the present time.
>
> The pages of my manuscript (many more than I thought to write at first) lie piled together on the table before me. I dare not look them over: I dare not read the lines *which my own hand has traced.* (*Basil* 311; emphasis added)

Through this gradual coordination of various Basils via our hero's act of pen-ning characters (letters), "character" comes to recapture a range of possible meanings: handwriting, personality, fictional entity, and projected autobio-graphical entity. The lack of self-possession that Taylor identifies is gradu-ally healed through the act of writing; Basil's difficult work of seeding his handwriting over page after page of manuscript allows him to effect the unification of his "split-personality."

As the retrospect catches up with its time of writing, Basil's "real" and manuscript worlds come to coincide. The conflation of the phenomenal and the textual evident here naturally takes on a good deal of importance in a book that would be implicitly lobbying to demonstrate how valuable writing is to its author. Collins in this novel implicitly asserts ownership over the text he is creating, tacitly suggesting that his handwriting and characters are as intimate a reflection of him as his character or personality.[32] The narrative of *Basil* is, by means of the repeated language games deployed in it—not the least of which being the conjunction of the narrative level and the real level in the name shared by the work and its protagonist/narrator—dedicated to bringing about the collapse of the author with his text, thereby strengthening the tie between the author and the "work" he creates.

Manuscript's End as Land's End

A particularly striking example of the strengthening of this proprietary tie is the way in which at the end of the narrative, through a figurative doubling, England literally becomes Basil's, the landless second son's, manuscript. The narrative's transformations of manuscript into land, as well as, conversely, of land into manuscript, have all along been necessitated by Basil's position in the birth order. As Basil is the "spare," the *secundo* in the fundamentally imbalanced system of primogeniture, he most likely, unless he, like the later characters Gwilt and perhaps Fosco, takes up murder as a hobby, is not going to inherit the family lands. So, he must necessarily make his own legacy, a task he has embarked on even before the necessity precipitated by his forceful disinheritance has come upon him. He will make that land out of his imagination and the labor of his pen. Collins has Basil emphasize, continually, at the beginning of the story his older brother Ralph's unfitness for assuming proprietorship over the family lands, an unfitness quite in contrast with Basil's more natural, because more intimate and more organic, tie to the work of his hands. For example, Basil writes,

> When a family is possessed of large landed property, the individual of that family who shows least interest in its welfare . . . is often that very individual who is to succeed to the family inheritance—the eldest son. . . . It was impossible to make Ralph comprehend and appreciate his position, as

---

32. Talfourd had had recourse to the example of the laws against slander and libel in his appeal on behalf of a longer term of copyright, saying, "[I]s the interest itself so refined—so etherial—that you cannot regard it as property, because it is not palpable to sense or to feeling? . . . If so, why do you protect moral character as a man's most precious possession, and compensate the party who suffers in that character unjustly by damages? Has this possession any existence half so palpable as the author's right in the printed creation of his brain?" (27 February 1839; *Hansard Parliamentary Debates,* vol. 45, col. 927).

he was desired to comprehend and appreciate it. The steward gave up in despair all attempts to enlighten him about the extent, value, and management of the estates he was to inherit. (11–12)

Not only does Basil seem obsessed with Ralph's landed inheritance, the younger son would also seem to be mesmerized by the older one's ill-suitedness to the role of proprietor, painting as he does here the picture of the stereotypical carefree eldest son—the son who can afford to be carefree thanks to that system of inheritance that allows that the first male bud gets all the leaves while the second must make his own. This stereotype is employed by Basil to contrast all the more starkly with his own serious-minded desire to work, and to labor, at making that land that is more dearly bought than inherited land, the estate made by the work of one's hands, the sweat of one's brow, and the scratching of one's pen.

It should be kept in mind that at the time that Basil is writing this he has been disinherited and thrown out of the family home by his father. That is, Basil has found it necessary to write not only as a result of birth order but also as a result of family circumstances. As Dickens puts it in his valedictory letter to Collins congratulating him on the fashioning of *Basil,* the novel shows "throughout . . . [that] you have taken great pains with it . . . [that] you have 'gone at it' with a perfect knowledge of the jolter-headedness of the conceited idiots who suppose that volumes are to be tossed off like pancakes, and that any writing can be done without the utmost application, the greatest patience, and the steadiest energy of which the writer is capable."[33] This compliment to our young author might extend to our young narrator and autobiographer Basil as well, given the degree to which the narrative stresses Basil's serious-minded dedication to his chosen profession. Dedication being the subject at issue in Dickens's comment, it is appropriate that he should be seen to be bestowing in this letter his imprimatur upon an assertion of Collins's own, made in the appropriately titled "Letter of Dedication" to the first edition of *Basil:*

> My only desire, in writing this letter, is to claim credit for one humble, work-a-day merit to which anybody may attain by trying—the merit of having really taken pains to do my best. . . . The mob of ladies and gentlemen who play at writing is increasing, in our day, to formidable proportions. With every new season appear additional numbers of the holiday authors, who sit down to write a book as they would sit down to a game

---

33. Dickens, "Letter to Collins," 20 December 1852; qtd. in Page 49.

at cards—leisurely-living people who coolly select as an amusement "to kill time," an occupation which can only be pursued, even creditably, by the patient, uncompromising, reverent devotion of every moral and intellectual faculty, more or less, which a human being has to give. . . . To escape classification with the off-hand professors of this sort of off-hand authorship, by the homely but honourable distinction of *being workers and not players at their task,* has really become an object of importance, now-a-days, for those who follow Literature as a study and respect it as a science.[34] (*Basil,* 1852 edition, 1:xv–xvii; emphasis added)

Here Collins prefigures the so very stark contrast to come in the narrative between Basil and Ralph, that one between the landless and the landed, between the worker dedicated to letters and the player dedicated to the pursuit of other desires.

Near the close of the novel, Basil, with Mannion pursuing him like a living curse, ends up in Cornwall, most significantly, near Land's End. Basil is hiding there in a cottage near a small fishing village. Mannion's discovery of him and his subsequent agitations among the villagers cause them to shun and finally to drive Basil from his place of residence. During a stormy and foggy morning Basil ends up walking along the English coast on his way to a new village, convinced, quite rightly as it will turn out, that Mannion is still pursuing him. This melodramatic gothic pursuit is set on a fog-bound coast offering the peril of Basil's not being able to rely on his sight to see the cliff's edge, to see where the land ends and the fall into the raging Atlantic begins. Basil, having only his ears to guide him by, keeps the sound of the ocean always on his right hand but then realizes that the sea is to be heard on both sides of him, for he has unknowingly walked out onto a promontory jutting into the ocean. Tunneling through a massive, wall-like section of this promontory is a large hole that Dorothy Goldman in her explanatory notes relates to a "geographic phenomenon near Kynance Cove" called "The Devil's Throat" that Collins had described in his early travelogue *Rambles beyond Railways: or, Notes in Cornwall Taken A-Foot* (1851). On his walking tour Collins had encountered "a wide, tunnelled opening . . . a black, gaping hole, into the bottom of which the sea is driven through the aptly-named 'Devil's Throat.'" The opening of the abyss on the promontory is a

---

34. Giving Dickens his due with respect to the question of priority on this standpoint, we might recall in *David Copperfield* (1850) David's allusion to the painstaking efforts expended in his literary labors: "I have never believed it possible that any natural or improved ability can claim immunity from the companionship of the steady, plain, hard-working qualities, and hope to gain its end" (672).

dangerous place as the rocks rise "wild, jagged, and precipitous, all around it."[35] The pursuing Mannion also journeys out onto this promontory, yet he is not so lucky as Basil in climbing past the abyss, precisely because of his extreme desire for vengeance. The work, or more properly unworkability, of Mannion's hands is prominently displayed in the description of his end:

> [Mannion] stopped—looked up and saw me watching him—raised his hand—and shook it threateningly in the air. The ill-calculated violence of his action, in making that menacing gesture, destroyed his equilibrium—he staggered—tried to recover himself—swayed half round where he stood— then fell heavily backward, right on to the steep shelving rock.
>
> The wet sea-weed slipped through his fingers, as they madly clutched at it. He struggled frantically to throw himself towards the side of the declivity, slipping further and further down it at every effort. Close to the mouth of the abyss, he sprang up as if he had been shot. A tremendous jet of spray hissed out upon him at the same moment. . . . For one instant, I saw two livid and bloody hands tossed up against the black walls of the hole, as he dropped into it. (*Basil* 325–26)

The providential hand of water turns out to be stronger than the force of Mannion's hand-hold as he tries unsuccessfully to find a purchase on what will become in a sense his tombstone. Here, it must be remembered, Mannion is not just falling down a hole in a promontory into the Atlantic; he is in fact falling off the extreme edge of England, falling off Land's End.

In sympathy with Mannion's fall off the land's edge, almost immediately afterwards, Basil falls off what might be called the "edge" of his reason. Having "traced" (*Basil* 326) his way off the promontory and to a nearby village, he falls seriously ill, not only courting delirium, but also—horror of horrors in a Collins novel—losing control of his text. The narrative suggests through a series of asterisked breaks that Basil is, in a manner similar to Mannion's failed attempts, losing his own "hand-hold" and falling into what an unknown editor in a postscript can only describe as "illegibility." Appropriately, Basil's delirium had begun with the memory of Mannion's hands:

> 23rd. . . . Waking or sleeping, it is as if some fatality kept all my faculties imprisoned within the black walls of the chasm. I saw the livid, bleeding hands flying past them again, in my dreams, last night. . . .

---

35. Collins, *Rambles* 75–76; qtd. in *Basil* 356.

26th.—Visions—half waking, half dreaming—all through the night. Visions of my last lonely evening in the fishing-hamlet—of Mannion again—the livid hands whirling to and fro over my head in the darkness— then, glimpses of home; of Clara reading to me in my study—(327)

The last two of the progressively disjointed entries in the diary complete Basil's fall off the manuscript:

I can't move, or breathe, or think—if I could only be taken back—if my father could see me as I am now! Night again—the dreams that *will* come— always of home; sometimes, the untried home in heaven, as well as the familiar home on earth—

* * * * *

Clara! I shall die out of my senses, unless Clara—break the news gently—it may kill her—

Her face so bright and calm! her watchful, weeping eyes always looking at me, with a light in them that shines steady through the quivering tears. While the light lasts, I shall live; when it begins to die out—*

Note by the Editor
*There are some lines of writing beyond this point; but they are illegible. (329)

The manuscript had been providing Basil with a hand-hold on his reason. Here he is figuratively doubling his double's fall. He is bloodying his hands trying to grab at seaweed-covered rocks, represented by the fading light of his sister's eyes, as he falls off the manuscript. We have others taking his papers, and then we have illegibility, and we know he has conclusively fallen off the edge. This conjoint falling off—Mannion's and Basil's—might seem to be serving as simply another Collins cliché of light and dark doublings such as that of the light and dark women of Basil's earlier dream.[36] However, this double fall does more than connect Mannion to Basil; it also connects the entities clutched at by these doubles' hands. Basil's failure to hold onto the *manuscript* replaying Mannion's failure to hold onto the *land,* the manuscript thus becomes, analogically, the landed estate Basil had always wanted it to be.

---

36. Catherine Peters begins her biography of Collins by noting that "[t]here is a question of identity at the heart of every one of his novels. . . . Doubles are often, though not always, involved" (1–2).

It is quite appropriate, then, that the false name that Basil had adopted while living among the people of Cornwall and writing the manuscript, a name that he neglects to mention until the end of the book when he writes his closing letter, had been the name of his sister Clara's estate, which she had inherited from their mother.[37] The writer of the manuscript has been going under the name of a piece of land. Furthermore, the name of that land itself is suggestive of the manuscript/land connection. The significance of this name, however, only appears when it is broadly contextualized. That Basil, while he is writing the manuscript (throughout the first four-fifths of the novel) should be living under the assumed name "Lanreath" initially means very little to us—especially as that name is never once mentioned during the preceding exposition.[38] But the context in which the name is finally disclosed, at the head of the last of the three letters that Basil appends to that manuscript, in a separate section called "Letters in Conclusion" (*Basil* 330), is a context giving a new significance not only to the name itself but also to that manuscript. These letters frame the latter end of the manuscript. Thus, the significance of this assumed name for my discussion should be at this point clear: it conjures up a connection between writing and land as the manuscript nominally becomes a sort of "Lan[d]" that these closing letters "[w]reath[e]." It is appropriate that after Mannion and the manuscript find their ends at Land's End, Basil should write his manuscript frame at Lanreath Cottage, thus wreathing his land/manuscript.

The name Lanreath is one that, despite its single "L," conjures up Welsh associations. And indeed Clara's estate will turn out in the final scene of the book to be most definitely located on the west coast of Britain. The book ends with a happy scene of rural contentedness:

> I have done. The calm summer evening has stolen on me while I have been writing to you; and Clara's voice—now the happy voice of the happy old times—calls to me from our garden seat to come out and look at the sunset over the distant sea. Once more—farewell! (*Basil* 344)

This final scene—in addition to providing a degree of narrative unity through its concluding a book that had opened with a sunrise with a sunset, fitting symbolic approximations of the acts of opening and shutting a book—once

---

37. Notice that Basil would seem to be the only member of his family not possessing a landed estate.

38. The novelist Dorothy Sayers, writing of the manuscript of *Basil* held by the British Museum—an early draft of the first edition—points out that originally throughout the tale "the hero was . . . called 'Philip Lanreath'" (90).

again conflates manuscript with land, for, as the readerly/writerly perspective looks off and away from the manuscript page, the narrator's perspective looks out beyond the land at the distant sunset over the sea. Appropriately, the end of the letter appended to the manuscript, the end of the manuscript-plus-appendage, coincides with the end of the land.

Anti-idealized Authors and Texts

Returning to Basil's dream, we might notice how its manifest sexual content could *itself* be used to support a textual interpretation. Basil writes,

> I was drawn along in the arms of the dark woman, with my blood burning and my breath failing me, until we entered the secret recesses that lay amid the unfathomable depths of trees. There, she encircled me in the folds of her dusky robe, and laid her cheek close to mine, and murmured a mysterious music in my ear. . . . (*Basil* 46–47)

As I have remarked, it is not surprising that this writing should at first glance seem "without much subtlety" (Thoms 18). It is *designed* to. However, we might follow the path I am suggesting if we think of the pen as penis or plow (the latter being a connection the corn-fields metaphor calls up)—the nascent writer tearing the paper with his implement, making ink blots, etc.—and if we notice the stress laid on the dark woman's connection to the soil through the earthy darkness of her dun-colored clothes. Here the vegetal associations of Basil's name should be highlighted as, having come to be "encircled" within the folds of her "dusky robe," the hero of the narrative comes to fulfill the requirement proposed for any good work of art by Collins's Letter of Dedication; that is, as Basil (or *Basil*) "take[s] root in earth" (*Basil*, 1852 edition, 1:xxxvi).[39] Thus, our hero and our author become one with the landscapes of their manuscripts and with the idea of the landscape-as-manuscript as their pens ink the sheets and the paper.

There is an oscillation here between the real and textual worlds. The merging of character (in both the sense of fictional entity and personality) and handwriting allows not only for the narrator to become one with his story, to become one with his autobiography, as Basil had by having come back to his own jaded, experienced self through the journey of "re-self-possession" that was his writing of the text, but also for seeing that written

---

39. In this sense, "dissemination," the scattering of seeds/texts, quite literally turns into land.

text to be a type of "land." It allows for, among other transformations, seeing the ownership of the work of the author's hands, the manuscript, to have come over into the realm of the "real," as opposed to remaining safely in the domain of the "incorporeal" where Justice Yates in 1769 would have had it stay. It subliminally persuades the reader toward seeing the text as a fertile field planted by its author—a "charac-terra" if you like—and as therefore sacrosanct to the same degree as might be landed property. The dream allegorizes an oscillation between the realm of the real and the realm of the fictive in which the fictive wins, thereby making the world into a system of signs; we, all of us, readers and writer, and world, coming down to the level of the text to find not only that the page itself is a world but conversely that all the world's a page.

To RETURN to our broader cultural context: as noted earlier, many commentators remark that Wordsworth was quite energetically involved in Talfourd's parliamentary campaign. With respect to Wordsworth's efforts in this debate, Susan Eilenberg points out that there came into being among the group surrounding the poet a desire to reject the typical Romantic idealization of the literary creation and the wish to replace it with a less aesthetically-oriented valorization of the work as a material product situated within commercial relations:

> The idealization of the literary having often proved hazardous to their finances, these writers were inclined to represent themselves as working men and their writings as the products of their industry. It was their object to claim the same property in their writings as other men had in their farms and grocery stores. (*Strange Power* 204)

The works produced by Dickens and his circle, especially after the passage of the Copyright Act of 1842, were involved in continuing this de-idealization of the literary product. Thus it was appropriate that *Basil* should have been not only one of Dickens's favorite books[40] but also the work that purportedly prompted him to take a serious interest in the future labors of the younger writer. Dickens writes in his congratulatory letter on *Basil* to Collins, "I have read the book with very great interest, and with a very thorough conviction that you have a call to this same art of fiction."[41] It is understandable, then,

---

40. Percy Fitzgerald, *Memories of Charles Dickens* (1913), 90; qtd. in Page 49.
41. Dickens, "Letter to Collins," 20 December 1852; qtd. in Page 49.

given the context of *Basil*'s manifest concerns with the nature of the author's
labor, that Dickens should, while encouraging Collins during the turbulent
writing of *No Name* a decade later, hark back to the earlier work:

> I cannot tell you with what a strange dash of pride as well as pleasure I read
> the great results of your hard work. Because, as you know, I was certain
> from the *Basil* days that you were the Writer who would come ahead of all
> the Field—being the only one who combined invention and power, both
> humourous and pathetic, with that invincible determination to work, and
> that profound conviction that nothing is to be done without work, of which
> triflers and feigners have no conception.[42]

For Dickens, a predilection for hard work, much more than God-given
genius, was a sign of the high seriousness necessary to prove one belonged
in the Field of Victorian literary endeavor. Collins having composed much
of the book while being personally trained in the profession by Dickens,
it comes as little surprise that he should have allegorized a transformation
akin to his own in Basil's dream of fair and dark women in what critics have
consistently taken as his sexually-charged first "sensation scene."

Copyright as Ideology before the Critique

In the year that Collins was writing *Basil,* an anonymous reviewer for the
Edinburgh Review described a somewhat surprising attitude to be exhibited
by some members of the Belgian publishing trade engaged in the controversial practice of pirating French books. Emphasizing the indecorousness
in Belgium of what seemed nothing so much as a sophistical malapropism,
the reviewer for the *Edinburgh* remarked:

> There, indeed, a party exists which, under pretence of cheap diffusion of
> knowledge, defends the *contrefaçon* trade, as a lawful branch of national
> industry, and inveighs against authors who expect a remuneration for their
> labours, and against publishers who purchase copyrights, denouncing them
> as "monopolists." (Rev. of *Projet de loi* 146)

The reviewer then expanded the purview of the epithet in a footnote:
"[a]ccording to this theory, any man who buys a house or marries a wife,

---

42. Dickens, "Letter to Collins," 20 September 1862; qtd. in Page 129.

might be termed a monopolist" (146*n*). Of course, now it was the reviewer who was overstating the case. Copying a man's book could hardly be considered to be on a par with having relations with his wife or occupying his home, those two flauntings of exclusion most apt to disturb the twin pillars of propriety maintaining the stability of the Westminster-based landed property system.[43] The act of copying a book hardly had the same resonance or would seem to have posed the same threat as those other acts—at least, that was, as long as the text and the land or woman in question were not made interchangeable, say, through ideological manipulation. Supposing these seemingly impossible collapsings to have occurred, we would be faced with the limitless dangers of finding lands or wives to be turning immaterial or of finding texts to be turning into immovable objects. They were essentially neither, as Collins well knew.

Apart from, presumably, the piratical Belgian publishers who are here being criticized, many disinterested people of the time also would have queried the reviewer's rhetorical equation of books with women and houses. Few would have been willing to allow the "sacredness" of the institution of marriage or of the system of landed property ownership to be perceived in the same light as any sort of "sacredness"—the term would have seemed absurd to them in this context—associated with the ownership of literary property. Copyright ideology was still at this time a thing in the early stages of its formation and, as such, something fairly easily contested. For instance, a writer for *The Times* of London had written the following on November 26, 1851, upon the successful negotiation of an International Copyright Treaty between England and France:

> The most hopeless subject of negotiation with the Governments of other countries has long appeared to be an international copyright law. Intellectual "produce" has been the only description of goods excluded from equitable conditions of exchange. . . . The various Governments of Europe and the United States of America have, from time immemorial, virtually declared that a work of literature or art, the property of a single individual in a single nation, was a fair mark for piracy and theft. . . . Nor, in fairness,

---

43. The exclusiveness of the mother's propriety guarantees and undergirds the proper passing on of the father's name and the inheritance of the house, as Catherine Gallagher, writing of Tocqueville, makes clear: "The natural signs of inequality are natural only insofar as women's sexuality and reproductive capacities remain proper. The assumed sexual propriety of women underlies both property relations and semiotics in the world Tocqueville inhabits. . . . The sexually uncontrolled woman . . . becomes a threat to all forms of property and established power" (Gallagher, Fineman, and Hertz 55–57).

> can the reprehension be confined to the leading statesmen of the time, no
> matter what their country, or what their political connexions. The real
> blame lay with the great bulk of the population, whether in Europe or in
> America. There has too long existed a profound immorality of thought
> with regard to the productions of literary genius. Men have said, "It is for
> our interest to have the readiest means of access to the works of literary
> men. Their labours cannot be the subject of property any more than the
> wild fowls of the air." . . . We are glad to be enabled to state that a treaty
> for the suppression of this most disgraceful system has at length been
> signed between England and France. ("The most hopeless subject" p. 4,
> cols. C–D)

Literary property occupied a special position when it came to determining "equitable conditions of exchange" between individuals and between
nations. It would continue to do so even up until the present day for very
determined structural reasons, reasons all inevitably related to the iterability
of language. Linguistic repeatability causes literary property to tend to be
seen as a less-than-solid form of property and its "theft" to be seen as a less-
than-criminal form of "crime."

Giving them the benefit of the doubt, I assume the Belgian publishers had not solely been motivated by a desire for specious self-justification
but also had genuinely been influenced by the socialist ideas pervading
certain sectors of French intellectual political thought in post-revolution-
ary France. Not the least influential of the proponents of ideas of this
type would have been Pierre-Joseph Proudhon who a decade earlier had
put forward arguments that would seem to justify the charge of unfair
"monopoly" against all styles, not just literary, of would-be ownership.[44] In
1840, when he had argued that property in general was an "effect without
a cause" (Proudhon 13), that neither arguments based on occupation, rule
of law, or the mixing of one's labor with the object adequately explained
the seeming unquestionableness of the connection between land and its
"owner," Proudhon had been attempting to unearth a deeply-rooted ideological construct, an ideological construct that had all along required the
deployment of a grand system of metaphors and rhetorics to hold it in
place. When he had stated, to put the conception in its more famous
form, that "property is theft" (13–14), he had been not only exposing a
fundamental illusion at the heart of capitalist ideology but also laying the

---

44. Rice points out (84) that the American economist-publisher and defender of the reprinting
of English books Henry C. Carey "went so far as to echo Proudhon's motto that 'property is robbery'" in his book *Letters on International Copyright*.

groundwork for Marx's later critiques of that ideology. In 1862 he would continue this line of argument in his critique of a proposed perpetual copyright:

> By enacting such a law, the legislature will have done far worse than paying the author an exorbitant price, it will have abandoned the principle of the *chose publique,* of the intellectual domain, and at great harm to the community. . . . Let us not disinherit humanity of its domain. . . . Intellectual property does not merely encroach on the public domain: it cheats the public of its share in the production of all ideas and all expressions. (Qtd. in Ginsburg, "Une Chose" 658)

The prevalent discourse of an "ownership society" (by that I mean individual as opposed to collective ownership) in this country in the early years of this century (for one example, see Hockett), would seem to indicate that we live in a time that would not be willing to understand this type of discourse. We are in a sense too "invested" in the ideology to be able to question it.

However, there were implications to Proudhon's critique that would not have pleased him. His argument led to the conclusion that all property was merely an ideological, and therefore fundamentally rhetorical, construct. As such, rhetorical manipulation could not only be disclosed to substantively found property but also to potentially *threaten* it after that foundation in its real-world solidity. This potential was manifestly put into practice when Macaulay used his rhetorical equation of copyright with monopoly to almost single-handedly stop copyright from being granted a duration of sixty years after the death of the author in his speech delivered to the House of Commons on 5 February 1841. The House voted to reject Talfourd's bill by a vote of 45 to 38. In his speech Macaulay remarked, "Copyright is monopoly, and produces all the effects of monopoly. . . . I may . . . challenge my honourable friend to find any distinction between copyright and other privileges of the same kind; any reason why a monopoly of books should produce an effect directly the reverse of that which was produced by the East India Company's monopoly of tea, or by Lord Essex's monopoly of sweet wines" (8:198–99). In a sense Macaulay and Proudhon proved, in very different ways, the lesson that he or she who manipulated the discourse also manipulated the property. This is the strategy that Collins adopted in his book *Basil.* There he attempted to represent the reification of the text as land and to enact its corollary effect of the conferral upon the author of the status as "owner" of that text, both as means of reinforcing the always threatened author–work relation.

One of the most memorable scenes in all of Collins's work, Basil's sensational eavesdropping on his cuckolding, is one in which we find him learning that "monopolistic" possession of his wife was always already going to
be impossible, even before the actual marriage had properly begun. He feels
violated in the same way that an author who had been pirated might. It
is not surprising to find that Mannion, the man conjoining with Margaret
in the infamy, had at one point in his life, as already mentioned, worked
as a "hack-author of the lowest degree . . . plagiarising from dead authors,
to supply the raw material for bookmongering by more accomplished
bookmongers" (*Basil* 231–32). *Basil* shows us an early example of Collins's
equating women with texts. Here the two different types of authors, one a
low-grade plagiarist and the other an autobiographer, engage in a contest
over sexual control of a particular woman. And the plagiarist wins, the self-
involved, implicitly narcissistic, autobiographer having instead to endure
the taunt "He calls himself a man doesn't he? A husband who waits a year"
(294). We might recall here Balzac's "jesting" equation of a pirating playwright with an adulterer in his 1834 "Letter to Authors":

> no sooner has a writer published a book, created various characters, come
> up with motives for their actions, sketched out a plot, than this plot, these
> motives, these characters, the whole book, as it were, are all taken and
> turned into a theatre play. A man of hounour, who would be incapable of
> taking from you the tongs with which you stoke your fire, takes away from
> you without any scruples your dearest possession, whereby his conscience
> will scarcely be more troubled than if he had taken your wife. But the point
> is that a lover takes a consenting wife, whereas the Cicisbeo of the theatre
> rapes your idea. Besides, this adultery cannot be excused in any way: it is
> horrible and all the more harmful given that so far there has never been the
> reverse case of a play being turned into a book. (71)

In the end, however, Basil, having broken beyond his self-absorption, wins
the final battle proving that the real author is the one who not only can call
himself a man, but a specific type of man, a literary working man, someone
who can use the strong "labor" argument to justify his ownership of the
literary text.

Proudhon had signaled that there was a specter haunting the capitalist
ownership system. That specter, not surprisingly, was a communism of a
certain type—the belief that property was fundamentally open to multiple
ownership rendering it in a sense subject to no ownership at all. Whether
or not this potential for the fundamental loss of control practically operates

in the real world with regard to commercial relations, it certainly does so in relation to the breaking function of the iterability of the mark as a result of the always precarious endeavor of claiming "ownership" of language. In writing *Basil,* Collins came to realize that words could, literally, create alternate worlds, but the corollary was also there: that iterability could eventually come to undo *this* world, down to the level of the author's personality. Iterability's breaking function continually threatens to radically transform the system, to turn an "ownership society" into one that believes "property is theft." And in this day and age, that potential transformation has conclusively come to pass, as the constant difficulties besetting the enforcement and legislation of the intellectual property trades clearly demonstrate. Those difficulties are a sign of the unstable theoretical grounding—a situation created by the legal and political decisions of late-eighteenth-century England— residing at the basis of the concept of "literary property." That unstable theoretical grounding was something Collins in his early career, especially in his novel *Basil,* had believed he could overcome through the sheer force of rhetoric. It was only in the 1860s, finally realizing that he could not win at this struggle in that way, that he would—whole-heartedly in novels like *No Name, Armadale,* and *The Moonstone*—learn to move the struggle to the level of generic manipulation and learn to give up the attempt at denying the significance of the breaking function of iterability.

3

The Woman in White

The Perils of Attempting to Discipline the Transatlantic, Transhistorical Narrative

Of the mistakes occasioned by the appearance of a picture bearing so strong a kindred resemblance to the one stolen, as to pass not only for a twin relative, but the very identical gem belonging to His Excellency Des-Chong-Fong, &c.

—William Collins, *Memoirs of a Picture* 3:270

"What an extraordinary people you are!" cried Martin. "Are Mr Chollop and the class he represents, an Institution here? . . . Are bloody duels, brutal combats, savage assaults, shooting down and stabbing in the streets, your Institutions! Why, I shall hear next that Dishonour and Fraud are among the Institutions of the great republic!"

The moment the words passed his lips, the Honourable Elijah Pogram looked round again.

"This morbid hatred of our Institutions," he observed, "is quite a study for the psychological observer."

—Dickens, *Martin Chuzzlewit,* chapter 34

Theory Surfacing

If existence were a case of, so to speak, history "all the way down," purely historical analysis (even that more than pure branch focusing on local histories known as "history written from the bottom up") might offer its practitioners some hope of its living up to its advanced billing. However, despite our present-day's stronger trends in literary criticism being set up to ignore the uncomfortable fact, there do indeed exist occasions, albeit slight, albeit fleeting, when theory necessarily will be breaking into the prison-house of history. Copyright piracy, that offshoot of book history, itself an offshoot of New Historicism, is one such theory-saturated phenomenon. At points where this particular issue and issues like it come into consideration, the generally acknowledged antagonism that the New Historicist and Deconstructive camps have for one another has to be transcended.

While the preceding points may seem obvious enough, their voicing is necessitated by the particular situation, the local historical context, in which literary criticism today finds itself. What we might loosely call "historicism"—in the sense of studies especially focused on particular and local contingent concerns, often in direct opposition to or defiance of that more generalized or generalizable hobgoblin "theory"—has undeniably come to hold sway in the critical analyses of nineteenth-century fictions produced in the last quarter century. In 1992 Paul Bové in his *In the Wake of Theory* was already acknowledging that the "move against theory" by the New Historicist critic Stephen Greenblatt "has been successful and . . . this makes Greenblatt 'king of the hill'" (161*n*22). This situation has only intensified over the last two decades, particularly in the field of Victorianist criticism. However, there are signs that the tide has recently begun to turn and this shift can only be welcomed, for the system had been facing the unhappy prospect of helplessly having to watch its tentacles fan out into innumerable individual dendrites and disappear into the sterile alluvial plain of rampant niche marketing and ever-thickening thick descriptiveness. The Romanticist Thomas Pfau was, already in 2007, formulating something akin to this critique:

> [A]n *a priori* commitment to historicism as a method sets inquiry on a course towards increasing specialization and professionalization such as will inexorably shrink the community for which one's findings can have any relevance at all. . . . Modernity's gradual journey from Cartesian skepticism via Lockean empiricism to nineteenth-century positivism thus intensifies the Nominalist creed that reality consists only of individual things. . . . The self-imposed restriction of recent models of inquiry to tightly localized and circumscribed chronotopes (biographically conceived time spans, the *punctum* of this or that local event, dates of publication, etc.) is . . . a familiar trait of nineteenth-century Historicism and has in equal measure enabled and constrained the project of Romantic Historicism for fully two decades now. (952–56)

Pfau is not alone in his worry about the danger inherent in historicism's hegemony. More recently, the co-editor of the journal *Victorian Literature and Culture,* John Maynard, has written,

> But the turn to history began to exhibit irrational exuberance, as these things will: everyone wanted a share, everyone rushed in. . . . As John Kucich has remarked, graduate students found the possession of one small subject an irresistible attraction in their actually steadily depressed area. As a journal editor, I see seven such articles, picking out one unexplored area of history, for every one doing any of the other major tasks we tradition- ally perform. Who needs theory? Graham and Derrida had their day; just do it. (73)

The winds, it would seem, are beginning to turn against New Historicism.

There were hints in the self-descriptions of the New Historicists' process indicating that the situation had been improperly set up from the beginning. According to H. Aram Veeser, one of the five fundamental propositions undergirding New Historicist practice is the hypothesis that "no discourse, imaginative or archival, gives access to unchanging truths nor expresses inal- terable human nature" (xi). This would, on the face of it, appear a fairly uncontroversial assumption, given the context. A literary critical school that privileges history is naturally going to be at its basis opposed to according significance to any and all types of transhistoricism, that is, for example, to claims that "humans have always been like this or that" or that dis- course gives "access to unchanging truths." To allow for the critical interest of notions like these would be to fatally undercut *the point* of historical inquiry.

There is, however, as there always must be, a bit more to this context. The agenda of distinguishing New Historicism from Deconstruction pervades Veeser's commentary. For instance, we find him, immediately after his list of propositions, adopting a commonly used less-than-flattering epithet for the latter approach: "New Historicists combat empty formalism by pulling historical considerations to the center stage of literary analysis" (Veeser xi). Empty formalism, however, can have its uses. Though discourse, *at the level of content,* may or may not give access to unchanging truths—and I leave that possibility open, in deference particularly to the aspirations of those pursuing the "harder" sciences—its *operations,* at the level of what could well be described as "empty formalism," can, I would contend, *themselves* be unchanging truths, truths that deserve critical attention (especially in the case of their being made the subject of significant intellectual interest by one's author in question). Indeed, the workings of linguistic iterability being ageless and universal, it is with good reason that Jacques Derrida is prompted to remark that "iterability . . . structures the mark of writing itself, no matter what particular type of writing is involved (whether pictographical, hieroglyphic, ideographic, phonetic, alphabetic, to cite the old categories)" ("Signature Event Context" 7). Deconstruction, or at the least the pursuit of empty formalism, is thus, in contrast to new, or old, historical contextualism, in a better position, I believe, to analyze a work directly thematizing—through its implicit interest in copyright piracy and explicit interest in the unsteady control of texts—the destabilizations made possible by the formal operations of language, that is, to analyze a work like Wilkie Collins's *The Woman in White*.

Indeed, I believe that contemporary Victorianist criticism—constantly eschewing "theory" (both overtly and covertly) as it does—faces the prospect of coming to find itself to have written itself out of a position from which to be able to properly assess a narrative such as *The Woman in White*. If this one of Collins's masterful plots is about anything, it is about the danger inherent in automatically assuming settling to be all there is, or to express the same outlook the other way, in presuming the breaking function of iterability to not exist. (It is that latter function that allows at a significant point in the story for Count Fosco to be able discreetly "to copy one and to intercept the other of two letters which [his] adored enemy had entrusted to a discarded maid"[1]). The gallant efforts of the heroes in the latter half of the plot are wholly given over to the goal of overturning this false assumption. At a particularly significant moment, the nurses in the asylum unknowingly participate in precisely the particular philosophico-literary effacement that this study has set out to undo:

> This was the Asylum. Here [Laura] first heard herself called by Anne Catherick's name, and here, as a last remarkable circumstance in the story of the conspiracy, her own eyes informed her that she had Anne Catherick's clothes on. The nurse, on the first night in the Asylum, had shown her the marks on each article of her underclothing as it was taken off, and had said, not at all irritably or unkindly, "Look at your own name on your own clothes, and don't worry us all any more about being Lady Glyde. She's dead and buried, and you're alive and hearty. Do look at your clothes now! There it is, in good marking ink, and there you will find it on all your old things, which we have kept in the house—Anne Catherick, as plain as print!" And

---

1. Collins, *Woman in White*, ed. Sutherland, 603. All further references in this chapter, unless otherwise noted, will be to this edition and will be cited parenthetically.

there it was, when Miss Halcombe examined the linen her sister wore, on
the night of their arrival at Limmeridge House. (436)

These nurses might well pass as modern day Victorianist critics. "Theory
is dead and buried; historicism is alive and hearty," they seem to be suggesting to the impressionable young novitiate. They assume the settling
function to be the sum total of the effects pervading the linguistic realm.
The New Historicists of the present day have less of an excuse but just as
much of a motivation to commit the same error. The hegemony of history
over theory, particularly common in this so economically difficult time for
humanistic inquiry, can leave this novel's more recessed folds not only at
first glance simply unperceived but potentially at second glance re-obscured
post-recognition, re-occluded by the profession's tendency towards enforced
historicization.[2] I will here be launching an attempt at beginning to rectify
this non- or anti-recognition. In this chapter, and this study in general,
rather than disclosing language's inherent conflict to be a product of its
time, that is, rather than endeavoring to put the genie (whether good or evil)
back into the lamp, by finding the apparently transhistorical construct to
have been in actuality a historically or culturally contingent issue all along,
I will be exploring the theoretical fundamental conditions of possibility for
language's conflicted nature and attempting, hopefully judiciously, to shift
what had seemed purely "historical" events back into the "theoretical" realm
from which many of history's conflicts often—seemingly almost, but not
quite, "of themselves" —actually had to have been arising.

The Introductory Anecdote

We might begin with a bit of history, but a history that is adduced here
more to display the theory peeking through than necessarily for itself; one
could do worse than to follow along in the wake of Barbara Johnson's efforts
at discovering "how to use history and biography *deconstructively,* how to
seek in them not answers, causes, explanations, or origins, but new ques-

---

2. To offer one example of this improper privileging of history over theory, I would point to
the New Historicist critic Clare Pettitt's argument in her *Patent Inventions: Intellectual Property and
the Victorian Novel* that Eliot's and Hardy's interest in what are, to my mind, clearly the conflicting
effects of iterability was actually the result of historically-contingent—respectively, gender-based and
technological—factors as opposed to theoretical ones (204–302). Pettitt fails to ask why—the point
where her inquiry should have *begun* rather than ended—she has been led to the conclusion that "The
conflict between the social and individual ownership of invention and information is open to endless
negotiation" (299).

tions and new ways in which the literary and nonliterary texts alike can be made to read and rework each other" (*World* 15). The American citizens of the mid-1800s were occasionally quite forward in their defiance of the, so to speak, "copyright morality" their recent adversaries the English appeared to be intent on imposing on them (in stark contrast to the present situation in which the United States is continually chastising China and Russia for international copyright violations).[3] The transatlantic struggle between the two powers in their century-long "copyright war" was in a certain sense a continuation of the Americans' earlier pursuit of independence. The copyright historian Catherine Seville notes,

> Independence is one of the great themes of American history. The history of copyright in America reflects this. Having first to develop her own domestic copyright law, America had then also to consider international copyright. There was much resistance to giving copyright to "foreigners." America's interaction with Britain over the matter was understandably coloured by their previous history, and the charged relationship between the two nations meant that feeling on both sides was strong and passionate. (*Internationalisation* 146)

This worship of independence spilled over, by analogy, to the linguistic realm as well. The decontextualizing operations of the breaking function of language could not but have suggested to Americans their own political history. We see something of this connection in Adrian Johns's point that "Since before the Revolution, reprinters had stressed the propriety of their enterprise, arguing that they were spreading enlightenment in the face of corrupt and monarchical monopolists" (*Piracy* 203). Why, the Americans might well have asked themselves, should English words not be broken "free" of their English "bindings" (with "s"s replaced by "z"s and extra "u"s left out) if that were possible? And, due to iterability, indeed it was. The English for their part simply saw the situation as a clear case of "injustice." The dispute between the two powers was, thus, on a certain level, one over who was to set the terms of the discussion, who was to determine the character of the highground—not for the Americans so much moral as implicitly philosophical—being contested. Was at issue the question of gauging "fairness" in dealing with intellectual property rights or that of assessing "normality" in the workings of language?[4]

---

3. See Alford and Butterton commenting on China's present-day relations with the United States. See also Reuters reporting in 2011 that "China, Russia top U.S. worst pirates list again."

4. There were, of course, other ways of describing the situation. For example, Henry C. Carey

This struggle is seen in, to offer a raindrop snatched from a deluge, the contest that took place in the mid-century between the "morality" of the most respected of the British journals and the "brazenness" of its American pirates, a struggle that, when viewed from a theoretical, less heated, perspective, could be re-characterized as British blindness to the reality of the fixed constitution of things in contrast to American pragmatic acceptance of things as they are. Sensational vitriol being particularly mesmerizing, that latter perspective is not one that is very easily perceived from its disadvantageous position behind the screen of energetic English claims of "immorality," "unfairness," or "piracy," but, I would argue, it is one that is nevertheless constantly in effect.

In a footnote to an article from 1848 published in *Blackwood's Edinburgh Magazine* (familiarly called Maga), we read of this magazine's American reprinters somewhat amusingly having the previous year advertised one of their "thefts" by having printed "as a *puff* of the reprint" a short extract from an article criticizing American piracy ("Blackwood and Copyright" 127*n*). Apparently, it had not been enough for the Americans simply to reprint without remuneration "How They Manage Matters in the Model Republic"—an article beginning with the condemnation that "in the absence of an international copyright law, Maga is extensively pirated in the United States, extensively read, and we fear very imperfectly digested" ("How They Manage Matters" 492). They—specifically Leonard Scott & Co. of New York[5]—had felt the need to add insult to injury by attempting to generate interest in that reprint through a particularly pointed quotation from it. The 1847 advertisement for the reprint, after listing the issue's table of contents, had cheekily proclaimed:

> Extract from the article on the "Model Republic":—"When these malignant pages arrive in New York, every inhabitant of that good city will abuse us heartily, except our publisher. But great will be the joy of that furacious individual, as he speculates in secret on the increased demand of

---

describes it as a contest between American "civilization" or "decentralization" and British "centralization," a centralization, he argues, that had led almost directly to the Irish famine: "half a century of international copy-right has almost annihilated both the producers and the consumers of books" (qtd. in Johns, *Piracy* 322).

   5. Scott would soon be forced to come to terms with the Blackwoods as their "official agent" in America. This arrangement and the circumstances leading up to it—including, quite sensationally, the disclosure of a surprise American author who had properly registered the American copyright of his October 1847 *Blackwood's* article "Maga in America" (Barnes 30–48)—were in fact being announced in the article "Blackwood and Copyright," the article citing the American advertisement. Thus *Blackwood's*, in referring to the advertisement, was tacitly emphasizing the *extent* of the Fosco-level hubris that had until recently been characterizing its soon-to-be chastened adversary.

his agonized public. Immediately he will put forth an advertisement, noti-fying the men of 'Gotham' that he has on board a fresh sample of British Insolence, and hinting that, although he knows they care nothing about such things, the forthcoming piracy of Maga will be on the most extensive scale." ("Blackwood and Copyright" 127*n*)

There are two ways to view this situation: the "agonized" ("agonised" in the original 1847 British publication ["How They Manage Matters" 496], but "agonized" in the 1848 British citation of the American reprint ["Black-wood and Copyright" 127*n*]) Americans can be seen here to be buying into the English view that they are doing something wrong, as they come to defy what they know to be the "proper" (or properly English-dictated) honor-able path *or* the not-at-all anxious revolutionary inhabitants of the Great Republic can be viewed to be simply championing and celebrating "free-dom," specifically the freedom both of one geographically-distant country to break away from the control of another *and* of the word to break away from its original context. As we saw in a previously-cited passage, Derrida recog-nizes a certain freedom to be associated with iterability: "[E]ven in the ideal case . . . there must already be a certain element of play, a certain remove, a certain degree of *independence with regard to the origin,* to production, or to intention in all of its 'vital,' 'simple' 'actuality' or 'determinateness,' etc." (*Limited* 64; emphasis added). The Americans' type of grand and cavalier defiance of an English code of propriety, exemplified here by the actions of these shameless breaking function–exploiting reprinters, sets the scene well for distinguishing the central opposition in Collins's narrative, that between the exemplary honorability of the manifestly good characters Walter Har-tright, Laura Fairlie, and Marian Halcombe and the unapologetic brashness of none other than Collins's most grandiloquent and memorable villain, Count Isidor Ottavio Baldassare Fosco.

The Larger Historical Context

This situation of, so to speak, "self-celebratory" piracy in the early days of American advertising had not arisen overnight. There was a substantial historical framework standing behind it. The belatedness of the passage of an Anglo-American copyright agreement—an American legislative change made, shamefully, only in 1891[6]—rendered U.S. publishers for most of

---

6. See Clark's chapter on Congress's 1891 "passage of the Platt-Simmonds Act," 149–81.

the nineteenth century free, legally, to republish English texts without paying the foreign authors for their work.[7] The text of the Copyright Act of
1790, the specific piece of legislation originally codifying the intellectual
property dispute between England and America and the act consolidating
different state copyright statutes under a federal umbrella statute, is, not
surprisingly, generally understood in political terms (as opposed to, as it will
be here, theoretico-linguistic ones). It is considered to have been solely an
attempt by the newly-independent Republic to defy the Mother Country.
Section Five of the Act served actually to license "criminality"—although,
the action being licensed, that term could be said to no longer apply, at least
when viewed within a local context. That remarkable, mutiply-negatively-
structured Section held,

---

7. While several American publishing houses regularly availed themselves of this freedom, not
all jumped at the chance to loot English intellectual property. There had informally come into being
a system of "trade-courtesy" among the more prominent American publishers. The fairly generous
amounts paid by one or another house for "advance sheets" allowed it not only to sell its edition
ahead of any "unofficial" reprinters but also to claim the work as its, hopefully sacrosanct, "property"
amongst the larger houses. The recompense offered by this system, arguably, succeeded more in assuaging the American conscience than in filling the English bank account. See Patten 97–98 and
Charvat 313. Trollope (309n1), Mott *(History* 386), and Barnes (15–19) offer several examples of the
breakdown of this system, particularly due to the invention of the "mammoth" weekly broadsheets.
Certainly, the payments granted English authors by the system were not considered quite enough
in Collins's opinion—and the opinions of many of his contemporaries—to successfully counter the
loss in profits. Anthony Trollope would write in 1876 in his *Autobiography,* "I have just found out
that £20 was paid to my publisher in England for the use of the early sheets of a novel for which I
received £1600 in England. When asked why he accepted so little, he assured me that the firm with
whom he dealt would give no more. . . . Many thousand copies must have been sold. But from these
the author received not one shilling. I need hardly point out that the sum of £20 would not do more
than compensate the publisher for his trouble in making the bargain" (313). In October 1867, just
before his second trip to America, Dickens would write the following to one of his legitimate American publishers, James T. Fields of the firm Ticknor and Fields, "Nor have I ever been so ungenerous,
as to disguise or suppress the fact that I have received handsome sums from the Harpers for advance
sheets." This seems a rather unconvincing acknowledgment, however, coming as it did immediately
after his statement that "For twenty years I am perfectly certain that I have never made any other
allusion to the republication of my books in America than the goodhumoured remark 'that if there
had been international copyright between England and the States, I should have been a man of very
large fortune, instead of a man of moderate savings'" (*Letters* 11:443). In 1912 the more honorable strains of the American publishing profession were still feeling the sting of remorse. Caroline
Ticknor, granddaughter of William Davis Ticknor, attempts in her memoir of her grandfather to
distance his memory from the practice of piracy by noting that he invented the advance sheet system
and by writing, "'[F]air play,' and not 'fair game,' was the motto embodied in the transactions of the
founder of the 'Old Corner Bookstore'" (3–4). Her Dedication also highlights this moral discourse:
"To Houghton Mifflin Company successors to the literary heritage of Ticknor and Fields and to
the just and honorable traditions of the earlier house which they to-day so steadfastly uphold this
volume is respectfully dedicated" (unpaginated Dedication page).

[N]othing in this act shall be construed to extend to prohibit the importa-
tion or vending, reprinting, or publishing within the United States, of any
map, chart, book or books, written, printed, or published by any person
not a citizen of the United States, in foreign parts or places without the
jurisdiction of the United States. (Rpt. in Patterson 198)

The multiple turnabouts make this a manifestly unrestrictive stricture, as
well as a very odd, even "contrary," type of "disciplining." This was a strange
clause for the newly independent States to have included in the Act. Since
non-citizens could not at this time secure United States copyright, it was
needlessly redundant to emphasize the fact that their works could be (more
precisely, that nothing prohibited their being) reprinted in America without
permission. Simon Nowell-Smith writes that this "quite unnecessary provision . . . was an encouragement to American publishers to reprint popular
English books without the author's consent and without remunerating him.
In fact the law was designed to benefit United States citizens—authors,
publishers, and printers—and to penalize the subjects of the kingdom from
which the states had successfully revolted" (18–19). When American copyright law was amended in 1831, 1870, and 1878 the clause was retained
(Kaplan and Brown 799). Solberg notes that the subsequent statutes not
only "failed to contain any provision for the protection of alien authors"
but, rather, each of the three revisions "in its turn included some provision
which in substance was in agreement with section 5 of the first Copyright
Act of 1790 to permit importing, reprinting, publishing and selling the foreign author's work" ("Copyright Law Reform" 50–51).

Reprinting the work of foreign authors thus was from 1790 to 1891
actually *encouraged* by the U.S. government. American publishers were for
a century invited to avail themselves of the various opportunities afforded
by the alienation(s) inherent in the breaking function of iterability. This
constitutes a near-farcical legislative situation, one destined to confound
thinkers, anti-theory historians and philosophers included, who would be
perceiving disciplinarial processes to be simply oppressive—or the cognate
productively repressive—historical mechanisms rather than as, say, also possibly, as here, satirical invitations to freedom, invitations to enjoy the "play"
made available by linguistic iterability. Thus, Michel Foucault's panopticism
as outlined in his *Discipline and Punish*—a type of self-disciplining by way
of internalized, implicitly straightforward prohibitions[8]—or D. A. Miller's

---

8. I agree with Michel de Certeau's opinion that Foucauldian panopticism, as an approach, is
itself rather too serious and "disciplinarial." Arguing that Foucault's analysis is itself indistinguishable
from the many micro-techniques of disciplinary power that he is intent on discovering to be operative

application to the novel form of Foucault's outlook in his *The Novel and the Police* are both going to be unable to "read" this type of move. Those aspects these two thinkers categorize as "normality" and "deviance" clearly are significantly complicated, if not indeed imperceptibly undone and re-assembled in the opposite camps, when a relatively young country takes, as here, to semi-satirically enforcing "un-disciplined" behavior. Anselm Haverkamp may well have been claiming correctly, albeit a century or two belatedly, that *Deconstruction Is/In America,* as he maintained in the title of his 1996 edited volume. Few situations are as quintessentially "postmodern" as that of the Americans allowing to remain in effect for a hundred years a clause that might be described as, when viewed from the perspective of the British authors, a thoroughly "un-policing" policing statute.[9]

Theoretical History and Biography

I seriously doubt that many mainstream historians, perhaps any, would unbraid from the history of this struggle a narrative that views the pirating Americans as champions of the breaking function of the iterability of the mark. To be fair to the historians, it is often a case of there simply being too much history, too many settling-function-instituted perturbations and permutations perturbating and permutating, to allow for anything else— anything "other"—being adequately kept track of. Naturally, then, the more "sensational" readings are going to be given precedence. However, I believe that sometimes the patently unemotional generalizations characteristic of theory can be of help in making sense of especially variegated and complex historical narratives. That is, occasionally theory has something to teach the established histories. Of course, the act of gratuitously disturbing orthodoxies should, where feasible, be studiously avoided. As Paul de Man remarks when defending one of his deconstructive essays on Hegel,

> There is no merit whatever in upsetting a canonical interpretation merely
> for the sake of destroying something that may have been built with consid-

---

within certain Western social structures of the last two centuries, De Certeau writes, "His own analysis . . . betrays an apparatus analogous to those whose functioning it was able to reveal. . . . Foucault's theory . . . is an effect and a network of these procedures themselves. It is a narrative, a theoretical narrative, which obeys rules analogous to those panoptic procedures. There is no epistemological and hierarchical break between the theoretical text and the micro-techniques" (190–91).

9. The perversity of the American statute is signaled in Meredith McGill's contention that "were it not for the double negatives in which it is couched, this provision would read like a ringing endorsement of international literary piracy" (80).

erable care. . . . The commentator should persist as long as possible in the canonical reading and should begin to swerve away from it only when he encounters difficulties which the methodological and substantial assertions of the system are no longer able to master. Whether or not such a point has been reached should be left open as part of an ongoing critical investigation. But it would be naïve to believe that such an investigation could be avoided, even for the best of reasons. The necessity to revise the canon arises from resistances encountered in the text itself (extensively conceived) and not from preconceptions imported from elsewhere. (*Aesthetic Ideology* 186)

It is my contention in this study that the perspective provided by a close analysis of Collins's works of the 1850s and his four masterpieces of the 1860s necessitates just such a "revision of the canon" of Collins criticism and, for want of a better term, a "complexification" of the situation of American piracy—indeed, getting started already, one might well be required to write here "piracy." The evidently pro–breaking function aspects of these narratives indicate that some part of Collins's multifaceted psyche viewed this situation (and textually-alienating situations like it) in a more variegated light than that made available by the view of the situation as a simple battle between the "good guys" and the "bad." After subjecting Fosco to his much-deserved punishment—settling's last hurrah, so to speak—at the end of *The Woman in White*,[10] Collins will soon enough be casting the breaking function no longer in the position of "bad" unwanted "side-effect" but rather—say, for instance, in *No Name*'s falsely conservative opening—in that of *essential component* of the workings of language. This acceptance of the breaking function will only intensify until finally it culminates in the *The Moonstone*'s concluding with Murthwaite's inability to go on with the story, his inability to any longer "tell." The Americans were putting into effect this legitimate theoretical possibility by acknowledging—and inviting to perceive it those English authors open-minded enough to do so—language's inherently alienatable nature, especially upon its passage beyond national borders, a nature that copyright law had been attempting in the nineteenth century, not always successfully, to bring under control over larger and larger areas through, among other regulators, international copyright agreements. It is my fundamental contention here that the plots of *The Woman in White*, *No Name*, *Armadale*, and *The Moonstone* gain their force from the growing acknowledgment of the existence of the breaking func-

---

10. Hutter offers interesting reasons for considering this punishment to be suspect in his article "Fosco Lives!" in which case we could argue that Collins's acceptance of breaking begins even earlier.

tion, and that it was the Americans who necessitated Collins's most overt confrontation with this function.[11]

In this chapter I will be attempting to undo the "orthodox" interpretation—as that of a battle between immorality and justice—that the English authors (and some American authors) were attempting at the time to impose on the situation. While Collins's comments on the American character after 1870 strongly suggest he felt an allegiance to this view, his fictions of the 1860s just as strongly direct one beyond this interpretation. The Americans' actions could be viewed either as a salvo designed to defy and hurt the general English sensibility, a sensibility that the Americans nevertheless shared even as they directly defied it, or as an acknowledgment of the true theoretical basis of (textual) things, specifically of the very real, very unignorable effects of the breaking function. In other words, when looking at the situation one is faced with the dilemma of deciding between the view of America as parasite (in a world in which settling holds sway) or as necessary and significantly-positioned corrective (with breaking coming to *balance* settling).

THE LOCAL and global effects of the American piracy of British works during the nineteenth-century copyright war between the two powers have only recently come to receive their full historical consideration.[12] Here in this chapter, before turning to the analysis of Collins's narrative itself, I will be attempting to tease out the theory from that history. Rather than being drawn into a discussion of this or that small-scale, esoteric (and therefore necessarily myopia-inducing) historical by-way, I will be looking at the historical narrative—specifically the mid-Victorian legal-cultural history and Collins's biography—schematically, that is, from the point of view continually advanced by Collins's subsequent major fictions, the theoretical one.

The nationalism-driven, large-scale piracy by the Americans elicited a countering nationalistic narrative on the parts not only of the British

---

11. I am attempting here to follow in the tradition of Welsh's admirably-ambitious claim in *From Copyright to Copperfield* that Dickens's interactions with American recalcitrance on the issue of copyright during his 1842 trip added new depth to his subsequent fictional character portraits. My argument differs only in my contention that the lesson that Collins learned from this recalcitrance was situated at a more "structural" or "empty-formalist" level than that learned by his friend and mentor.

12. Johns's recent *Piracy* offers a good history of the situation. See also Barnes and McGill for discussions focusing on the early phase of the dispute as well as Seville's *Internationalisation*. Baker et al. address the copyright dispute in the introduction to the four-volume edition of Collins's letters (Collins, *Public Face* xxx–xxxix). See also Law's chapter on the later Collins's well-documented interest in this issue, "Collins on International Copyright," in Mangham, *Wilkie Collins* 178–94.

literary establishment but also of its legal culture. Although the author-as-disseminator model remained the dominant one in British copyright cases, certain judges were prompted to adopt an always-available perspective of the author-as-creator in their decisions. While the former standpoint focused strictly on the work itself and the rights to the profits derived from it, the latter viewed copyright as a defense of the "personality" of the British subject.[13] It was difficult to defend convincingly the violation of the faceless British "product," that product being bound up as it was with the to-ings and fro-ings of unfeeling transatlantic economies. Turning the discourse to that product's producer and the producer's family made the violation all the more personal. This bodily focalization of the rationale for copyright helped to set in clear relief the distinction between the "moral" British and the "immoral" Americans. Pursuing this author-as-creator path, the English legal culture gradually came to effect a conjunction between corporeality and textuality along the same lines as that conjunction evident in *The Woman in White*'s easily-moved-about girl-woman/easily-alienated published text conflation. Thus, more was at stake, I am arguing, in the re-assignment of the misrecognized Laura Fairlie to her proper place in society than might have at first seemed.

My main contention in this chapter will be that *The Woman in White* is a covert allegory, simultaneously published in both Britain and America, lobbying against the contemporary American practice of pirating British works.[14] In the hands of the conflicted Collins—awkwardly situated as he

---

13. Justin Hughes writes of this dichotomy, "The main alternative to a labor justification [of property in copyright] is a 'personality theory' that describes property as an expression of the self. This theory . . . is relatively foreign to Anglo-Saxon jurisprudence. Instead, its origins lie in continental philosophy" (288–89). "Disseminator" more clearly signaling the concept of breaking than "laborer," I find the dichotomy disseminator/creator to be more appropriate to this situation than that of laborer/personality. While it may seem I am bringing together two separate entities by equating an "author-as-creator" approach with a personality-based one, that is, in equating the possession of creativity with the simple possession of an individual personality, I do not do this without precedent. The Supreme Court has already made such an elision in its decision in *Feist v. Rural Telephone* (1991): "To qualify for copyright protection, a work must be original to the author. . . . Original, as the term is used in copyright, means only that the work was independently created by the author (as opposed to copied from other works), and that it possesses at least some minimal degree of creativity. . . . To be sure the requisite level of creativity is extremely low; even a slight amount will suffice. The vast majority of works make the grade quite easily, as they possess some creative spark, 'no matter how crude, humble or obvious' it might be" (345). Here the standard for creation has been brought down to the level of an individual "creative spark," a requirement at least as low as the possession of the markers of a unique personality.

14. While the narrative was in large part based on the Madame de Douhault case, I will in what follows not only be dealing mainly with Collins's peculiar additions to the story, for example, the other woman—briefly mentioned in the case and then only posthumously as "le corps d'une autre personne" (Mejan 3:229)—becoming the titular focus of the story and honorability becoming a ma-

was between the perspective of his literary father Dickens (and real father as well) and that of the theoretically perspicacious Americans who were actuating that aspect that Justice Yates (and Collins's own grandfather perhaps) had been arguing should not be denied—the representation of the remarkable exchange of the two women in the narrative brought about by the two villains came to mimic that act perpetrated by the illicit American reprinters, that of stealing the contents of the legitimate English version of the book. His villains' derisive ridiculing of "copy-book morality" (*Woman in White* 235) thus takes on a new meaning when it and the narrative that contains it are viewed—a particular contextualization I am keen, at least provisionally, to effect—from the perspective of English moralizing about American copyright violations.

Overt Moralizing

The immediate issue that my admittedly rather elaborate formulation of a "covert allegory" raises is the question of why Collins would have wanted to avoid making explicit his criticism of American piracy in 1860, especially since he would have no compunction about doing so after Dickens's death in 1870, publically and forcefully. The answer lies, I believe, in the cautionary example offered by the effect that Dickens's pointed comments on the issue had had during his 1842 trip to America, an effect that we need to consider if we are to understand the context out of which this one of Collins's narratives arises.

Looking at Collins's comments on (literally) the narrative of *The Woman in White* we find evidence that he connected the issue of American reprinting with it. We see a private hint of a concern with illicit reduplication left us in Collins's own hand, in the description of the publishing history of his novel given at the head of his manuscript (now held, somewhat ironically, in the United States, institutionalized in the Morgan Library in New York): "[*The Woman in White*] was first published, in weekly parts, in 'All the Year Round.' . . . During the same period it was periodically published in New York, U.S. (by special arrangement with me)[15] in 'Harper's Weekly'" (*Woman*

---

jor theme, but I will also be implicitly suggesting why Douhault's story should have initially appealed to Collins at this moment in both publishing history and his unified novel series.

15. The need for this arrangement was specified in the Harper brothers' contract with Dickens for reprinting in America selected contents of *All the Year Round* from advance sheets. Reprinting of serials longer than three months' duration required that an agreement be made with the individual authors (Drew 147). Robert L. Patten argues that "all things considered" *in actuality* Dickens was not

in White 647). We find Collins in this manuscript comment obliquely giving voice to the worry that during this period his novel could have been published, quite legitimately as far as American law was concerned, in the States *without* "special arrangement" with him—as indeed it was. In 1880, Collins, looking back on this period of his career, has no trouble voicing in an article titled "Considerations on the Copyright Question Addressed to an American Friend," quite clearly, his anger at the Americans:

> It has been calculated, by persons who understand these matters better than I do, that for every reader in England I have ten readers in the United

hard done by by the advance sheet system (342; see also Kappel and Patten 32), a difficult proposition to concur with when the difference between actual English and American revenues is contrasted with the difference in the countries' populations and literacy rates, both higher in America (see Kaestle et al. 18–25). Appeals such as this for retrospective analyses of the "actual" monetary situation threaten to distort and obscure the more pertinent issue here, that of the contemporary subjective impressions of infringement and exploitation in the minds of Victorian English authors subjected to both this system and to the ill-treatment of the American "pirates." But, giving these critics the benefit of the doubt, if only *possibly* losing out in the matter of money, the British authors *certainly* lost out to the Americans in the matter of time. To counterbalance traveling time to America, the advance sheet system required that an earlier deadline, of twenty to thirty days, be set for weekly or monthly parts than would otherwise have been the case. This could only have worsened the sour impression left by the Americans on writers who had difficulty meeting these deadlines as was occasionally the case with Collins, due to the effects of a mysterious unabating illness and other misfortunes. See, for example, Dickens's letter to Collins during the writing of *No Name:* "[W]hat follows . . . I hope may save you some mental uneasiness. For I was stricken ill when I was doing Bleak House, and I shall not easily forget what I suffered under the fear of not being able to come up to time. . . . [S]ay you are unequal to your work, and want me, and I will come to London straight and do your work. . . . I could do it, at a pinch, so like you as that no one should find out the difference. . . . [But] [y]ou won't want me. You will be well (and thankless!) in no time. But here I am; and I hope the knowledge may comfort you" (14 October 1862, *Letters* 10:142). (It is said by many commentators that Collins did not need this help; see, for example, Peters 245. However, I find each opening paragraph or two of the eight scenes in *No Name* to be suspiciously Dickensian in style. On 24 January 1862 Dickens had written the following to Collins: "It seems to me that great care is needed not to tell the story too severely. In exact proportion as you play around it here and there, and mitigate the severity of your own sticking to it, you will enhance and intensify the power with which Magdalen holds on to her purpose" [*Letters* 10:20]. One has to wonder if Collins, in the throes of his illness, might not have agreed in his scene openings to take up—or allowed passively at some later compositional stage—Dickens's severity-mitigating [in various senses] aid.) See also the Preface to the revised edition of 1871 of *The Moonstone* in which Collins comments on the effects of his mother's death and an illness that nearly derailed the serial composition: "While this work was still in course of periodical publication in England, and in the United States, and when not more than a third of it was completed, the bitterest affliction of my life and the severest illness from which I have ever suffered, fell on me together. . . . Under the weight of this double calamity, I had my duty to the public still to bear in mind. My good readers in England and America, whom I had never yet disappointed, were expecting their regular weekly instalments of the new story" (29). The advance sheet system also disturbed a specific aspect of Dickens's work, its topicality, as the requisite long lead time hampered timely journalistic commentary: "the perpetual sliding away of temporary subjects at which I could dash with great effect, is a *great* loss" (qtd. in Drew 147).

States. How many unauthorized editions of this one novel of mine—published without my deriving any profit from them—made their appearance in America? I can only tell you, as a basis for calculation, that *one* American publisher informed a friend of mine that he had "sold one hundred and twenty thousand copies of 'The Woman in White.'" He never sent me sixpence. (618)

Collins also offered a more general condemnation of the Americans' practice by opening that particular article with a parable, a "little anecdote," that bears a striking methodological resemblance to *The Woman in White:* the anecdote is a fictional allegory of copyright infringement. The parable is set in the early days of North American settlement by the Dutch and recounts the "theft" by an Iroquois chief from a Dutch settler of a watch "made by [the Dutchman] and containing special improvements of his own invention" (Collins, "Considerations" 609). When requested to return the watch, the chief refuses, saying, "Possibly your watch is protected in Holland. . . . It is not protected in America. There is no watch-right treaty, sir, between my country and yours" (610).[16] Collins ends the parable with the key to its decipherment: "[t]he prototypes of modern persons have existed in past ages. The Iroquois chief was the first American publisher. [The Dutchman] was the parent of the whole European family of modern authors" (610). Here we have Collins, by characterizing the American publishers as more-native-than-the-Native-Americans in their "lawlessness" and "savage" immorality, coyly taking to its logical extreme a pervasive rhetoric of American republicanism and sovereignty that was being used throughout the century to support the publishers' contention of feeling like absolute "foreigners"—consistent with those taunts about "moral clap-traps" (*Woman in White* 236 and 604) aimed by Fosco at the two scandalized, excessivly-forthright heroines—in the face of British understandings of honor and civility.

"Considerations" was not Collins's only protest against American piracy. On 27 February 1874, during the last engagement of his winter reading tour in America, in the spirit of Dickens's first American trip, he had upset some members of his Boston audience by bringing up this point of contention

---

16. Collins's analogy here may well owe something to Richard Bentley, his publisher from 1850's *Antonina* to 1854's *Hide and Seek*. After George Bohn, the English reprinter of certain of Bentley's American authors, agreed to settle with him in late 1851, Bentley's celebratory indignation in print was such that his lawyer Devey had to warn him towards tempering it: "Bohn is a pirate—but he is not a felon! Your illustration, therefore, of a man robbing you of your watch, seems to me to lack a very rank ingredient in order to work it into an analogy" (Barnes 165).

in Anglo-American literary relations (Ashley 102). Additionally, in 1870 he had collaborated with the novelist and editor James Payn on an article entitled "A National Wrong," allowing Payn to quote extensively from two of his piqued responses to potentially-pirating Dutch publishers. The second of Collins's letters concluded with the following forceful pronouncement:

> For the rest—whether you do or do not take my book from me—I persist, in the interest of public morality, in asserting my right to regard as my own property the produce of my own brains and my own labour, any accidental neglect in formally protecting the same in any country notwithstanding. I declare any publisher who takes my book from me with a view to selling it, in any form, for his own benefit—without my permission, and without giving me a share in his profits—to be guilty of theft, and to be morally, if not legally, an outlaw and a pest among honest men. (Payn 109)

In the article, Payn himself referred to the age's most significant market denying profits to British authors:

> The idea of our "spry" cousins is, that they will not be the gainers by an honest reciprocity. They can import the works of our most popular writers for nothing, and how, say they, can they hope to get them cheaper? . . . [I]f [the "spry" American senator] could apply [America's] lack of International Copyright to every other article under heaven, and thereby rob the whole world of all they possess, as he now robs authors of their offspring, he would do so—slick. (107)

Admittedly, it seems hardly creditable that an author who felt this way later in his career could have been writing in 1860 a *covert* allegory on this heated topic. However, I believe that at that time the lesson of 1842 was still in effect, in a way it would not be after Dickens's death in 1870. It was a lesson so stinging in its rebuke as to be hard to forget. On January 22, 1842, Dickens had arrived in America full of hope. In the years—and, in one case, even months—leading up to his trip, bills attempting to establish a recognition of British copyright had been presented several times by Henry Clay, Senator for Kentucky, and defeated or allowed to die without debate in Congress (in 1837 [twice],[17] 1838, 1840, 1842) (Solberg, "Bibliography"

---

17. As a means of attacking its enemy Clay and the report of his Select Committee of 16 February 1837, *The United States Magazine and Democratic Review* adopted in 1838 the sly practice of disingenuously calling for no action to be taken on the question of international property until authors had had restored to them a perpetual copyright in their works, an impossible ideal in the America of that

788). Dickens's trip had been, undoubtedly, among other things an attempt to help Clay along in his project.[18] However, the author's efforts were, to say the least, not well received. Fred Kaplan writes,

> Only a literary lion, Dickens walked into the political and economic den of [American] public pressure groups like an ignorant Daniel. . . . With no sense of the economic reality or of American irritability on such matters, Dickens had one overriding feeling: A great injustice was being done. . . . Of all living writers he stood to gain most by a copyright agreement. Though most of his English fellow-authors supported his lobbying, some, like Bulwer, as well as numbers of his American friends, thought his speeches unseemly and his position awkward. (127–28)

Part of the problem was that Dickens's concern for "justice" overrode any concern for local economic circumstances. David Saunders comments that "the early 1840s was a time of recession in the United States economy, a fact that made Dickens's campaign to have Americans recognize and pay for use of British copyright material singularly ill-timed, given that such recognition was alleged to threaten the American industry with much higher costs" (158). Though Dickens had imagined he would be able to positively influence the situation, his directly-stated criticisms resulted in the American public's turning largely against the cause. Given the particularly forceful nature of Dickens's "lobbying" endeavors this is not surprising. To give a sense of these efforts, we might quote a long passage from one of his letters written from New York back home to England:

> I spoke, as you know, of international copyright, at Boston; and I spoke of it again at Hartford. My friends were paralysed with wonder at such audacious daring. The notion that I, a man alone by himself, in America, should venture to suggest to the Americans that there was one point on which they

---

time as the magazine well knew: "We hope . . . if a bill similar to that which was passed through the Senate in February of last year, is again introduced by its author, that it will be postponed until after a bill shall have passed restoring literary property to its proper level of equality with all other kinds of property, recognizing its equal inviolability and perpetuity. . . . Then, and not till then, will it be time to take up the subsequent question *for consideration,* to be decided on calm and statesmanlike views of public justice and public policy" ("Literary Property" 311; emphasis in original).

18. McGill remarks, "The American press . . . reads Dickens's assertions . . . as proof that he was both mercenary and plotting—that he came not voluntarily, to be celebrated by his readers, but as a national emissary on behalf of British trade. This theory gains considerable momentum as Dickens's trip wends south toward Washington, where the last of Henry Clay's international copyright bills is under consideration" (113).

were neither just to their own countrymen nor to us, actually struck the boldest dumb! . . . It is nothing that of all men living I am the greatest loser by it. It is nothing that I have a claim to speak and be heard. The wonder is that a breathing man can be found with temerity enough to suggest to the Americans the possibility of their having done wrong. I wish you could have seen the faces that I saw, down both sides of the table at Hartford, when I began to talk about Scott. I wish you could have heard how I gave it out. My blood so boiled as I thought of the monstrous injustice that I felt as if I were twelve feet high when I thrust it down their throats.

I had no sooner made that second speech than such an outcry began (for the purpose of deterring me from doing the like in this city) as an Englishman can form no notion of. Anonymous letters; verbal dissuasions; . . . assertions that I was no gentleman, but a mere mercenary scoundrel; coupled with the most monstrous mis-representations relative to my design and purpose in visiting the United States; came pouring in upon me every day. The dinner committee here (composed of the first gentlemen in America, remember that) were so dismayed, that they besought me not to pursue the subject, *although they every one agreed with me.* I answered that I would. That nothing should deter me. . . . That the shame was theirs, not mine; and that as I would not spare them when I got home, I would not be silenced here. Accordingly, when the night came, I asserted my right, with all the means I could command to give it dignity, in face, manner, or words; and I believe that if you could have seen and heard me, you would have loved me better for it than ever you did in your life. (Dickens, "Letter to Forster" 24 February 1842, *Letters* 3:82–84; emphasis in original)

Dickens's description of his feeling of righteous indignation during his American speeches conforms well with the self-description that his character Pip provides in *Great Expectations:* "In the little world in which children have their existence whosoever brings them up, there is nothing so finely perceived and so finely felt, as injustice. . . . Within myself, I had sustained, from my babyhood, a perpetual conflict with injustice" (63).

Given this standoff between Dickensian moral righteousness and American brazenness, it is no surprise to find a critic remarking that "one may question whether Dickens's intervention . . . did not, by all the journalistic opposition it aroused, contribute to delay the passage of an international copyright bill rather than to further it" (Houtchens 27). The assertions that Dickens was "a mere mercenary scoundrel" referred to in the letter above continued even after he had left the States, occasionally appearing in the most galling of contexts. For instance, the next year the American "mammoth" newspaper *Brother Jonathan,* in introducing the American sections of its *piracy* of *Martin Chuzzlewit,* prefaced the following comment:

> if ever a man left our shores in the humor to write an ill-natured, illiberal book upon America, that man was Charles Dickens. His reception here was most brilliant. The fuss made about him was such as almost to lay those who were concerned in it, open to the charge of fulsome adulation. . . . Still, he did not come here to be *feted* and feasted, and toasted and lionized. He came on a pure business errand, by the success of which he expected to put money in his purse. . . . On the day after his arrival [in Washington] he discovered . . . that, whatever might be the general opinion in this country upon the abstract justice of an international copyright law, to talk or think of passing such an act was idle. Now, Mr. Dickens dearly loves the dollars, and here was the most promising scheme for scraping them together, ever presented to his imagination, crushed, utterly annihilated. All those glittering visions of heaps of the yellow boys . . . were entirely, remorselessly swept away. The blow was a cruel one, and, as it were, knocked him all of a heap. Of course he made up his mind on the instant that the Americans, both in the aggregate and individually, were naturally, constitutionally, and from inveterate habit, no better than they should be, and, if anything, a good deal worse. ("Martin Chuzzlewit" 379–80)

This type of provocation could have done nothing to change Dickens's opinion of the Americans, an opinion that seems to have solidified by early May of his trip. The observations he offers in another letter—similar to those expressed satirically in the second epigraph from *Chuzzlewit* at the beginning of this chapter—indicate that he did not think much of the American character:

> I'll tell you what the two obstacles to the passing of an international copyright law with England, are: firstly, the national love of "doing" a man in any bargain or matter of business; secondly, the national vanity. Both these characteristics prevail to an extent which no stranger can possibly estimate. With regard to the first, I seriously believe that it is an essential part of the pleasure derived from the perusal of a popular English book, that the author gets nothing for it. It is so dar-nation 'cute[19]—so knowing

---

19. The placement of the hyphen in "dar-nation" here is meant, one imagines, at some level to suggest not only an American regional colloquialism but also an overweening American nationalism. This implicit reference to nationalism is not out of place because, as we saw with Nowell-Smith's

in Jonathan to get his reading on those terms. . . . The raven hasn't more joy in eating a stolen piece of meat, than the American has in reading the English book which he gets for nothing. (Dickens, "Letter to Forster," 3 May 1842, *Letters* 3:231–32)

Dickens undoubtedly also shared these sentiments with his friend Collins when the two grew close in the early-1850s. As a result, his younger colleague, I am arguing here, chose to make his own attempt at remedying the problem, this time under the surface of the discourse.[20]

The American context that Collins encountered when beginning to plan and compose *The Woman in White* in 1859 was a little more welcoming— despite the looming war—than the one Dickens had encountered in the early 1840s. There were renewed hopes (after an 1852–54 treaty effort had miscarried)[21] in the late 1850s that the Americans might be persuaded to establish a copyright agreement. After a 15-year period of congressional legislative inactivity on the issue, two American bills were presented, both

---

interpretation of the U.S. copyright clause, an anti-English republicanism was at the heart of the resistance to granting English authors American copyright. The Irish nationalist Mathew Carey, who fled Ireland to avoid imprisonment for republican activities, and his political-economist son Henry C. Carey both worked through their very successful Philadelphia publishing dynasty to defend the practice of reprinting English works. See particularly the latter Carey's *Letters* of 1853 and Johns, *Piracy* 175–211, 309–26.

20. Dickens may have tried his own covert allegorizing with regard to this issue in Pecksniff's appropriation of Martin's design in the Liverpool grammar school episode in chapter 35 of *Martin Chuzzlewit* (1844) (coming one chapter after Pogram's remarks about the English hatred of American institutions in the second epigraph to this chapter). Noting that in his "mission" Dickens "entirely, humiliatingly failed," Gerhard Joseph goes on to argue that "the American piracy of Dickens's novels . . . gets displaced in *Martin Chuzzlewit* onto a meditation on Pecksniff's theft of Martin's grammar-school plans. . . . [I]t is surely true that the dispute about authorial rights to an intellectual property within a fiercely individualistic humanist/capitalist ethos is what is at issue for both Martin the apprentice and Dickens the author" (260, 268–69).

21. In 1852 the secretary of state Daniel Webster had drafted an Anglo-American international copyright treaty and his successor Edward Everett had authorized it on 17 February 1853, but it failed, due to a variety of factors, to receive ratification by the Senate (Barnes 241–62). Solberg remarks, "the matter was allowed to drop, the convention never being put into force" ("Copyright Law Reform" 59). Henry Carey's *Letters* of 1853 may have had some effect in causing it to be tabled. Dickens agreed to hold a meeting on the matter of monetarily supporting the treaty at Tavistock House, writing to invite, among others, the publisher Richard Bentley on 18 May 1852: "Sir Edward Bulwer Lytton is in possession of some very curious papers having reference to the passing of an International Copyright law with America. He has communicated them to me, and we agree that they ought to be *privately* imparted to you and one or two others interested in like manner in the question. . . . Will you meet Sir Edward here on Saturday next, at 3 o'Clock in the afternoon?" (*Letters* 6:675). See Barnes describing the skepticism Dickens exhibited at this meeting about the feasibility of this eventually unsuccessful campaign (223–25). In general Dickens "felt that American legislators could never be brought to do anything other than serve their own self-interest" (Barnes 92).

authored by Representative Edward Joy Morris, in relatively quick succession, on January 18, 1858 and February 15, 1860 (Solberg, "Bibliography" 788). In addition, in December 1858 *Blackwood's* had published a report on the International Copyright Congress held that September in Brussels.[22] This was the environment in which Collins contemplated beginning the composition of *The Woman in White,* a task he started on 15 August 1859 and completed on 26 July 1860 (Collins, *Woman in White* 647).

Thus, Collins entered an arena in which, though it was still clear that direct appeals published in a journal conducted by Charles Dickens would be ineffective, there was nevertheless some hope that a clever-enough author could offer a subtle push in the right direction. Authors such as Marryat, G. P. R. James, Ainsworth, Cooper, Irving, Bryant, Emerson, and Poe, both in England and America, had been overtly complaining about the widespread practice of the American piracy of British works for several years before Collins would come to compose *The Woman in White.* Direct appeals to the Americans having not worked, Collins, one imagines, decided to carry out his critiques of literary piracy—and to deploy his references to textual ideology in general—sub rosa. That approach may have been risky, in the sense that it would have allowed the message often to be missed, but it was nevertheless a way of avoiding once again stirring up ill-will of the sort that the speeches given by Dickens during his trip had generated. Dickens himself, though remaining a strident advocate for various other causes, subsequently gave up the direct approach in relation to this issue, reportedly avoiding mentioning it in public forums (*Letters* 11:634). In short, I would argue that Collins's novel, coming to be composed during this renewed phase of American legislative activity, should be seen as a surreptitious ideologico-literary salvo—and as potential redemption of his friend's political misstep—in this war for the minds and moral wellbeing of his American readers.

---

22. The article began with the obligatory complaint that "English authors and publishers are infinitely more interested in the question [of international copyright] than the authors and publishers of any other country. . . . [A]lmost every English book that appears . . . is caught up by the race of American Harpers (an obvious corruption of harpies), and circulated for a few cents throughout the length and breadth of the United States" and concluded with a recapitulation of the Congress's resolutions, the first of which was aimed at establishing a globalized unity of approach: "The Congress is of opinion that the international recognition of property in literary and artistic works, ought to be adopted in the legislature of every civilised people; that it ought to be extended from country to country even in the absence of reciprocity; and that legislation in all countries where the principle is adopted, should be founded on an [*sic*] uniform basis" ("International Copyright Congress" 687, 698).

The Face and the Text in *Jeffereys v. Boosey*

Having established the local context for Collins's covert allegorizing, we might now attempt to establish the larger legal context encouraging the collapse of look-alike texts with look-alike faces, a collapse on which Collins's allegory relies. An early instance of this collapse appears in the English legal case of *Jeffereys v. Boosey* (1854),[23] described by the nineteenth-century copyright authority Eaton S. Drone as "the leading copyright case of this century, as *Millar v. Taylor* and *Donaldson v. Becket* were of the last" (223). This legal dispute is a consideration of the right of foreign authors to claim copyright in England. While it appears very much an Italian–English case—at issue is the piracy of the printing of an aria from Vincenzo Bellini's opera *La Sonnambula*[24]—it is not solely concerned with that context. The more important contemporary group being addressed by the decision is unquestionably the Americans, as is signaled by some of the Justices' musings on the decision's potential impact on the current transatlantic international copyright dispute. Barnes notes, "It was not entirely coincidental that most of the copyright cases involving foreigners [in England] during the first half of the nineteenth century had to do either with American authors or European musical composers. . . . There was no need to translate either, and as a result they were the natural targets of unauthorized republication" (165–66). Lord St. Leonards, the former Lord Chancellor, delivering his opinion (along with the other two Law Lords deciding the case, current Lord Chancellor

---

23. This was the appeal of the decision in *Boosey v. Jeffereys* (1850). That decision had concluded that an American author had copyright in England if the book had been first *published* there, the author's place of residence on publication day being immaterial. Thus, from 20 May 1851 (when the decision in *Boosey* was handed down) onwards, it appeared American authors had solid rights covering all their works in both the American and British markets. In response to the *Boosey* decision, Richard Bentley, "the largest publisher of American works in Britain" (Barnes 176), was prompted to write the following to his most valuable and valued author, James Fenimore Cooper: "At last we have had a decision of the Question—whether a foreigner can hold Copyright—by the Lord Chief Justice and five other judges sitting in a court of Error, deciding this point affirmatively. I am therefore now proceeding against those who have interefered with the novels by you and published by me. . . . Not but that the pirates threaten to carry the matter to the court of last resort—The House of Lords—but we shall see whether they will like to spend more money" (3 June 1851; qtd. in Seville, *Internationalisation* 179). Unfortunately for Bentley, they did like, and this state of affairs would be undone by the decision handed down in *Jeffereys* in 1854. Barnes notes that the decision in *Jefferys*, the House being the last recourse in appeals, put the nail in the coffin. It had a serious effect on American writers such as Cooper, Irving, Stowe, and Melville, for, their unprotected earlier works having become much less valuable and exclusive, "[p]ublishers of American books . . . were faced with having to renegotiate all their contracts with American authors" (173). The effect of the decision in *Jefferys* was that "Prices offered American authors for the British market plummeted" (Seville, *Internationalisation* 188).

24. Collins will have Lydia Gwilt, Ozias Midwinter, and Allan Armadale attend the performance of a different opera by Bellini, *Norma*, in Naples late in *Armadale* (555–56).

Cramworth and Ex-Chancellor Lord Brougham) feels of necessity called on
to comment on that particular dispute:

> I may remark, in passing, that, although nothing could be more improper
> than to consider the state of international law in deciding a question upon
> our own municipal law, (for here we must decide this question, not with
> reference to the relation in which we stand to the United States, or any
> other country with respect to copyright, but as it regards our own law in the
> abstract, without reference to any other country at all), yet I may observe,
> that the strained construction which would give to a foreigner the right
> which is now claimed, would have the effect of placing this country not
> on a level with the United States. For example, the United States do not
> allow a foreigner resident out of them to obtain a copyright there; but the
> American publisher imports his [the foreigner's] books the moment they
> are published, and sells them without difficulty and without interruption.
> In the United States they attempted to bring in a Bill in order to reconcile
> the laws of the two countries, and to put authors upon the same footing in
> each country. That attempt did not succeed.[25] . . . [Thus] we are not called
> upon to put any strained construction upon our own Act of Parliament [of
> 1844] in order to give to foreigners a right which their law denies to us.
> (*Jeffereys* 749)

St. Leonards's reasoning would be instrumental in leading the presiding
judges to decide that a foreigner could indeed hold English copyright but
only if that work's first publication had taken place in England or its Colonies and the author had been resident on publication day within those
dominions.[26] The British here, even more markedly than in the "Interna-

---

25. Of that unsuccessful treaty agreement, in which he played a part (Seville, *Internationalisation* 182; Barnes 250), William Makepeace Thackeray would write, "I hear the most cheering accounts . . . of the International Copyright bill, which on my conscience will make me 5000 dollars a
year richer" (Letter of 16 February 1853; qtd. in Seville, *Internationalisation* 182–83n114).

26. See Drone 227. The House of Lords' decision in *Routledge v. Low* (1868) would clarify the
requirement that to secure British copyright an American author's residence had to be on publication day in the British Dominions "however temporary" that residence might turn out to be (Seville,
Internationalisation 198). Thus, the English understanding of "residence" was not as stringent as the
American. The American attitude was expressed in *Carey v. Collier* (1837). There the U.S. Circuit
Court of New York had decided that Captain Marryat would not be granted American copyright
protection for *The Phantom Ship* because the evidence, despite the filing of a declaration of intention
to become a citizen, pointed to his actually being merely what the judge described as a "transient
visitant" (59; see also Drone 233n2). Mark Twain would make use of this British provision, as would
other American authors. Twain would be writing in 1887, "To-day the American author can go to
Canada, spend three days there, and come home with an English and Canadian copyright which is
as strong as if it had been built out of railroad iron" (qtd. in Matthews 47). Barnes writes that the

tional Copyright Acts" of 1838 and 1844, effectively are offering to meet the Americans half way in resolving the issue of the lack of an international copyright agreement. St. Leonards's reference to the Americans was not a simple aside. They may well have been the intended audience for the judgment, if not precisely the case. Seville remarks, "The *Jurist* reported that the 'commonly received explanation' of *Jeffereys v. Boosey* was that it was decided with a view to the renewal of the abortive treaty negotiations [with America]. If so, the attempt failed" (*Internationalisation* 190).

In *Jeffereys,* William Erle, a Justice of the Court of Queen's Bench, had been called on (along with nine other judges), as was the practice for especially significant cases, to offer an advisory opinion to the presiding Law Lords. In the course of delivering his opinion (that the work of an alien in residence, even manifestly transitory residence, *does* merit British copyright protection), Erle had put forward an analogy that located copyright securely within the realm of the control of personhood rather than, as had often before been the case, in the realm of the control of landed property (as has been outlined in the examples in the previous chapter). Arguing against those who would be considering literary property to be an "evanescent and fleeting" concept that entailed "a claim to ideas which cannot be identified," Erle equated a literary composition's individuality with that of the face of its author:

> [T]he claim [in copyright] is not to ideas, but to the order of words, and . . . this order has a marked identity and a permanent endurance. . . . *The order of each man's words is as singular as his countenance,* and although if two authors composed originally with the same order of words, each would have a property therein, still the probability of such an occurrence is less than that there should be two countenances that could not be discriminated. (*Jeffereys* 703; emphasis added)

---

immediate effect of *Routledge*—with regard to American works already published without the safety of authorial residence on publication day in Canada (i.e., the vast majority of them)—was "to throw open the floodgates to the republication of American works [in England]. Reprinters no longer feared court injunctions" (172). The question of American authors' rights in England had been very much up in the air since the Court of the Exchequer in *Chappell v. Purday* (1845) had held it to be "doubtful whether a foreigner not resident [in Britain] can have an English copyright at all" (499). Seville points out that the decision in the case of *Boosey v. Purday* (1849) had prompted the English publisher Bentley to warn his American author Herman Melville that the justices of the Court of Exchequer "have decided that a foreigner has *no copyright.* This driveling absurdity can scarcely be suffered to remain, I trust, but in the mean time this decision will expose publishers like myself, who am so largely engaged in this department of publishing to the risk of attack from any unprincipled persons who may choose to turn Pirate" (Bentley to Melville, 20 June 1849; qtd. in Seville, *Internationalisation* 176–77).

The specter of American piracy haunted Erle's words here, particularly his formulation of a text that looked the same as another but that should not have come into existence except through an entirely separate process of composition. We are not far from the logic implicit in the narrative of *The Woman in White* allowing look-alike women, actually half-sisters, to pass for look-alike texts, the British original and the American reprint.

Theory continually obtrudes into the historical domain, but we can only see this if we are open to noticing theory's effects. This scenario, implicitly touching on the precarious balancing of the repetition (breaking) and originality (settling) characteristic of linguistic iterability, will be conjured up by jurists and writers again and again down to our own age. In 1936 Judge Learned Hand notes that copyright attaches in different ways to different works, even if those works happen to look the same: "[I]f by some magic a man who had never known it were to compose anew Keats's 'Ode on a Grecian Urn,' he would be an 'author,' and, if he copyrighted it, others might not copy that poem, though they might of course copy Keats's" (*Sheldon v. Metro-Goldwyn* [54]). One might copy Keats's poem of course because it would be out of copyright. In 1938, Jorge Luis Borges composes the story "Pierre Menard, Author of the *Quixote*" in which the title character does "not want to compose another *Quixote*—which is easy—but *the Quixote itself*" (39). Unlike Cervantes's real-world rival Avellaneda de Tordesillas, Menard has not set out to write a false continuation. Nor has he set out to plagiarize the original but rather to recompose the book itself: "Needless to say, he never contemplated a mechanical transcription of the original; he did not propose to copy it. His admirable intention was to produce a few pages which would coincide—word for word and line for line—with those of Miguel de Cervantes" (39). Given that the particular words used—though only *seemingly* infinite in their possible permutations and combinations—are *definitely* infinitely reusable, there always exists the chance, however remote, that two compositions could turn out the same. This is the type of situation that Erle, by tying iterability to faces, was trying to bring under control.

However, the situation, as formulated in *Jeffereys*, then posed the opposite threat, of perhaps having copyright infect the realm of facial gestures and singular authorial identity. This possibility was not welcomed by some of the other judges advising in the case. Lord Chief Baron Pollock, presumably intending mockery but actually laying out the future directions of copyright and its offshoot the "right of publicity,"[27] attempted to counter Erle's type of

27. See Gaines's chapter "*Dracula* and the Right of Publicity," in *Contested Culture* 175–207, and the California Celebrities Rights Act of 1985.

author-as-creator argument, and thinking like it, by following such propositions to their logical conclusions:

> The ground taken by the learned Counsel for the Defendant in Error, on this part of the case, has been that an author has the same property in his composition, being his own creation or work, as a man has in any physical object, produced by his personal labour. If such a property exists at Common Law, it must commence with the act of composition or creation itself, and must, it seems to me, be independent of its being reduced into writing. . . . [If so it] must apply to every other offspring of man's imagination, wit, or labour . . . to whatever belongs to human life. . . . And it is difficult to say where, in principle, this is to stop; why [copyright] is to be confined to the larger and graver labours of the understanding? Why does it not apply to a well-told anecdote, or a witty reply, so as to forbid the repetition without the permission of the author? And, carried to its utmost extent, it would at length descend to lower and meaner subjects, and include the trick of a conjuror, or the grimace of a clown. (*Jeffereys* 729)

Here Pollock transformed Erle's "each man's countenance" into each clown's grimace as a means of disclosing the apparent absurdity of the basic presumptions underlying such an analogy.

However, despite Pollock's general objections to this type of thinking, Erle's analogy would take hold. The legal scholar Jane C. Ginsburg considers Erle's remarks a nascent moment "when courts began to recognize an individual personality basis for copyright"[28] and connects this trend to the creation of a Right to Privacy in the United States at the end of the 1800s: "Samuel Warren and Louis Brandeis's 1890 article, *The Right to Privacy*, argued that common law copyright, and its new corollary, privacy, found their source in rights of personality" (Ginsburg, "Creation" 1882–83). Erle's opinion would join a series of copyright decisions culminating in Warren and Brandeis's article founding what they would be calling the "right to be let alone" (205) on the common-law right to keep the unpublished manu-

---

28. I believe this opinion, rather than being the origin of anything, to be actually one of those always possible periodic reemergences, as in *Feist* (1991), of the author-as-creator construct. See, for another example, Justice Aston in *Millar* in 1769 suggesting that the right to keep the manuscript back from publication stems from the author's role as originator. He holds, "there is a material difference in favour of this sort of property, from that gained by occupancy; which before was common, and not yours; but was to be rendered so by some act of your own. For, *this is originally the author's:* and, therefore, unless rendered common by his own act and full consent, it ought still to remain his" (221; emphasis added).

script back from publication, a right that had previously often been closely allied to copyright.[29]

Another opinion that could be said to exemplify what Ginsburg characterizes as the "copyright as personality approach" was a decision serving as a seminal precedent for Warren and Brandeis, Vice-Chancellor J. L. Knight-Bruce's decision in the first hearing of the celebrated case of *Prince Albert v. Strange* in 1849 (Ginsburg, "Creation" 1882). In that case, the mere cataloguing of unauthorized printings made from engravings created by the Prince Consort and Queen had prompted Knight-Bruce to defend not only the royal palace but also the no less sacred institution of the general Victorian home:

---

29. The Right to Privacy derives directly from eighteenth-century copyright decisions, specifically from K. Knight-Bruce's misinterpretation of Yates's arguments in *Millar*. It is somewhat appropriate, given Yates's liberal attitude towards the ownership of published writing, that his own recorded thoughts on the author's lack of control of his "sentiments"—in Yates's time a synonym for "ideas"—should have been taken so far afield, co-opted to such an extent, as to have been interpreted to be referring to "feelings" by later judges and legal authorities wishing to found, in America, a Right to Privacy. For the most significant manipulations of Yates's published sentiments on "sentiments," see Knight-Bruce, V.C., in *Prince Albert v. Strange* (1849), 303; and Warren and Brandeis's "The Right to Privacy" (198–200). Knight-Bruce (310) quotes Yates's assertion that "it is certain every man has a right to keep his own sentiments, if he pleases" (*Millar* 242). This statement is re-cited by Warren and Brandeis (198n2) as significant, indeed crucial, precedential authority for the concept of a common law legal protection of the subject's "feelings" and thus a grounding for the new right to privacy the two were in the process of formulating. But this characterization of Yates on "sentiments" as "feelings" would seem to stand in stark contrast to the spirit of Yates on "sentiments" as "ideas": "when the sentiments are made common by the author's own act, every *use* of those sentiments must be equally common" (*Millar* 234; emphasis added). Compare also Yates at 230, 231, 233, and 242, and, more generally, William Blackstone in the well-known *Commentaries on the Laws of England* (1765–69): "the identity of a literary composition consists intirely [sic] in the *sentiment* and the language; the same *conceptions,* clothed in the same words, must necessarily be the same composition" (2:405–6; emphasis added). It would seem that once Yates had himself let those "sentiments" fly they were no longer his to control in the way that his immediate context or argument might be supposed to have wished. See also Lord Chancellor Eldon failing in 1825 to uphold the distinction between sentiments and feelings by failing to consistently tie the former to ideas. At certain points, the distinction between sentiments and feelings is upheld: "[in *Millar v. Taylor* and *Donaldson v. Becket*] there was a great deal of argument concerning the question of what sort of property a man may have in his unpublished ideas or sentiments, or the language which he uses" (*Abernethy v. Hutchinson* [1825] 213). As *Abernethy* was a case dealing with the unauthorized publication of medical lectures on the principles and practice of surgery, it is highly unlikely that it was Abernethy's feelings that were being referred to here. See also the same case at 217: "In *Millar and Taylor* there is a great deal said with respect to a person having a property in sentiments and language, though not deposited on paper." However, at a certain point the distinction breaks down: "That legal question, in the shape in which it is now put, namely, with respect to an oral delivery of ideas and sentiments, has occasioned much abstruse learning" (215). My reason for focusing so closely on these usages/misusages of "sentiments" is to show how the reader-centered breaking function of iterability was able to infiltrate another system designed to exclude or control it, this time corrupting not the system of copyright but rather that of legal precedent.

I think . . . not only that the defendant here is unlawfully invading the plaintiff's rights, but also that the invasion is of such a kind and affects such property as to entitle the plaintiff to the preventative remedy of an injunction; and if not the more, yet, certainly, not the less, because it is an intrusion,—an unbecoming and unseemly intrusion,—an intrusion not alone in breach of conventional rules, but offensive to that inbred propriety natural to every man,—if intrusion, indeed, fitly describes a sordid spying into the privacy of domestic life,—into the home (a word hitherto sacred among us), the home of a family whose life and conduct form an acknowledged title, though not their only unquestionable title, to the most marked respect in this country. (*Prince Albert* 312; qtd. in Warren and Brandeis 202*n*1)

Taken together, Erle's and Knight-Bruce's comments signaled the advent of a culture in the England of the 1850s in which reproducible and distributable artistic creations in general and word orderings in particular were coming to be considered on a par with identities, those presumably most private of entities, and, concomitantly, in which the theft of those word orderings was coming to be seen as tantamount to that modern crime that so worries us today, identity theft.[30] Legal decisions such as these would establish the perspective from which the seemingly disconnected crimes of Collins's vil-

---

30. One significant implication of Collins's attempt at allegorizing the breaking function was that the relatively novel crime of identity theft would have to come, of necessity, to replace murder in the villain's arsenal. This is precisely what occurs in Collins's narrative. Reveling in the ingenuity of his successful plot, Fosco remarks, "I might have taken Lady Glyde's life. . . . [I] took her identity, instead" (*Woman in White* 628). Thus, he marks himself out as an individual made more for our "identity theft"-obsessed times than for his own. The substitution of the identity for the life made here can be found to have its model in Dickens's two major productions published just before Collins began composition. In Dickens's *Little Dorrit* (1857), Monsieur Rigaud/Blandois—that other self-proclaimed "citizen of the world" (24 and 373)—having graduated from the simple art of murder to the more complex crime of identity theft, shifts from perhaps having taken his wife's life when she refused to relinquish her rights (25) to making a market of his fellowship with, if manifestly not Jeremiah Flintwinch himself, then his twin brother (745). And of course the scene at the close of *A Tale of Two Cities* (1859)—the work immediately preceding, and for one installment overlapping with, *The Woman in White* in *All the Year Round*—in which Sydney Carton famously substitutes himself on the guillotine for his look-alike Charles Darnay is a far, far better example of identity theft than it is, technically speaking, of suicide or self-murder. Nevertheless, Fosco's maneuver—imposed against Laura's will and coming after his usurpation of the identity of our narrator—suggests that *all* our identities are vulnerable to usurpation and figurative "rewriting." Thus Collins's strategy is more reminiscent of the "postmodern" artists of the recent past, such as Nabokov, Borges, and Philip K. Dick, or, on the other hand, of those masters of pre-postmodern postmodernism Laurence Sterne and Miguel Cervantes than it is of Dickens. This change in the usual practice of the villain's opting simply for murder is the result of the real world being made to come into line with the theoretical implications of the breaking function, of bodies coming to be textualized, a conjunction that takes place in both Erle's opinion in *Jeffereys* and, as we saw in Chapter 1, in the significant Tombstone Scene in *The Woman in White*.

lain Fosco, namely, the textual theft committed against Marian Halcombe and the identity theft committed against Laura Fairlie, could come to be seen to be related. However, the *criminality*, from a theoretical perspective, of those "crimes" would have to remain an open question. It all depended on whether the person judging them was an excessively morally upright citizen of some particular place or a presumably jaded "citizen of the world" as Fosco styles himself (*Woman in White* 237) or, in other words, to reduce the situation to the metaphors most relevant to Collins's life, on whether one was a sober English author-citizen or incredibly perceptive idealist heavily dosed on laudanum.

Immorality vs. Linguistic Pragmatism

As I have already remarked, there were competing ways of viewing the situation of copyright theft in the mid-nineteenth century: the English (or locally historical) and the "theoretical" perspective. There was, not surprisingly, little variance, at least when one considers solely their conscious, daylight comments, in how English authors, including Collins, regarded the state of affairs. The "successful" English author of the nineteenth century was simply and plainly appalled by the situation—and nothing else. While composing, he or she was continually plagued by the prospect of the American reprinters always waiting, so to speak, in the wings. This was a situation bound to elicit a bit of ill will on the part of the pirated authors. Dickens had, as we saw, made up his mind about the Americans as a result of his first-hand experience of them during his trip.

However, the young Collins had a mind of his own, or, more precisely, a subconscious of his own, and Dickens could not have predicted how far afield that subconscious would be taking his fellow writer. Catherine Peters notes that Collins's opium use increased significantly from 1859 onwards (240). Not surprisingly, his works' psychic bifurcation, mirroring that one always already plaguing his language, dates from about this same time. Collins remarks on his apprehension in composing the serial to follow *A Tale of Two Cities* in Dickens's new journal *All the Year Round* writing in the Preface to the contemporary French translation *La Femme en Blanc*, "When I accepted the responsibility of speaking to one of the largest readerships England can offer, after the greatest novelist in our country had just enchanted it by his talent, I was naturally rather nervous as I wondered if I would show myself worthy of such a sign of confidence" ("Preface" 622). I will in this chapter be contending that the issue of American piracy must have weighed

heavily on the mind (both the waking and opium-influenced parts, or conscious and subconscious to use the standard terms) of the up-and-coming
author Collins as he approached the task of writing his inheritance-theft-
through-doppelganger-exchange story for Dickens's journal—and, of course,
for that tale's American reprinters, both authorized and unauthorized—and
that the pressure he was already under could only have increased as Collins's
intellectual honesty led him to entertain the necessity of showing "disloy-
alty" to Dickens's, and the general English populace's, confirmed "settling"
views.

Dickens's perspective was an understandable one. In a world (especially
one menaced by profiteering American publishers) where settling had come
so often—albeit always only temporarily and unstably—to eclipse breaking,
"piracy" (or "reprinting" as it was less sensationalistically known)—the terms
characterizing it emphasizing, and perhaps attempting to keep in place, its
secondary status—was naturally going to appear a parasitical "deviance" living off the seemingly-incontestable normality of controllable texts. This was
what the majority of the English saw when they assessed literary relations
between England and America in the nineteenth century. But it was not, I
am arguing, what Collins, in his darker, more profound, moments perceived
or at least intuited.[31] I do not mean to suggest that he for a moment took
seriously the Americans' self-serving and conscience-assuaging rhetoric of it
going "against nature" for the law of copyright to extend beyond national
borders. No English writer of the nineteenth century could have been that
naïve. And Collins was certainly no idiot—or saint. Rather, the laudanum
addict Collins, seeing past the emotions permeating the issue—perhaps as
a result of the seductiveness of the villain he had created to represent it—
intuited American defiance and general self-interested recalcitrance to be
pointing in the direction of a fundamental and necessary intellectual *lesson*.

Indeed, in contrast to Dickens's singular perspective, there was another
way of viewing the situation. The Americans' practice could be understood,
rather than as simply "bad," to be bringing along with it the exposure of a
fundamental, but continually disowned, truth about language. Indeed, from
a certain perspective, the Americans could be seen to be, à la Justice Yates
in *Millar,* simply manifesting more intellectual honesty than the tradition-

---

31. This was not the first time Dickens and Collins had differed in their responses to international political issues. Nayder notes that in 1857 there were already significant "political differences
between the two writers," particularly evident in their reactions to the 1857 Indian rebellion: "Collins's response . . . differed markedly from Dickens's . . . and . . . the virulent racism that characterizes
Dickens's remarks about Hindus . . . is notably absent from Collins's writing. . . . In 'A Sermon for
Sepoys,' published in *Household Words* in 1858, Collins . . . advocates the moral reform of Indians
rather than their extermination" (*Unequal Partners* 103–4).

bound English. The breaking function—allowing the receiver of a written communication to make what use he would of it ("[e]very purchaser of a book is the owner of it" [*Millar* 234])—was as legitimate a cause/effect (take your pick) as the settling process, and just as deserving of acknowledgment. Thus the American market—rather than simply being a zone filled with "immoral" reprinters—could be considered a clear and present manifestation of that particular function that the Enlightenment-influenced author's intellectual culture would have been implicitly persuading him or her to deny. It is understandable then that the open-minded—or at least so schizophrenically-minded as to have rendered himself unobstructedly other- or breaking-minded—Collins, when looking at the broader picture, might well have found himself to be fundamentally conflicted when approaching this situation, since the Americans, who seemed from one point of view so patently "in the wrong," could be viewed to be merely restoring the balance that European intellectual culture had improperly skewed toward one side.

In other words, while writing *The Woman in White,* near the cusp, that is, of the turn in his novel series, Collins must have felt this conflict acutely and, even while in his more sober moments consciously resenting the U.S. publishers for their profiting from his efforts, he must have at some laudanum-induced or -accessed level recognized that their "theft" was one that was coming to bring his Old World views more into line with what Yates had called "the fixed constitution of things" (*Millar* 234). This acknowledgment of expanded horizons was gestured at by the settled complacency of the character he created to champion that expansion, the well-traveled Count Fosco, an individual whose self-description shows him to unapologetically uphold very "liberal" views, particularly regarding the lack of a universal virtue that would be regulating the commission of certain socially-relativistic "crimes":

> I am a citizen of the world, and I have met, in my time, with so many different sorts of virtue, that I am puzzled, in my old age, to say which is the right sort and which is the wrong. Here, in England, there is one virtue. And there, in China, there is another virtue. And John Englishman says my virtue is the genuine virtue. And John Chinaman says my virtue is the genuine virtue. And I say Yes to one, or No to the other, and am just as much bewildered about it in the case of John with the top-boots as I am in the case of John with the pigtail. . . . Ah! I am a bad man, Lady Glyde, am I not? I say what other people only think; and when all the rest of the world is in a conspiracy to accept the mask for the true face, mine is the rash hand that tears off the plump pasteboard, and shows the bare bones beneath. (*Woman in White* 237–39)

In the continuation of this monologue, Fosco points out that society rewards deceit and punishes what is usually called virtue. The thieving dressmaker becomes a rich lady. The woman who sells herself in marriage for gold is applauded by her friends.

Fosco's worldliness also extends to the textual realm. The Count will later, in his written confession—the penultimate narrative in this story composed of a series of narratives—explicitly acknowledge the vulnerability to theft of all writing that has, to quote Derrida, "fall[en] from the body" ("*La parole*" 175) when he offers the scene of his carrying Anne Catherick's clothes to the house where Laura Fairlie lies drugged by him—an allegorical representation of iterable English contents being shifted to American bindings—freely, on a sort of international trade model, to the public domain: "What a situation! I suggest it to the rising romance writers of England. I offer it, as totally new, to the worn-out dramatists of France" (*Woman in White* 626). He might well be repaying an intellectual debt here, for we are reminded of his description of the "innocent follies" of his early literary life when he "ruled the fashions of a second-rate Italian town, and wrote preposterous romances, on the French model, for a second-rate Italian newspaper" (260). While composing the confession, the Count is more aware than anyone that he is in fact potentially rendering himself vulnerable to the same theft he had perpetrated overtly in the initial theft of Marian's diary, what we might call her "characters," and to that later one he had perpetrated covertly in a type of replaying of the earlier crime in the switching of Laura's character for Anne's—of perhaps having his writing, his "characters," stolen from him. (Recall his tacit allusion to the etymological tie between "character" and "type": "Percival! Percival! . . . Has all your experience shown you nothing of my character yet? I am a man of the antique type!" [336]). The sophisticated visitor to England thus evinces on more than one occasion a "foreign" or "worldly" reconcilement to his writing's (indeed to any and all writing's) inherent tendency to become alienated from its primary producer.[32]

---

32. The struggle between an English and a "worldly" sense of virtue can be found also in Collins's first full-length novel to be simultaneously serialized transatlanticly, the one written just before *The Woman in White*, *The Dead Secret*, which ran in both *Household Words* and *Harper's Weekly* from January to June 1857 (Ashley 52). In that novel, we can perhaps see Collins making explicit his conscious feelings about the unwillingness of the Americans to recognize British copyright through his having one of his characters espouse what must have seemed at the time, to anyone but a British author trained as a lawyer, as Collins was, quite excessively fastidious copyright principles. When Rosamond Frankland, née Treverton, naively asserts her wish to pay her uncle Andrew's duplicitous servant Shrowl five pounds for a copy—taken from the "Rare. Only six copies printed," *History and Antiquities of PORTHGENNA TOWER*—of the plan of the Treverton family home, the key to solving the mystery of the location of the elusive Myrtle Room that contains the secret referred to in the book's title, her husband Leonard has to shame her into a proper understanding of the intricacies

The "worldly" characterization of this perspective understates the radically "un-charitable" nature of the theoretical one that it is screening. The breaking function of iterability cannot, and does not, care whose feelings it hurts. It would have been difficult for Collins to justify the active promotion of this standpoint in a serial appearing in Dickens's journal. He thus was willing at this point only to place it in the mouth of a clear villain, one who ends up being apparently punished in the end. Justice Yates may have failed at converting his colleagues to his world-view, and, as I will be arguing here, Collins may have drawn back at the conclusion of this particular novel from fully acknowledging the breaking function, but that function, once seriously entertained, was not something that it would be thereafter easy to ignore. The possibility of the breaking function's more than merely transitory "eruption," that is, of its taking over the whole scene, was one that Yates had already envisioned in his attempt in *Millar v. Taylor* to label as "normal" this particular perspective. His more conservative brother judges, on the other hand, had attempted to wrest control back to the settling side by characterizing such a perspective as deviant. The conflict in 1769's *Millar* would be replayed in the nineteenth century—both parties' outlooks proving that literary property was anything but secure—with American piracy standing in for Yates's standpoint while English indignation stood in for the majority's opinion in the case. In short, say what Dickens might about them, the Americans, like Yates, were at some level continually demonstrating that there was only a very tenuous (or at least severely mitigated) moral high ground for those defending an artificially-constricted view with regard to the workings of language.

Collins, the Good Son and the Bad Grandson

Collins's submerged lobbying grew out of not only a desire simultaneously to learn from and abjure the negative example of Dickens's trip but also a

---

involved in honoring copyright. The narrative has laid the ground earlier by pointedly explaining to us Shrowl's reasoning in making a copy rather than stealing the plan outright. Shrowl chose to make "the best copy he could of the Plan, and to traffic with that, as a document which the most scrupulous person in the world need not hesitate to purchase" (*Dead Secret* 206). Shrowl had not reckoned, however, on the existence of a character like that one possessed by the admirably-principled Leonard Frankland. Rosamond complains, "What harm are we doing, if we give the man his five pounds? He has only made a copy of the Plan: he has not stolen anything" (221). However, the blind Leonard, sensitive to copyright issues to an unusual degree, protests against his wife's "reason[ing] like a Jesuit," emphatically replying, "He has stolen information, according to my idea of it" (221). Of course, Rosamond will acquire the plan in the end, and just as implacably—since this is early in Collins's project—that "theft of information" will be her undoing.

profound belief in the power of fiction. Manipulating tastes in reading was considered a real possibility in Collins's early journalism. Just two years before *The Woman in White,* Collins was making it clear that he believed he could successfully manipulate his readers' psyches in matters of literary taste. Having discovered a newly-literate audience, an "unknown public" of three million penny-journal readers, that according to him simply needed to have its literary taste elevated, he had ambitiously concluded that such manipulation on a mass scale was possible: "there [is] the great . . . difficulty . . . of accustoming untried readers to the delicacies and subtleties of literary art. An immense public has been discovered; the next thing to be done is, in a literary sense, to teach that public how to read" (Collins, "Unknown Public" 222). As is indicated by Collins's narrative's intense concern with maintaining the sometimes very fine distinction between Laura and Anne, between the Lady in White and the Woman, connoisseurship in literary tastes and literary artifacts was a subject that interested him a great deal, at least when he was being a good son and dutiful employee. The apparent unfairness of the situation of American piracy—as well as the vehemence of his employer's unhappiness with respect to the issue—did not allow at this point for Collins's conscious adoption of his usual worldly equanimity, a wordliness that would have reveled in the playful possibilities lying at the basis of a potentially irresolvable ambiguity or paradox. He was not able in this novel to maintain the same judiciousness that he would—as a world famous novelist in his own right—exhibit later in, for instance, *Armadale* when it came to remaining balanced with regard to the impossibility of settling on a single interpretation for Ozias Midwinter's dream narrative.

Given the history of Collins's familial involvement in the creation of paintings—his father William Collins having been a very popular artist of his day and member of the Royal Academy—a concern with forgery on Collins's part should not be surprising. It is likely that the son inherited from the father a family "tradition"—albeit extending back only one generation—of opposing the attenuation of payments to the artist resulting from false wares being circulated on the market. Early in the 1856 novella *A Rogue's Life,* a story appearing in both *Household Words* and *Harper's Weekly,* we find a passage implying that piracy had been a prominent issue throughout Collins's lifetime, for it possibly indirectly affected the payments his eminent painter father—perhaps referred to in the following passage's allusion to the "famous artists of the English school"—received for his paintings. The Rogue's championing of the wronged contemporary English artists turns into a discoursing upon the evils of the nobles' lack of an ability to discriminate between the good and the bad, the original and the forgery, when buying Old Masters:

> The unfortunate artist had no court of appeal that he could turn to. . . . For one nobleman who was ready to buy one genuine modern picture at a small price, there were twenty noblemen ready to buy twenty more than doubtful old pictures at great prices. The consequence was, that some of the most famous artists of the English school, whose pictures are now bought at auction sales for fabulous sums, were then hardly able to make an income. They were a scrupulously patient and conscientious body of men, who would as soon have thought of breaking into a house, or equalising the distribution of wealth, on the highway, by the simple machinery of horse and pistol, as of making Old Masters to Order. They sat resignedly in their lonely studios, surrounded by unsold pictures which have since been covered again and again with gold and banknotes by eager buyers at auctions and show-rooms, whose money has gone into other than the painter's pockets—who have never dreamed that the painter had the smallest moral right to a farthing of it. (*Rogue's Life* 41–42)

Disclosing the vast number of forgeries circulating in the marketplace was one way to help the struggling contemporary artist, working in either paints or ink, to put food on his table. For Collins, it was a moral imperative to find a means of educating the connoisseur as to the difference between an original and a copy of an Old Master, consonant with sensitizing the reader with regard to which copy of the woman in white, or perhaps that should be *The Woman in White*, was the Fair(lie) copy and which the bad.[33]

On the other hand, Collins's unusual *openness* to the breaking function can *also* be ascribed, in part, to what seems a family tradition, only one extending one generation further back. Collins's grandfather William Collins wrote in 1805 a novel—providing the first epigraph to this chapter—drawing on his experiences in the picture-dealing trade entitled *Memoirs of a Picture*. In that story an original renaissance masterpiece by a painter named Guido is continually confused with one of its two illicit reproductions over the course of a series of changes in possession and its movement through several European countries. The grandson devoted

---

33. Along these lines, it is appropriate that Collins should have had a major part of the narrative of *The Woman in White* be taken up with the reestablishment of the lost tie between Walter Hartright, called "the artist" (191), and the Fairlie copy, or that late manuscript revision before printing, the "fair copy." Laura Fairlie thus becomes when viewed from this perspective the literary artist's stolen manuscript.

several early pages in his biography of his famous painter father, his first major published work, to a painstaking summary of the complicated plot of his grandfather's novel. In his précis of his grandfather's life, Collins mentioned William Collins's two careers "as a man of letters and a dealer in pictures" and the "remarkable influence that his knowledge of art and artists had in determining his son in following the career in which he was afterwards destined to become eminent" (*Memoirs of the Life* 5). Like Charles Darwin, Collins may have ventured forth on his chosen career path—also, quite literally, as a "man of letters"—in an attempt simply to perfect his own paternal grandfather's muddled thinking. At one point in the story we come across a passage expressing a surprisingly cavalier attitude toward authenticity, a passage that might not be expected in a novel written by a professional picture dealer. A very "worldly" perspective on the trace's borderlessness is expressed by the aptly-named Sir Disney Doubtful, the belief that being happy in one's ignorance about an entity's originality, being happy in a fiction, might be better than having an expert come along and disabuse one:

> You must know . . . that there are now, and ever have been, a number of ingenious artists, in various places upon the continent, whose sole employment is copying the works of the great masters of antiquity; and, by a singular species of legerdemain, well known to some of their brethren here, contriv[ing] to give them the fascinating mellowness which resembles the tint which can only be effectually given by time; and in this species of trick they are too often successful. Such has been the case with me, repeatedly; and I make no doubt but every one of our friends here has experienced in his turn the same deception, and has been as much pleased with it, till some stern obtruding judge has made us *wise,* at the *expence* of our *delight.*
> (William Collins, *Memoirs* 3:163–64; emphasis in original)

There are two very different ways of reading this situation: (1) as the valorization of settling in Doubtful's exhibiting such a respect for originality as to lose all delight on having fabrications disclosed, or (2) as the acceptance of breaking in Doubtful's wishing for a near-complete divorce from reality as a means of remaining happy in his ignorance. The transition between these two standpoints maps out the concerns of the fictions of the major phase of the career of William Collins's grandson. It is as Wilkie Collins (christened William Collins, like both his father and grandfather before him) matures as a writer that he begins expressing a more open-minded attitude toward the possibility of controlling traces, finally accepting, even as he may well regret having acquired the knowledge, that they will always face the peril of potentially becoming alienated from their source.

Poe's Warning

During his 1842 trip to the United States, Dickens had met twice with Edgar Allan Poe in March in Philadelphia (Poe, *Complete Works* 184). Whether or not they discussed The Inimitable's desire to save the American moral character by pushing through the passage of an international copyright agreement is impossible to determine, though highly likely.[34] It is noteworthy that Poe would be predicting in late 1845 in one of his "marginalia" the coming of a resultant backlash against American piracy:

> We get more reading for less money than if the international law existed; but the remoter disadvantages are of infinitely greater weight. . . . The last and by far the most important consideration of all . . . is that sense of insult and injury aroused in the whole active intellect of the world, the bitter and fatal resentment excited in the universal heart of literature—a resentment which will not and which cannot make nice distinctions between the temporary perpetrators of the wrong and that democracy in general which permits its perpetration. The autorial [*sic*] body is the most autocratic on the face of the earth. How, then, can those institutions even hope to be safe which systematically persist in trampling it under foot?[35] (Poe, *Works* 3:580–81)

---

34. They showed a fellow feeling on this issue. Poe, in the first number of his *Broadway Journal,* explained in early 1845 why he would predominantly be reviewing American books: "this liberal feeling will compel us to give our first attention and widest space to the authors of our own country, because they have the greatest odds to contend with, having a forestalled opinion against them in the minds of their own countrymen, and the best paid and most fertile authors in the world for competitors, whose works are imported scot free to our markets" ("Reviews" 2).

35. Similarly, Emerson would write in his journals in March of 1854: "The lesson of these days is the vulgarity of wealth. We know that wealth will vote for the same thing which the worst and meanest of the people vote for. Wealth will vote for rum, will vote for tyranny, will vote for slavery, will vote against the ballot, will vote against international copyright, will vote against schools, colleges, or any high direction of public money" (Emerson 150–51). In the anonymous *A Plea for Authors and the Rights of Literary Property* of 1838, a work possibly co-authored by Washington Irving (Rice 90), we read, "The national welfare of a people, in the time of our forefathers, was considered to have no surer basis than independence and moral honesty. Robbery has in no code of modern political science been made the basis of national aggrandizement" ("Literary Property," *New York Review* 301). These American authors' sentiments, while not the only, and indeed perhaps not the prevailing, ones in everyday American intellectual culture, adequately reflect, I believe, the daylight opinions of the young Collins.

Ominously, there was—according to Poe, arguably the king of the porten-
tous statement—no "safety" for those committing textual wrongs.

It is not surprising to find these sentiments expressed by an author who
elsewhere has one character comment to another, "[D]id there not cross
your mind some thought of the *physical power of words? Is not every word
an impulse on the air?*" (Poe, "Power of Words," *Poetry* 825; emphasis in
original) and who composes stories of unruly guilty consciences undoing
individual characters, such as "The Tell-Tale Heart" (1843) and "The Black
Cat" (1843). Not surprisingly, "The Purloined Letter" of 1844 would also
fit this scenario of revenge being exacted for textual crimes. At its end we
have revealed to us the words that Dupin writes in the letter substituted for
the purloined one: "—Un dessein si funeste, / S'il n'est digne d'Atrée, est
digne de Thyeste" (Poe, *Poetry* 698). Barbara Johnson writes of this riposte,
"Atreus, whose wife was long ago seduced by Thyestes, is about to make
Thyestes eat (literally) the fruit of that illicit union, his son Plisthenes. The
avenger's plot may not be worthy of *him,* says Atreus, but his brother Thyestes deserves it. What the addressee of the violence is going to get is simply
his own message backwards" (Johnson, "Frame" 466). Receiving "[one's]
own message backwards" is a good description of what Poe fears might happen to the Americans at the hands of the British authors whom they had
been wronging since 1790. Poe is worried that the British will counter this
American textual violence with some textual violence of their own, which
might not be worthy of them but which *would* be worthy of the Americans.

It is not surprising to find in 1860 an author of a best-selling English
novel of this period—and additionally an intimate friend of Dickens—
to be fulfilling Poe's fears. Emrys argues that "Collins's most important
detection-relation antecedent for his multiple testaments is not . . . trials
and cases but Poe's stories" (25). Collins may well have taken more than
just lessons in narrative style from Poe's works. The narrator of "A Stolen
Letter" leaves behind in place of the incriminating letter one that reads
"Change for a five hundred pound note" (*Mad Monkton* 37). This is a literary foreshadowing of the somewhat longer "backwards message" he will
deliver to the Americans in the form of *The Woman in White.* As we saw
in the last chapter, Collins was not averse to using his fictions for the purpose of ideological manipulation. In that novel he will once again deploy
tactics like those employed in *Basil,* this time with the particular political
goal of shaming the Americans into adopting an international copyright
agreement, albeit with his villainous creation Fosco ending up more seductive (even for his creator) than Collins had expected. One sort of "sharp
practice" often engendering another, the covert shaming of the Americans

is a move of which his friend and publisher Dickens, if not also the judges in *Jeffereys v. Boosey,* most certainly would not have disapproved.

The Boat-House Scene

There can be no better entrée into understanding what Collins is attempting to do in the narrative of *The Woman in White* than that provided by a close study of the boat-house discussion between the male and female residents of Blackwater Park. Taking place about one-third of the way through the narrative and containing "one of [Fosco's] most sustained monologues in the text" (Tromp 85), this is, to my mind, a pivotal episode, for it stands out, in this otherwise non-stop narrative, for its temporizing and precise nature. No other scene of comparable length is so patently lacking in forward impetus with regard to the setting up or resolution of the plot. Thus the significance of the scene (given that this is a Collins novel) must rise in direct proportion to its apparent lack of necessity. As well, in the process of introducing the scene our narrator Marian Halcombe gives us an indication that Collins may be attempting to pass on some sort of coded message in it. Marian writes,

> At the old boat-house [Sir Percival] joined us again. I will put down the conversation that ensued, when we were all settled in our places, *exactly as it passed.* It is an important conversation, so far as I am concerned, for it has seriously disposed me to distrust the influence which Count Fosco has exercised over my thoughts and feelings, and to resist it, for the future, as resolutely as I can. (233; emphasis added)

Despite Marian's attempted justification, the ensuing conversation hardly warrants, on the face of it, this concern with verbatim recording. The practical effect of her fastidiousness, however, is to have certain especially suggestive phrases entered into the literary Record (as well as into the larger context of the Anglo-American copyright dispute going on at the time). In addition, we readers will have the opportunity to be graced with the Count's already-cited wisdom regarding the relativity of morality in an international context and the need for latitude in assigning blame with regard to moral issues.

It is not surprising that during the conversation the Count should ridicule Laura's naive moral sentiments as being appropriate to a child's handwriting primer. He remarks, "My dear lady . . . those are admirable sentiments; and I have seen them stated at the tops of copy-books" (235).

Indeed, the American publisher whom Fosco represents would presumably ridicule in a similarly belittling manner (and so does[36]) any attempt at ascribing a simple moral schema of good-versus-bad—Percival Glyde's label for this schema is that of a "copy-book morality" (235)—onto the nineteenth-century Anglo-American "copy-book" system or—to use less childishly literal, more traditional terminology—the publishing trade. Here this potentially politically-charged phrase that ostensibly would be attempting to pass itself off as a simple reference to the school-age practice of repeatedly copying out a particular phrase in order to fill up blank pages and, aside from improving one's handwriting, *learning a moral lesson* in the process (such as, to propose a not so random example, "Pirating this book is wrong. Pirating this book is wrong. . . .") concisely encapsulates the allegory at the heart of *The Woman in White*. There is good reason for the latter half of the text's reading less like a standard sensation novel and more like a morality play. It is a sign of Collins's attempt at turning their practice against the American pirates, that is, at creating a situation in which they can be seen to be, so to speak, hoist with their own petard. It is not surprising that Hartright should condemn "the vile manner in which the personal resemblance between the woman in white and Lady Glyde had been *turned to account*" (*Woman in White* 439–40; emphasis added) as though he were commenting on some sort of specific usage of other people's literary creations for personal monetary gain. Nor is it surprising that the critic Walter Kendrick should characterize Glyde's deception in words that could work as well to describe a nineteenth-century American pirate publisher: "Sir Percival owes his power and position to a few lines of writing where there ought to be a space" (30). These signs all suggest that, ironically, this book, generally acknowledged as having given birth to the "immoral" genre of sensation fiction, is instead

---

36. See for example the argument of Henry C. Carey: "Read *Bleak House,* and you will find that [Mr. Dickens] has been a most careful observer of men and things. . . . He is in the condition of a man who had entered a large garden and collected a variety of the most beautiful flowers growing therein, of which he had made a fine bouquet . . . [yet he] insist[s] that he is owner of the bouquet itself, although he has paid no wages to the man who raised the flowers" (*Letters* 20, 25). Carey would also reference England's introduction of slavery into her colonies and her ill-treatment of the Irish as justifications for denying English authors American copyright. As absurd as these arguments and analogies must strike us now, Carey's was at the time a significant standpoint: "the *status quo* had its defenders also; their argument was most ably presented by Henry C. Carey, economist and publisher, in his *Letters on International Copyright* (1853)" (Mott, *History* 1:393). Not every American was convinced, however. E. L. Godkin in 1868 in *The Nation* was writing, "a man of Mr. Carey's powers is inexcusable in bringing such loose thinking as we have in the pamphlet before us to bear on a question which so deeply affects the national morality as well as the national culture" (148); and in 1879 an anonymous author comments, "Henry C. Carey . . . wrote several pamphlets *against* international copyright, which contained some of the best arguments in *favor* of that only practical remedy for the wrong and injustice done to authors, American and foreign" ([Stylus] 17).

actually concerned with instructing a young nation in how to have a moral conscience.

These "copy-book morals" that the sophisticated Fosco so urbanely deprecates as "comfortable moral maxims" (*Woman in White* 236) and that he so manifestly lacks will prove more astute than he had given them credit for when—in the scene at the opera in which he self-incriminatingly flees from a startled Professor Pesca—the otherwise accomplished equanimity that had allowed him to bring off the audacious plot of substituting one woman (or *Woman*) for another will be completely overthrown, thereby teaching him, as himself the case in point, the moral and literal lesson that crimes indeed *do* "cause their own detection" (235). Laura's cipher-like vacuousness, which has been remarked by many critics—D. A. Miller included: "The same internment that renders Laura's body docile, and her mind imbecile, . . . fits her to incarnate the norm of the submissive Victorian wife" (172)[37]—may or may not mark her as the prototypical Victorian wife, but it certainly serves well as an analogue for that fundamental uncontrollable transferability (the breaking function), and therefore fundamental vulnerability to violation, that characterizes writing (or indeed any form of expression), thereby quite effectively highlighting her allegorical status as the stand-in for the inanimate book that is in danger of being pirated. That is, when the allegory has been demystified, Collins's Angel in the House is disclosed to be, rather, the book in the closet.

The Marian–Fosco Scene

Returning to our framing discussion, I would point out that "empty formalism" while it may lead on the one hand to a radical interpretation of Anglo-American copyright history leads on the other to a fairly standard one—up to a point—of *The Woman in White*. In fact my analysis here will be following closely in the tradition—attention however this time being paid primarily to the American literary market—established by the breaking function–focused critic U. C. Knoepflmacher, a commentator intent on discovering Count Fosco to be introducing into the narrative a Victorian rebellious "'counterworld' that is asocial and amoral, unbound by the restraints of the socialized superego" (352).[38] Knoepflmacher contends that "*The Woman in*

---

37. See also Barickman, MacDonald, and Stark similarly writing, "[Laura] is so passive, so acquiescent to the various men who rule her life, and so incapable of assisting in her own rescue that she seems a parody" (114).

38. Following in the tradition of Knoepflmacher's assertion that Collins gives a "fuller hearing than any of his English predecessors to the antisocial voice of the [English] Rebel" (366–67), the

White depicts a collision between a lawful order in which identities are fixed and an anarchic lawlessness in which those social identities can be erased and destroyed" (362). As such, his interpretation acknowledges an aspect of this narrative that must remain more or less opaque—or visible only in the guise of its opposite—to a perspective influenced by Michel Foucault's concept of "discipline," a concept growing out of, as outlined in his *Discipline and Punish,* the consummately settling-valorizing procedures deployed to combat the plague's effects on bodies in seventeenth-century France:

> The plague is met by order; its function is to sort out every possible confusion. . . . A whole literary fiction of the festival grew up around the plague: suspended laws, lifted prohibitions . . . individuals . . . abandoning their statutory identity. . . . But there was also a political dream of the plague, which was exactly its reverse: not the collective festival but strict divisions; not laws transgressed, but the penetration of regulation into even the smallest details of everyday life through the mediation of the complete hierarchy that assured the capillary functioning of power; not masks that were put on and taken off, but the assignment to each individual of his "true" name, his "true" place, his "true" body, his "true" disease. The plague as a form, at once real and imaginary, of disorder had as its medical and political correlative discipline. (197–98)

Knoepflmacher's analysis thus finds evidence in the social sphere of the narrative, and literary culture at large, of what I am describing here as the eruption of the breaking function from its home in the theoretical realm into that of the social while the Foucauldian perspective, in focusing on procedures for ensuring that bodies are tenaciously tied to names, suggests an allegiance to (or at least serious focus on) settling. This tension will not be easily resolved. That the Foucault-inspired critic D. A. Miller should have chosen a narrative by Collins, the creator of some very determined identity

---

most recent adherent to the line of breaking-function-oriented-but-Anglo-limited interpretations is Cannon Schmitt who, sensing a particular non-Englishness to be at work in the novel, endeavors in his article "Alien Nation: Gender, Genre, and English Nationality in Wilkie Collins's *The Woman in White*" to make that alienness comment back upon a split English psyche. Schmitt finds a schizophrenic distanciation to be imposed by the novel on its English reader that the narrative then works to recuperate through the mechanics of a difference-respecting type of assimilation. Using Foucault's understanding in the first volume of *The History of Sexuality* of the way in which repression and subversion are both eventually equally co-opted (not quite through a production of the same but rather of a manageable difference) by the System through a collapse into the more general "discourse of sexuality," Schmitt finds the sensation novel's mixing of Realist and Gothic conventions to be resulting in a momentary schizophrenia that is thereafter successfully contained within the singular psyche of an English national consciousness.

changing and exchanging characters, a tendency especially prevalent in this particular one of his narratives, to be the exemplar of Foucauldian disciplining must already set off alarm bells. Knoepflmacher's contention that "Unlike Dickens . . . Collins never disguised his fascination with the amorality of the counterworld" (360) makes much the same point. We will in this section be investigating the radical difference in interpretation to which these differing philosophical ideals lead and demonstrating once more the danger inherent in considering solely the settling function at the expense of its breaking counterpart as well as that inherent in positing solely the existence of a "manageable" type of breaking as opposed to one that might be managing *us*.

KNOEPFLMACHER'S position serves as an excellent foil against which to judge the impressive novelty of D. A. Miller's gender-history- and Foucauldian-settling-influenced construal of that narrative. Miller acknowledges his debt to Foucault early on in his book:

> What has been standing at the back of my argument up to now, and what I hope will allow me to carry it some steps further, is the general history of the rise of disciplinary power, such as provided by Michel Foucault in *Surveiller et punir*. . . . Traditional power founded its authority in the spectacle of its force, and those on whom this power was exercised could, conversely, remain in the shade. By contrast, disciplinary power tends to remain invisible, while imposing on those whom it subjects "a principle of compulsory visibility" ([*Discipline and Punish*] 187). . . . The aim of such regulation is to enforce not so much a norm as the normality of normativeness itself. Rather than in rendering all its subjects uniformly "normal," discipline is interested in putting in place a perceptual grid in which a division between the normal and the deviant inherently imposes itself. (16–18)

This disciplinary power is, in Miller's hands, very much one operating in a straightforward, settling-valorizing manner. Earlier Miller has described his variety of discipline as one leading to "a regime of the norm, in which normalizing perceptions, prescriptions, and sanctions are diffused in discourses and practices throughout the social fabric" (viii). Millerian discipline, in content as well as form, would seem to be proving itself to be as old as the hills here.

In a surprising interpretive move, Miller, in stark contrast to Knoepflmacher, finds *the Count*, as opposed to the narrative's more "upright" characters, to be an agent working in behalf of this "regime of the norm." He understands him to be a character whose only-apparently-trangressive actions turn out actually to be quite in line with—when viewed from the context of Victorian discourses about sexuality, as well as Foucauldian ones about a prevalence of "hierarchical surveillance, normalization, and the development of a subjectivity supportive of both" (D. A. Miller 18)— contemporary social mores and other disciplinary processes. According to Miller, the Count is a conservative agent working to effect society's wish for a normative heterosexuality to come to discipline the novel's readers' illicit homosexual desires. Adopting Karl Ulrichs's formulation casting (and caging) the male homosexual as a person exhibiting symptoms of the woman inside or "the woman-in-the-man," he argues—through a virtuoso reading of Walter Hartright's panic at being touched on the shoulder at night by Anne Catherick on the road near Hampstead Heath (D. A. Miller 152–56)—that the narrative's dual projects of recapturing a particular woman escaped from an asylum and of bringing under control the assumedly male reader's recurrent nervousness, that femininity inside to which the novel insistently will nevertheless be bringing him to consciousness, are linked in the novel's generalized desire to keep "the woman" bound. Appropriately, Miller has qualified Ulrichs's ambivalently valedictory woman-in-the-man formulation beforehand. Not only does it participate in a misogynistic cultural strategy of incarcerating females; it also participates in the homophobic caging or self-closeting of the male homosexual: "Meant to win a certain intermediate space for homosexuals, Ulrichs's formulation in fact ultimately colludes with the prison or closet drama—of keeping the 'woman' well put away—that it would relegate to the unenlightened past" (155). This rescinding of the release-order suggested by Miller's teleological phrasing here, his laying stress on the "ultimate" loss of the legible "intermediate" space for homosexuals, foreshadows, it would seem, his subsequent carceral interpretation of the progression of the entire narrative of *The Woman in White*. It is not only Walter Hartright who would seem to need to make recourse to a "violent counteraction," a panicked self-enforced recloseting, when the feminine nervousness inside threatens to break free (as he does when he "tightens his fingers round 'the handle of [his] stick'" in order to "reaffirm" his ostensible-but-threatened gender identification [152]). The novel as a whole would, according to Miller, also seem to need to proscribe in its latter half what it had in its reckless earlier sections practiced.

If either of Knoepflmacher's or Miller's starkly opposed stances regarding the Count's role in the narrative—as lawless versus lawful entity— is to maintain its validity, it must convincingly correlate with the

startling turnabout encountered in the scene of Fosco's most shocking
transgression/disciplinary exploit in the narrative, his usurpation of the role
of narrator of the story when he takes Marian Halcombe's diary from her
after she has fallen into a delirium at the close of an eavesdropping adventure. This changeover—both an actualization of the breaking function of
iterability at the same time that it is an instance of unexpected surveillance,
or as one critic puts it, "a remarkable moment of reversal in which our
readerly intimacy with Marian is violated, our act of reading adulterated
by profane eyes" (Brooks 169)—delivers a considerable readerly shock and
neurasthenic lesson. The fact that I would, following Knoepflmacher, propose viewing this scene to be actuating all the uncanniness inherent in the
disquieting potential held out by the breaking function of the iterability of
the word—through its mimicking of the especially prevalent nineteenth-
century Anglo-American experience of having writing deviate toward
"improper" readers—is as unsurprising as the fact that Miller's settling-
influenced precepts should lead him to see precisely the opposite to be
occurring. Placing textual considerations ahead of gender-based ones, I
believe that we American readers of Collins's allegory of piracy are being
situated *in the position of the textual thief Fosco*—tellingly, a somewhat differently nuanced, in both structure and content, situation than the characterization Miller gives to the scene: "the Count's postscript only puts him in
the position we [readers in general] already occupy" (164). Miller's particular understanding of the situation—with Fosco seen as a settling-valorizing
reader rather than a breaking-valorizing textual thief—is necessitated by his
argument's emphasis on the internalization of discipline through "containment," specifically of a nascent homosexuality by heterosexuality. In launching this argument, Miller makes the scene of Fosco's reading of Marian's
diary the fulcrum of his analysis:

> It is not only, then, that Marian has been "raped." . . . We are "taken" too,
> taken by surprise, which is itself an overtaking. We are taken, moreover,
> from behind: from a place where, in the wings of the ostensible drama, the
> novelist disposes of a whole plot machinery whose existence . . . we never
> suspected. . . . To being the object of violation here, however, there is an
> equally disturbing alternative: to identify with Fosco, with the novelistic
> agency of violation. For the Count's postscript only puts him in the position
> we already occupy. Having just finished reading Marian's diary ourselves,
> we are thus implicated in the sadism of his act, which even as it violates
> our readerly intimacy with Marian reveals that "intimacy" to be itself a
> violation. The ambivalent structure of readerly identification here thus

condenses—as simultaneous but opposite renderings of the same powerful shock—homosexual panic and heterosexual violence.[39] (164)

For Miller, the Count, in surprising the reader here, is putting him through a degree of panic by once more bringing out his feminine nervousness and at the same time re-educating that excessively nervous reader by training him in "heterosexual violence." Here, it would seem, we have played out in front of us, on more than one register, that "penetration of regulation" described at one point by Foucault (*Discipline* 198). In other words, the male reader is being disciplined by Collins's narrative in the common Victorian homophobic strategy of closeting the woman-in-the-man at the same time that he is being taught to want to be inside the woman.[40]

---

39. The manifest difficulties of shifting from the situation in which Fosco "takes" the reader to the situation of the reader "taking" Marian is a sign of the effort involved in Miller's turn against the tide of the narrative.

40. Miller's interpretation goes on to contend that the Marian–Fosco scene is itself serving to transform the genre of Collins's narrative. The scene's radical alteration of perspective, the usurpation of narratorial control that it recounts and the consequent viewing of the situation from the other side that it effects, reproduces for him the path of Ulrichs's ultimately collusive formulation, the change in narrators offering a local rendering of the larger shift of the novel's plot from the genre of Victorian sensation fiction to that of domestic fiction, from the genre of homosexual panic to the genre of heterosexual violence. The established paradigms of homosexual panic and the woman-in-the-man reach their logical conclusions, and collusions, at the point where this narrative comes to close off that intermediate space in which homosexual panic had once found haven, finally, allowing the narrative to successfully do what it had only been threatening to in the Walter–Anne scene, that is, when it finally successfully "jumps out of its skin" the more effectively to be able to turn back on itself and slap on the normative cuffs. Thus, according to Miller, we have homosexual panic countered and contained by the traditional story of heterosexuality. Indeed, that it is in this case a violent heterosexuality is all the more understandable as this "rape," to use Miller's term for Fosco's act, elaborates an earlier-introduced, and quite unpersuasive, discussion of reading-as-usual being a figurative "raping" of the text, with the exception somehow in the case of sensation fiction, in which case the act of reading becomes necessarily a figurative being-raped (D. A. Miller 162–63). As marking the transfer, then, of readerly identification from the figuratively raped Marian Halcombe to the figuratively raping Count Fosco, the scene, as interpreted by Miller, is *doubly* marking—as a conforming to genre specifications both with regard to reader-manipulation as well as with regard to content (tumultuous sexuality being replaced by strict heterosexuality)—the transition from sensation fiction to "normal," or more properly normalized, fiction. Punning on the narrative's apparent "straightening" out, Miller writes, "Foremost on the novel's agenda in its second half is the dissolution of sensation in the achievement of decided meaning. What the narrative must most importantly get straight is, from this perspective, as much certain sexual and gender deviances as the obscure tangles of plot in which they thrive. In short, the novel needs to realize the normative requirements of the heterosexual menage whose happy picture concludes it. This conclusion, of course, marks the most banal moment in the text, when the sensation novel becomes least distinguishable from any other kind of Victorian fiction" (165). I would argue, however, that we do not have in this particular scene a generic (or genericizing) *change* in its reversion to the norm, but rather a *continuation* of the earlier "breaking genre" with which we had begun, a taking of the earlier warnings announced by the narrative to their dreaded conclusions or horizons. In Fosco's indiscretion we have a radicalization, as opposed to normalization, of the

There are two significant collapsings occurring in Miller's rather breezy pronouncement, "To being the object of violation here, however, there is an equally disturbing alternative: to identify with Fosco, with the novelistic agency of violation" (164). First, Miller's loose employment of the term "novel"—potentially meaning either text or book—in the description of Fosco as "the novelistic agency of violation," unfortunately hides more than it illuminates. While it is true that both Marian and Fosco take turns serving as first-person narrators of the story and that they describe the same scenes from differing vantage points, that is, adopting Gerard Gennette's narratological terms, that they occupy the same "extradiegetic-homodiegetic" standpoint of "a narrator in the first degree who tells his [or her] own story" in a multiply-zero-level-focalized epistolary-style narrative (Genette, *Narrative Discourse* 248 and 190), it is a mistake to find them to be situated at precisely the same level. Their positions vary with regard to the issue of what I would describe as their "worldliness" or "archness" in relation to the concept of linguistic "discipline," in other words, to their attitudes towards the workings of iterability. Marian's is a sincere and very English or England-bound settling approach to discipline, one that acknowledges that "crimes cause their own detection." Fosco's, on the other hand, is a worldly or breaking one in which "foolish criminals . . . are discovered, and wise criminals [and presumably also texts] . . . escape" (*Woman in White* 236). He could be described as a "resident alien" with regard not just to England—"In the summer of eight hundred and fifty, I arrived in England, charged with a delicate political mission from abroad" (614)—but also to English values and straightforward disciplining. Consequently, he possesses, unlike Marian, the startling capability of ascending from what I might call, figuratively, the "level of the narrative" to the "level of the book." Second, we should note a subtle collapse to be occurring when Miller refers to our "identify[ing] with Fosco, with the novelistic agency of [implicitly sexual] violation." We need not too quickly follow him here in allowing the sensationalism of his final clause to overpower and efface the significant ramifications of his previous one, that is, to cancel the identification taking place *apart from* the Count's being seen as "the novelistic agency of [Marian's text's, and therefore body's] violation." The already-mentioned ambiguity inherent in the word "novel" is allowing Miller at this moment also to effect this collapse. "Novelistic" here is clearly intended to mean narrative-level as opposed to book-level. Thus, the term "extra-novelistic" might more accurately have been used

---

narrative's "sensations." Only after this scene is *complete*—admittedly, a slight, but crucial, distinction—as I will argue later in this chapter, do we have the narrative altering to a common, conservative "settling genre" production.

to describe Fosco's—as opposed to Marian's simply "novelistic"—immediate position. Here Miller has improperly collapsed the beyond-England-diegetic and England-diegetic domains, having put the former turn by the reader, the turning to Fosco's perspective of "extra-novelistic violation," on the same level as the reader's turn to Marian's perspective of "novelistic violation."

Having broken ourselves out of the cage of "the novel," we might consider, pausing for a moment to emphasize the breaking aspects of this scene more than its straightforward disciplining, what it means simply to "identify with Fosco," as textual thief rather than sexual violater or mere reader. Despite Miller's significant investment of rhetorical and critical energy in establishing Marian's body as the gravitational center of the interactions taking place in this scene, this effort is not enough to completely obscure the scene's explosive, expansive, and indeed expatriate, elements. At its end, we learn that we have Fosco's own "strict sense of propriety" (*Woman in White* 344) to thank for his having restored Marian's diary (the form at least, the content having already been viewed and reviewed) to her desk so that she might have the chance of passing it along through a process of verbal transcription, at the conclusion of a veritable assembly-line of book production, to Walter Hartright, our general editor, so that we might now be reading it. This scene replays the overall narrative's structure, an initial unsuccessful flirtation with the powers of breaking that ends up in a turn back to settling, Marian's diary's replacement in her desk standing as a prefiguring of Laura Fairlie's reestablishment in her identity at the conclusion. To put it simply, I contend that it is a literal rather than sexual (or, if you like, a theoretical rather than historical) criminality that interpellates the Fosco-identifying reader of this scene. Indeed, the outward and upward movement of the reader identifying with Fosco, that shocking extra-novelistic distention that carries her into the circumscriptive region of the beyond-narrative, would seem seriously to put in question Miller's carceral and containing characterization of the scene.[41] For, contrary to his depiction, nothing's boring inwards here. Rather, I would hold, the narrative is exhuming or exiling itself outwards, as it erupts into the book level. In Collins's allegory of the U.S.

---

41. It is strange for Miller's rhetoric of containment to have fixed upon Fosco as its hero. For it would seem the narrative had specifically marked him out as manifestly defying all would-be restrictions. "[H]e is immensely fat," Marian writes in her diary, apprizing us of perhaps his most memorable characteristic (*Woman in White* 220). Continuing her description, once again she remarks his "excessive grossness in size" (220). This physical "excess"—rendering the Count a character in a sense both within and without his body (he may be wearing a fat suit as part of a disguise)—will be matched by his excesses in the diegetic domain.

piracy of English works, Fosco mimics America's undisciplined discipline, or disciplining in non-discipline, through the deployment of a "shadow" or "worldly" disciplining that merely looks like straightforward Foucauldian disciplining. To read this state of affairs as an example of simple settling-valorizing disciplining is to improperly cancel out one half of iterability's workings as well as to foreclose on the possibility for the existence of other, less straightforward forms of discipline that might be arising from the uncanny effects of the breaking function. To see more clearly the distinction that I am proposing we need to look at the precise point at which Collins's thinking parts from that of Miller's model Foucault.

Parody as an Oversight for the System of Oversight

Once again, it should be emphasized that Foucault's theory of discipline is developed strictly in relation to the control of material entities, specifically bodies, as opposed to iterable traces. He finds the type of radically one-sided and deeply internalized disciplining he labels Panopticism to be the end product of two distinct social mechanisms, the mechanisms for dealing with plague and with lepers:

> Underlying disciplinary projects the image of the plague stands for all forms of confusion and disorder; just as the image of the leper, cut off from all human contact, underlies projects of exclusion. . . . All the mechanisms of power which, even today, are disposed around the abnormal individual, to brand him and to alter him, are composed of those two forms from which they distinctly derive. Bentham's *Panopticon* is the architectural figure of this composition. (Foucault, *Discipline* 199–200)

It should go without saying that bodies are not the same things as words. Yet, as I have been arguing, the two entities are continually conflated by outlooks that would be finding material-world settling to be the sum total of the effects characterizing iterable traces.

The direct result of the attempted imposition of a body-centered philosophy onto textual elements is the shunting off to the side—as "negativities"—the breaking aspects of iterability. The critic is forever thereafter obliged to expend time and energy on the project of actively ignoring these, for, unfortunately, the breaking function will keep returning. Foucault assumes a standard, single form of discipline to be at work. But with language there exist *two* forms, one growing out of a desire to control the characteristics of the settling view characterizing its material and meaning-determining aspects (Marian's perspective) and another growing out of a desire to control those of the breaking view characterizing its immaterial and decontextualizing aspects (Fosco's perspective). All of the negativities ignored by the settling world-view can be ecompassed within the non-normative, even in some ways anti-normative, concept of "parody." That concept, a direct offshoot of breaking, allows here for the coming into being of a situation where disciplining, while still operating as "disciplining," comes, from outside, to instruct an inner normality in deviance, all the while allowing the critic (or historian) arriving later to read it "seriously" as does Miller when he perceives the situation to be one of an inner "deviance" being taught by a surrounding normality to closet itself. It is a mark of Miller's considerable versatility that his rhetoric should have been able to successfully render the former an instance of the latter.

Derrida sorts out a similar self-blindering when he considers the work of the English language philosopher J. L. Austin. Austin's attempt at solidly founding his distinction between constative and performative speech acts is, according to Derrida, an attempt wholly given over to actually ignoring language's fundamentally uncontrollable negativities:

> [Austin] says that "we need to develop a general theory," but at that moment he doesn't construct it. Now, what's remarkable is that the general theory concerns precisely all the phenomena of failure, all the phenomena of negativity, of what we call the nonserious, the anomaly, the parasite, etc. What seems to me unfortunate in this incompleteness is that the fact of taking account of a negativity—let's summarize all of these [phenomena] under the heading of negativity—coextensive with all of discourse would have led him to define this negativity not as an accidental fact in the sense traditional philosophy most often takes the negative, like an accident, but as a structural element of the law of speech acts. While developing this general theory, he wouldn't have been able to push all the parasites aside. Under the heading of the parasite we find precisely the phenomenon of citation which seems to be indissolubly linked to the structure of every mark. This means that I don't think a mark can be constituted without its being able to be cited. Therefore, the entire graphematic structure is connected to citationality, to the possibility of being repeated. (Derrida and Ricoeur 154)

Miller, like Austin, does not adequately address the breaking-function negativities being passed over, as a matter of structural constitution, by his outlook. Thus, it is necessary for the consistency of his argument (despite

Miller's attestation to the contrary) that his ideal reader never be allowed to *actually* assume Fosco's position, that is, his position as break-out artist with respect to Collins's fully realized representation of the readerly linguistic moment. Indeed, Miller's interpretation, in attempting to make Marian into Fosco and vice versa, that is, to merge the two, is more *disciplining* than the actual scene.

MILLER acknowledges that he is taking Foucault's thinking, through a self-described "intellectual gamble," into a region that the French philosopher studiously avoided: "[P]erhaps the most notable reticence in Foucault's work concerns precisely the reading of literary texts and literary institutions, which though often and suggestively cited in passing, are never given a role to play within the disciplinary processes under consideration" (D. A. Miller viii*n*1). I do not believe that Miller's gamble pays off. For it requires him to collapse bodies with iterable traces. Bodies not being subject in the same way as traces to the vagaries of iterability[42] (before the days of cloning and 3D printing at least), the latter are inevitably going to escape any restricted economies of disciplining or surveillance that might have been effective for the former.[43] The materiality of bodies is a hindrance to the ready passage from place to place characterizing traces. Thus, the "disciplining" that might work on them will not apply to iterable traces, or, to be precise, will apply in a similar manner *only to the settling side of those traces*. (Naturally then, a philosophy of straightforward disciplining [here I intend a reference more to Miller's would-be panoptical New Historicism applied to texts than to Foucault's historical/sociological panopticism applied to bodies] will have an interest in seeing solely the settling aspect of iterability). As a result of the incommensurability between texts and bodies, the laws of discipline, of social control, of political economy—specifically the logic of the economics of equivalent exchange and wealth from scarcity—will not apply in the

---

42. This is a distinction that Collins, with his puppet-like characters continually subject to breaking, does not always respect, as we will see in the next section's discussion of Laura Fairlie's vacuity.

43. I would cite in this context a remark—intimating in its excessively qualified structure the complex relationship between books and bodies—made by J. L. Knight-Bruce in his decision in *Prince Albert* (1849) when discussing the protection of literary property from "invasion": "this class of property, by nature not corporeal at all, or not exclusively corporeal, require[s] to be defended against incorporeal attacks, and not at all or not exclusively against bodily assaults" (312). Knight-Bruce touches on the fact that books and bodies require that different laws and disciplinary structures be applied to them. Therefore, to apply a discourse founded on bodily concepts and control to the situation of books or language, which are certainly not "bodies"—or at least not exclusively so—is eventually going to end up being distortive.

same way to books as they will to bodies. That particular form of economic logic that was labeled by Georges Bataille a "restricted economy" is constitutionally incapable of completely accounting for the movement of the trace. Iterable traces—on their immaterial side—are *also* subject to what Bataille labeled a "general economy":

> Sovereignty differs in no way from a limitless dissipation of "wealth," of substance; if we limited this dissipation, there would be a reserve for other moments, which would limit—*abolish*—the sovereignty of an immediate moment. . . . The question of this *general economy* is situated on the plain of the *political economy*, but the science designated by this name is only a *restricted economy* (restricted to market values). This is a question of the problem essential to the science treating the use of wealth. The *general economy* makes evident in the first place that a surplus of energy is produced that, by definition, cannot be used. Excess energy can only be lost without the slightest goal, in consequence without any meaning. It is this useless, senseless loss that *is* sovereignty. (284n5)

Leaving aside Bataille's liberational hyperbole, here we glimpse the other economic (and perhaps disciplinary) model that would be pertaining with regard to iterability. That other model accounts for some of the more disturbing (to systems founded on a restricted economy model) aspects of iterability. It is no accident that Bataille's rhetoric suggests the rhetoric of the French or American Revolution. It was the particularly "liberational" nature of the breaking function that was allowing the Americans in the mid-1800s to associate the "sovereignty"—or general economy of excessive and non-recuperable expenditure, to paraphrase Bataille—of iterable words with their own.

Thus, Miller's interpretation of an instance in Collins's text of a radical *breaking out* as one of a radical *settling in* is the result of his philosophical model's predisposition in favor of settling when that predisposition is faced with the Americans' parody of disciplining. America is able in the mid-nineteenth century to effect a "parodistic" disciplining, making an actual "something" out of the many bitter "nothings" contained in its copyright clause—in one case, as we saw, transforming English criticisms into American advertising matter—thereby fashioning out of the breaking function something that appears very much akin to straightforward, active discipline. The acts of breaking ourselves out of the prison-house established by Miller's outlook and of viewing the supplanting in the scene from a sufficiently detached perspective—a nineteenth-century transatlantic

one—allow us to perceive it as not so much an inwardly collapsing, con-
servational, carceral compulsion as an outwardly averting event or *escape.*
That is, we find ourselves presented with not so much an author-centered,
psychological redisciplining as an externally focused, readership-centered,
usurpation—one founded on the conceptualization of the book's readership as composed of "bad" American readers lifting the book from the
hands of the "good" English ones.[44] Fosco's illicit reading (and hence the
identification with him by the reader) is a fundamental shift at the level
of perspective. Miller's focus on the apparently conservative re-education
of the reader misses that radical perspectival alteration experienced by him
or her as a result of the to this point fundamentally carceral world of the
narrative being transformed into the fundamentally anti-carceral one of the
book. We have here a radical break out of the carceral modality (as indeed
we should have also out of the carceral critical mentality, since the narra-
tive-turning-to-book here is leaving behind Miller's hermetic body- and
prison-metaphors—or at least their constrictive charge) as now it would
seem that *the criminals were running the institutions.*

This is a more complicated situation than those simplistic [English]-
rebel-vs.-[English]-society-type interpretations (but nevertheless one that
can look exactly like them) of the type put forward by the long line of critics following Knoepflmacher. The "empty formalism" perspective has shown
us, shockingly, an entire society and social structure brazenly defying what
we had thought was a generalized normality coming to be only occasionally harassed by deviance. This enforced and unexpected recontextualization
is certainly shocking. The existence of an American culture that is at the
time effectively *parodying* disciplinarity, a sort of otherness within otherness (that does not collapse back into the self) casts the scene in terms of
a normality (Marian) that is being assaulted by a more populous deviance
(Fosco), in contrast to Miller's less-powerful deviance (homosexuality) being
"closeted" by—or closeting itself in response to—a surrounding normality
(heterosexuality). This situation causes us readers to realize that we have
been all along, in Wilkie Collins's eyes, deviants. The author has not been
on our side. We are indeed "brought into line" by Collins's narrative but

---

44. Gaylin argues that "By surprising us with the information that we are not the only readers
of this private document, Collins draws . . . [an] analogy between Fosco's intrusive behavior and
our sanctioned eavesdropping on Marian's private words and thoughts; he makes us recognize the
potentially transgressive nature of all reading" (129). I would of course revise this contention to read
" . . . the potentially transgressive nature of the reading by the nineteenth-century American readers
of their pirated editions." Later on in his project Collins will, of course, shift his focus of investigation
to the (self-)transgressive nature of all *writing.*

not into line with normality but, rather, into line with deviance, with the deviance of the nineteenth-century United States's attitude towards foreign intellectual property ownership. The shock that most definitely assaults the reader here is that which inheres in conclusively disclosing for herself, in Jean Baudrillard's term, "the satellization of the real,"[45] as the reader's belief in her essential goodness is turned into a satellite at the same time that England is turned into a satellite nation. In other words, Miller's at first glance seemingly outré interpretative standpoint turns out to be, in the final analysis, too conventional and conservative to properly come to terms with the power dynamics set in motion by what one might characterize as a struggle between particular national codes, that is, by the anomalous situation of the larger rogue state.

Foucault's hierarchical mechanism is too rigidly established to admit the entrance into the system of the "play" represented by parody. Foucault writes, "The enclosed, segmented space, observed at every point . . . in which power is exercised without division, according to a continuous hierarchical figure . . . all this constitutes a compact model of the disciplinary mechanism" (*Discipline* 197). This is a very humorless, or at least whimsy-less, philosophy. An example of the non-seriousness that evades Foucauldian discipline would be the copy that mimics the iterable shape of the shadow-imaged prisoner of the Panopticon, that is, the cardboard cut-out of the prisoner's body that fools the surveillance while the prisoner escapes. The disciplinary mechanism as it is understood by Foucault in *Discipline and Punish* makes no provision for false or deviant—take your pick—"disciplining" of the type represented by the Americans' proviso that nothing in their Copyright Act should be taken to prohibit the piracy of British books. It had been the bizarre effects of that former function that had allowed for the surprising situation of the Americans *encouraging* (or "disciplining") their citizenry in the practice of pirating English books. This is a world wholly beyond the ken of Foucauldian philosophy. Foucault's implicitly, so to speak, *Matrix*-embedded philosophical outlook is too "disciplined" to envision the possibility for the Americans to be recontextualizing on the other side of the Atlantic (as in the case of the *Blackwood's* advertisement and Fosco's intrusion into the diary) and redeploying criticisms *of* their practice as advertisements *for* it.

In contrast to the philosophers and literary critics, the novelists were more sensitive to the power and potential held out by parody or secret

45. *Simulations* 149. Another description of this process might be the "Red Pill moment" in the film *The Matrix*. See the discussion of the opening of *No Name* below for another example.

agency. Joseph Conrad remarked on the danger posed for a disciplinary system by the existence of parody in his *The Secret Agent*. In that story, the Assistant Commissioner, the most philosophically disposed disciplinary character, notes that it is the sham anarchist who presents true problems for the disciplinarial organizations operating in a standard (Foucauldian) manner that come into contact with them. The situation of the secret agent or *agent provocateur* working for a disciplinarial organization who infiltrates anarchist groups in order to lead them to overreach is one that marks a blindspot for any solely uni-directional system of disciplining, for, as the Assistant Commissioner reminds us, "the existence of these [government] spies amongst the revolutionary groups . . . does away with all certitude." He remarks similarly later, "We can put our finger on every anarchist here. . . . All that's wanted now is to do away with the *agent provocateur* to make everything safe" (Conrad, *Secret Agent* 145 and 209).[46] The *agent provocateur*—not the straightforward criminal—is the genuine threat to the system of disciplining. The obverse of this situation of the secret agent would be the society seemingly fulfilling a disciplinarial role—as societies in the modern age (i.e., without provision for carnival) *ex officio* must—but actually turning out to be unexpectedly deviant *as a whole*.[47] This might seem a situation solely characterizing petty dictatorships, but a little over a century ago it was precisely the situation of the United States.[48]

---

46. Similarly, in Vladimir Nabokov's novel *Pale Fire* the narrator Kinbote tells us that the supporters of the ousted King of Zembla, Charles II, disguised themselves as the fleeing king in order to lead the authorities astray: "He never would have reached the western coast had not a fad spread among his secret supporters, romantic, heroic daredevils, of impersonating the fleeing king. They rigged themselves out to look like him in red sweaters and red caps, and popped up here and there, completely bewildering the revolutionary police" (99). Further on we read that "[t]he illusion of the King's presence in the wilds of Zembla was kept up by royalist plotters who decoyed entire regiments into searching the mountains and woods of our rugged peninsula" (149). The ruse is so successful that the Zemblan authorities at one point mistake the king himself for an imposter and take away his "disguise" (144).

47. William St. Clair writes of the point at which America passes, so to speak, "through the looking-glass," that is, shifts over from the realm of parodic disciplining to that of standard (Foucauldian) disciplining: "In 1891, after nearly a century of Anglo-American dispute, the United States, having by this time built up a strong local publishing as well as printing industry, and having become a net exporter of the potential intellectual property implicit in printed texts, joined the international copyright treaties. Since that time . . . intellectual property has become one of the main instruments through which the United States dominates the modern world" (393; see also 488).

48. Echoing Martin Chuzzlewit from our epigraph, the nihilistic Professor in Joseph Conrad's *The Secret Agent* comments about America, "They have more character over there, and their character is essentially anarchistic. Fertile ground for us, the States—very good ground. The great Republic has the root of the destructive matter in her. The collective temperament is lawless. Excellent. They may shoot us down, but—" (96).

The Powerlessness of Woman as Text/Text as Woman

Of course to justify the covert allegory argument, one would need to prove that Laura Fairlie and Anne Catherick (perhaps that should be "Laura Fairlie" and "Anne Catherick") are more iterable texts than material entities, more books than bodies. And indeed I do believe we see this "textualization," or flattening, of character occurring in Collins's narrative: Laura's doppelganger being a character composed of as little substance as could be understood to be characterizing Laura, we have a contest between competing "blank-page" vacuities taking place in this novel, and I use that term purposefully. Thus, I would argue, the plot's center-piece, the substitution of Anne Catherick, the Woman in White, for Laura Fairlie, effectively enacts the central move in the drama of literary piracy. We learn near the end of the book that Laura and Anne are actually half-sisters, Anne being the offspring of an affair between the now-deceased Mr. Philip Fairlie and the maid of a friend. Fairlie's having published two copies of himself—in the Shakespearean sense of printing copies of oneself[49]—one legitimate and one not, has led to the possibility of his estate being shifted away from its proper course. In the end it will be Walter Hartright who takes on the task of reassembling and re-establishing—literally, in the narratives he gathers—the single, proper line of descent. And it is a curiously filial, rather than sexual, interest—"The sad sight of the change in her from her former self, made the one interest of my love an interest of tenderness and compassion, which her father or her brother might have felt, and which I felt, God knows, in my inmost heart" (464)—that he, our moral exemplar, displays in his quest for the re-establishment of Laura's claim to her proper identity and her proprietary rights over the family lands. In the end, Hartright will be the one who has successfully controlled the possibility of the loss of property and coin opened up by Mr. Fairlie's hither-thither "dissemination" (that sexual/textual pun in this case being appropriate).[50]

Hartright's disclosure of Percival Glyde's crime, in the most obvious "copy-book" instance in the narrative, highlights the connection between women and books on which Collins's allegory implicitly relies. As a result of his forgery of the registering of his parents' marriage, Glyde is described

---

49. See, for example, Sonnet 11, ending with the memorable peroration "Thou shouldst print more, not let that copy die."

50. In this sense, the drama between Walter Hartright and Anne Catherick on Hampstead Heath has always already taken place, for their meeting and Walter's vacillating as to whether or not to let her go (the act that symbolically re-enacts Phillip Fairlie's sin of having let himself go) is simply a replaying of the moment of Anne's conception.

by Hartright, in a characterization resonating with Fosco's earlier crime, as having "usurped" a "whole social existence" (521). One might recall here Hartright's earlier distress at Laura's having been rendered, as a result of the almost total triumph of Fosco's machinations, "socially, morally, legally—dead" (421). The success of Glyde's crime, his addition of his parents' names within a fortuitously-positioned blank space in the register at Old Welmingham, is overthrown by the existence, unknown to him, of another copy in lawyer Wansborough's strong-room in Knowlesbury, that other register still containing a blank space where there indeed should legitimately be one. The other copy renders "illegitimate" the one on which Glyde has come to (to borrow a phrase Hartright uses to describe the effects of incarceration on Laura) "set [his] profaning marks" (443). The existence of the other copy reveals his crime, in effect, to be that of having substituted one book for another, an illegitimate for a phantasmal (yet thanks to iterability, always potential and therefore theoretically always already extant) legitimate copy. The parallel in the crimes is further heightened by Glyde's ultimate "incarceration," so to speak, within the vestry. It is structurally appropriate that the false baronet, having been one of the two principal agents responsible for the incarceration of women in madhouses, should himself die as a result of having been locked—incarcerated as a result of the "hampering" of an old lock on the outer door—within an asylum of his own, in the dilapidated vestry housing the "marked" copy as the room around him begins to burn. Women and books in this narrative continually seem to be finding themselves locked up. Through this re-presentation to us of Fosco's crime of substituting women in Glyde's crime of substituting books, the narrative suggests not only that books can stand in for women but also, conversely, that women can stand in for books—a quite significant allegorical transformation in a story recounting, as I have been arguing, the redirection through the substitution of those women of legacies, as one is then prompted to consider whether the narrative might not also be representing at a symbolic level the redirection of literary profits.

This woman/text conjunction is also seen earlier in the narrative, in the diary-stealing scene. An unascribed Note introducing Fosco's "Postscript by a Sincere Friend" tells the reader,

> [At this place the entry in the Diary ceases to be legible. The two or three lines which follow, contain fragments of words only, mingled with blots and scratches of the pen. The last marks on the paper bear some resemblance to the first two letters (L and A) of the name of Lady Glyde.

On the next page of the Diary, another entry appears. It is in a man's handwriting, large, bold, and firmly regular; and the date is 'June the 21st.' It contains these lines:] (342–43)

The note's textual reference to Lady Glyde hints at a connection, in the phrase "some resemblance," between this "bold" act by Fosco and his later one of stealing Lady Glyde's body. His remarks in the postscript reinforce that connection. In his praising of Marian's delineation of character and detective abilities, he comes close to perpetrating the same conflation that had been effected by Collins's having titled his book *The Woman in White* in the first place, the conflation of woman with text:

> The illness of our excellent Miss Halcombe has afforded me the opportunity of enjoying an unexpected intellectual pleasure.
>
> I refer to the perusal (which I have just completed) of this interesting Diary. . . .
>
> Admirable woman!
> I allude to Miss Halcombe.
> Stupendous effort!
> I refer to the Diary. (343)

The excessive interest in clarifying referents here suggests more than just the introduction into the narrative of a Humbert Humbert–like fancy prose style; it also suggests the possibility for a momentary confusion between the references to the woman and the references to the book. This confusion is one that Collins will exploit, understandably, on more than one occasion in his allegory of piracy.

Marian having fainted, her text is completely at Fosco's mercy. So is her body. Since the villainous Count clearly does not hesitate in violating the one, it is within the realm of possibility that he violates the other also. This situation has suggested to some critics that Marian is raped by the Count. Miller places the word within qualifying quotation marks yet continues in a tone that would seem to disavow the need for qualification: "Marian has been 'raped,' as both the Count's amorous flourish ("Admirable woman!" . . .) and her subsequent powerless rage against him are meant to suggest" (D. A. Miller 164). I do not wish to be taken to be suggesting that it is necessary to conclusively prove, with respect to this fictional literary creation, the case one way or the other with regard to the "actuality" or not of Marian's physical rape. The mere suggestion of bodily violation, in connection with this instance of manifest textual violation, is enough to fulfill

Collins's purpose here. This is simply another instance of his favored sexual/ textual mixing. Unlike the case in *Basil,* here that mixing is not screening a subliminal influence working on behalf of copyright *extension* but is rather furthering Collins's implicit agenda of allegorizing the act of copyright *violation* through having this Victorian woman's physical powerlessness represent the powerlessness of the trace to resist the breaking function of iterability. Collins would seem to want to use this veiled sexual violence that comes in the form of a manifest textual violation to once again bind the woman and the text together so as to render his covert lobbying in behalf of international copyright even more morally virtuous than it already was.

This textual violation does not, however, immediately announce itself as identity theft. That transformation requires us to turn outwards, toward the contextual surroundings. Indeed, Fosco's two acknowledged crimes in *The Woman in White* would at first glance seem markedly unrelated. The crime he commits against Marian—for the sake of argument I will characterize it simply as textual theft—is never *overtly* represented as being similar to the crime he commits against Laura, identity theft. Only through a metaphorical leap—albeit a fairly understandable one—could one come to equate the theft of the diary of one woman with the theft of the identity of another. However, the context in which these thefts occur is not neutral with regard to the issue of connecting texts with women's bodies. The book containing these scenes happens to be titled after the cognomen of a woman, the Woman in White. Thus, before the reader has even picked it up, Collins is asking her to make exactly that metaphorical leap of connecting women with texts toward which Fosco's crimes will later be prompting her. Viewed from this perspective, Fosco's two crimes—the theft of a woman's identity and of a woman's text—become one. This conjunction of woman and book, I am arguing, when it is situated within an even larger context, that of mid-Victorian, transatlantic book piracy—as *The Woman in White* itself could not have helped being—comes to render Fosco the allegorical stand-in for nothing less than that most hated of Collinsian real-world villains, that state-of-the-art exploiter of the breaking function of iterability, the immoral mid-Victorian American publisher.[51]

---

51. At the end of the story "A Rogue's Life" (1856), Collins has Doctor Dulcifer, the counterfeiter and last "employer" of the Rogue, having escaped the Bow Street runners, flee to America and there adopt a profession that Collins must have loathed; remaining consistent with prior practice, the unregenerate Dulcifer ends up engaging in a different form of theft in the New World, "editing a newspaper in America" (188). Old File, his accomplice in the English coining operation, serves as his publisher. Many nineteenth-century American newspaper editors having been unrepentant "reprinters" of English texts (Mott, *History* 2:128–30), it is not surprising that Dulcifer should have been cast by Collins in the iniquitous situation of having turned his already tainted hand to, in essence, if not

IT MUST be admitted that Collins, both for good and ill, is no Dickens. That is, he is a writer who, though having been praised for the unequaled plotting exhibited throughout his major phase, was nevertheless throughout the whole of his career also criticized, to my mind legitimately, for the flatness and puppet-like nature of his characters. An anonymous reviewer in the *Saturday Review,* commenting on 16 June 1866 on *Armadale,* notes this failing:

> There is a sort of unearthly and deadly look about the heroes and heroines of [Collins's] narrative, and though it is necessary for the purpose of the plot that they should keep moving, we feel that every one of their motions is due, not to a natural process, but to the sheer force and energy of the author's will. They dodge each other up and down the stage after the manner of puppets at a puppet-show, and after watching their twistings and turnings from first to last we come away full of admiration of the strings and the unseen fingers that are directing everything from behind the curtain. . . . Contrasted with [Becky Sharp], Miss Gwilt is a waxwork figure displayed from time to time in every conceivable sort of garish light.[52] (Rpt. in Page 151–52)

This shallowness of characterization may or may not serve as a valid reason for valuing Collins's works less highly than those of some of his contemporaries, but what it certainly does is suggest a means of assigning priority between his two favorite screenings. That is, were his characters more "well-rounded" one might be tempted to think twice before finding the sexuality or gender-relations in his tales to be mere window-dressing as I have been doing here. Indeed, I believe the sociologically-focused critic's attempts to draw out the cultural implications of Collins's theoretically-oriented, schematic fictions to be fundamentally amiss, unless, that is, that critic is considering Collins's implicit denigration of women via his having equated the effects of their many oppressions in Victorian society with the flatness and mobility of texts.

---

quite a different type of forgery, then certainly a different type of thievery, or false "circulation"—at least in English moral terms, if not American legal ones—on the other side of the Atlantic.

52. See also M. W. Townsend writing in an obituary of Collins in the *Spectator* on 28 September 1889, "With the possible exception of Count Fosco, about whom we are doubtful, Mr. Collins having not only failed, but consciously failed to find him a governing motive, he has never created a character; but he has sketched-in an enormous number, a dozen or two of whom the spectator will never forget. . . . Compare Alfred Jingle with Captain Wragge, in *No Name,* who is very much the same kind of swindler, and the difference between genius and cleverness becomes at once apparent" (rpt. in Page 264).

Indeed, Collins's characteristic strategy of screening textuality behind sexuality has to be seen through if his allegory of piracy is to be properly perceived. It is remarkable how close feminist and gender criticism, two approaches that would seem dedicated to not demystifying that screening, nevertheless come to doing so nevertheless (albeit sometimes unconsciously). Once the melding of the violation of the individual identity with the violation of the text has occurred, there are two clear ways in which instances of it can be interpreted: the critic can find, as was true in our earlier consideration in the Introduction of the Tombstone Scene, bodies and identities coming to be textualized or texts coming to be embodied, and perhaps even gendered. That latter viewpoint is, understandably, the one adopted by many feminist critics of the 1980s and early 90s. The arguments about female powerlessness in *The Woman in White* that are so common in that era are intent on disclosing that instances of the vulnerability of Collins's textualized femininity abound in *The Woman in White*.

Feminist critics, acknowledging Collins's careful balancing act between female and textual vulnerability, are forced, however, by this text to eventually shift toward the materiality of the literary endeavor. Thus, they can be found in their more recent interpretations to be nearly writing their way past their own particular *raison d'être* and entering the domain of materialist textual criticism proper as the more prominent analyses of the purported textualized femininity in this novel uncover a Collins more interested than the critics might wish in a feminized textuality (with the stress placed on the latter term). In 1979, Gilbert and Gubar in their famous study *The Madwoman in the Attic* focus on Anne Catherick and comment that her "white dress, which gives Wilkie Collins's *The Woman in White* its title, suggests the pathos of the Victorian child-woman who clings to infancy because adulthood has never become a viable possibility. . . . Anne's white dress tells a realistic story of female powerlessness" (619–20). The vulnerable text/vulnerable child-woman connection is of course fairly well submerged here. However, traces of it can be seen in the connection between the child-like woman in white and the iterable text's "powerlessness." The connection is even more manifest in later readings. In 1990, Perkins and Donaghy contend that "Laura [Fairlie] . . . functions from her first appearance in the story merely as a heroine to be loved, a blank to be filled by male desire" (393). In 1993, approaching Collins's novel from a similar perspective, Diane Elam notes that "[i]n Collins's text . . . the body of the woman in white is *figured as a blank page,* as virginal space, to be inscribed by the pen of the authorial and authorizing male, after the contours of a by-now-familiar critical and sexual analogy" (50; emphasis added). Familiar indeed. Here textual criticism and feminism have come nearly to acknowledge the struggle for priority with regard to this particular text that they had been in (often unknowingly) since 1979. This connection that the critics are continually making is symptomatic of the fact that in the man-handled woman in white—her status as cultural commonplace serving more Collins's purposes than the actual abused Victorian woman's—the male Victorian author found an excellent metaphorical stand-in or screen for the man-handled text.

In other words, it requires only a slight shift in emphasis, moving from the textualizing of the feminine to the feminizing of the textual, to turn a proto-feminist Collins into if not quite an anti-feminist one then into a self-absorbed author more interested in textuality than real-world personhoods. And I believe this shift to be warranted as, given the concerns of the allegory at the basis of *The Woman in White,* the textuality is more important than the feminism, indeed, to a great enough extent that it is not a misrepresentation to find the latter to be a mere screen for the former. Despite the arguments made by several critics, I am unpersuaded by the view that considers the author of this book to have been a feminist author. Leaving aside the various critics intent on drawing out the parallels between the story and the advent of the Matrimonial Causes Act of 1857 and its corollaries, the Married Women's Property Acts of 1870 and 1882, I would mention as exemplary the claims by Barickman, MacDonald, and Stark that of the four novelists they consider Collins is "the most directly concerned with issues of women's rights and the most openly irreverent toward Victorian sexual conventions" (111) and by Lyn Pykett that "Collins uses Marian's proto-feminist pronouncements . . . as a way of questioning and challenging current gender roles" (*Wilkie Collins* 126). While he would certainly take up feminist causes during the "mission fiction" phase characterizing the latter half of his career, in such works as *The New Magdalen* (1873), *The Law and the Lady* (1875), *The Fallen Leaves* (1879), *Heart and Science* (1883), and *The Evil Genius: A Domestic Story* (1886), Collins here was merely *making use of* (as opposed to making hay with) the Victorian woman's plight to represent that entity that was much more important to him at this time, the vulnerable text. In this novel, Collins, far from bemoaning woman's subjection, exploits the affinities between the situations of mid-Victorian woman and manuscript. That is, while seemingly grieving over the sad fate of womankind, he actually mourns for his text, rendering himself, effectively, indistinguishable from the worst sort of anti-feminist. Thus, it should come as no surprise that instances of the powerlessness of the text—which Derrida describes thus: "the force of the rupture is . . . important: . . . a written syntagma can always be detached from the chain in which it is inserted or given . . . [and] inscrib[ed] . . . or *graft[ed]* . . . onto other chains" ("Signature Event Context" 9)—should have been, Collins having represented them as instances of female powerlessness, recoverable through analyses of the "misogynistic" dynamics at work in *The Woman in White*.

By "the powerlessness of the text" and "the force of rupture," I mean, of course, to suggest the breaking function, that fundamental lack of grounding always already rendering the text vulnerable to the process of American copyright violation. Viewed from this perspective, Marian Halcombe's rhetoric of an invariably unhappy destiny for a female joining adult society thus becomes in effect an unhappiness with regard to the publication process: "Men! They are the enemies of our innocence and our peace—they drag us away from our parents' love and our sisters' friendship—they take us body and soul to themselves, and fasten our helpless lives to theirs as they chain up a dog to his kennel" (183). This ability for a woman to be "dragged" away from home and "fastened" elsewhere—like a piece of writing that is "cut" from one context and "pasted" into (or merely onto, depending) another—is the breaking function of linguistic iterability embodied. As soon as the text is created, it has entered a region of potential subverters from whom one will thereafter be trying to protect it, despite one's having known from the beginning that it would eventually be sent out some day to face them, that it was being "raised," in a sense, precisely for that purpose. This situation has more than a few affinities with that of the bringing up of the average Victorian girl.

Anticipating the interests of future psychologically-focused readers, Collins's text pre-established a trap that was sure, at least for a while, to ensnare those readings and the critiques that followed in their wake. Collins intuited that this particular "cover" would serve, almost as well as the overt sexuality in *Basil* had, to effectively camouflage his copyright allegory. However, not having foreseen that body-centric (Freudian, feminist, gender, postcolonial) interpretations would dominate the literary critical domain in the West for a significant portion of the twentieth century, his camouflage may have been more effective than he might have wished. The degree to which Collins uses the sexual to hide the textual renders the understanding offered by those approaches of his major fictions always already confidently self-affirmed. During his 1860s phase, Collins might well, if he had been able to foresee Twentieth-Century methodologies, have said the same thing that Vladimir Nabokov declares in the Introduction to *Bend Sinister:* "all my books should be stamped Freudians Keep Out" (xviii). Casting Laura and Anne both as child-like women ensured for decades to come—due to the unforeseeable advent of the particular styles of literary criticism growing out of Freudian psychoanalysis—that the critics would view the two substitute versions of the Woman in White as, if not necessarily oppressed women, at least culturally-embedded subjectivities *before* viewing them as violated texts.

Putting the "You" Back in Honor

As we have seen, the discourse of independence underwrote the refusal by the Americans to honor British copyrights. Collins, by having Hartright insist at one point on a "common honour" (539), was attempting to undercut that rhetoric. Recall Thomas Carlyle putting forward in a letter to Dickens the argument that England and America are

> not two nations, but one; *indivisible* by parliament, congress, or any kind of human law or diplomacy, being already *united* by Heaven's Act of Parliament, and the everlasting law of Nature and Fact. . . . In an ancient book, reverenced I should hope on both sides of the Ocean, it was thousands of years ago written down in the most decisive and explicit manner, "Thou *shalt not* steal." That thou belongest to a different "Nation," and canst steal without being certainly hanged for it, gives thee no permission to steal! So it is written down, for Nations and for Men, in the Law-Book of the Maker of this Universe. . . . How much more [for] two Nations, which, as I said, are but one Nation; knit in a thousand ways by Nature and Practical Intercourse; indivisible brother elements of the same great SAXONDOM.[53] (Qtd. in Forster 1:332–33)

53. See also Charles Reade's book of 1860 arguing against American literary and dramatic thefts, which in its title, *The Eighth Commandment,* emphasizes this same common root. Recall also the reference to an Anglo-American Divine Christian Retribution signaled in Marian's use of capitalization in her recounting of the speech delivered by a dream-Hartright in Central America: "The night, when I met the lost Woman on the highway, was the night which set my life apart to be the instrument of a Design that is yet unseen. Here, lost in the wilderness, or there, welcomed back in the land of my birth, I am still walking on the dark road which leads me, and you, and the sister of your love and mine, to the unknown Retribution and inevitable End" (278). See Collins's distinction in the Foreword to *Armadale* (1866) between "the Clap-trap morality of the present day" and "the Christian morality which is for all time" (5). Many Americans, however, saw themselves as clearly distinct from the English. For example, one anonymous reviewer for the, at that point in its history, rabidly anti-international-copyright *Democratic Review* not surprisingly emphasizes, repeatedly, the distance between the United States and Great Britain: "[The British author] has no reason to complain, if in *another country,* the antipodes perhaps of his own, and a *totally distinct* political organization, his work is reproduced, for the benefit of a *new* population, without any injury to any of the rights or interests of his secured by law *at home.* . . . [T]o this *foreign* nation it is a question of expediency whether or not to grant him, to any greater or less extent, a privilege of copyright; and . . . actually in the case of the present demand upon *our government* on behalf of *English* authors, the preponderance of the expediency—an expediency coincident with the moral right of the matter—is against its concession" ("Note" 615; emphasis added).

Similarly, from Collins's perspective, our American cousins were not all that different. They were half-siblings who at the current moment simply lacked the will to be honorable in the same way as the British. Turning away, for the moment, from the theoretico-linguistic lesson being offered by Fosco of the need to acknowledge breaking, Collins in the latter third of this book, simply wished to bridge the gap in the two differing understandings of honor/honour prevailing on the differing sides of the Atlantic.[54] Walter Hartright, that returned Central American explorer, serves as that bridge. Not only are we readers taught by this narrative to contest counterfeit writing (on tombstones, on marriage registers) and to equate woman with word in a way that is important to Collins's underlying allegory, but we are also at the same time taught by the last volume's constant discoursings on honor to contest false writing and to pay attention to moral actualities thus completing the narrative's fundamental allegorical lesson. We are taught to assume a virtue if we have it not as we come to realize that sometimes writing can be *mis*-representing truth (as in the blank space in the marriage register having been falsely filled) and that to have taken one woman in white to be as "valid" as another was to have abetted a villainous injustice.

True to his name, Hartright throughout the story acts the perfect English gentleman—not to mention perceptual savant, as seen in his unerring and unquestioned capabilities of discriminating at a glance between the doppelgangers Laura Fairlie and Anne Catherick[55]—thus also serving as the perfect agent of moral instruction for those readers across the ocean so much in need of it. After Glyde's death, Walter considers what he would have done had Glyde lived. Having been in a position to blackmail him with the threat of the disclosure of Glyde's secret and of his usurpation of a legacy that was not legally his, Walter decides that properly he could have done only one thing: "In common honesty and common honour I must have gone at once to the stranger whose birthright had been usurped—I must have renounced the victory" (539). It should be noted that "common honesty and common

---

54. Noah Webster, in consultation with Benjamin Franklin, had decided to change the spelling of "honour" in his *Dictionary* so as to more effectively mark American independence. In 1789 in his *Dissertations on the English Language* he famously declares, "As an independent nation our honor [*sic*] requires us to have a system of our own, in language as well as government" (qtd. in Mencken 48). Franklin was also a significant influence on, and at one point employer of, Mathew Carey, the father of Henry (see Johns, *Piracy* 175).

55. Walter Kendrick calls the recognition scene "an immediate vision which transcends the lies of language—just the sort of direct felt sympathy which was the ultimate goal of mid-Victorian realism" (32). Rachel Ablow contests this reading, commenting, "although *The Woman in White* invites this interpretation, ultimately it destabilizes the notion of 'direct felt sympathy' to the same extent that it undermines the reliability of documentary evidence" (159).

honor" in Hartright's quotation are meant to signify not just an English honor but at the least an Anglo-American and ultimately universal honor, as Collins's disseminal hopes for this book are that it might imbue each of its readers with that same sense of common honesty and honor repeatedly exemplified in Hartright's good actions and almost too-upstanding-to-be-believed moral rhetoric. This interest of Collins's may have been derived from Balzac, who in his letter to authors on the subject of literary property of 1834 had written, "peoples are in need not just of good institutions, but also of morals. 'We must have morals!' is Rousseau's great battle-cry" (63).

A drama of grand moral dimensions is being played out in the scene in question here, since one could imagine, the rightful heir being thoroughly absent and even unknown in the immediate context, that someone in Hartright's position, with a Laura to resurrect, might be tempted to blind himself to the bad karma that might inhere in choosing the path to suppress the correct heir's rights. (And what is the frame story of *The Moonstone* if not an exploration of this same bad karma—specifically as it is manifested in the Indian "Brotherhood's" exacting a [seemingly] Indian rather than English form of vengeance according to the dictates of a [seemingly] Indian rather than English form of honor?) Yet Hartright chooses the strictly honorable path, implying that the Americans should do the same, despite any possible adverse effects that might eventuate with respect to their base monetary or fundamentally non-justifying national (and, in the case of their Anglo-influenced conceptions of "honor," unjustifiably nationalistic—they are after all at this time reading more English than American novels[56]) interests.

This rhetoric of English honorability deployed in the latter half of the narrative is, from the standpoint of the task of lobbying against piracy, at least as important as Hartright's and the Italian Brotherhood's eventual concluding exactions of reparations and/or blood from the villains of the story. These two aspects of the narrative end up working conjointly. The sub-plot of the moral instruction of the reader is rendered more forceful at the conclusion by the unhampered mobility, especially across international

---

56. Charles Reade comments in 1860, "in America, where genius and labour are swindled by the competition of stolen genius, five great writers out of six retire from that unfair competition to salaries and ephemeral comments on passing events" (*Eighth Commandment* 336). The anonymous author of the pamphlet *American Publishers and English Authors* writes in 1879, "At present, our authors, having to compete with books stolen from English authors, cannot find a market for their works. Their manuscripts are 'declined with thanks,' because the American publisher employs his capital more profitably in printing foreign books which cost him nothing. What is the result? The young American poet and novelist . . . is compelled to do hack work in order to live, while American publishers become millionaires from the unpaid books of English authors" ([Stylus] 7).

borders, of that shrouded secret society "The Brotherhood." In contradis-
tinction to Fosco's insistence on the nation-specific nature of virtue which
we had cited earlier—"Here, in England, there is one virtue. And there, in
China, there is another virtue . . . " (237)—the ubiquitous nature of the
providential vengeance wreaked by the Brotherhood's agents[57] is designed to
suggest that there does indeed exist a uniformity of virtue, a commonality
of morals, everywhere, expressing itself in the form of that virtue that Hartright has been continually invoking. We learn from Pesca that a member's
"serving other interests" will potentially result in death "by [the] hand of
a stranger who may be sent from the other end of the world to strike the
blow" (590). This novel dreams that the category of bad readers that has,
before the narrative's beginning and throughout its course, been allowed to
come into being through a lack of policing, will be reassimilated by some
(admittedly paranoid and panoptic, the man with the scarred cheek having
been eavesdropping amazingly coincidentally in the right place at the right
time) inter-national, indeed supranational, Brotherhood.

That organization thus in the end brings into being what initially had
been the narrative's foundational desire: a positing in its opening gambit
that there could be established a domesticity everywhere, through Professor
Pesca's sheer energetic willfulness if nothing else. The narrative had covertly
attempted to found this universal "domesticity" when our secret operative
of the association, at the "starting-point of the strange family story,"[58] had
answered the door—no "accident," despite Walter's off-hand pronouncement to the contrary—when Walter had rung at his mother's and sister's
cottage home: "I had hardly rung the bell, before the house-door was opened
violently; my worthy Italian friend, Professor Pesca, appeared *in the servant's
place*" (*Woman in White* 7; emphasis added). This appearing in the servant's,
the domestic's, place is not the only assumption of a domestic role attempted
by Pesca: "The ruling idea of his life appeared to be, that he was bound to
show his gratitude to the country which had afforded him an asylum and a
means of subsistence, by doing his utmost to turn himself into an Englishman" (7). It seems that Pesca is intent on, one way or another, becoming
"domesticated." The Brotherhood will at the end of the narrative successfully

---

57. "Agents" will certainly be the operative word in the works of those authors writing in Collins's
wake and living in just as internationally intriguing times: Conan Doyle, Buchan, Fleming, Le Carré,
among others.

58. We might recall at this point the pun being set in operation—in contrast to that enacted in
a title such as *Dealings with the Firm of Dombey and Son, Wholesale, Retail, and* for Exportation—by
Collins's subtitling *The Evil Genius* (1886) "A Domestic Story," which we saw in the Preface to be a
tale especially concerned with America's iniquitous stance on international copyright.

complete this task broached at the beginning by its member Pesca, only on a much larger, in fact universal, scale. Serving to allegorically represent a domesticity everywhere (and a domesticatability of everything), the Society's implacable non-restrictability will be the *deus ex machina* resorted to finally (if you cannot bring the Americans to the legal system, bring the legal system—or, at least, common legal sense—to the Americans) by this narrative intent on establishing one system of honor across the entirety of the Anglo-American literary domain.

This universality of the honoring of copyright is just what *The Woman in White* as narrative—not content with simply diverting the world but believing the point is to change it also[59]—is trying to bring about, even, or rather *especially*, as it in its book form haplessly falls "victim" to the American pirates. One could thus offer for it a description much like that one characterizing the diamond in that later Collins novel, a "native production" that can be seen to be "carrying its curse with it" (*Moonstone* 112 and 35). The narrative's ultimate moral can be nothing else than that there *is*, counteracting Fosco's repeated assertions to the contrary (*Woman in White* 237, 604), an ultimate sense of universal justice. It is no accident that by the end of *The Woman in White* the reader sees quite clearly which, or whose, type of virtue is the wrong. For the common goal of the two separate parts of the book (the first two sensational volumes standing in contrast to the moralistic last) had been to teach her through the various incursions they had made, respectively, into her nervous and moral systems that there was more than one way to establish a commonality of virtue, if not through the reinforcement, via disconcerting, sensational shocks, of the threat of the possibility of coincidentally meeting up with some agent of retribution coming around any and all corners, or turnings of the page, then perhaps through a morality tale in which the reader was made to read of himself continually self-satisfactorily—"Stupendous effort! I refer to the Diary" (343)—committing his textual crime—and continually eventually *paying* for it.

---

59. In this sense we might say that the effective "realism" that the sensation novel is so often found by contemporary reviewers to be lacking is more than made up for, at least in this case, by a grandly propagandistic, fundamentally political, practical effectivity or "effectual realism."

PART TWO

The Fictions of Breaking

4

Overdoing Things with Words in 1862

Pretense and Plain Truth in *No Name*

If you will promise not to be alarmed, Mamma Oldershaw, I will begin
this letter in a very odd way, by copying a page of a letter written by somebody else.

—Lydia Gwilt, in *Armadale* 282

Transhistorical Sensationality

Collins is most often remembered as a writer of sensation novels, thrillers,
and mysteries, alarming styles of writing generally understood—as a result
of the "brow" with which they are most commonly associated—to be tied
firmly to their particular historical milieu. However, it is my contention in
this study that his major fictions are to be illuminated more by investigations
into their universal theoretico-philosophical aspects than their journalistic
ones. That is, I believe the critic will get further in reading Collins's masterpieces by considering them from the perspective of comparisons to and
contrasts with Immanuel Kant than Constance Kent.[1] Though the almost-

---

1. Brantlinger argues that "Historically there is a direct relationship between the sensation novel
and sensational journalism, from the extensive crime reporting in the *Times* and the *Daily Telegraph*
to such extensive crime tabloids as the *Illustrated Police News*. Collins based some of the details of *The
Moonstone* on the sensational news stories of the Constance Kent murder in 1860 and the Northum-
berland Street murder in 1861" ("What Is 'Sensational'?" 9).

183

obtrusive "immediacy" of the styles that Collins adopted continually tempts critics toward seeing only the local issues at hand, it is important also to register the movements of that essential background element always of significant concern to him, the strange effects produced by language's breaking function. Iterability is not something that itself can or should be "historically-situated." Of course, as contended earlier, anything so fundamental is going to be making itself felt in the culture at large, and thus there always exists the possibility that its eruption will come to be confounded with and obscured by "simple history," that is, that it will be considered to have used up all of its interpretative "force" through its simply having manifested itself in one or another seemingly-contingent "historical" guise, such as mid-nineteenth century transatlantic literary disputes over piracy or Collins's particular conceptualizations of the English sensation and mystery novel forms, as well as in our own age's obsession with the "new" mass-publishing freedom made possible by the Internet and the need to properly restrict that freedom's scope.[2] This situation makes possible the mistaking of one of the most theoretically-minded of Victorian authors for the "father" of one of the most historically-situated of Victorian literary genres.

To offer one example of Collins's enforced "journalization," I might turn to Lillian Nayder's seemingly-uncontroversial statement that the novels comprising the sensation genre are categorized as such on two grounds, their depictions of a particular set of crimes and their stirrings of strong readerly emotions, that is, as a result of "their scandalous revelations, which center on acts of adultery, bigamy, and domestic abuse; and the physiological effects these novels allegedly produced in readers, whose pulses were quickened and whose nerves were electrified with every new twist in the plotline" (*Wilkie Collins* 71). There is a certain historically-defaulting undirectedness, in the guise of an innocuous academic neutrality, inherent in Nayder's taxonomy of crimes, implicitly suggesting that Collins was intent on creating journalistic fictions commenting on differing modes of Victorian domestic strife.[3]

---

2. For a recent example of the, to my mind misdirected, practice of tying Collins's transhistorical studies of iterability in his major fictions directly to sterile historical happenstance see Mangham, *Violent Women* 79–86 and 169–209. It should be clear by now that, at least in the 1860s, Collins was nothing if not a writer who looked for his work to have other and "larger" implications than those ascribed to journalistic reportage; thus we can trust that any choice of this or that historical issue (and/or screen)—*à la* the misleading openness of the ex-employee Davager or over-blownness of the pseudonym "Ozias Midwinter"—will have been motivated by a deeper agenda.

3. To offer another example of this conflation, I would quote one critic recently writing, "Notorious for exposing bigamy, adultery, and false identities in the midst of seemingly ordinary and often genteel milieux, the novels of Wilkie Collins, Mary Elizabeth Braddon, Ouida, Ellen Wood,

I am arguing, however, that these particular crimes appealed to Collins not for their own sake, that is, as instances of topical social commentary, but because they offered paths towards representing the breaking function. In his major works, Collins is intent on finding common cultural analogs for the linguistic trace's ability to change meaning and significance on its entrance into different contexts, and in the accomplishment of that particular task these social transgressions are the ones to which he most often has recourse. Domestic abuse (leading a certain Mrs. Waldron to poison her husband and subsequently change her name or a Lady Glyde to defy the wishes of hers and therefore end up one of the dead-alive), adultery (leading to the birth of a half-sister doppelganger named Anne Catherick who might eventually replace one), and bigamy (allowing, perhaps, an infamous Mrs. Waldron to begin her practice of moving to less sensational identities through marriage—and/or deceit—by initially turning herself into the unexceptional Mrs. Manuel) as well as the corollary acts of taking on a new name after marriage or passing oneself off under a false name without having undergone the proper formalities all provide Collins with real-world stand-ins for the workings of iterability. A man very much of his time and yet also very much "beyond" it as well, Collins would continually make use of iterability's capacity—a capacity that was simultaneously both access point and facilitator to screening—to erupt into and leave its traces within the social realm.

Repeatedly, Collins's characters' textualized identities are stolen or reinvented through legitimate or illegitimate marriages, or other means (the documents attesting to those changes always being of particular significance), actions that rehearse or gesture toward his final goal of representing, seemingly impossibly, the more disturbing and foundational crime of the theft of the textualized authorial identity. This funding by Collins of seemingly purely "historical" or "social" incidents or models with covert theoretical significance necessarily offers his contemporary sensation writer disciple, and the future literary critic, a fork in the road: (1) of coming to understand Collins's purported participation in "the" sensation genre to be eclipsing any and all individuality of approach on his part, including that theoretical significance, or (2) of coming to find Collins to have launched a profound theoretical critique aimed at undoing the primacy of systems based on the hegemony of settling, such as, in the case of *No Name,* literary realism. Thus, a possible screen is set up. This screening invitingly leaves

---

and Rhoda Broughton shifted emphasis from the perils of the marriage market to the sanctuary of the household—revealing marriage itself to be equally crowded and unstable" (Steinlight 502).

open one particular interpretive path through which contemporary sensationalists would have been able to understand (as many did)[4] themselves to
be "following" Collins without actually participating in his actual critique.
Although considering Collins to be their progenitor and leader, the other
sensationalists do not actually properly understand the project to which they
have signed on. Collins's sensationalism, based as it is in large part on various exploitations of the breaking function, should properly be described, I
would argue, as a "linguistic sensationalism," and not as a simple "cultural
subversiveness." To limit Collins's goal in his unified novel series to a desire
to redress, or merely address, particular local historical crises and concerns
is to miss completely the serious theoretical stakes involved in that project.
Collins's was an endeavor that went to the limits of the theoretical conun-
drums that most of his era's other sensation novelists' explorations into
"subversion" merely gestured towards. Neglecting to follow Collins in his
project of writing iterational reality *first* and then iterational fiction based
on that already-selectively-manufactured reality *second,* his acolytes chose
merely to write "manageable" critiques of the center from the periphery.

However, having said that, I do not believe that Collins should be understood to stand completely apart from other novelists; the similarities and differences are just distributed in a different manner than is currently allowed
by the gross generalizations characterizing contemporary literary history.
I would contend that Collins, in intellectually grappling with language,
an element common to *all* his contemporaries, was implicitly offering in
his negotiations with iterability a model for the ways in which the other
authors of his time must in their more honest or perspicacious moments
(that is, when they were not assuming settling to be all there is or mistaking their negotiations with the workings of language for legal or cultural
difficulties) have experienced their relations to the linguistico-theoretical
underpinnings of Victorian authorship. I would simply insist that Collins
was exceptional in the *degree* to which he was attuned to these "theoretical"
textual considerations.

INSISTING ON a particular distinction between Collins and his contemporary sensation novelist colleagues has far-reaching implications. For one, it
allows his achievement to shine forth unimpeded. The strategy of collapsing
Collins's form of sensation with that of the other sensationalists of his era
has, since that time, been a literary critical mechanism working almost of

---

4. Braddon commented, "I always say that I owe 'Lady Audley's Secret' to 'The Woman in
White.' Wilkie Collins is assuredly my literary father" (qtd. in Rance 121).

itself implicitly to reinforce his secondary status in the galaxy of Victorian novelists as well as to entrench his status as mere protégé of Dickens. However, Collins differed from his mentor in some profound ways. An example might clarify my point: Dickens, described by one critic, paradoxically but correctly, as a "sensational realist" (Meckier 96), was prompted to declare in his journal sensationalism to be a mere offshoot of realism, as a means of, paradoxically, defending the former as a legitimate style of fiction. In *All the Year Round* in 1864 he asked,

> [W]hy is all art to be restricted to the uniform level of quiet domesticity? To say nothing of the super-natural regions of imagination and fancy, the actual world includes something more than the family life; something besides the placid emotions that are developed about the paternal hearthrug. It has its sterner, its wilder, and its vaster aspects; adventures, crimes, agonies; hot rage and tumult of passions; terror, and bewilderment, and despair. Why is the literary artist to be shut out from the tragedy of existence, as he sees it going on around him? Why is it necessarily immoral to shadow forth the awful visitations of wrath and evil and punishment, or to depict those wonderful and unwonted accidents of fortune which are just as real as anything that happens between Brixton and Bank, only of less frequent occurrence? It is very easy to cry "Sensational!" but the word proves nothing. Let it be granted that such things *are* sensational; but then life itself is similarly sensational in many of its aspects, and Nature is similarly sensational in many of her forms, and art is always sensational when it is tragic.[5] ([Dickens], "The Sensational Williams" 14)

This is not very far from Ellen Wood's narration's description in that quintessential sensation novel *East Lynne* of Barbara Hare's need to tell Archibald Carlyle that she loves him: "There are moments in a woman's life when she

---

5. Anthony Trollope also did not consider the two styles of writing to be opposed. Summarizing this debate in 1876, Trollope in his *Autobiography* writes, "Among English novels of the present day, and among English novelists, a great division is made. There are sensational novels and anti-sensational, sensational novelists and anti-sensational, sensational readers and anti-sensational. The novelists who are considered to be anti-sensational are generally called realistic. I am realistic. My friend Wilkie Collins is generally supposed to be sensational. The readers who prefer the one are supposed to take delight in the elucidation of character. They who hold by the other are charmed by the continuation and gradual development of a plot. All this is, I think, a mistake,—which mistake arises from the inability of the imperfect artist to be at the same time realistic and sensational. A good novel should be both, and both in the highest degree. If a novel fail in either, there is a failure in art. . . . Let an author so tell his tale as to touch his reader's heart and draw his tears, and he has, so far, done his work well. Truth let there be,—truth of description, truth of character, human truth as to men and women. If there be such truth, I do not know that a novel can be too sensational" (226–29).

is betrayed into forgetting the ordinary rules of conduct and propriety; when she is betrayed into making a scene" (211). Collins's sensationalism, on the other hand, was a sensationalism different in kind, rather than degree, from that practiced by Dickens, Braddon, Reade, Le Fanu, and Wood.

Collins's linguistic sensationalism was not a case of an easily manageable attack from the periphery against the center, a center then as now occupied by realism and social propriety, but rather a critique working its way up and outwards from the very core of that center. Collins's sensation fiction, in attacking the philosophical underpinnings of realist fiction itself, particularly its implicit reliance on a strong signifier–signified bond, was protesting the denial of breaking implicit in that bond. For him, literary realism turned out to be a style of fiction based on a significant, and indefensible, *denial* of "reality," the reality of at least half of the operational aspects of language. Collins's critique's interest in iterability's breaking function—allowing that critique to cut more deeply than those offered by the other sensation novelists—is what keeps it standing before and beyond common history-writing and literary realism, two systems manifestly predicated on an assumption of the automatic precedence of (the one-to-one correspondence grounding) the settling function. Their obsessive interest in textuality—as well as their profound explorations into the theoretical underpinnings of it—sets the novels of Collins's major phase apart from the mass of novels surrounding them, while—the seams becoming blurred—he, as was his storytelling nature, worked to have his fiction nevertheless "tak[e] root in earth" (*Basil,* ed. Goldman xxxvi) thereby successfully camouflaging his productions amongst the sensation novel masses. At the same time, his followers would be working, on their side, to passably mimic his style, without, alas, quite comprehending the actual theoretical import of his particular compositional choices. From their unique position, Collins's narratives come to disclose that the uncanniness of the act of impersonating "respectability" or "high seriousness" can never be fully repressed, that in the end the citational potential, if not indeed perhaps fundamentally citational nature, of that impersonation (no matter how "seriously" intended or brought off) will surface. In essence, Collins's fictions turn out to be more all-encompassing than the realist works they might have seemed to be merely attempting to subvert or add drama to, and his sensationalism turns out to be more fundamentally—and more theoretically—subversive than the usual mid-Victorian sensationalism with which it is usually confounded.[6]

---

6. Judith Butler says something similar about the deinstituting potential of drag: "Drag constitutes the mundane way in which genders are appropriated, theatricalized, worn, and done; it implies that all gendering is a kind of impersonation and approximation. If this is true, it seems, there is no

DICKENS'S was a common standpoint. Throughout the heyday of the genre of sensation, generally understood to be confined to the decade of the 1860s, these books were considered merely an extension (albeit a grotesque one) of realist fiction. Nearer our own time, Patrick Brantlinger argues that because writers of sensation novels were interested in challenging and critiquing Victorian domestic conventions, they put themselves directly in contention with Victorian realist novelists. However, according to Brantlinger, they went about their task as if it were a matter of an attack on a dominant center from the periphery, that is, they operated "not by pushing the conventions of realistic fiction to the limits . . . but by subverting those conventions themselves, importing romantic elements back into contemporary settings, reinvesting the ordinary with mystery . . . and undoing narrative omniscience to let in all kinds of knowledge that realistic fiction had often excluded" ("What Is 'Sensational'?" 26). Accordingly, the sensationalists were self-condemned to remain subordinate to the realists:

> In place of the empiricist realism that strives for objective, direct mimesis, the sensation novel seems to substitute a different measure of reality, based on primal scene psychology, that now reads objective appearances as question marks or clues to mysteries and insists that the truth has been hidden, buried, smuggled away behind the appearances. But this subversive attitude is also felt to be regressive, inferior to traditional realism: the sensation novel never directly challenged the dominance of more serious, more realistic fiction. (26–27)

Brantlinger's perspective is one with a long history.[7] After Ann Radcliffe's popularity had given way to Jane Austen's in the 1820s, the gothic and New-

---

original or primary gender that drag imitates, but *gender is a kind of imitation for which there is no original*; in fact, it is a kind of imitation that produces the very notion of the original as an *effect* and consequence of the imitation itself" (127).

    7. He points out that the connection between, on the one hand, the primal scene disclosure, the child's viewing of parental intercourse, and, on the other, the discovery of the perpetrator or reconstruction of the criminal moment in detective fictions dates back at least to 1949 when it was first proposed by Pederson-Krag ("What Is 'Sensational'?" 25*n*42). The connection is then taken up by Rycroft in 1957, Hutter in 1975, Brantlinger, of course, in 1982, and, somewhat archly, D. A. Miller (152) in 1988. One should note that not all critics find sensation fiction to be as monolithic in approach as Brantlinger. See for example Nemesvari arguing that "The first-person, multinarrative mosaic of detection in *The Woman in White* has relatively little in common with the third-person, linear domestic melodrama of *East Lynne*, while *Lady Audley's Secret*'s combination of the two creates a hybrid effect which is itself unique" (18). Nevertheless, for him sensation is still a mere backdrop to realism: "Sensation fiction is constructed not as a unified form, but as an alterity against which opposed literary/cultural expectations may be recognized" (18).

gate novels, as well as their offspring the sensation novel, never had much chance of being considered a serious threat to the dominance of the realist novel. Indeed, Austen's many satiric references to Radcliffe in her fiction (especially in *Northanger Abbey*) would seem to indicate that she was already in her own time acknowledging the victory of realism over the gothic.

Collins in *No Name* sought to restore sensationalism to its proper status with regard to realism, as there could be no latter without Collins's particular type of the former. This particular project was an extension of Collins's larger one of bringing the breaking function out of the shadow cast over it by the settling. I will be contending in this chapter, as well as the next, that Collins's sensation novels do indeed push "the conventions of realistic fiction to the limits"—and beyond. *No Name* and *Armadale* threaten to subvert the realist novel from the ground up. By parodying the domestic novel in *No Name*'s opening phase, and by having Magdalen's parents impersonate a lawfully wedded couple throughout the first scenes, Collins not only directly contests the variously-characterized improper/proper dichotomies that the critics and many novelists were in the process of establishing at the time but also offers an implicit critique of the Biblical incipit of "In the beginning was the Word," rewriting it to read "In the beginning was the [iterable] Word." While the critics and novelists had been attempting to set up a game of fiction writing that would have had the literary scene be read as an inside (the realm of domestic/realist fiction) that might remain safe from an outside (the realm of sensation fiction) if only enough precautionary boundaries were erected and effectively policed, on the other hand, Collins was intent on showing—along the future lines of Derrida's critique in "Signature Event Context" of J. L. Austin's performative/constative distinction—that the violation had always already taken place, had been operating at the level of the home, the domesticity, through that domesticity's necessary foundation in citation and the inherent re-citeability/re-siteability of the trace. Thus, for Collins, sensationalism, at least as he practiced it, turned out to be a more "honest" style of fiction than realism.

As a result of language's iterability, specifically its breaking function, the word—composed of the more or less arbitrarily linked signifier and signified—is disclosed by Collins's fictions itself to be "sensational," to be operating in a shocking manner. Collins is dedicated to having that sensationality express itself in all its uncanny glory. In *Armadale*, in a clear attack on the proprieties of naming and a clear exploitation of Saussurean "arbitrariness," five characters (albeit across three generations) are allowed to claim the name "Allan Armadale." Clearly, we are not dealing here with your "average" sensation novels, that is, with your ordinary extraordinaries. *No Name* and *Armadale* are different in kind from other sensation fictions. It is no accident that Collins's sensation narratives are so interested in the possible complications, screenings, and misidentifications possibly resulting from the change of name that occurs when a Victorian woman marries, an instance of the radical recontextualization of the trace. This particular set of interests sets his works apart. While the goal of the usual sensation novel arguably can be seen to be the reenactment of the remarkable opening quest of the genre's founding text *The Woman in White,* that is, the reabsorption of a sensationalism that had (always illegitimately) momentarily broken free of the larger category of "real life," the goal of Collins's subsequent works of the 1860s is to show that that "real life," in all its seeming complacency, had never been constituted by anything other than a misreading, a willful self-blinding to the many other modes of correspondence always already possible. Rather than attempting to "come home" to the realist center, to the asylum, *No Name*'s thoroughly-sensationalized Combe-Raven Estate shows that center to be, in fact, less "central" than the citation-founded and citation-funded sensationalism it had been attempting to denigrate and/or exclude.

Ordinary Language

In Walter C. Phillips's classic study of 1919, *Dickens, Reade, and Collins, Sensation Novelists,* there comes a point at which the critic believes himself to have caught the last of his novelists in a moment of artlessness. Remarking on the comforting and seemingly-conformist opening of *No Name,* Phillips comments that "in the early sixties . . . the popular drift toward realism—stories of domestic life—had compelled some modification of Collins's . . . original melodramatic scheme" (133). However, Collins's predilection for artfulness being well-established we are called on—nay, forced—to question Phillips's complacency. Rejecting Collins's suggestions for an earlier hinting at the Dr. Manette subplot in *A Tale of Two Cities,* Dickens on 6 October 1859 comments, "I do not positively say that the point you put, might not have been done in your manner; but I have a very strong conviction that it would have been overdone in that manner." He goes on to characterize Collins's suggested revision as potentially off-putting for the readership because it would inevitably be found out and the situation consequently judged "too elaborately trapped, baited, and prepared" (*Letters* 9:127). This chapter will be an exploration of the special utility inherent in the elaborately prepared trap. The elaborate plan can sometimes go places, make certain philosophical critiques, that the accommodative plot cannot. Collins was not known to be a writer who changed course easily in the face of criticism. Thus, it is surprising to find Phillips, as well as other literary critics, taking Collins's opening in *No Name* seriously and as a sort of conservative stylistic retreat on his part.[8] But traps being what they are, that is, made to be fallen into, Phillips's misreading is understandable. The opening of *No Name* does most assuredly invite such an interpretation. I will be arguing here, however, that far from attempting to accommodate a newly emergent popular Victorian domestic taste, and pulling back from a previous subversive stance, Collins especially in his opening but also throughout this non-canonical[9] masterpiece is actually covertly attacking that taste at its very foundations.

In a manner similar to Collins's previous fiction *The Woman in White*, which had concluded with an allegorical parody of the conventional, happy domesticity,[10] *No Name* begins with an illegitimate "happy home." In the "First Scene," that idyllic opening in which the reader is presented with a portrait of ideal aristocratic family life in what would seem the model Victorian country setting, that is, in that introductory parody of the domestic novel that appears—to resurrect that thankfully now discarded critical solecism—to "carry conviction" for critics like Phillips, the issue of impersonation, which we will see to be so important to the thematic level's recounting of the adventures of the story's heroine Magdalen Vanstone, that "born actress"[11]

---

8. Amidon writes that "The novel opens quietly, with an image of blissful domestic rectitude that was sure to warm the hearts of Collins' critics" (97).

9. This masterful narrative deserves more critical attention than it has thus far received. The most prominent treatments of this book are those offered by Taylor (1988), Michie (1989), David (1990), Horne (1991), Peters (1991), A. Jones (2000), and Pykett (2006). See Stange perceptively commenting in 1979 that "no one has recently claimed that [*No Name*] was a finer novel than *The Moonstone* or *The Woman in White*. And yet, reading *No Name* again, necessarily in the light of our present preoccupations with the theory of fiction, I have come to feel that it displays more clearly and more compendiously than the better-known novels what now appears to be the distinctive interest of Collins's work" (96).

10. The conjunction of Walter Hartright and Laura Fairlie in the new "*Heir of Limmeridge*" produced at the end of the narrative would appear to have Collins deploying that most conventional of Victorian conclusions, the couple-with-child tableau. However, he is, I believe, merely imitating (offering a doppelganger of) the conclusion offered, more or less seriously, by so many of his contemporaries. In actuality, what we have at the end of *The Woman in White* is a convention-screened bit of Collinsian wish-fulfillment that, in its merging of the *Fair(lie)-copy* of the Woman in White and the *Hart-right*, offers us the cheering prospect of a wronged author advocating the hopeful symbolic re-establishment if not within the American reader of a fair heart then at least within her legal system of his claims to his copy-right.

11. Collins, *No Name*, ed. Ford, 43. All further references in this chapter, unless otherwise noted, will be to this edition and will be cited parenthetically in the text.

(already we can sense the critique of realism in this bizarre phrase), redounds to the authorial level also. (Similarly, the twelve year old Lydia Gwilt will begin her writing career in *Armadale* not with a "serious" literary production but rather with the forgery of a letter written in a hand intended to be taken for that of someone else.) Collins here is not only parodying the domestic novel in general but may be—like Captain Wragge in his "imitation of the great Imitator himself" (191), that is, in his imitation of Charles Mathews's "At Homes"—setting his sights on a particularly famous representative of his chosen genre, Jane Austen's *Sense and Sensibility,* a more "serious" treatment of the theme of disinherited girls of contrasting natures. Wragge's labeling of Mathews as "the great Imitator" naturally implies a critique of the realist novelists of the mid-century. Collins here suggests that realist authors such as Austen, in their own fictionally imitative "At Homes," were not so much offering originary models as imitating them (the terms "citing," "imperson-ating," "falsifying" would do as well here)—models that themselves might be found to be no more foundationally solid since they themselves could be seen to be based on the imitation of models of their own. No matter how much their genre, especially in its constatively/performatively ambiguous names "Realism" and "the domestic novel,"[12] might have wished to hide the fact of this serial and unanchored imitability, it could not cover over, or undo, a persistent artificiality. In *No Name,* Collins is directly parodying (or impersonating) in the First Scene the "homely" style of the domestic novel, citing it, all the more perhaps to disclose both the artifice at its basis and, by extension, the artifice inherent in its models, the upstanding Victorian and pre-Victorian citizenry and society.[13]

But, as is implied by Phillips's mistake, this would at first glance not seem to be the case. Indeed, *No Name*'s opening lines could hardly be more pacifyingly comforting, more lullaby-ish, in their prototypical domesticity:

> The hands on the hall-clock pointed to half-past six in the morning. The house was a country residence in West Somersetshire, called Combe-Raven. The day was the fourth of March, and the year was eighteen hundred and forty-six.

---

12. I will throughout this essay be using the terms *domestic fiction* and *realist fiction* interchange-ably, considering them offshoots from the same parent source: whether or not this collapse is justified with regard to object, it is so with regard to subject, as both "sincerity" in congenial domesticity and "propriety" in referentiality are attacked by Collins in *No Name*'s First Scene.

13. Collins would himself undergo a similar parodying in the opposite direction when *The Moonstone* (1868) was perhaps "domesticated" by Trollope in *The Eustace Diamonds* (1873). See Mil-ley and Ashley 94.

> No sounds but the steady ticking of the clock, and lumpish snoring of
> a large dog stretched on a mat outside the dining-room door, disturbed the
> mysterious morning stillness of hall and staircase. (3)

The text continues on in this vein set going by ticking clocks and snoring
dogs, with the pretty, privileged daughter commencing for the next hundred or so pages to fall in love with and become engaged to the penniless
neighbor lad. We will soon enough, however, be asked to contrast the
equanimity of this opening with Magdalen's anguish at several unforeseen
turns of events, as the narrative comes to reveal itself at the end of the First
Scene in all its sensationalist glory: "'Yes,' she replied. 'Strange things happen sometimes. If strange things happen to *me,* will you let Frank come
back before the five years are out?'" (134). The coldly rational neighbor Mr.
Clare, ominously foreshadowing *No Name*'s sensational continuation, fore-
sees that Magdalen's future "will be no common one" (134). And indeed it
is not. This latter sensational context forces us to look again at the narrative's
beginning and to revise our understanding. Now, having been awakened
by sensation, we realize that Collins had *artfully constructed* the opening
Scene so that it might turn out a *mere imitation* of the realist, specifically
domestic, novel. Collins's virtuosic exercise in parody had been meant at
first to be taken "seriously" (and seriousness in its stoic opposition to artifice will be an important facet of this chapter's argument). Jeanne Bedell
remarks that in *No Name* "[t]he placid opening scenes of the novel disarm
readers and lull them into a false sense of security, one they share with its
characters" (21). Here at the beginning of his narrative Collins has done
a very good job—showing himself a kindred spirit to his chameleon-like
heroine—of impersonating, or mimicking, a writer of domestic fictions.

The argument pursued here will attempt to demonstrate that the narrative's complacent domesticity had always already been haunted by the specter of textual repetition's undelimitability. In his introduction to the novel
Mark Ford writes that "Combe-Raven, where the story begins, is a placid,
utterly commonplace country residence which Collins takes pains to evoke
in the opening pages in the most realistic of ways. . . . [But] [s]ubliminally—
and because this is a Wilkie Collins novel—one intuits everything is about
to go horribly wrong" (*No Name* vii). I will here be attempting both to formulate a rationale for Collins's having placed his readers and characters on
such a precarious precipice of immanent realist referential catastrophe—that
master of breaking Count Fosco having been capable of doing little better—
and to describe the precise coloring—a peculiarly "linguistically sensational"
one—of that catastrophe's manifestation.

The Fake Name as Real Name

The story of the tortuous process through which Collins determined on the—admittedly, rather off-putting—title of this one of his books is an interesting one. Collins consulted Dickens about the name and the latter sent him several suggestions, all of which Collins eventually rejected. Dickens's list ran to around 25 possibilities all tending, according to Collins's earlier direction one imagines, toward an overt banality. For example, we find Dickens suggesting titles such as "Below the Surface," "Pitfalls," "Behind the Veil," "Playing out the Play," and "The Beginning and the End" (Dickens to Collins, 24 January 1862, *Letters* 10:20–21). Other suggestions include "The Twig and the Tree," "Latent Forces," and "Work in the Dark." The naming of what would become *No Name*—his follow up to the runaway success *The Woman in White*—was important to Collins. A few days before first installment publication day Collins was still pondering eight options. In a letter to his mother he asks her for an opinion on them: "The Forbidden Fruit" [Collins]; "Man and Wife" [Collins]; "Nature's Daughter" [Dickens]; "The Beginning and the End" [Dickens]; "Behind the Veil" [Dickens]; "The Pitfall" [Dickens]; "Our Hidden Selves" [Collins]; and "Magdalen" [Dickens] (Collins to Harriet Collins, 4 February 1862, *Letters* 1:204–5). Interestingly, "No Name" is not an option. The titles of novels of this time were not generally especially lively or specific, so it is not surprising to find a certain plainness and generality of style being employed here. But there seems to be an especially pronounced desire for referential vacuity in these choices. What sensation novel could not be titled "Our Hidden Selves"? What book of whatever stamp could not be titled "The Beginning and the End"? That last option is close to *no title at all*—but, obviously, not in the right way. Collins seems to have desired a title that would be—like the First Scene—undoing itself even in the process of fulfilling its function. No more extreme example exists of the conflict between the settling and breaking functions of iterability than that encapsulated in the name he finally determined on, "No Name."

Collins's potential titles, while tending toward a certain plainness of face or unpaintedness—something Magdalen our heroine will not be able to abide—are still fundamentally acquiescing to the tyranny of reference. The title *No Name,* however, does not do this. It is an outright rejection of reference, masquerading as a proper title, one that only afterwards, after an initial demurral, allows itself to be resubsumed into the system of reference. It is a non-naming in the act of naming (or a naming in the act of non-naming). Titling one's novel *No Name* is a dangerous form of subversiveness

as it potentially can be understood as a failure of the creative imagination—
a risky move for anyone but an author safe in the knowledge that he was
at this time at the "top of the tree," as Collins described himself (see Peters
235–36). Here in the title *No Name* we see a rebelliousness to be evident, a
rebelliousness against the necessary act of giving one's book a title, of publishing. Many of the earlier options had tended toward this rebelliousness
("Latent Forces," "Our Hidden Selves," "Behind the Veil") but none had
gone quite this far. Indeed they had all remained within the conventional
parameters of reference in a way that "No Name" does not. This title in a
sense breaks *beyond* reference, turning back and taking reference by surprise.
Reference in this sense thus becomes a *secondary* effect rather than remaining the primary one, becomes the aftereffect of an initial *failure*.

This story of the book's naming is thus a good place to begin our interpretation of its narrative as it offers a microcosmic representation of the
novel's macrocosmic relationship to its larger literary context. Collins refuses
to compromise when it comes to naming this one of his novels. Instead of
choosing, while under severe pressure, a name that might suggest a primacy
of realism out of which a secondary sensationalism might be seen occasionally to be erupting (such as "Below the Surface" or "Pitfalls"), Collins, from
his title onwards, *overturns* that relation. We will find this type of overturning to be repeated throughout the rest of our inquiry, and overturning Collins no doubt learned from his observations of the struggle always already
taking place between the breaking and settling functions.

Mad to Act

The characters in Collins's text are intent on "doing" things with words—
indeed perhaps, as Dickens had characterized Collins's tendency, on *over-
doing* them. The marriage vow, that arch performative, will prove an
especially significant access point for this "doing." As was mentioned in the
Introduction, the "performative utterance" was named such for the first time
by the analytic philosopher J. L. Austin in his 1955 series of lectures on *How
to Do Things with Words.* This term describes words that actually do what
they say: "The name is derived . . . from 'perform,' the usual verb with the
noun 'action': it indicates that the issuing of the utterance is the performing
of an action—it is not normally thought of as just saying something" (Austin, *How to Do Things* 6–7). Austin finds a most useful, and pithy, example of
these "doing" words in the common conception of the wedding ceremony:
"for instance, the utterance 'I do' (take this woman to be my lawful wedded

wife), as uttered in the course of the marriage ceremony. . . . [I]n saying these words we are *doing* something—namely, marrying, rather than *reporting* something, namely *that* we are marrying" (12–13). The marriage vow is also a significant structuring component of Collins's narrative. Here, however, I will not be arguing that Collins is an analytic philosopher before his time. Quite the contrary. I will instead be attempting to show that Collins's novel of 1862, in its relentless attack on the institution of marriage, sets out through various instances of parody to undo the idea of the sacredness of the marriage vow and, in so doing, also undoes the proprieties founding both J. L. Austin's approach to performatives and the fortuitously similarly-named Jane Austen's approach to realist narration. It performs both these undoings as a result of its explorations into the realm of parody, a parodicity made possible by Collins's investigation into and utilization of the implications of the iterability of language.

Collins's story parodies the marriage vow in both obvious and subtle ways. The first example encountered in the narrative is a parody by omission. By having a loving couple turn out to have bypassed the necessity for the exchange of vows, Collins implicitly critiques society's imposition of that necessity. While the estate at Combe-Raven headed by Andrew Vanstone seems at first to be the ideal, indeed even extra-ideal, Victorian country home, it will soon enough turn out that the master and mistress are, shockingly, not married and that their daughters Norah and Magdalen are illegitimate. The daughters have, in effect, "no name." The parents are disclosed to have been only pretending to be married, falsifying the exemplary Austinian performative of "I do" at the same time that their story, quite appropriately, had been falsifying the conventions of the standard nineteenth-century domestic novel. They have, due to Andrew's already having been married,[14] been merely play-acting at marriage without having gone through the proper formalities. This rift, like those innumerable "infelicities" catalogued by Austin, only leads to "unhappinesses"—Magdalen being described on more than one occasion as the "unhappy girl" (110, 142, and 323).[15]

Over the course of the narrative, we follow our heroine's adventures as she endeavors, through recourse to the aid offered by her scoundrelish

---

14. This detail may have been autobiographical, as Collins is rumored not to have married Caroline Graves because of an earlier, secretly contracted marriage (see Peters 198).

15. While these descriptions undoubtedly refer to Magdalen's new-found distance from the conventional "happy home," that label itself also connects her to Austin's "infelicities" as both she and Austin would seem nostalgic for a happiness based on the illusion of solid Victorian domestic propriety.

quasi-relation Captain Horatio Wragge[16] and via a masterfully-handled series of deceptions and counter-deceptions, to recover from her miserly cousin Noel Vanstone the legacy of eighty thousand pounds left by her father.[17] The cousin's having ended up with that legacy is solely the result of the father's ignorance of a technical quirk of the law, that is, a result of Andrew's having failed to draft a new will after his belated official marriage to his girls' mother had taken place, rather than the result of any active desire on his part to see his daughters left destitute. Her father's manifest intention having been thwarted, Magdalen feels justified in repeatedly assuming one disguise after another in her quite artful efforts at recovery—the model for this practice having been perhaps furnished not only by her early experience in the Marrables' private theatricals but also by an impersonation carried out at the extradiegetic level, our author's opening impersonation of the style of a serious-minded author of nineteenth-century domestic fiction. Thus, the central theme of the story at both the narrative and authorial levels is repeatability—of manner, of tone, and of literary style.

It comes as little surprise, then, that *No Name* should be written on the plan of a stage-drama. This theatrical frame establishes, as many critics have remarked, the appropriate backdrop for Magdalen's many acts of taking on disguises throughout the story.[18] The story is broken up into eight "Scenes," with several series of documents being presented "Between the Scenes." The eight Scenes in the narrative are of varying lengths and for the most part each takes place at an individual location. In the First Scene the story opens with a domestic establishment that has always already been fissured, an establishment rifted before the narrative has properly begun. We find, in essence, as will be suggested by the title of one of Miss Clack's pamphlets in *The Moonstone,* that the serpent is in the home. The fact that all the action in this narrative filled with impersonations is taking place so to speak "on

---

16. Magdalen's maternal grandmother had been Wragge's step-mother for a time, before she came to marry Mrs. Vanstone's father and to give birth to the daughter who would become Magdalen's mother. The complex family dynamics connecting Wragge to Magdalen's mother suggest a foreignness in the home; that is, they imply the existence of other possibilities for defining a family than that one presented to us by the fantasized ideal of the unified nuclear family with which *No Name* begins.

17. In his insightful review Stange considers these intrigues to be the main interest in the story, trumping the climax in importance: "Collins is at his most exuberant in handling the continually inspissating pattern of intrigue that dominates the middle section of the novel. . . . [T]he reader's interest is not in the outcome of the main plot but in the succession of plots and counterplots the characters devise to ensnare each other. It would not be far wrong to say that the subject of *No Name* is *plotting*. It is a tale of trappers trapping trappers, devised by a novelist who, we are continually reminded, is himself an addictive contriver" (97). Stange in his comment here is alluding to the situation in *The Moonstone* in which we have an opium addict (Collins) writing of an opium addict (Jennings) in his turn writing of a man operating under the influence of opium (Blake).

18. See Horne 283–84 and Peters 239.

stage" puts into effect from the beginning a mechanics of "doubled imita-tion." A single imitation would at first glance at least *seem* to be control-lable. A doubled imitation, however, being patently uncontrollable, might as well be infinite.[19] Infinite contexts necessarily result in infinite intentions. Extrapolating from the radical resituatability of one's language (including one's thought-language), Derrida will continually over the course of his career point out that all intentions are fundamentally doubled, or to use his favored term "impure," and therefore potentially infinite.[20] This situ-ation leads to an illimitability of imitations and split intentions from the beginning and the possibility (but not necessity—contexts having after all a significant effect) of referential madness.

Not surprisingly, there exists an always uncomfortably controlled mad-ness surfacing in this Collins story so taken up with the issue of rampant imitability. The entry of the Marrables' play, appropriately, is what sets off the madness of the main character (her name probably properly being pro-nounced Mad-lin).[21] When she promises to be a "good girl" for the rest of her days if allowed to participate, her father mockingly replies: "'A good girl?' repeated Mr Vanstone—'a mad girl, I think you must mean. Hang these people, and their theatricals!'" (33). Later, her father will describe her as "mad to act" (38). Magdalen's theater-madness is an analog for the ref-erential madness with which Collins's story had begun. Indeed, if we take the initially complacent domesticity at Combe-Raven to be symbolic of a general referential complacency, we can see both these aspects—referential- and domestic-complacency—being threatened jointly when the narrative describes Magdalen as "the one ever-disturbing element in the family seren-ity" (39). Collins's heroine's fierce need to act (a better term might be "act out") poses a threat, it would seem, both to the domesticity and the funda-mental referential grounding of the domestic/realist novel.

Irrepressible Iterability

Austin's fundamental project throughout *How to Do Things with Words* is one of active repression. The demonstration he is trying to effect in his lecture

---

19. It is significant that in Collins's grandfather's book *Memoirs of a Picture* there are not one but *two* imitations of the original masterpiece in circulation.

20. See for two examples, among many, "Freud and the Scene of Writing": "We must be several in order to write" (226), and *Monolingualism of the Other*: "We never speak only one language—or rather there is no pure idiom" (8).

21. Virginia Blain, the editor of the Oxford edition of the novel, suggests the name should be "possibly pronounced as it was sometimes spelt 'Madlin,' from the French form, Madeleine" (*No Name*, ed. Blain, 743).

series is predicated on the possibility of discovering a means of conclusively distinguishing between performative and constative utterances. More than once he finds himself unable to establish a firm basis for his distinction.[22] Austin endeavors to keep rigorously excluded all the possible "infelicities"— "the things that can be and go wrong" (*How to Do Things* 14)—acting on the occasion of the utterance of performatives, to effectively show them the door, in a sense, so as to safely establish the happy, secure domesticity as one in which the constatives (words that merely report things) can always be distinguished from the performatives. As his study is for the most part simply an unsuccessful definition by negation of the elusive "pure performative," he understandably spends a good deal of time classifying various categories of failed performatives. Austin uses terms such as "Non-plays," "Misplays," "Miscarriages," "Misexecutions," "Non-executions," "Disrespects," "Dissimulations," "Non-fulfilments," "Disloyalties," "Infractions," "Indisciplines," and "Breaches" to describe the various different types of failed performatives (18*n*1). (This impressive proliferation of categories of infelicitous would-be performative utterance should have given Austin pause, should have stood for him as a sign that perhaps his task was futile.)

Derrida, in a brilliant critique (or more appropriately continuation) of Austin's project entitled "Signature Event Context," describes why he fails. That failure is the result of Austin's having ignored a fundamental principle of language (one known to the narrative of *No Name* in 1862): that "infelicity" begins "at home," that is, in the act of citation itself. Derrida, in solving Austin's problem, or rather in showing why it cannot be solved, will mine his way below the level at which one is able to distinguish between these two "entities" labeled the performative and constative utterance. He will take Austin's inquiry into a region where the "iterability" of language must be encountered and acknowledged. Derrida makes clear that writing must have an effectivity beyond a given addressee and given addressor in order to be "readable." Once one grants these propositions—and I myself am inclined to do so because a form of communication that had been so structured as to be effective solely for one particular pair of communicators and for one particular context is not my experience of communication—one has effectively granted everything to follow in Derrida's critique. Derrida holds that "a written sign carries with it a force that breaks with its context, that is, with the collectivity of presences organizing the moment of its inscription. This breaking force [*force de rupture*] is not an accidental predicate but the very structure of the written text" ("Signature Event Context" 9). Admitting

---

22. See Bearn for a good exposition of these points of failure.

the necessary existence of the possibility for the repetition of the trace—that is, of the "structural unconsciousness" of language (18)—means admitting the possibility for the alteration of a given statement's tone, its speaker's intentions, indeed also its constative or performative nature. This breaking force has radical implications for the Self that would be attempting, vainly it turns out, to appear unified in language, as Derrida makes clear when he comments, "the entire graphematic structure is connected to citationality, to the possibility of being repeated. And since a mark is repeatable, this means that it no longer needs me to continue to have its effects. *Insofar as I make use of an instrument that bears within itself its repeatability, I am absented from what I use.* And it's necessary to take account of this absence" (Derrida and Ricoeur 154; emphasis added). In short, language's inherently mobile qualities cause it always to fit uncomfortably within the typical regimes of determinate reference, analytic grammatical categorization, and thoroughly consistent self-representation, not to mention the context stressed in the previous chapter, regimes of property ownership.

To help Austin's failed inquiry to get beyond its impasse, Derrida decisively poses the following questions about the general possibility for his serious-minded language to be attacked or parasited by non-serious usages:

[I]s this general possibility necessarily one of a failure or trap into which language may *fall* or lose itself as in an abyss situated outside or in front of itself? . . . In other words, does the quality of risk admitted by Austin *surround* language like a kind of *ditch* or external place of perdition which speech [*la locution*] could never hope to leave, *but which it can escape by remaining "at home"* [emphasis added], by and in itself, in the shelter of its essence or *telos?* Or, on the contrary, is this risk rather its internal and positive condition of possibility? *Is that outside its inside, the very force and law of its emergence?* [emphasis added] . . . In excluding the general theory of this structural parasitism, does not Austin, who nevertheless claims to describe the facts and events of ordinary language, pass off as ordinary an ethical and teleological determination (the univocity of the utterance [*énoncé*]—that he acknowledges elsewhere . . . remains a philosophical "ideal"—the presence to self of a total context, the transparency of intentions, the presence of meaning [*vouloir-dire*] to the absolutely singular uniqueness of a speech act, etc.)?

For, ultimately, isn't it true that what Austin excludes as anomaly, exception, "non-serious," *citation* (on stage, in a poem, or a soliloquy) is the determined modification of a general citationality—or rather, a general iterability—without which there would not even be a "successful" performative? So that—a paradoxical but unavoidable conclusion—a successful performative is necessarily an "impure" performative, to adopt the word advanced later on by Austin when he acknowledges that there is no "pure" performative. ("Signature Event Context" 17)

Derrida's critique discloses that Austin's implicit reliance on propriety, in various guises, in his formulation of the "speech-act situation" is always already rifted by language's necessary iterability, its ability to be repeated. The honest intentions of Austin's unified subject are never going to be as pure as Austin wants them to be.[23] When discussing the logic of supplementarity, Derrida writes, "the indefinite process of supplementarity has always already *infiltrated* presence, always already inscribed there the space of repetition and the splitting of the self" (*Grammatology* 163). Derrida's point is that the bottom line is complexity: that the end result is iteration and its various manifestations, polysemia, muddled intentions, improper or uncertain self-understanding, noise, etc. Derrida thus effectively maps out a world manifestly working not according to the proper/improper dichotomy founding Austin's inquiry (as well as, as we will see, Jane Austen's realism) but rather according to a different set of rules. He maps out a world in which artifice is rendered not a controllable supplement to the otherwise art-less world but rather a necessary precept. Austin's mistake was to have assumed (or to have attempted to create through a process of selective viewing) artlessness in the face of the inherently so-very-artful practice of citation.

Derrida's essay goes on to reform the contours—as Austin has set them out—of the landscape figuring the domain of language and leaves us with a system of language that works not along the lines of the "usual" model, that is, not a system of language that works because just enough meaning gets through for understanding to take place but rather a system of language that works because a disturbing excess of information gets through. Along with what will, perhaps after-the-fact, be claimed to have been the necessarily serious-minded speaker's "actual intention(s)" come along various other meanings and intentions. Derrida's point is that while those multiple meanings can indeed be placed in a hierarchy with regard to the dictates of a

---

23. Mary Louise Pratt holds that the "lone pairs of speakers and hearers are generally taken in speech-act theory to be much more monolithic entities than people really are. In fact, the speakers and hearers of traditional speech-act theory are clear instances of the notorious unified subject.˙ . . . Speech-act theory . . . supposes the existence . . . of an authentic, self-consistent, essential subject, a 'true self.' . . . It's all a matter, as Austin loved to say, of a man's (*sic*) word being his bond. The idea is of an authentic self, fully realized through speech, and speech fully adequate to the self—speech from the heart. Derrida's critique of speech-act theory addresses this aspect of the theory" (8).

given context, language owes its greatest debt for its functionality not to that process of hierarchization (often called "contextualization" or the application of "tradition" or proper contextual/historical understanding) but rather to the preceding process of multiplication of meaning. Language does indeed function, but this functioning is never "pure," and indeed this functioning is in actual fact *the result of* that impurity:

> Rather than oppose citation or iteration to the noniteration of an event, one ought to construct a different typology of forms of iteration, assuming that such a project is tenable and can result in an exhaustive program, a question I hold in abeyance here. In such a typology, the category of intention will not disappear; it will have its place, but from that place it will no longer be able to govern the entire scene and system of utterance [*l'énonciation*]. Above all, at that point, we will be dealing with different kinds of marks or chains of iterable marks and not with an opposition between citational utterances, on the one hand, and singular and original event-occurrences, on the other. . . . The "non-serious," the *oratio obliqua* will no longer be able to be excluded, as Austin wished, from "ordinary" language. (Derrida, "Signature Event Context" 18)

Titling one's book "No Name" could be viewed as a very "non-serious" or "improper" response to the necessity of naming. It poses the potential for being (seen as) a very cheekily parodistic act. Adopting, *à la* the American pirates and the reprinters of *Blackwood's*, his own parodistic stance toward Austinian-style disciplining, Collins in *No Name*—and continuing on into *Armadale*—will deploy a peculiarly linguistic style of sensationalism, a sensationalism that will, in a manner similar to that of the Americans, capitalize on the distance between signifier and signified. Here in this novel we will find a certain type of seriousness being fundamentally undermined by the unforeseen possibility for parody. We will see Collins taking the lesson he learned from his shameless reprinters and applying it to the attempt at the illusory Holy Grail of conclusively unifying signifier and signified. Derrida exposed the same type of illusion to be at the heart of Austin's performative utterances. This is a goal Austin had taken over from the settling-valorizing tradition founded by Jane Austen's realist fictions. Here we will see Collins performing a demystification similar to Derrida's. It is the limitations of the seriousness underlying these discourses, Austin's and Austen's, that Collins was most concerned with exposing in *No Name*.

Collins's brand of sensationalism manifests itself in *No Name* as a critique of the "natural" bond between word and world undergirding Realist fiction, among other disciplinary regimes. Collins is opposed to what he considers a false and dishonest "naturalism" and "naturalization." The literary critic Paul de Man offers a comparable critique of the reductivist ideology underlying realism. Commenting that "the privileged adequation of sign and meaning that governs the world of literary fictions is taken as the ideal model toward which all semantic systems are assumed to tend" ("Roland Barthes" 172), De Man notes that this regime of adequation is contested only at one's peril: "One can see why any ideology would always have a vested interest in theories of language advocating correspondence between sign and meaning, since they [those ideologies] depend on the illusion of this correspondence for their effectiveness. On the other hand, theories of language that put into question the subservience, resemblance, or potential identity between sign and meaning are always subversive" (170). Collins's sensationalism of the mid-1860s is one such "subversive practice."

Collins's text is intent on unearthing hidden precepts, particularly those associated with realist novel writing. It is always useful, in coming to understand a society, to look at its repressions—especially fertile ground with regard to Victorian culture. The excluded entity *par excellence* for Victorian realist fiction is, as is signaled by its name, the evidence of its own fictionality, of its constructedness or non-"realness." While realist fiction, like any narrative-centered fiction, relies on the possibility of mimesis, that is, on the possibility of the world being re-rendered through a system of signs, what it most desperately needs to exclude is the coming to consciousness of that practice. Parody, or the mimesis of mimesis, brings realism's repressed basis in artifice out into the open, brings it back to consciousness and out from behind the somnolescence that had been the reader's suspension of disbelief. By having his story transform from domestic to sensational novel in the latter half of its First Scene, Collins will be bringing home—much like Derrida in his critique of Austin—the fact of the undelimitability of parodic reference, the fact of linguistic iterability's irrepressibility.

While Collins's previous novel *The Woman in White,* in its recounting of the Madame de Douhault Affair, had been the retelling of the story of an impersonation,[24] the citation of impersonation so to speak, *No Name* in its appearing to veer toward the arena of domestic fiction, in contrast, is the *impersonation of citation.* The narrative begins, as we have seen, by impersonating the realist novel, a type of novel whose authors tend to understand their role as one of effecting something that we might call a "simple citation" of the world. The Victorian realists, following in the tradition established

---

24. See Hyder; and Collins, *Woman in White,* ed. Sucksmith, appendix E, 599–600.

by Jane Austen, attempt to record reflections in a desire to "faithfully" represent (and re-present) the world. In a realist touchstone even more seminal than Chapter 17 of *Adam Bede,* the Reverend Richard Whately writes in his *Quarterly* review of 1821 that Austen's is

> *that unpretending kind of instruction which is furnished by real life*; and certainly no author has ever conformed more closely to real life, as well in the incidents, as in the characters and descriptions. . . . Her fables . . . have all that compactness of plan and unity of action which is generally produced by a sacrifice of probability: yet they have little or nothing that is not probable; the story proceeds without the aid of extraordinary accidents; the events which take place are the necessary or natural consequences of what has preceded.[25] (360; emphasis added)

Collins mimics that simple "unpretending" citation practiced by Austen. Indeed, he could be said quite simply to be *citing* that citation. But in citing it he introduces—necessarily through the simple act of citation if nothing else—a foreignness into the home. (It is no accident that the plotting in this novel should be instigated by an instance of oxymoronically-named "private theatricals").

Once he doubles it, the situation is no longer as "simple" as it had been. However, one is prompted at this point to wonder whether things had been all that simple in the first place. Is it possible to distinguish between simple citation and the impersonation of citation, between simple and doubled citation? The fact that, like Phillips, we could have been, and indeed at any time could be again, "taken in" by Collins's opening suggests these two types of citation can easily pass for one another, thus posing serious ramifications for the suspension of disbelief. Always already facing the potential of being disclosed to have been overly-credulous, we would-be "suspenders" will tend to resent this type of revelation. It halts the uncomplicated enjoyment of the suspension of disbelief so desired by a narrative like *Sense and Sensibility,* makes it something that from then on has to be willed rather than "simply" being enjoyed. Collins is suggesting that, unpleasant as it may be, this is in fact the more honest standpoint. In *Armadale,* noting the look of appeal the seemingly-artless Neelie Milroy casts in Allan Armadale's direction, Lydia Gwilt will comment in her diary, "For downright brazen impudence, which a grown woman would be ashamed of, give me the young girls

---

25. Levine describes Whately's review as "an invaluable guide to historical understanding of what, to the sensible contemporary, Austen seemed to be doing, and in what consisted her newness" (36).

whose 'modesty' is so pertinaciously insisted on by the nauseous domestic sentimentalists of the present day!" (432). Collins's critique of the "brazen impudence" behind the apparent "artlessness" of the domestic novelists of his day had already begun one novel previously. He is in *No Name* out to disabuse the reader who wants nothing more, it seems, than to stay under the sway of the domestic novelist's illusions. In this narrative Collins is "pretending" to be unpretending, and this "pretense" turns out to be radically subversive as Collins discloses all *realist* novelists to be potential *parodists*.

"I do pretend . . . " and the Disarticulation of the Soul from the Body through the Copy

We turn now to a particular example of Collins's parodying of the marriage vow, one with—as had been true of this opening parody—surprisingly profound implications. At the end of the First Scene of this theatrical narrative, the character Mr. Clare makes the following pronouncement to our heroine Magdalen: "I don't pretend to enter into your feelings for Frank, or Frank's for you. . . . The subject doesn't interest me. But I *do* pretend to state two plain truths" (132). This statement, given its particular emphasis and general context, is, at a certain level, clearly parodying the marriage vow. It is significant that immediately after Magdalen's parents' marriage has been disclosed to have been a sham a character should be making the statement "I *do* pretend. . . . "

Clare's statement comes as the first explicit "I do" in a series of what Austin would have called performative "misfirings." There are other instances in the narrative of a type of misuse or "mis-reference" in relation to the marriage vow. For example, there are the elliptical "I do"s interchanged by Magdalen and her cousin Noel late in the novel. At the particular moment when Noel and Magdalen are meant to exchange their vows, the narrative takes on a surprising reticence:

> The clergyman opened the Book.
>
> It was done. The awful words which speak from earth to Heaven were pronounced. The children of the two dead brothers . . . were Man and Wife. (418)

Few performative failures could be more patent than the complete absence evident in this bodiless soul, that is, in this instance of Collins's strategic use of what he liked to term—characteristically giving substance to what is usually ignored—"white lines." (For Collins even emptiness could signify, as is evident in Walter Hartright's excitement at finding "a space evidently left because it was too narrow to contain the entry of the marriages of the two brothers, which in the copy, as in the original, occupied the top of the next page. That space told the whole story!" [*Woman in White,* ed. Sutherland 520]). Collins's somber phrasing, "[t]he awful words which speak from earth to Heaven," suggests that he recognizes there to be a power particular to certain words and phrases. It is Collins's profoundly-insightful focus on linguistic cruxes such as this one that tempts one to style him a speech-act theorist, only of a more worldly type than most twentieth-century practitioners. After intuiting the possibility of speech-acts, Collins tends to revel in that category's failures rather than to prop it up through the deliberate imposition onto the system of language of unworkable proprieties (or falsifying normalizing conventions). For Collins, domesticity, whether residential or literal, cannot be rendered fundamentally unassailable, secured from the always-possible return of the repressed, the return of the "unserious" performative specifically and of unseriousness in general.

If one were to attempt to sum up his work in a single statement, it would be that in Collins's novels no one is safe at home. *No Name* is no different from the rest of Collins's major novels in this respect. The most forceful assault made in the narrative on complacent domesticity is that one we have begun to trace, the assault made on the marriage vow, that basic grounding for the propriety, if not perhaps also the happiness, of the average Victorian home. One of the titles Collins was considering up to the last minute before serialization of *No Name* had begun—*Man and Wife,* a title he used in 1870—particularly emphasized the domestic and matrimonial aspects of his narrative.[26] The marriage vow is explicitly parodied in the tensely dramatic scene in which Magdalen agrees to take the fatal step of giving herself over to the mentorship of Captain Wragge:

> "Place your departure from York, your dramatic career, and your private inquiries under my care. Here I am, unreservedly at your disposal. Say the word—do you take me?"
>
> Her heart beat fast; her lips turned dry—but she said the word.
>
> "I do." (181)

---

26. See Peters 241. The later novel was itself a sustained attack on—when it was not criticizing the amorality of narcissistic athletes—the Scottish and Irish marriage laws of Collins's day.

This particular "I do" is most probably intended to remind us of that other one, the one that Magdalen did not have the chance of saying in the First Scene to Frank Clare, her young love interest, because her happy domesticity had commenced—like a less-than-solidly-built stage set—literally crumbling around her. As *No Name*'s manifest emphasis on stage mimicry and on the phrases "I do" in the act of marrying and "I will" in the act of bequeathing make clear, a principal interest of the narrative rests in "performatives," those "awful words which speak from earth to Heaven," those words, that is, to put it in the discourse of the narrative, that make body and soul work together as one in a common goal.

There are other implications to Mr. Clare's words. He shies away from the pretension of weighing Magdalen's and Frank's feelings for one another but does not shy away from the pretension of stating plain truths. The term "to pretend" can of course also mean to falsify, and it is in this sense that his statement implies a reference to Collins's opening domestic gambit in *No Name.* "I *do* pretend to state . . . plain truths": this might well be Collins speaking in his own person—or indeed any *realist* novelist. This is what Collins the writer had been doing throughout the First Scene of his novel, that is, in the pages that had preceded Mr. Clare's admonition.

What does it mean to "pretend" to state plain truths? Is this something different from lying? Is *pretending to be* different from *merely* stating plain truths, i.e., representing straightforwardly in language? It is impossible to distinguish these (three?) situations and it is *this truth* that this fiction is ultimately attempting to convey. In *No Name,* Collins shows the representation of "truth"—insofar as it would want to manifest itself through something called domestic *fiction*—to always already have been based on pretense. However, Collins is not content with this degree of subversive overturning of the true/false, real/sensational, and real/unreal binaries. He will go on to attempt to disclose intentions to be, as a direct result of iterability, always already potentially false or inherently falsifiable at their basis.

Several critics have noted the unifying role played by nineteenth-century domestic fiction in upholding the general domestic proprieties.[27] The narrative of *No Name* represents, then, a very serious threat, as it shows those proprieties to be fundamentally violable, bringing it all home, down to the level of the propriety of the "proper" citizenry from which the realist author draws for his or her models. As we have seen, imitability, at various levels, is the main issue with which this narrative occupies itself throughout its

---

27. See for instance Nancy Armstrong's discussion in *Desire and Domestic Fiction* of the establishment and upholding by eighteenth- and nineteenth-century domestic fictions of the proprieties concerning sexuality and gender.

course, as it transitions from staid, average Victorian domestic novel to sensational story of our heroine Magdalen's disinheritance upon the untimely deaths of her father and mother and her subsequent sensational efforts to see that justice is done to her and her sister Norah. The assault on the safe domesticity in *No Name* takes on its most radical formulation in the narrative's assault on the safe home of the integral self, the unique body. We should recall in this context not only Magdalen's impersonations of Norah, of the girls' governess Miss Garth, and of Magdalen's own maid Louisa, but also her impersonation of the spirit of her father, that impersonation that calls forth the plotting in the story. After her father dies, Magdalen takes on herself the task of seeing his last wish realized, of embodying his last intentions. By comparison, after Noel Vanstone makes a new will in order to thwart Magdalen from in effect inheriting back her father's eighty thousand pounds, that will is described as a speech-act empty of Noel's actual intention, empty, that is, until one considers a further document. To discover that intention one also needs to know the contents of the Secret Trust. That Trust being the necessary link putting into effect Noel's wishes, it becomes the document that renders the will a viable performative, as Mrs. Lecount makes clear: "Your will there, is a body without a soul . . . until the letter is completed and laid by its side" (467). And was not the sad story of Andrew Vanstone's so-very-ineffective intention—specifically the intention to leave a will—with which we had begun the narrative, on the contrary, the story of the spirit being cruelly deprived of the official means, that is, an instance of a soul without a body?

The plotting in *No Name* only truly begins after Andrew Vanstone's death has resulted in the thwarting of his manifest intention to have provided for his two daughters. Because Andrew has not made a new will after having taken the step, apocalyptic in testamentary terms, of finally having married the girls' mother—his common-law wife of many years—the whole of his estate passes to his heartless and already wealthy brother Michael, Noel's father. This circumstance renders Andrew a character a bit like Hamlet's father, doomed to walk the earth decrying the usurpation of his (e)state by his brother and demanding the actualization of his intentions. (Captain Wragge at more than one point will quote Osric's judgment from *Hamlet,* "a hit, a palpable hit" [159 and 171]). It is this thwarted "will"-ingness that causes Magdalen so to resent her uncle Michael's refusal to give the sisters their father's money. In his last letter, directing his lawyer Pendril to begin the process of drafting a new will, Andrew presciently writes, "If anything happened to me, and if my desire to do their mother justice, ended (through my miserable ignorance of the law) in leaving Norah and Magdalen disin-

herited, I should not rest in my grave!" (108). Once Andrew is dead, however, there would seem to be no way for his intention to be put into effect.
As Andrew's last words make clear, it is in this case absolutely a matter of
the spirit being willing but of the flesh needing to be . . . well, somebody
else's. The rest of the narrative of *No Name* is largely a recounting of Magdalen's dedication of her body, in various ways, to the goal of effecting her
father's last wish. Magdalen not only sacrifices her self-regard by taking on a
series of disguises and commencing a career as a stage actress in the pursuit
of the eighty thousand pounds, but she also sacrifices her purity—scandal-
izing most every novel reviewer of the day. Her marriage to Noel may be
an improper use of her body that only goes the more to show how "vulgar"
and "polluted"—to repeat Margaret Oliphant's descriptions of Magdalen's
actions and of Magdalen herself ("Novels" [1863] 170)—the genre of sensation fiction had become by that time, but it nevertheless also makes a sort
of thematic sense in the context of her quest to actualize her father's disem-
bodied and as yet ineffectual wish.

Another turn-about of the soul/body duality is effected by the two marriages in the narrative. Magdalen's sacrifice in marrying Noel is one that we
are called on to compare with her parents' "marriage." While Magdalen's
marriage (disregarding the fact that she has married under an alias) has
undergone the requisite formalities, her parents' common-law union had
actually possessed the spirit so very lacking in this "official" one; that is,
while the parents' marriage may have been a soul without an official body,
their daughter's marriage is most decidedly a body without a soul. Magdalen's many hesitations along her path toward her wedding day with Noel not
only serve to highlight Wragge's role as Svengali, and perhaps to mitigate
the immorality of her marriage, but, in a speech-act context, also go toward
proving that the soul in this shape-changing body is not as willing as it
should be, that Magdalen is most decidedly not that most desired of speech-
act entities, a unified subject. Her hesitations provide a good indication that
the narrative of *No Name* is much more interested in the "space between,"
so to speak—that is, in the distance between thought and action, between
word and deed, between motivator and actor—than in "pure" performatives. It is fundamentally interested in—as Collins puts it in the preface to
Basil (1852), that earlier novel that was being carefully revised during the
early stages of the writing of *No Name*—"the broad line of separation which
distinguishes between the will and the deed" (Collins, *Basil*, ed. Goldman
xxxvii).[28]

---

28. The title of *How to Do Things with Words* when it was being formulated as lectures at Oxford

At one point during the intrigues at Aldborough, Magdalen orders Captain Wragge (masquerading as her uncle "Thomas Bygrave" for the purposes of their con-game) to take her away from the scene of action for a few days: "I can't get over the horror of marrying him, while I am in this hateful place—take me somewhere I can forget it, or I shall go mad!" (358). Consequently, she, the Captain, and his wife spend four days at the town of Woodbridge. On returning, Magdalen has recovered her composure, having reconciled herself to her original plan: "Vibrating perpetually from one violent extreme to another, she had now passed from the passionate despair of five days since, to a feverish exaltation of spirits, which defied all remorse and confronted all consequences" (364). One is again tempted to compare her with Hamlet as we find her, after a bout of near-madness, once more resolute of heart in her purpose of seeing her father's wishes honored. However, this resolve does not last, and soon enough she is on the point of another, this time much more serious, hesitation. When she is on the brink of having achieved the union toward which she had been so dedicatedly maneuvering, Magdalen nearly decides *not* to be, stopped only by the appearance of an eighth ship at her window: an odd number of ships during the fateful half hour, she had arbitrarily decided, would have meant she must drink the fatal dose of laudanum she held ready in her hand.

Just before the scene of the ships, she asks herself where her amazing endurance under her many trials comes from: "[W]hat is my heart made of! How it lives and lives, when other girls' hearts would have died in them long ago!" (400). Her "heart" it will turn out, not surprisingly, is made up of *textual citations*. Throughout the plotting, Magdalen keeps with her in a white bag tied round her neck, resting over her physical heart, two extracts, one copied from her father's defunct will, the other from his last letter to his solicitor Pendril. While it is certainly Magdalen's heart, in the physical sense, that allows her to commit her acts throughout the narrative, it would seem that her father's spirit, "heart" in the figurative sense, all the while motivates them. Magdalen's impersonations take not only their impetus but also perhaps their analogical model from these textual extracts that she carries about with her in her little white bag. The narrative makes it clear that these words are citations, iterations. Norah comments on Magdalen's refusal of the original documents, "I was the eldest [*sic*] (she said), and those last precious relics ought to be in my keeping. I tried to propose to her that we should divide them; but she shook her head" (138). Showing the bag containing the extracts to her sister, Magdalen replies, "I have *copied* for myself . . . all

---

was "Words and Deeds" (Austin, *How to Do Things* vi).

that he says of us in the will, and all that he says in the letter. . . . This tells me in his own words what his last wishes were for both of us . . . and this is all I want for the future" (138; emphasis added). (Here we have the two girls treating these texts as a type of legacy. This is an important conflation, since an issue of some interest to the narrative is the question of the control of Andrew Vanstone's other [monetary] legacy. What would have made the money and the texts work together would have been Andrew's successfully wrought last performative.) Iterability has shown up in the center.

The situation of Andrew Vanstone's failed performative brings to prominence the linguistic iterability at the basis of the will/deed distinction. More properly, this should be termed a will/will distinction (since Magdalen and her father represent two aspects of the same will). In this non-unified will we find there to be a foreignness disclosed to exist at the basis of the Self. This situation is another manifestation in Collins's major fictions of the Other being lodged securely in the Self, that situation of course having come into being as a result of "one" being via linguistic iterability, as Derrida puts it, "absented from what one used," absented from the language one had been using to express the Self. The constantly failing performatives in *No Name* are meant to invoke and disclose this Otherness in the Self.[29] In *Armadale* and *The Moonstone,* Collins will extend his explorations into this Otherness that has the potential for manifesting itself within the region of the Self as a result of the iterability of language.

Sensationalism in a New Sense

As we have observed, the opening scenes of *No Name,* this novel so dedicated to theatricality, cleave to the line between simulation and origination and disclose the former to be subverting the latter. But theatricality had already been extant in the name given to the genre that it helped found, the "sensation novel." The term "sensation fiction" was continually to haunt the composition and reception of *No Name.* It was labeled a "sensation novel," to offer but one example, by an anonymous reviewer in the London *Daily Telegraph* on 2 January 1863. The term "sensation novel" had been coined as early as September 1861, when a reviewer in the *Sixpenny Review* had used the label in the course of commenting on the startling effect *The Woman in White,* among other novels, had had on contemporary fiction (see Page 17).

---

29. As will also the alienations of the name and non-singularity of the event in Collins's next novel *Armadale* and the scenes of self-alienation in *The Moonstone.* The second-most-prominent failed performative in *No Name* is Mrs. Lecount's stamping with Noel's seal the envelope containing Noel's Secret Trust after he refuses to do so (474–75).

No Name's initial serialization, in *All the Year Round,* had begun on 15 March 1862 and ended on 17 January 1863 (*No Name* xxiv). Collins's next novel *Armadale* famously would be labeled by the reviewer H. F. Chorley "a 'sensation novel' with a vengeance."[30] This lumping with "the masses" implies the presence of similarities. However, I contend that from the beginning, specifically *No Name*'s First Scene, Collins was attempting to write a "sensation novel" with a peculiarly linguistic focus rather than one specifically critiquing his culture's unstable priorities.

Collins's agenda was more ambitious than that of the typical sensation novelist of his time. A lack of revolutionary ambition on the other sensationalists' part is evident in the defenses they offer for the "legitimacy" of this genre, arguing that, in actuality, there exist occasional eruptions of sensationality in the real world, as in, for example, Dickens's earlier-referenced contention that "It is very easy to cry 'Sensational!' but the word proves nothing. Let it be granted that such things *are* sensational; but then life itself is similarly sensational in many of its aspects, and Nature is similarly sensational in many of her forms, and art is always sensational when it is tragic" ([Dickens], "The Sensational Williams" 14). But Collins believed that it was more productive, rather than suggesting sensation was an occasional eruption in regular life, to ask what made the eruption always already possible in the first place. In order to adequately address this problem of nineteenth-century fiction we were forced to turn, surprisingly, to a twentieth-century literary critical context, Derrida's critique of speech-act theory in the early 1970s. Applying Derrida's insights about Austin to Collins's context, we have seen that his eruptions of sensationality all turn out to have been the result of sincerity being based on a fundamental insincerity, and insincerity so fecund that some of its manifestations could be sacrificed to the mundane task of mimicking the effects of what we like to call "sincerity." It is now time to turn our attention to those manifestations left over.

EARLY in the narrative of *No Name,* Magdalen has an argument with her sister Norah. Magdalen has the night before impersonated the latter while playing the role of Julia in the Marrables' private production of *The Rivals,*[31] and she can tell that her sister is not at all pleased:

---

30. Chorley, unsigned review, *Athenaeum* (2 June 1866): 732–33; rpt. in Page 146.

31. Helena Michie—in her discussion of the way in which "fallen sisters . . . are frequently recuperable through their sisters' efforts" in both Rossetti's "Goblin Market" and *No Name*—suggests there to be in Collins's recourse to private theatricals a covert tie to domestic fiction, specifically to the fictions of Jane Austen: "Amateur theatricals are used, of course . . . from *Mansfield Park* onward, as vehicles for the expression of inappropriate erotic feelings" (17–18 and 30).

"Dear me, how black you look this morning! I'm in disgrace, I suppose. Haven't you forgiven me yet for my acting last night? I couldn't help it, love; I should have made nothing of Julia, if I hadn't taken you for my model. It's quite a question of Art. In your place, I should have felt flattered by the selection."

"In *your* place, Magdalen, I should have thought twice before I mimicked my sister to an audience of strangers." (52)

Given the starkly contrasting natures of the two Vanstone girls, expressed here and throughout the story, it would seem *No Name* could just as appropriately have been titled *Sense and Sensationality,* the difference in the sisters' natures having served to highlight the distance being bridged by, and degree of violation inherent in, Magdalen's impersonation. Mark Ford, the editor of the Penguin edition, insightfully focuses on this particular scene: "Norah's distress is interesting because it so clearly illustrates society's aversion to having what it likes to believe is natural and unique revealed to be conditioned and imitable" (*No Name* xii). Here the would-be integral identity encounters the danger of perhaps having to acknowledge its always potential disruptibility by iterability.

If we extend the implications of Ford's comment about Norah's distress also to the macro-mimicry in the First Scene, we see that Collins is implying with his parody of realism that the realist novelists of his day could all along have been writing parodies, an insight for which they, like Norah, would have been unlikely to thank him. The only things hampering this undecideable whirligig of uncontrollable interchangeability are certain contextual cues. There is nothing, in theory, distinguishing the elements at the basis of realism from those at the basis of the parody of realism. Both are disclosed by the opening of *No Name,* at different points and from the points of view of different contexts, to bear the possibility of being constituted by the same words, the possibility of looking the same—reminding us of the sensation-generating similarity in appearance of Anne and Laura in *The Woman in White.*

At the beginning of *No Name,* Collins shows that the domestic novel, like any form of fiction, can itself be cited and impersonated—even at the level of its founding principles: in the case of domestic fiction, the happy home, the young lovers headed altar-wise. It is all the more appropriate, then, that Magdalen should take, after that home has broken up, the most conservative character at Combe-Raven, her governess Miss Garth, as her model when she begins performing "At Homes" under the direction of Captain Wragge—parodying the form of domestic fiction within the narrative

itself. A clue to the always already unstable propriety at the basis of the
paradigmatic domestic picture afforded by Combe-Raven can be found in
the novel when Wragge describes his plan for utilizing Magdalen's powers
of mimicry. Wragge writes in his Chronicle of Events,

> I have discovered that [Magdalen] possesses extraordinary talent as a
> mimic. She has the flexible face, the manageable voice and the dramatic
> knack which fit a woman for character-parts and disguises on the stage. . . .
> Train her in the art of dramatic disguise; provide her appropriate dresses
> for different characters . . . *advertise her as A Young Lady at Home* . . . and
> what follows as a necessary consequence? Fame for my fair relative, and a
> fortune for myself.[32] (190–91; emphasis added)

For Collins, once again, home is where the mimic is. We have seen Derrida come to a very similar conclusion for a very similar reason. This conjoint discovery about the workings of language made by these two cultural
authorities—albeit a discovery that was staggered over time and made in
markedly different disciplines—should come as little surprise, as both had
involved themselves in a similar project, that of analyzing the ramifications
for "propriety" (whether philosophical or social) of the *fundamental illimitability of the act of citation*. Both having involved themselves in disclosing
that the disturbance caused by the possibility of citation reaches all the way
down to the level of the hearth and home and the very essence of the "self,"
it was inevitable that the cracks in the essentially vulnerable foundations of
the proprieties holding up the school of John Austin's speech-act theory and
of Jane Austen's realism should have come to disclose themselves.

Mine is not an altogether original formulation. The spirit of our two
Aust(i/e)ns has been brought together before. Margaret Anne Doody comments on J. L. Austin's implicit claim to philosophical kinship with Jane
Austen, noting that the Oxford philosopher "paid tribute to Austen's philosophical title and concerns when he named his own book *Sense and Sensi-*

---

32. This role played by Magdalen is foreshadowed when the narrative has Miss Garth look in
on the tableau of the future star of the Marrables' play preparing for her role: "There sat Magdalen,
in an arm-chair before the long looking-glass, with all her hair let down over her shoulders; absorbed
in the study of her part. . . . And there behind her sat the lady's-maid, slowly combing out the long
heavy locks of her young mistress's hair, with the sleepy resignation of a woman who had been engaged in that employment for some hours past. . . . The luxurious tranquility of the scene; the cool
fragrance of flowers and perfumes in the atmosphere; the rapt attitude of Magdalen, absorbed over
her reading; the monotonous regularity of movement in the maid's hand and arm, as she drew the
comb smoothly through and through her mistress's hair—all conveyed the same soothing impression
of drowsy delicious quiet" (39).

bilia" (xxxiii–xxxiv). Doody's further point suggests one reason for Austin's choice of title: "J. Aust*i*n was doubtless stimulated by the similarity of his name to that of J. Aust*e*n into seeing some resemblance in their concerns" (xxxiv*n*21).[33] However, I here have been arguing that the similarities lie deeper, especially with respect to the issue of repressive capacity, than Doody would seem to envision. This similarity between Austin and Austen is not surprising as the philosophers of propriety (as we might term them) are always going to be involved in campaigns designed in one way or another to repress, control, and discipline the iterability of the mark, be that mark the improper arching of the brow, the speaking or writing of the wrong word, or, most disturbing of all, the mimicking or counterfeiting of the proper gesture. Collins, through the project of showing that the world works according to a different set of rules than those provisional ones mapped out by Jane Austen and by the more proper Victorian domestic novelists of his own time, is also posing a fundamental challenge to the world of Austen's heirs, the world of the twentieth-century speech-act theorists. Collins thus could be seen in *No Name* to be, in general, a deconstructionist *avant la lettre* and, in particular, to be prefiguring Derrida's deconstruction of J. L. Austin's speech-act theory.

The argument might be posed that what realists do is done "seriously" and according to rules that sensationalists do not believe in or follow. This is the position that would be espoused, and undoubtedly continually is in the present day, by what I am calling the "School of Austen/Austin," a position disclosed by Derrida's critique to be patently inadequate to the complex task of dealing with Yates's "fixed constitution of things." I would summarize Derrida's critique of Austin by way of a simple question: Is there not a degree of artifice *inherent in* any act of citation, no matter how "faithful"? Is not the act of simply moving something to a different context a radically transformative act, an act structurally constituted to fatally undermine the transparency of "honest" intentions? Conversely, can one's good-willed intentions—as Magdalen implies they do in the case of her impersonation of Norah—ever sufficiently mitigate the threat posed by the act of citation? Is the artless citation ever really possible? According to Derrida, the answer to this last question would have to be—as is Norah's answer to Magdalen—a resounding No.

---

33. In the Foreword to *Sense and Sensibilia,* G. J. Warnock writes, "Austin lectured many times on the problems with which this book is concerned. The first lectures were those which he gave in Oxford in Trinity Term, 1947, under the general title 'Problems in Philosophy.' He first used the title 'Sense and Sensibilia' in Trinity Term of the following year, and this was the title that he subsequently retained" (Austin, *Sense and Sensibilia* v).

Constantly Saying "Relly!"

The issues raised in this chapter about this book entitled paradoxically *No Name*—a story very much taken up with the sensational legal fiction of the illegitimate child being considered Nobody's Child—are all encapsulated in a particular story that Wilkie Collins includes in his first book, his biography of his painter father. The amusing anecdote is related in a letter written by Collins's father and has special resonance with the issue of naming since the man being spoken of by William Collins is Wilkie Collins's godfather, the painter Sir David Wilkie, the bestower of Collins's middle—later first—name. Both these gentlemen, one as character and one as author but both conjoined in the name "Wilkie Collins"—our author's original "models," in a sense—play significant roles in the following story regarding the impossibility of distinguishing a real "re(a)lly" from a faked "re(a)lly." William Collins writes,

> Chantrey and Wilkie were dining alone with me, when the former, in his great kindness for Wilkie, ventured, as he said, to take him to task for his constant use of the word "*relly,*" (really,) when listening to any conversation in which he was much interested. "Now, for instance," said Chantrey, "suppose I was giving you an account of any interesting matter, you would constantly say, '*Relly!*'" "*Relly!*" exclaimed Wilkie immediately, with a look of the most perfect astonishment. (Qtd. in Wilkie Collins, *Memoirs of the Life* 1:194)

This scene has resonances with Magdalen's quest in *No Name* to become "Magdalen Vanstone," a name she had mistakenly thought was hers for her first 18 years. After she has married her cousin Noel and thereby become "properly" entitled to use that signature, near the end of one of her letters to her former governess Miss Garth she writes the following:

> I have made the general sense of propriety my accomplice this time. Do you know who I am? I am a respectable married woman, accountable for my actions to nobody under Heaven but my husband. I have got a place in the world, and a name in the world, at last. . . . You forget what wonders my wickedness has done for me. It has made Nobody's Child,[34] Somebody's Wife. . . . If you ever speak about me to Norah, tell her that

---

34. Magdalen refers here to the legal designation of the illegitimate Victorian child as *filius nullius.*

a day may come when she will see me again—the day when we two sisters
have recovered our natural rights; the day when I put Norah's fortune into
Norah's hand. . . .

MAGDALEN VANSTONE (484)

In Magdalen's allusion to her "natural right" there is a suggestion of that
"moral right" of the author over his literary creation that characterizes certain strains of French and English copyright law. Along these lines, it is
appropriate that Captain Wragge, her helpmeet, should be a self-professed
"Moral Agriculturist" (169) and should describe himself as "the publisher,
so to speak, of [Magdalen's] book" (200). Magdalen is all along passionately fighting, as she writes that "book," for the reestablishment of a natural
right—related quite closely to paternity—that she feels has been unfairly
slighted by the culture around her.

The narrator of the story at one point asks, "What did Magdalen care
for satire?" (78). Quite a bit, it would seem. Here in this letter, her name
"Magdalen Vanstone" could be seen to be a type of satire on society's proprieties. She has been able to play by the rules and nevertheless to end up in a
position that seems "real" but that has been reached by unrelenting "wicked-
ness." Similarly, Lydia Gwilt in Collins's next novel *Armadale* cannot believe
her luck when she learns that the real name of her husband Ozias Midwinter
is "Allan Armadale." This fortuitous circumstance suggests to her a wicked
plan for establishing a similar false legitimacy having to do with naming:
she resolves "to pass [herself] off for the widow of one man, while [she is]
all the while the wife of the other" (*Armadale* 447). Both of these women
are able to establish that powerful oxymoron, a false reality, through a clever
manipulation of the proprieties. They have reached that region where one's
"relly," or one's reality, is fundamentally ambiguous.

Language's always-operative iterability opens up vast realms of possibility for diversity of meaning and intention. For one thing, it frees up those
possibilities that Austin's act of having summarily labeled them more or less
"improper" (recall Austin's extensive list of misexecutions) would seem to
have successfully pushed off into exile. What is the act of titling one's book
"No Name" if not a potentially very "improper" response to the necessity
of naming? No matter how much the philosophers of propriety desire their
exclusion, the infelicities are never going to be conclusively excised. Here
in this story of Sir David Wilkie's always-potentially-ambiguous reply, iterability allows for the second "Relly!" forever to oscillate between the performative and constative domains, between use and mention, between the

realistic and the parodic. We can never be sure whether Wilkie was joking or being serious (just as you can never be sure whether I intend here a formal reference to the painter or an informal one to the writer), citing (himself) seriously or parodically, when he exclaimed, *"Relly!"* And this uncertainty was undoubtedly fine with Wilkie.

⊰5⊱

Ingesting the Other in *Armadale*

I was startled just now by a shadow on the wall. It was only after a moment or two that I mustered sense enough to notice where the candle was, and to see that the shadow was my own. . . . I see my own hand while I write the words—and I ask myself whether it is really the hand of Lydia Gwilt!

—Lydia Gwilt, in *Armadale* 440 and 507

The Receiver and Sender
Modes of the Breaking Function

The sensation novel reinforced a particular fear of the English populace. The dread of the possibility of the invasion of the Homeland by the Other while of course not originating with the genre was nevertheless buoyed up by it. This worry is evident in an anonymous reviewer's description of sensation fiction, in a review of *No Name* in the *Reader* in 1863, as "a plant of foreign growth [that] comes to [at?] us from France" (rpt. in Page 134). The Reverend Francis Edward Paget, in the polemical afterword to his 1868 parody—a more successfully rendered imitation than he might be presumed to have intended—*Lucretia or, The Heroine of the Nineteenth Century: A Correspondence, Sensational and Sentimental,* feels similarly called on to characterize the threat posed by this genre as one of a potential invasion by the Other, or at least Otherness:

The staple commodity of our sensation novels is scoundrelism of the lowest type. . . . If such filthy Yahoos . . . do really exist . . . there is at least this comfort, that, as yet, . . . they do not obtrude themselves on our notice; they are a race as strange to us as the Fuegians would be, or the Andaman islanders. But strange they will not long continue, if the rage for sensational novels continues. (301)

Paget is onto something, certainly with regard to Collins's longest and most complicated narrative *Armadale* (1866), the goal of which is, on one level, to effect precisely this "noticing" of Otherness.[1] But Collins's is actually a more radical meeting up with alterity than Paget in his worst fantasies—his reference to two purportedly cannibalistic tribes suggesting those fantasies to be pretty extreme already solely hampered by the hurdle of the ingestion moving in the wrong direction—would have been envisioning, as it involves the eventual acknowledgment that the Self *is* that Other. That is, the operational strategy in this one of Collins's narratives is to represent an initial encounter with Otherness that then modifies into the attendant stage of that Otherness's incorporation. Collins understood that a direct result of this ingestion of the Other/of Otherness—the distinction between integration at the minimal level (inclusion in the form of a sealed "crypt") and maximal level (absorption and conjoining) being precisely the aspect most distinguishing, respectively, *Armadale* from *The Moonstone*[2]—would be the bringing home of the fact, in a pre-playing of a particular Postmodernist tenet, that those problems (particularly the unsettling effects of the breaking function of language) usually automatically shunted off as entirely the fault of the Other are actually to some degree native to the Self. The latter thus loses its protective/projective disguise, its chance of scapegoating the Other. This incorporational desire is evident in the story of the Bedouin brothers, that reverse-Russian-nesting-doll situation, that Collins has Allan Armadale 4[3] relate at one point in *Armadale*:

---

1. Many critics—especially those influenced by the Profession's turn toward postcolonial criticism—halt in their analyses of Collins's strategy of "Otherness ingestion" at this simple encounter stage. See for example Reitz, who argues in her punningly titled article "Colonial 'Gwilt': In and around Wilkie Collins's *Armadale*" that "*Armadale* demonstrates an Englishness that is strengthened by recognizing colonial mistakes" (101).

2. See Derrida writing in "*Fors*" of the process of the "encrypting" of the Other leading to "a redefinition of the Self" (xv). He notes that there are two possibilities of dealing with the mourned person: as a locked safe within the self—"The inner forum is (a) safe, an outcast outside inside the inside" (xiv)—or as an element that is eventually broken open and completely melded with the self—"the break-in technique that will allow us to penetrate into a crypt . . . consists of locating the crack or the lock, choosing the angle of a partition, and forcing entry" (xv).

3. In an attempt to clear up a baroque confluence that continually has (almost by design?) the

Deuce take the pounds, shillings, and pence! I wish they could all three get rid of themselves like the Bedouin brothers at the show. Don't you remember the Bedouin brothers, Mr. Brock? "Ali will take a lighted torch, and jump down the throat of his brother Muli—Muli will take a lighted torch, and jump down the throat of his brother Hassan—and Hassan, taking a third lighted torch, will conclude the performances by jumping down his own throat, and leaving the spectators in total darkness." Wonderfully good, that—what I call real wit, with a fine strong flavour about it.[4] (*Armadale* 62)

Whether or not this is wonderfully good as wit, it is certainly wonderfully good at representing the Otherness-internalizing strategy being deployed at this point in Collins's long–novel project. In both *Armadale* and *The Moonstone*, Collins, like the last Bedouin brother Hassan, will be moving the public spectacle, the performance, inside, will be shifting the complications from the realm of the Other (specifically that big "O" other for Collins, the reader) to the realm of the *Self*, or writer, and as a result we will in Collins's next novel have Franklin Blake, the stand-in for the writer of *The Moonstone*, end up being described as having had "so many different sides of his character . . . that he seemed to pass his life in a state of perpetual contradiction with himself. . . . He had his French side, and his German side, and his Italian side—the original English foundation showing through,

---

critics making mistakes (for example, Pal-Lapinski 46, Tondre 595, and Dames 170 all confuse Allan Wrentmore/Armadale with his father Mathew), I will be denoting the five Allan Armadales according to the order of the dates they were either born into this name or changed their given names to it. Allan Armadale 1 was the original owner of the estate in Barbados who disinherited his son (Allan Armadale 2, aka Fergus Ingleby) in favor of Allan Wrentmore (Allan Armadale 3). The two sons of these Allan Armadales are, respectively, Allan Armadale 4 (the "light" Allan Armadale) and Allan Armadale 5 (alias Ozias Midwinter, the "dark" Allan Armadale), born one year apart. I will refer to these last two as Allan Armadale and Ozias Midwinter respectively. Such an unknotting, in avoiding misunderstanding, goes against the spirit of the readerly confusion Collins clearly was for some reason actively intent upon encouraging in his narrative. See Taylor noting that *Armadale* "exploits the links between names and inherited property to question the stable boundaries of the self, as well as to explore social construction" (*Secret Theatre* 154). Obviously, Allan Armadales 4 and 5 are meant to be conflated with each other in an enaction in the reader's mind of the theme of the Other coming to be the same, or at least a brother (indeed, Young-Zook incorrectly understands these two main Allan Armadales to be "stepbrothers" [235]), while, on the other hand, their conflations with their fathers are intended to suggest the fear (eventually proved incorrect) that a murdering mindset may possibly be inherited from one generation to the next, namely from Wrentmore, the murderer of Allan Armadale 2, to Midwinter.

4. The critic Peter Caracciolo confesses himself to be "tantalized by this bizarre, dream-like story" (165). I am in this chapter simply attempting to account for Collins's inclusion—a clumsy one, but all the more significant for being so—of this instance of "wit" in his narrative.

every now and then, as much as to say, 'Here I am, sorely transmogrified, as you see, but there's something of me left at the bottom of him still'" (*Moonstone* 76–77).

In this particular installment in Collins's project, this incorporation of Otherness is, not surprisingly, correlated with the workings of language. The locally "historical" guises taken by Otherness in *Armadale* (racial-, gender-, and class-oriented ones) inevitably come to be outweighed by the linguistic manifestations—for example, the Otherness arising upon the word changing context (or "ownership" through "publication") or the signifier attempting but failing to seamlessly substitute itself for its motivationlessly connected signified—that those guises had been on the verge of obscuring (successfully, in the case of postcolonialism trumping deconstruction in this novel's criticism) in the process of representing them. Iterability opens a space through which alterity can enter the world. Derrida remarks, "In a tangential and elliptical way, a difference always causes repetition to deviate. I call that *iterability,* the other . . . appearing in reiteration" (*Paper Machine* 136). This deviating creates a rift in what had seemed simply a situation of the Same being repeated elsewhere. This Otherness is present in the term's name itself: "*iter,* again, [*sic*] probably comes from *itara, other* in Sanskrit, and everything that follows can be read as the working out of the logic that ties repetition to alterity" ("Signature Event Context" 7). A space or, more properly, spacing, is always extant—whether it is utilized through recontextualization or not—at the basis of the Self represented through iterable traces. This spacing brings into being an ever-present (but not always acknowledged) "shadow" self or paradoxical "ghost presence" that potentially can be substituted for the so-called "real" self and then perhaps spirited away, a possibility that has fascinated authors throughout literary history, especially science fiction writers in the vein of Philip K. Dick and William Gibson.

That repetition-based Otherness can, however, manifest itself in the form of two different *modes,* that of "the receiver" and that of "the sender." We saw in Chapter 3 the receiver-mode Otherness of the breaking function being exploited by the American publishers through their pirating of *The Woman in White,* especially in the scene of their representative Fosco illicitly purloining and reading Marian Halcombe's diary. The primary goal of Collins's project having been to progress toward fundamentals, it is not surprising to find reader-mode Otherness transforming at this point into the authorial "internal complaint" (*Moonstone* 429) of sender-mode Otherness, as we have, in a figurative sense, the textual violater Fosco, as the result of an impressive act of ingestion, becoming a mere projection of

Marian Halcombe's diseased imagination (a situation very much akin to that self-conflicted one taking center stage in *The Moonstone*).[5] This progression offers the possibility of moving us past that chimera that had mesmerized the eighteenth-century copyright commentators, the publication moment.

The possibility for deviations in the receiver mode is evident enough in our own lives; we hear of such misdirections every day, the pirated song, software, or movie being only today's most sensational manifestations. Literary piracy would have been an especially prominent example of obtrusive reader-mode disruptiveness in the nineteenth century. These situations allow us, as senders or authors, to be lulled into a false sense of complacency. We believe, like Austin in *How to Do Things with Words,* that all we need to do to "settle" the situation and control our "language" is to keep it "safe" by avoiding some sort of dangerous region "outside," a wish that is also motivating Paget's comments. In other words, we believe that that zone to be avoided if we want our writing to remain safe—that "*ditch* or external place of perdition" ("Signature Event Context" 17) representing for Derrida the illusory locus beyond which the breaking function is rumored by solely settling-valorizing perspectives to lie safely confined[6]—is the region of the Other, the region not (currently) under control. But what if it is the *Self* that is actually the site of tumult? In that case, one's self-complacency—to say nothing of one's imperializing imperative, distress at the publication moment, or entrenched resistance to "theory"—must, to say the least, be reassessed, if not quite, at this point, overthrown.

Humanizing the Other as a Means of Disclosing the Complications of the Self

As we have already seen in this study, Collins was devoted to the practice of screening his primary intentions behind misleading secondary ones (a practice rendering him conclusively opaque to many critics, paradoxically as a result of his seeming *too* transparent). His linguistic sensationality, as we saw in Chapter 2, was often passing itself off as the standard type of sexual

---

5. *Armadale*, like any good transition point, is obsessed with the concept of mid-ness. Not only is the main character pseudonymously named "Midwinter" but both he and Allan Armadale end up at one point stuck for the night on a half-sunken boat located half-way between the Calf of Man and the Isle of Man—islands to which Collins had made a taxing research visit in 1863, finding them eminently suitable for his "occult literary purposes" (*Letters* 1:232).

6. This locus for Collins in 1859 took the form of the Atlantic Ocean and for the eighteenth-century judges that of the moment of release to publication.

sensationality. Having guessed correctly that sexuality would not fade in its attractiveness for critics, Collins established that particular one of his screens on firm ground. In *Armadale,* the screen misdirecting the critics this time seems more their fault than Collins's. The subject of glamorous "exoticism" running a close second to sexuality in capturing critical attention, his move towards counteracting one of his earlier strategies in *The Woman in White,* the fomenting of a distrust of the Other, is bound often to be read as an instance of "reverse colonization," instead of as, as I will be interpreting it here, a simple "clearing of the decks" so that the complications of the Self can now come into their own. This situation leads directly to a critic like Lyn Pykett finding both *Armadale* and *The Moonstone* to be

> early examples of the "reverse colonization" narrative, a type of fiction which Stephen Arata has associated with the "cultural guilt" of the end of the nineteenth century. . . . Both *Armadale* and *The Moonstone* problematize the relationship between colony and metropole in narratives in which the "home country" is invaded by Creoles (Ozias Midwinter and Ezra Jennings) or Hindus (the Indians who have travelled to England to reclaim the Moonstone). (*Wilkie Collins* 156–57)

Pykett's interpretation slots nicely into a niche carved out beforehand by the recent vogue for postcolonial criticism. Because Collins was always on the "edges" of significant historical/political trends without actually being a true adherent of them (note the difficulties critics have had in conclusively labeling him a defender of women's rights), it is very important, even more than usual, for the critic to be sticking with the movements of the text—in this case Collins's long–novel project, a multi-volume "text" that would be encouraging him or her to look beyond the available and enticing local screens thrown in the way by this author seemingly constitutionally compelled to do so—and not allowing transient critical fashions to dictate the interpretation. In that spirit, here I will be not only attempting to demonstrate to the fullest the institutional and narrative structures that would be pushing the critic toward reading Ozias Midwinter's humanization simply as a postcolonial move on Collins's part—that is, as an undoing of a "cultural guilt" stemming from colonialism—but also endeavoring to show that Collins's is actually nevertheless *moreso* a theoretical movement toward the basis of the author's dealings with language.

It has been generally remarked that Collins's sensation fiction's "sensationality" had begun with a harking back to the xenophobia associated with the influx of foreigners coming to visit the Crystal Palace of the Great Exhibition of 1851. The prospect of that influx had played a central role in the establishment of the intrigues in that earlier narrative, the event providing the motivation for the visit to England of Fosco and for his continuance in the capital even after his plot of stealing Laura Fairlie's identity and inheritance—his invasion into the heart of the domesticity—had succeeded. Late in the story Walter Hartright makes reference to the Exhibition:

> The year of which I am now writing, was the year of the famous Crystal Palace Exhibition in Hyde Park. Foreigners, in unusually large numbers, had arrived already, and were still arriving in England. Men were among us, by hundreds, whom the ceaseless distrustfulness of their governments had followed privately, by means of appointed agents, to our shores. My surmises did not for a moment class a man of the Count's abilities and social position with the ordinary rank and file of foreign spies. I suspected him of . . . being entrusted by the government which he secretly served, with the organization and management of agents specially employed in this country.[7] (*Woman in White,* ed. Sutherland 578)

Ronald R. Thomas clarifies the historical context standing behind this passage's worries:

> It is not only the invasion of foreigners that is of concern here, but the invasion of suspicious foreign influences—specifically, the anarchistic impulses that fueled the revolutions of 1848 in Europe. . . . The juxtaposition of the economic spectacle of the Crystal Palace with the political intrigues involving imported agents from the revolutionary movements . . . forms a striking image of the very historical transformation with which the sensation novel is centrally concerned. ("Wilkie Collins" 485)

In short, sensation fiction could be said, from a certain perspective, to have established its basis upon a fear of revolution.[8] In *The Woman in White*—that

---

7. Collins may have been drawing on newspaper reports such as the following: "Two police-agents, who had been sent from Frankfort to the Exhibition of London, says the *Constitutionnel,* were, on their arrival in that capital, relieved by some adroit thieves of all their luggage and papers, amongst which happened to be the description of several famous German thieves, whom they had been ordered to seek out and observe" ("Report in a London Newspaper"; qtd. in Gibbs-Smith 29). Hartright elsewhere notes that the Count's assistant Mrs. Rubelle and her husband "had taken a house in the neighbourhood of Leicester-square, to be fitted up as a boarding-house for foreigners, who were expected to visit England in large numbers to see the Exhibition of 1851" (*Woman in White* 426).

8. In this sense, my argument could be said to a certain extent to overlap at this moment with Jonathan Loesberg's contention that sensation novels "evoke their most typical moments of sensation response from images of a loss of class identity" (117).

is, at the inception of the genre that he was criticizing—we find Paget's fear of invasion being eminently justified.

It is not surprising that latent British fears about foreigners should have been raised by the prospect of their "German Prince"'s Exhibition coming so soon after the 1848 revolutions and inviting an alarmingly large number of Continentals and Easterners to gather in the heart of the Empire. In *The Shows of London,* Richard Altick remarks that "So many pickpockets, confidence men, cut-throats, prostitutes, foreign spies, stealers of trade secrets, and other illicit practitioners were expected to descend on the metropolis that to dispassionate observers it might have seemed likely that they would be most effectively foiled not by the police but by the law of diminishing returns" (457).[9] By some accounts, two million people were eventually to view the displays (but of those probably only 3% were aliens).[10] The event provided the perfect backdrop against which to establish a culture awash in spying by, and suspicion of, foreigners. Literally "under invasion," the isle had as a result come to be filled with strange accents and languages as well as by a patently un-English ingenuity by a people possessed of an ability to create crimes of impersonation foreign to the English nature (if not, albeit, the opium-influenced mind of the Victorian literary man). Collins, speaking years later of Fosco's crime, says, "I thought the crime too ingenious for an Englishman so I pitched upon a foreigner" (Yates 591).

The lead-up to the Exhibition had been tinged with a paranoia growing among the residents of London, and among their politicians as well. Up until its opening on May 1, 1851—the Exhibition would close on October 15—various Victorian notables would be foreseeing an unhappy outcome for the event. Benjamin Disraeli, future Prime Minister and close friend of

---

9. Elsewhere Altick notes that "no crime wave ever materialized" (*Presence* 422). Even Dickens's *Household Words*—not a journal generally supportive of the Exhibition (Dickens remarked of the Exhibition, "I don't say 'there's nothing in it'—there's too much. I have only been twice. So many things bewildered me. I have a natural horror of sights, and the fusion of so many sights in one has not decreased it" [*Letters* 6:428])—would be forced to acknowledge in mid-October that those people who had predicted disasters ranging from plague to famine to fire to the "unchristinisation" of England, who "amid the fogs of November, 1850, [had] wagged their heads, and sibilated evil predictions awfully," had been conclusively proven wrong: "The threatened invasion has taken place: the Gaul, the Teuton, the Muscovite, and the Moslem have arrived—and to the extent of some thousands, too—yet, I am proud to say that the flag of England, named 'Meteor' by Thomas Campbell, does 'yet terrific burn' above the gates of Buckingham Palace, and Mr. Cutmore's European Dining Rooms. . . . [O]ur foreign visitors have neither burnt our houses about our ears, nor endeavoured to overturn our government, nor run away with our daughters" ([Sala], "Foreign Invasion" 64).

10. Indeed, the threat posed turned out to have been more fearsome than the actuality. The Royal Statistical Society was informed that "The number of visits to the Crystal Palace were 6,039,195,—and the number of persons who visited it were 2,000,000; nevertheless, the landing of only 65,233 aliens was reported in the year" (Cheshire 45).

the recently dethroned Louise Philippe, was prompted to confide the following warning to Lady Londonderry on April 20: "You may rely upon it, as a fact, for it reaches me from a quarter that never misled me—that the Ministers are really alarmed about the concourse of foreigners to the Exhibition, & that the Socialists have been making, & are making, extensive arrangements for our regeneration, apropos of that gathering. This affair has been the subject of cabinet councils" (*Letters* 430). "Regeneration" here is Disraeli's euphemistically sanguine manner of alluding to the general fear of a Continentally-based revolutionary movement coming to raise havoc in England. Collins had been thus in *The Woman in White* most decidedly guilty of propagating, or perhaps resuscitating, a fear of the encounter with the Other—taking the form of a grandly unscrupulous Exhibition visitor— by purposely setting his story at a time when that fear had been especially operative in his culture.

THUS, taking that context into account, the critic can be forgiven for viewing Collins's project of humanizing Ozias Midwinter in *Armadale* as, say, an imitation of his friend Dickens's move in 1865 of having attempted to compensate for his portrayal of the criminal Fagin in *Oliver Twist* with the creation of the sympathetically-rendered Jewish moneylender Riah in *Our Mutual Friend*.[11] Or another interpretation—the result of a "reading backward" from the reformist zeal evident in his later "mission fictions"—could be to find this move to be of a piece with his later humanitarian endeavors in such overtly polemical laters works as *The New Magdalen* (1873), *The Two Destinies* (1876), *The Fallen Leaves* (1879), and *Heart and Science* (1883). Prior to his mental breakdown of 1870 or so, Collins was a literary theorist before he was a defender of the oppressed (not to suggest that the two are necessarily mutually exclusive). Either way, Collins's intent could well appear in *Armadale* to be simply the atonement for his earlier having sensationalized the fear of the Other in *The Woman in White*. In offering such a reading, the critic is happy and the Profession (self-)satisfied. However, it is important to see what is *actually* occurring, for the crudely "political" interpretation of this situation will be—while perhaps advancing the Collins critic's career—unfortunately immuring him or her within

---

11. Collins's move also could be seen simply as an attempt to broaden the insular perspectives of his English readers, readers exhibiting a tendency toward closed-mindedness that Dickens, in 1856 in *Household Words,* had been warning against: "We English people, owing in a great degree to our insular position . . . have been in particular danger of contracting habits which we will call for our present purposes, Insularities" ([Dickens,] "Insularities" 1).

that region that our author is, I believe, at this moment in his project, precisely engaged in leaving behind. Only by taking a long-range perspective, that is, by considering the whole of Collins's long–novel project, can we observe his rejection of the false earlier path offered by the simple undoing of xenophobia as he moves on to the investigation of the more ontological zone. At one point in *Armadale,* Collins has Allan Armadale and Pedgift Jr. visit the Exhibition (348), but in this instance that reference, in direct contrast to those in *The Woman in White,* serves no major plot function. Instead, its ancillary nature stands as a clear indication that Collins has progressed past his earlier xenophobia-fomenting. Collins's humanization of Midwinter is not one carried out for itself, but rather in order to remove the possibility of the Other's potential complicatedness obscuring the perception of the complicatedness of the Self.

We should look at that process of humanization in the narrative in detail: the character Ozias Midwinter—one of the many Allan Armadales who nevertheless chooses to go under a radically strange assumed name Otherness-ingesting (as a sort of double feint)—is obviously an Other. Leaving aside his name, the "strangeness" of which is remarked on by several characters—Mrs. Armadale will describe him as "the man with the horrible name" (63)—there is his parentage. He is the son of a white Englishman (Allan Armadale 3) and his mulatto wife.[12] On first meeting, Midwinter gives the impression of being from elsewhere: "His tawny complexion, his large bright brown eyes, and his black mustachios and beard, gave him something of a foreign look" (60). Collins has this foreignness invariably become in the narrative the impetus for sparking a distrust in the incontestably English characters. Reverend Brock, guardian of the other Allan Armadale of Midwinter's generation, fears him at first because of his foreign looks. His appearance we are told "tended to discompose the rector" (64):

> The rector's healthy Anglo-Saxon flesh crept responsively at every casual movement of the usher's supple brown fingers, and every passing distortion of the usher's haggard yellow face. "God forgive me!" thought Mr. Brock, with his mind running on Allan, and Allan's mother, "I wish I could see my way to turning Ozias Midwinter adrift in the world again!" (64)

But Collins will eventually have that distrust be overturned. Late in the narrative, in a posthumous letter Brock will urge Midwinter not to acqui-

---

12. Young-Zook describes Midwinter as "a racial hybrid" and a "Lacanian split subject" (236–37).

esce to his current fears and in so doing will call this character whom he had initially distrusted by a significant epithet: "Look up, my poor suffering brother—look up, my hardly-tried, my well-loved friend, higher than this! Meet the doubts that now assail you from the blessed vantage-ground of Christian courage and Christian hope" (513). This transformation from discomposing stranger or Other to "brother" is highly suggestive of the tenets of the abolitionist movement in the United States. The narrative of *Armadale* was, of course, being planned from 1863–1865, the latter part of the American Civil War.[13] I believe that John Sutherland is right, in a general sense, to refer to the movement when he remarks of Midwinter's request of Allan—as the two stand on the deck of the half-sunken ship—to shake hands "while we are brothers still" that "The abolitionists' slogan, 'Am I not a man and a brother?,' would echo for many readers here, given the fact that Ozias is black and Allan white" (*Armadale* 688*n*1). Perhaps a better example of this concern with abolition might be seen to come, however, on the last page of the story when Midwinter makes a clear claim to brotherhood:

> All I can sincerely say for myself is, what I think will satisfy you to know, that I have learnt to view the purpose of the Dream with a new mind. I once believed that it was sent to rouse your distrust of the friendless man whom you had taken as a brother to your heart. I now *know* that it came to you as a timely warning *to take him closer still* [italics added]. Does this help to satisfy you that I, too, am standing hopefully on the brink of a new life, and that *while we live, brother, your love and mine will never be divided again?* (677; last two emphases added)

The Other has successfully turned brother here. This could be viewed as a consciousness-raising move on Collins's part—and is so by some critics[14]—

---

13. In 1862, Margaret Oliphant would connect the English desire for sensation fiction with the turns and turnabouts occurring in the American Civil War: "That distant roar has come to form a thrilling accompaniment to the safe life we lead at home. On the other side of the Atlantic, a race *blasée* and lost in universal *ennui* has bethought itself of the grandest expedient for procuring a new sensation; and albeit we follow at a humble distance, we too begin to feel the need of a supply of new shocks and wonders" ("Sensation Novels" 564).

14. See, for example, Young-Zook writing that "Collins uses his characters Ozias Midwinter and Lydia Gwilt, both class, gender, and racial hybrids, to sensationally subvert the ideals of British nationalism and undermine dominant Victorian racial and gender ideologies. . . . Of Collins's non-British characters in this novel, one is its loveliest woman—Midwinter's mother—and the other is its most loyal and capable man—Midwinter himself. Thus the novel sublimates these critiques [of British nationality and manhood] into questions of friendship and proper romantic ties while simultaneously suggesting that the ideal of masculinity is not reckless and patriarchal but collective and fraternal and not necessarily only British" (234 and 239).

or as a means of having the sender, the receiver having exited from intellectual consideration, come to be in a position to disclose him- or herself as
the truly complicated and self-threatening/self-threatened entity.

Collins is primarily interested in facilitating the revelation of the potentially destabilizing threat to be coming from the inside rather than the
outside and thereby extending the foundation-reaching-after goals of his
long–novel project. The settling-valorizing interpretations (of, say, D. A.
Miller's Foucault or J. L. Austin, among others) are not only half-blind but
are accompanied by unfortunate corollary implications, as they result in
constant mis-ascriptions and displacements onto, say, a fear of the "outside,"
of the potentially-invading racial, gender, class, or political Other. Collins's
transition from receiver-mode to sender-mode breaking in *Armadale* (and
The Moonstone as well), at the same time that it will be requiring an undoing of this xenophobia—and thereby rendering itself in danger of being
understood as solely a consciousness-raising "political" maneuver—will be
bringing with it an implication that, being drawbridge–indefensible, is far
more disturbing, for the ruse of compassionately doting on the Other as a
means of avoiding the Self will no longer be available to us.

Sender-mode Complications and the
Other Side of the Paradox of Publication

In *Armadale* the internalization of Otherness occurs not just at the diegetic
level, in scenes such as the story of the Bedouin brothers, but at the extradiegetic level also. Collins uses this process specifically to explode the
usual—but incorrect—understanding of the process of publication. When
publication is viewed from the settling perspective, as it so very often is, it is
seen as a type of "making one's mark" on the world. Publishing is considered
a "birth," a coming to be noticed. However, there is also a "death-of-the-
author" aspect potentially manifest in the act, as Roland Barthes famously
asserted, a "death" resulting from the action of dispersal characteristic of
publication. The conflict between these two aspects of the process creates
what I will be labeling here "the paradox of publication."

The dispersive threat to the Self posed by publication is seen more
clearly when one moves from the receiver-mode to sender-mode view of the
breaking function. Derrida acknowledges that the text will always already
be breaking away and venturing into regions filled with "others," that is
with "improper" readers: "To be what it is, all writing must, therefore, be
capable of functioning in the radical absence of every empirically deter-

mined receiver in general. And this absence is not a continuous modification of presence, it is a rupture in the structure of the mark" ("Signature
Event Context" 8). While Derrida does not hierarchize between the two
modes, simply pointing out that "What holds for the receiver holds also,
for the same reasons, for the sender or the producer" (7–8), Collins's ever-
deepening exploration of the moment of publication in his transition from
The Woman in White to *The Moonstone* allows him to perceive that the
undeniable terrors threatened by those reader-mode alienations, represented so gallingly and obtrusively by the nineteenth-century Americans,
are themselves being funded by an unacknowledged terror residing within
the sender's psyche. While the author might well blame illicit readers as
the sole cause of her own disturbing, but re-assignable, schizophrenia (and
thereby reinforce the denial of her own difficulties the more ardently she
does so—a situation that I believe the later works of Dickens were never
able to transcend),[15] the knowledge of a sender-mode alienation will nevertheless continually be reintroducing itself.

In Collins's hands the fear of the foreigner turns out to be a fear of a
consciousness that might be as valid as one's own, a necessary step in bringing to the fore that schizophrenia lodged at the core of the writer's selfhood.
Unlike many writers of his time, Collins does not recoil from the situation of a contest between two equally-weighted entities. Indeed, far from
it. Collins relishes watching the fight between the two. Before memorably
exemplifying the unsituatedness characteristic of the encounter with a consciousness as valid—or as "own"—as one's own in Franklin Blake's meeting
up with an unknowingly previously-alienated "second self" on the beach
in *The Moonstone,* Collins performatively enacts this circumstance for the
readers of *Armadale* by having the two interpretations of Allan Armadale's
dream fight it out for priority, a priority that is never conclusively decided
on, or decidable upon.[16] Both of these contests will stand as attempts by
Collins to represent the author's selfhood in the process of its being split by
the peculiar workings of iterability.

We see the paradox of publication played out for us at both the beginning and end of the narrative. Early on, Allan Wrentmore (Allan Armadale

---

15. Perhaps Collins was attempting to teach his excessively-aggrieved (see Welsh) friend this
lesson in his three masterpieces of breaking, *No Name, Armadale,* and *The Moonstone.*

16. Taylor argues that "meaning is rendered problematic in the novel": "By continually replaying
a plot with modifications the novel elicits distinct interpretations which succeed and overlap with one
another, and which form a set of interlocking but dissonant frameworks. In this respect, *Armadale*
generates a sense of mystery by continually undermining the terms on which its own cognitive assumptions are founded while allowing them, on another register, to remain intact" (*Secret Theatre* 156
and 154).

3) dictates his biography, in a letter intended eventually as a warning to his infant son, to the Scotsman Mr. Neal while Wrentmore still has the self-control and life to do so. Paralysis will soon be taking away his speech, as it has already his ability to write, and he therefore requires aid to convey his message, that is, to, in a sense, "publish" it. The Doctor tells Mr. Neal, "The paralysis is fast spreading upwards, and disease of the lower part of the spine has already taken place. He can still move his hands a little, but he can hold nothing in his fingers. He can still articulate, but he may wake speechless to-morrow or next day" (15). The illness is slowly cutting off Wrentmore's means of articulation: it could be said that it is his final act of "publication" that actually kills him, the palsy overtaking him to such an extent that he cannot seal the envelope himself.[17] When his letter is completed, in response to Mr. Neal's question, "Do you insist on my posting it?" Wrentmore makes a great effort: "He mastered his failing speech for the last time, and gave the answer. 'Yes!'" (50). Mr. Neal leaves the room for the post-office and Wrentmore immediately dies. Here we have a sort of death-of-the-author resulting from publication.

Similarly, in the sensational conclusion of the narrative we are presented with another (this time more symbolic) instance of death-via-publication. This episode is a clear transition point between the materiality outlook expressed by Collins so many years before through the manuscript's having been equated with land in *Basil* and the acknowledgment of the legitimacy of the claims of immateriality in the publication situation. The nefarious Dr. Le Doux uses intriguingly suggestive terms to describe to Lydia Gwilt the killing mechanism built into the architecture of his asylum:

> Do you see that bottle? . . . that plump, round comfortable looking bottle? . . . Suppose we call it "our Stout Friend"? Very good. Our Stout Friend, by himself, is a most harmless and useful medicine. . . . *But* bring him into contact with something else—introduce him to the acquaintance of a certain common mineral Substance, of a universally accessible kind, broken into fragments; provide yourself with (say) six doses of our Stout Friend, and *pour those doses consecutively on the fragments I have mentioned,*

---

17. Collins was mesmerized by the situation of the legal document being signed by one person but sealed by another. This situation had already occurred in *No Name:* "With that final act of compliance, [Noel Vanstone's] docility came to an end. He refused, in the fiercest terms, to seal the envelope. There was no need to press this proceeding on him. His seal lay ready on the table; and it mattered nothing whether he used it, or whether a person in his confidence used it for him. Mrs Lecount sealed the envelope, with its two important enclosures safely inside" (*No Name,* ed. Ford 475). I will be arguing that such an instance recurs once more in *The Moonstone* only in that case with regard to Collins himself.

at intervals of no less than five minutes [emphasis added]. Quantities of little bubbles will rise at every pouring; collect the gas in those bubbles; and convey it into a closed chamber—and let Samson himself be in that closed chamber, our Stout Friend will kill him in half-an-hour! . . . What do you think of *that,* my dear lady, in the way of mystery and romance? . . . Don't suppose I am exaggerating! Don't suppose I'm inventing a story to put you off with, as the children say. (*Armadale* 642)

Armadale was of course initially published in twenty monthly serial parts in the *Cornhill Magazine* from November 1864 to June 1866 (*Armadale* xxxi). Collins can be seen here to be re-presenting that process of seri- alized publication in the sequenced aspects of the very elaborate murder scenario that concludes his narrative—an intricately-choreographed dance recalling the automatons of Major Milroy's clock—in which Gwilt will end up both murderer and victim, akin to Blake's serving in *The Moonstone* as both detective and thief. Collins's immateriality-respecting position here stands in stark contrast to that of his good friend Charles Reade. The lat- ter would be publishing a series of letters in September and October 1875 addressed to the editor of the Pall Mall Gazette and entitled "The Rights and the Wrongs of Authors." There Reade would inveigh against the par- ticular "delusion," resulting directly from the immaterial side of textuality, he called "The Aetherial Mania":

The aetherial mania intermits, like every other. Its lucid intervals coincide with the visits of the rent-gatherer, the tax-gatherer, and the tradesmen with their bills. On these occasions society admits that an author is a solid, and ought to pay or smart; but returns to aether when the funds are to be acquired, without which rent, taxes, and tradesmen cannot be paid, nor life, far less respectability, sustained. No Anglo-Saxon can look the aethe- rial crotchet in the face and not laugh at it. Yet so subtle and insidious is Prejudice, that you shall find your Anglo-Saxon constantly arguing and act- ing as if this nonsense was sense: and, pray believe me, the most dangerous of all our lies are those silly, skulking falsehoods which a man is ashamed to state, yet lets them secretly influence his mind and conduct. (131-32)

At the conclusion of *Armadale,* Collins far from confusing the iterable with the purely material, as he had in *Basil,* comes to honor writing's ethereal qualities, representing them through the toxic ether that results from the chemical reaction between rocks (perhaps limestone—paper?) and an ener- getic acid (perhaps carbonic acid—ink?) (see *Armadale* 710), an ether that will kill Gwilt when she substitutes herself for her unconscious husband

Midwinter.[18] Thus, the text here is equated with an initially solid mineral substance that *dematerializes*—into a toxic ether no less—through the publication process.[19]

Thus, both at the beginning and end of this narrative, characters are expiring *while* publishing. It might not be wrong to say that they die *through* publication. These scenes thus enact one side—the breaking function—of the paradox that has plagued publication from its very beginnings, particularly in the legal realm. The paradox-of-kind associated with the act of sending one's writing off on a mass scale has always posed the question of whether publication should be seen to constitute an *assertion* of the author's proprietary right or, on the contrary, represent a *relinquishment* of it, and by extension whether it should be seen to be a consolidation or dispersal of the author's "identity."[20] The paradox-averse judges in *Millar v. Taylor* in 1769 were, not surprisingly, divided on this issue. Justice Aston, upholding the "consolidative" view, understood the act to be a straightforward laying claim by the author to the ownership of the work:

> [W]ithout publication, 'tis useless to the owner; because without profit: and property, without the power of use and disposal, is an empty sound. In that state, 'tis lost to the society, in point of improvement; as well as to the author, in point of interest. Publication therefore is the necessary act, and only means, to render this confessed property useful to mankind, and profitable to the owner: in this, they are jointly concerned. (*Millar v. Taylor* 222)

18. Collins is committed, in a direct recantation of *Basil,* to dematerializing land in this narrative. The Norfolk Broads, the site of a memorable picnic scene in the narrative, are a marshy region of shallow lakes that seem to be both land and water at the same time. They are paradoxically described as "quite a watery country": "With the ancient church towers and the wind and water mills, which had hitherto been the only lofty objects seen over the low marshy flat, there now rose all round the horizon . . . the sails of invisible boats moving on invisible waters. All the strange and startling anomalies presented by an inland agricultural district, isolated from other districts by its intricate surrounding network of pools and streams . . . began to present themselves in closer and closer succession. Nets appeared on cottage pailings; little flat-bottomed boats lay strangely at rest among the flowers in cottage gardens; farmers' men passed to and fro clad in composite costume of the coast and the field, in sailors' hats, and fishermen's boots, and ploughmen's smocks,—and even yet the low-lying labyrinth of waters, embosomed in its mystery of solitude, was a hidden labyrinth still" (244–45). Here where church towers can be obscured by the sails of "invisible boats moving on invisible waters" the aquatic and the terrestrial domains are intertwined.

19. It is appropriate in this context that the names of the estates, Combe-Raven and Thorpe-Ambrose, in both *No Name* and *Armadale* should be split—representing fissured land and stability?—by hyphens.

20. Peter Thoms remarks a similar duality to be characterizing the substitutions occurring at the end of the narrative: "In *Armadale* the idea of substitution . . . possesses . . . duality, being interpreted either as an eradication of identity or as a confirmation of identity in which one so identifies with another that one assumes the other's troubles" (125).

Championing the "dispersive" view, Justice Yates, that strong advocate for the acknowledgment of the effects of the breaking function, on the other hand, held the opposite opinion. He considered publication a clear handing over to the public of the proprietary right:

> From these observations, this corollary, in my opinion . . . does naturally follow; "that the act of publication, when voluntarily done by the author himself, is, virtually and necessarily, a gift to the public." . . . To this I might add, that in every language, the words which express a publication of a book, express it as giving it to the public.[21] (*Millar v. Taylor* 233–34)

Aston's response to Yates's outlook was not surprising: "[T]o construe this only and necessary act to make the work useful and profitable, to be 'destructive, at once, of the author's confessed original property, against his express will,' seems to be quite harsh and unreasonable" (*Millar v. Taylor* 222). John Dunning, co-counsel along with Wedderburn for Becket in *Donaldson v. Becket,* in 1774 claimed something similar:

> My Lords, it is to me most extraordinary to admit an Author hath a Property originally in his Composition, and that the first Moment he exercises his Dominion over that Property, and endeavours to raise Profit from it, he looses [*sic*[22]] it. Publication I cannot conceive to be of such a Nature as to destroy that Right to the Matter published, which is acknowledged an Author hath before it is published. (*Cases of the Appellants* 30)

In the late 1700s the effects of publication were clearly ambiguous, but they were such not as a result of inadequate previous policies or laws. Nor was

---

21. To offer a more timely expression of this outlook we might quote from a letter published in *The Springfield Republican* by George Merriam, at the time the publisher of "Webster's Dictionary." This letter is excerpted in an article entitled "Who Owns an Author's Ideas?" from *The Nation,* 27 June 1867. Merriam writes, "What are the true grounds for a claim for an international copyright? . . . It is said an author has a natural, perfect, perpetual, and inalienable—but by his own act— right to the coinage of his own brain, as fully as the mechanical workman to the product of his own hands. . . . I deny the premise, and the conclusion therefore fails. It is true that while the manuscript is in his own possession he may do what he will with his own. . . . But when he publishes, he parts with his exclusive ownership, and gives it to the public under a contract with that public which for the benefit thus received secures to him in return certain valuable unexclusive rights and enjoyments, and extends over him the shield of its protective law. In other words, literary property is the creature of law. If it were not so, if the author's property in his works is founded on natural right, then, is he entitled to the exclusive enjoyment not only in all lands, but through all time" (520).

22. This particular instance of eighteenth-century freedom with spelling is unfortunate, as the whole point of copyright would seem to be that to loose is *not* to lose.

this ambiguity, as Collins came to learn in the transition from *The Woman in White* to *Armadale,* the result of the actions of illicit mid-Victorian readers across the Atlantic. Rather, it was the direct result of the timeless linguistic structures grounding the author's self-expressed-through-language. At the moment of publication, the Other, rather than being safely cordoned off outside, was instead disclosed to be, shockingly, solidly located inside.

Writers Proliferating

While the deinstitutions deployed in *Armadale* do not quite reach the depths of those deployed in *The Moonstone,* we do on occasion see signs of a type of fundamental undermining of the author's stability in the former novel. As the goal of Collins's incorporational process is to remove the mesmerizing screen of readerly complications and to disclose them to be writerly ones, it is not surprising that *Armadale* should be a narrative filled with writers, and complicated ones at that. Allan Armadale 3, as we have seen, and his son Ozias Midwinter both strenuously work to create texts, the latter presumably "tak[ing] to Literature" (676) after a period of laboring as a foreign correspondent for a London newspaper. But it is the character of Lydia Gwilt who most clearly presents to us the complictions of the author. A character who is, in a prefiguring of *The Moonstone*'s Franklin Blake, self-avowedly "inconsistent with [her]self" (559), she is from the beginning shown to be uncomfortable with—or at least complicatedly-situated with regard to—the process of writing. She begins her career of iniquity at the age of twelve through an exercising of her "imitative dexterity" in the forgery of a letter, the embodiment of someone else's text. She is during the story not only constantly writing letters, many to be included in the narrative, but also writing a diary, excerpts from which end up making up nearly a fifth of the completed text. In "breaking off" that diary—a hint at her approaching suicide?—she expresses herself as if she were bidding adieu to her life rather than to a mere recreation: "Good-by, my old friend and companion of many a miserable day! Having nothing else to be fond of, I half suspect myself of having been unreasonably fond of *you.* What a fool I am!" (612). At one point she asks herself, "Why do I keep a diary at all?" and responds as any born writer might, "I don't care why! I must write down what happened between Midwinter and me to-night, *because* I must" (559).

Gwilt is also, like Collins, a consummate plotter, and the plots she formulates are not just of any old variety but scenarios that show the Self to be surprisingly profoundly vulnerable to substitution. She at one point comes up with an effective intrigue through which to mislead Reverend Brock as he observes her door from his own rooms across the street. She will, mimicking her earlier forgery of text, have her housemaid be seen leaving the house clothed in her previous day's walking dress, that is, in the iterable or imitable markers of her identity. Gwilt's accomplice Mother Oldershaw suggests additionally having the housemaid lift her veil so as to have her face (ie, to Brock's understanding the London Miss Gwilt's face) be noted clearly as a means of further establishing her difference from the Miss Gwilt who will soon be showing up at Thorpe-Ambrose Cottage to take up the position of governess. Oldershaw's own particular contribution to the con game is described by her as one worthy of reality: "Don't suppose I'm at all over-boastful about my own ingenuity. Cleverer tricks than this trick of mine are played off on the public by swindlers, and are recorded in the newspapers every week" (219). Here "publication" leads to a type of "death" of the person and, of course, the birth of her substitute.

Of her original scheme, Gwilt comments,

> The thing would be quite impossible, of course, if I had been seen with my veil up; but, as events have turned out, it is one advantage of the horrible exposure which followed my marriage, that I seldom show myself in public, and never of course in such a populous place as London, without wearing a thick veil and keeping that veil down. If the housemaid wears my dress, I don't really see why the housemaid may not be counted on *to represent me to the life*. (216; emphasis added)

This concept of being represented "to the life" suggests the type of destabilizing contestation between equals that Collins came to realize is always occurring between an author and her words. Being "represented to the life" suggests that the literal reaches down to the very bases of the Self. Textuality—and therefore iterability, in all its aspects—can be seen to be a fundamental aspect of "being." Indeed, once her strategem has succeeded, Gwilt will crow about her having been *"proved not to be myself"* (284; emphasis in original)[23]—a statement Franklin Blake could also make. Here we have the Self and its texts disclosed to be launched on a perpetual whirligig of substitutions and screenings. Here we have "Hassan" jumping down his own throat.

---

23. Even when she *is* herself, as the wife of Ozias Midwinter—really Allan Armadale 5—that is, when she is finally officially "Lydia Armadale," she is attempting to use that name to pass herself off to the citizens of Thorpe-Ambrose as the widow of the *other* Allan Armadale of Midwinter's generation. Those citizens will turn out to be more credulous than the real-world critics and her plan will have a fair chance of success until, that is, Allan Armadale 4 returns from his presumed death at sea.

This concept of the author being proved not to be herself is seen also at the climax of the novel. In the asylum scene, it will be recalled, Midwinter will exchange bedrooms with Allan Armadale 4 and Gwilt will then, upon discovering the change, commit suicide by substituting herself for her overcome husband in the poisoned air, an air poisoned, it should be recalled, by figurative serial publication effects. Here we have "the author" living on as one Self while a different side of the Self dies as a result of "publication." The substitution of Gwilt for Midwinter shows us a writer with a split psyche. Both are writers, as already noted, as well as being husband and wife. If man and wife are truly "one person," as Blackstone's *Commentaries,* an authority amusingly cited in the narrative on marriage in a different context (455–59), famously has it, one writer-Self of "the happy couple" can be seen here to be substituting for another aspect of itself. Here the extroverted and introverted (Midwinter is more than once described as "shy" [118 and 221]) sides of the author are undergoing the publication process and one side is—as a result of self-sacrifice—ending up overcome by it while the other lives on. This move is very close to, as we will see in the next chapter, Collins's in the writing of *The Moonstone.*

6

The Return of the Author

Privacy, Publication, the Mystery Novel, and *The Moonstone*

[I]t was at the moment when a system of ownership and strict copyright rules were established (toward the end of the eighteenth and beginning of the nineteenth century) that the transgressive properties always intrinsic to the act of writing became the forceful imperative of literature. It is as if the author . . . was compensating for his new status by reviving the old bipolar field of discourse [sacred vs. profane, licit vs. illicit] in a systematic practice of transgression and by restoring the danger of writing which, on another side, had been conferred the benefits of property.

> —Foucault, "What Is an Author?" *Language* 124–25

If opium-eating be a sensual pleasure, and if I am bound to confess that I have indulged in it to an excess, not yet *recorded* of any other man, it is no less true, that I have struggled against this fascinating enthralment with a religious zeal, and have, at length, accomplished what I never yet heard attributed to any other man—have untwisted, almost to its final links, the accursed chain which fettered me.

> —De Quincey, *Confessions of an English Opium-Eater* 4; emphasis in original

---

ALWAYS already involved in a struggle between a purportedly stable self and a potentially unstable self-in-language—a struggle set going by the act of clothing oneself in linguistic form—the English author in the mid-nineteenth century also faced the unenviable task of attempting to negotiate a different conflict, that between the opposed roles he or she was being forced to assume by the legal discourse of the time, specifically those of pre-publication author-as-creator and post-publication author-as-disseminator.[1] In this chapter, I will be bringing to light Collins's strategy of having the linguistic disarticulations serve as a model for a strategy for undermining the legal ones. In *The Moonstone,* Collins deploys two authorial extra-legal defense mechanisms against his legal culture's divestments, one effected through his manipulation of the mystery novel form and the other through his use of opium. In the scene in which Franklin Blake passes the diamond named "The Moonstone" to Godfrey Ablewhite while under the influence of opium (hereafter we will be adopting the narrative's own appellation for it, describing it as the "door of communication" scene) Collins will be exploring the connection between the relocation of texts and the alienation of authorial intentions. At the same time, in his own situation, Collins will be both *enacting* this alienation and *counteracting* it at the same time. Writing the conclusion of this work while under the influence of opium, Collins will be saying, "I published this ending (to my novel, to my project), but I didn't *mean* it."

The Author's Dilemma

Many nineteenth-century authors felt a degree of discontent with the legal situation in which they found themselves. That situation was marked by the law's concession of a strong pre-publication proprietary right in the work but a weak post-publication one at the same time that the author was also given by the system no pre-publication authorial identity while being granted a post-publication one.[2] An anonymous writer in the *American Law Review* in 1876 notes the absurdity of the Victorian author's situation:

> It is a ridiculous doctrine which recognizes the existence of a species of property, and yet pronounces its only use unlawful and self-destructive. If

---

1. Kant touches on a similar type of distinction when discussing the two radically different roles adopted by a publisher who also happens to be an author: "If the publisher is an author at the same time, it must be taken into account that the two occupations are quite different: that is, he publishes in the capacity of a businessman what he has written in the capacity of a scholar" ("Unlawfulness" 413). This distinction may also be related to his distinction between *opera* (exertion or activity) and *opus* (finished work) (406).

2. The agitation by Wordsworth and Dickens, among others, for a longer term of copyright in the late 1830s could be seen as a manifestation of a lack of contentment with this particular bargain (see Chapter 2). In addition, the situation of large-scale foreign, especially American, piracy of English novels during the Victorian era must have brought home only the more the threat of this usurpation of identity inherent in the act of publication (see Chapter 3).

the property is recognized, a mode of use must be conceded. To say that authors have rights of property in their literary productions, and that they are lost by publication which is their only source of value is absurd. It is destructive of the first principles, the essence, the very notion of the right of property. "Property," says Pufendorf, "implies a right of excluding others from your possession . . . 'twould be in vain for you to claim that as your own which you can by no means hinder others from sharing with you."[3] ("Is Copyright Perpetual?" 28)

One "mode of use" that was found for this untenable property was to cast it in the form of a mystery novel. Distinguished as it is by the, so to speak, "exclusions" inherent in that genre, the mystery is a style of storytelling that splits author-as-disseminator from author-as-creator in a manner commensurately counter to the splitting demanded by the movement from manuscript to published book undergone by the text, the latter movement being stressed in the drawn-out serial publication method characteristic of the more prominent novels of the Victorian era. Instead of author-as-disseminator predominating over the course of publication, in the mystery novel the author-as-creator does so. Even in the single-volume mystery we can see this unusual counter-poised splitting occurring. Even there we see the holding off of the demands of publication at the same time that we have the author-as-creator role thrust to our attention through the prominence of the author's role as creator of suspense. As a matter of course, any mystery narrative holds off the devastations wrought by publication for the longest possible time, usually almost its full length, while still allowing the author to enjoy the benefits of being known as the creator of that text. The truly perfect mystery would of course be a story that could overcome the enervational effects of the publication of its last, or climactic, page. Falling short of that, most mysteries are content to merely gesture toward this ideal through the pervasive sense of extended suspense that they create. In the case of *The Moonstone,* this suspense, or at least its force and necessity, is imposed *on* the author rather than *by* him, that is, until the end when Collins turns his early

---

3. This was a fair representation of the situation, as is evidenced by a comment made by Warren and Brandeis in 1890 about the common-law proprietary right in the manuscript, "The right is lost only when the author himself communicates his production to the public,—in other words, publishes it. It is entirely independent of the copyright laws, and their extension into the domain of art. The aim of those statutes is to secure to the author, composer, or artist the entire profits arising from publication; but the common-law protection enables him to control absolutely the act of publication, and in the exercise of his own discretion, to decide whether there shall be any publication at all. The statutory right is of no value, *unless* there is a publication; the common-law right is lost *as soon as* there is a publication" (199–200).

"mystery novel" into a story allowing its author to remain creator despite publication's relentless demands on him to also be disseminator.

The ridiculousness of the situation referred to by the *American Law Review* critic above would have been felt keenly by our author-lawyer Collins. It required a good deal of strategic manipulation on the Victorian author's part, faced as he or she was by this formidable degree of theoretical and legal resistance, to establish a solid proprietary right nevertheless. The ideal solution for that author would have been either to have been known despite not having published (harbinger of our present age of celebrity) or to have published without having been "known" to publication, that is, to have published but to have at the same time somehow forged a strong post-publication proprietary right. It was in the mystery novel form, especially in its serialized version extending over several months, if not years, that some Victorian authors found what they were looking for. This form of fiction had an inherent exclusionary character giving it an advantage over other forms of literature in the task of defending against the divestment threatened by law. As Edmund Wilson, in his characteristically acerbic style puts it, "detective stories in general are able to profit by an unfair advantage in the code which forbids the reviewer to give away the secret to the public—a custom which results in the concealment of the pointlessness of a good deal of this fiction and affords a protection to the authors which no other department of writing enjoys" ("Why Do People Read?" 233).[4] This protection to which Wilson refers should be read not solely as a protection from reviewers but also as a protection from the eighteenth-century legislators who had established the Victorian author's legal situation as a radically unfair one.

I believe that the peculiar legal predicament of the author was a significant factor bringing about the circumstance in which certain well-known authors in the mid-nineteenth century, namely, Collins and Dickens, adopted the mystery novel form, particularly in their novels *The Moonstone* (1868) and *The Mystery of Edwin Drood* (1870), and thereby set in motion a trend we see continuing today, that present-day situation in which so many authors in Western literary culture choose to write mystery stories. That these authors should have chosen the role of both not wanting to tell and telling their stories characteristic of the mystery novel was a result of their peculiar legal situation, that is, of the general writer's split desire to keep alive what Dr. Johnson had described as a "metaphysical right of creation" (Boswell, *Life of Johnson* 2:259) and at the same time to establish

---

4. We should recall in this context Collins's admonition in the Preface to the first edition of *The Woman in White* that the reviewers take care not to give any of the crucial plot twists away.

a greatly desired post-publication identity as "author." I believe that the author-as-creator's adoption of this particular genre is ascribable to the decision by the House of Lords in 1774 in *Donaldson v. Becket,* a decision that denied the claims of the author-as-creator, replacing them with the claims of the author-as-disseminator and thereby bringing into being a situation in which the only safe place left for the manifestation of the author *in toto* (the one desiring to manifest both sides) was an in-between zone that found its most amenable, and in the late twentieth century most common, form of expression in the provisional withholding of disclosures characteristic of the mystery novel form. Apart from supplying the reader with the shock of surprise or thrill of horror at the eventual disclosure of the actual culprit, the mystery novel also, I would argue, fulfills a deep-seated desire in the author, a desire harking back to the late eighteenth century when that metaphysical right of creation was revoked in legal discourse. The mystery novel thus is to some extent a protest novel, a protest bemoaning the loss of the author's perpetual proprietary right. During the Victorian era, far from being conclusively silenced, a certain conception of the author took up residence, in defiance of the Lords and of late-eighteenth-century legal discourse, in the mystery where we find it happily residing today. Others having tried to explain why we read mysteries,[5] this chapter will be trying to explain why Wilkie Collins *wrote* them.

Disseminating and Not Disseminating the Moonstone

Dorothy Sayers's comment that "[b]y comparison with [*The Moonstone*'s] wide scope, its dove-tailed completeness and the marvellous variety and soundness of its characterization, modern mystery fiction looks thin and mechanical. Nothing human is perfect, but *The Moonstone* comes about as near perfection as anything of its kind can be" and T. S. Eliot's contention that *The Moonstone* is "the first, the longest, and the best of modern English detective novels," while debatable on several points, when taken together make a forceful case for suggesting that this novel possesses a privileged position with regard to the long tradition of English and American mystery fiction that has followed in its wake.[6] Here in Collins's most popular

---

5. See for example Wilson, "Why Do People" and "Who Cares"; Auden; Hutter, "Dreams"; and John Anderson.

6. Sayers, *Omnibus* 25; and Eliot, "Wilkie Collins," *Selected Essays* 464. Gavin Lambert calls the

story we have the insightful and intelligent detective, the crime defying his ingenious attempts at solution, the red herring, etc., all before Conan Doyle would come along to enshrine them in Anglo-American literary practice. But most importantly we also have at work that other, definitive, characteristic of the mystery novel: the secret withheld by the author from the knowledge of the readers until near the very end. It is this last characteristic that will for me be tying Collins's deployment of the mystery genre to the culture of privacy (authorial and otherwise) that was coming into being in legal discourse in the mid-1800s, that culture having been made explicit as we saw earlier in the decision in *Jeffereys* and *Prince Albert*. And the keeping of that secret will be helped along by the inveterate reticence characterizing the personalities of so many of the characters of the narrative, as the contrary impulses of the interests of the right to privacy and the effects of publication come to an accommodation in this limit-approaching (and -broaching) example of what would come to be called the "mystery novel."

I will here be arguing that Collins used the relatively new genre of English mystery fiction in order to ground and assert his authorial proprietary right over the published text. As writing was coming to be more and more connected to the author's "identity" (in a public as opposed to legal sense) over the course of the eighteenth and first half of the nineteenth century, the act of publishing one's work was coming to be poised on an especially sharp knife-edge so that, by 1868, publication—an act both undermining and asserting ownership over one's writing—was coming to be seen as tantamount to—in a refinement of our last chapter's "paradox of publication"—both a loss of "essence" (for the author-as-creator) and a claim to the unification of the author's "self" (for the author-as-disseminator). It is no accident, then, that at this time a genre promoting authorial control to an alarming extent should have come into prominence. To put it another way, it is no surprise that an author as interested as Collins was in protecting his authorial proprietary right should have been attracted to the mystery novel form.

That form, as used by Collins, was intended to solve the problem of the owned yet disseminated, disseminated yet owned text. The mystery of *The Moonstone* allowed Collins's personality to be safely contained even while his story offered itself up to be subjected to the dangerous proprietary undermining characteristic of part or volume publication. This genre allowed for an accommodation to be reached with the pharmakon of publication. The

---

book a "*tour de force* [that] exhausted the best possibilities of a form destined to click into formula" (28).

need for an antidote to that poison and cure had been voiced by Rachel
Verinder in her plea to Godfrey Ablewhite in the narrative:

> Oh, how can I find words to say it in! How can I make a *man* understand
> that a feeling which horrifies me at myself, can be a feeling that fascinates
> me at the same time? It's the breath of my life, Godfrey, and it's the poison
> that kills me—both in one![7]

If publication was both poison and cure for the author, the mystery story
was more cure than poison. The mystery genre having exploded in popularity since Collins's time, both with authors and readers, one can reasonably
claim that all the mystery stories that might trace their origins back to *The
Moonstone* have as their basis the mystery of authorship, for, when one comes
right down to it, the mystery of *The Moonstone* is—to resurrect that archaic
(but also quite prescient) term for that one-time novel technology—the
"mystery of printing" (Eisenstein 9).

NOT SURPRISINGLY, then, the act of publication is one of this mystery novel's major obsessions. *The Moonstone* is particularly interested in the
problem of forcing closed books open. It is no accident that when the three
Indians following the lost Indian diamond referred to in the title turn Godfrey Ablewhite's and Septimus Luker's pockets inside out the lure they use
to initially distract their proposed victims' attention is an open, illuminated
manuscript. The most intriguing "closed book" in the narrative is of course
Rachel Verinder. Indeed, there would be no mystery were Rachel willing to
speak with regard to who it was she saw stealing the Moonstone from the
cabinet in her sitting room on the night of her birthday dinner. That she is
unwilling to speak is quite out of character for the standard young girl who
would, according to the lawyer Mr. Bruff, have almost immediately given
all her secrets away: "The first instinct of girls in general, on being told of
anything which interests them, is to ask a multitude of questions, and then
to run off, and talk it all over with some favourite friend. Rachel Verinder's
first instinct . . . was to shut herself up in her own mind, and to think it
over by herself" (319). Instead she keeps her secrets to herself, chief among
these being the solution to the mystery.

Rachel's reticence is not simply reactive but also proactive. Indeed, not

---

7. Collins, *The Moonstone: A Romance*, ed. Stewart, 279. This printing reproduces the 1871
revised text. All further references will be to this edition and will be cited parenthetically in the text by
page.

only is she continually locking her bedroom door in the faces of the two inquisitive policemen who come into her home in order to solve the mystery, but she is reported by Betteredge to have had a tendency when young to energetically assert her refusal to disseminate. Describing what could be considered a voicing of the mystery writer's credo, he comments, "She looked you straight in the face, and shook her little saucy head, and said plainly, 'I won't tell you!'" (87–88). A strong implication of the ungentlemanly course of action later contemplated by Bruff, "[s]he must be persuaded to tell us, or she must be forced to" (384), is the suggestion that the act of having one's story go over to dissemination is akin to having one's body be subjected to violation. Here we have the implicit suggestion put forward that writing, or at least the trace, is an intimate reflection of the author's person. In its desire to open the "closed books" of its characters and read their "stories," particularly in its desire to violate Rachel's inveterately reserved nature, the narrative suggests that the personality is analogous to a textual entity, and, as such, as open as texts to violation.

Publication, even in a limited form, being a potentially self-contradictory, a potentially self-diluting act, the author's only means of truly declaring an intention to keep control over his or her literary effort, and indeed perhaps identity, is to keep the manuscript strictly private. This is a lesson markedly brought forth by the circumstances in which Ezra Jennings, the assistant to the physician Mr. Candy, finds himself. Jennings at one point refuses to communicate to Blake the specifics of the scandal pursuing him: "I don't profess, sir, to tell my story (as the phrase is) to any man. My story will die with me" (427). Here, in deploying this conjunction between Jennings's telling his life history and publishing a novel in the word "story," the narrative of *The Moonstone* is supporting the hypothesis put forth by Susan Eilenberg that publication is a forfeiture of identity: "the author, by the fact of publication, loses control over something he had regarded as his. The question I would like to raise is whether he loses control of *himself*. Is publication—is allowing another access to one's thoughts—an implicit alienation or forfeiture of identity?" (Eilenberg, "Copyright's Rhetoric" 20–21). It is quite appropriate, then, that Blake should have earlier described Jennings as possessing that *"unsought self-possession,* which is a sure sign of good breeding, not in England only, but everywhere else in the civilised world" (419; emphasis in original). Jennings the self-possessed does not disseminate. The suggestion of "good breeding" in this quotation should be seen, I would argue, as a pun. For, as the rest of the narrative will make clear, it is the lack of "self-possession," particularly that lack marked by indiscriminate "dissemination" that is itself a manifestation of bad "breeding."

In the end the story will turn out to have been, at a certain level, merely the tale of Franklin Blake no longer disseminating "inappropriately," say, in the middle of the night with another man in his bedroom or with the two "unmentionable" (48) women who keep him from returning to England at earlier stages of his travels, but, at the end of the story quite traditionally, when he and his first cousin Rachel produce an heir. Indeed, Rachel succeeds in doing what, for Betteredge, had seemed the impossible: "there was a hole in Mr Franklin's pocket that nothing would sew up" (48). The self-collapsing family tree that comes to contain and control a potentially dispersive dissemination on Blake's part could itself be represented in the form of a diamond. The movement of the Moonstone, from the Hindu statue to the West and toward the potentially dispersive threat of "Amsterdam" (to be possibly Amsterdam[ned]?) and back to the statue, is another example of this process of potentially uncontrollable dissemination being recuperated and once more controlled.

In contrast to Blake, Jennings, as already mentioned, is distinguished by a self-possession that extends to all aspects of his personality, including his literary output. Mr. Candy has good reason for writing after his death that "the world never knew him" (516), for in this story so focused on the issue of making reluctant people and texts speak it is only Jennings who will not have been forced or cajoled into disseminating. Candy's letter to Blake after Jennings's death makes clear the extent of Jennings's reticence:

> At [Jennings's] request, I next collected the other papers—that is to say, the bundle of letters, the unfinished book, and the volumes of the Diary—and enclosed them all in one wrapper, sealed with my own seal. "Promise," he said, "that you will put this into my coffin with your own hand; and that you will see that no other hand touches it afterwards."
>
> I gave him my promise. And the promise has been performed. (515–16)

Here—in stark contrast to the memorable *Life, Letters, and Labours of Miss Jane Anne Stamper,* which have reached their forty-fourth edition (*Moonstone* 300)—the life, letters, and work of Mr. Ezra Jennings are not going to be disseminated, to be published. Immediately after this passage, the earthly existence of our presumably Anglo-Indian doctor's assistant—very much like T. S. Eliot's most celebrated poem—comes to a close with that repeated cry: "Peace! peace! peace!"[8]

---

8. Suggesting that perhaps both references spring from the same subcontinental source? Eliot's

The fate shrunk from by Jennings is undergone on the other hand by Godfrey Ablewhite. After his encounter with the Indians, the story of that encounter—and, in a sense, Ablewhite's identity—is taken up by the media. While Ablewhite would seem to want to play down the incident, commenting that as a result he has lost "[n]othing but Nervous Force—which the law doesn't recognise as property" (246), it would seem that he has lost a good deal more through the loss of his privacy:

> If I could have had my own way, I would have kept my adventure to myself—I shrink from all this fuss and publicity. But Mr Luker made *his* injuries public, and *my* injuries, as the necessary consequence, have been proclaimed in their turn. *I have become the property of the newspapers,* until the gentle reader gets sick of the subject. I am very sick indeed of it myself. May the gentle reader soon be like me! (246; last emphasis added)

The publication of his adventure has caused Ablewhite to lose control of his personality. He has become the "property" of the newspapers. The print media have gotten a hold of him and they seem to be threatening to turn him—as the Indians had his pockets—inside out. Soon his own malady might be resembling that of Jennings: he too might be dying of "an incurable internal complaint" (429), only one now funneling outwards rather than inwards. Thus, Ablewhite and Jennings represent the two poles of the author's dilemma: to publish or not to publish. The story suggests that only by reaching some sort of balance between these two extremes can the author maintain a workable accommodation with publication—not fully in control of himself and his personality but not dangerously out of control either.

Postcolonial Iterability

Having explored the significant interest that the narrative of *The Moonstone* demonstrates in the complementary discourses of reticence and publication, we might now turn to the issue of the story's adoption of a colonial metaphor to represent the theoretical issues at the basis of the workings of language. *The Moonstone* is often read from a postcolonial perspective. This trend was begun by John R. Reed, who in a ground-breaking analysis held

note to the last line of "The Waste Land" reads: "Sha[a]ntih. Repeated as here, a formal ending to an Upanishad. 'The Peace which passeth understanding' is our equivalent to this word" (T. S. Eliot, *Selected Poems* 74, note to line 433).

that the largely English original audience for Collins's novel was being subjected to a critique of English imperialism. Reed remarked,

> [T]he Moonstone represents England's gains from its Indian adventures, and therefore the conveyance of this gem implies an important question. Does a nation inherit the evil of its forebears if it accepts the benefits derived from their crime? . . . It is a national not a personal guilt that is in question in this novel, and national rather than individual values that are tested. (287–88)

While it is of course impossible to dismiss interpretations of this novel that would be situating it within the context of a critique of colonialism or empire, here I will be reading the Indian aspects of the plot as representations not of actual colonial Indians or a colonial India but rather as representations of the workings of language. Once more arguing, as I have been doing throughout this study, that in Collins's long–novel project the locally historical is working in the service of the representation of the theoretical and linguistic (and *not* vice versa), I will be finding the black and white relations in this narrative, as well as the Blake and Ablewhite relations, to be situated more within the realm of textuality, say in the form of ink on paper, than in the domain of colonial discourse. (Of course one has only to ask exactly what kind of ink that could be in order to be led inexorably back into the colonial domain). As with the fable of the Bedouin Brothers in *Armadale,* here the problems of the seemingly outré Other will turn "backwards" and be disclosed to be actually the problems of the Self, specifically that Self's attempts at manifesting itself through a paradoxically-operating iterability.

As already noted, it is language's iterability that allows for copies to be created—necessarily uncontrollably—and from this proliferation of copies a proliferation of meanings to be produced as a result. Iterability allows for the fundamental absenting of the user, creating an inherent precariousness in the necessary reliance on language for the representation of one's identity. The same words appearing in different contexts can come to mean different things. I would stress that a proliferation of meanings does not occur without a proliferation of copies having preceded it (if only in phantom cognitive form). This proliferation of copies, the result of iterability, allows would-be-consolidating repetitions to turn into disintegrational iterations and provides the basis for the split between the author-as-creator and the author-as-disseminator. The resultant proliferation of meanings can be represented in various ways. It often is called a proliferation of Others, of meanings "foreign" to oneself and to one's intention. This split is often seen as an "Othering" or "alienation" of the author-as-creator. There is no inherent connection, I would stress, between alterity and the proliferation of meanings, but it is in the metaphor of Otherness that we find the latter's most common expression given. However, I would argue that this metaphor can tend to give the wrong impression, especially given the extensive interest in Postcolonialism in current literary discourse. For the proliferation originally takes place not in some far-away zone but rather within the mind of the person using language, the person thinking in language, and therefore the "split" manifests itself first and foremost as an Othering of the Self. We will therefore need to be aware of the possibilities of this potential internalization of Otherness and its contrary the potential colonially-metaphorized manifestation of consciousness as we explore this seemingly-patently-Postcolonial story's representation of the self-absenting resulting from language's repeatability.

Thus, I will here not be emphasizing a consideration, as tempting as that situation might be, of the circumstance of three Indians having come to England in search of a stone they consider theirs but rather, moving from the inside outwards, a consideration of Franklin Blake's leaving of himself. Collins's interest in textuality having, I believe, been proven by this point, the latter situation clearly occupies a more central role in his long–novel project than the former. Through its most shocking plot disclosure, Collins's narrative acknowledges the perils that language poses for the unity of the self. An acknowledgment of the deep-seated nature of the foreignness to which the act of writing renders one subject comes in the book at perhaps the story's tensest point and allows for the narrative's most dramatic moment of "self-recognition." At the crescendo of the plotting of this most masterfully-plotted of English fictions we find our hero Blake making his way out onto a rocky spit of land while following the directions left him by the dead housemaid Rosanna Spearman. Believing Rosanna's posthumous memorandum to be leading him to the location of the lost Indian diamond, and manfully overcoming the dread prompted by the horror-show fantasy of possibly meeting up with the dead girl's body as it surfaces from beneath the sands in which she had died, Blake dredges up instead her varnish-sealed tin case. Sufficiently intriguing as this situation itself is, beneath the surface of this remarkable scene something else—perhaps the more appropriate term in the case of this book would be something Other—is taking place. As often happens with other interpretations, however, this one can on first reading tend to go unnoticed.

We might look more closely at the scene in order to plumb its submerged depths. Here we have Blake describing his suggestive use of his walking-stick in the recovery of Rosanna's case and his struggles with that case back on the beach:

> I own I closed my eyes at the moment when the point of the stick first entered the quicksand.
>
> The instant afterwards, *before the stick could have been submerged more than a few inches,* I was free from the hold of my own superstitious terror, and *was throbbing with excitement* from head to foot.
>
> . . . I drew [the chain] up without the slightest difficulty. And there was the japanned tin case fastened to the end of it.
>
> The action of the water had so rusted the chain, that it was impossible for me to unfasten it from the hasp which attached it to the case. *Putting the case between my knees, and exerting my utmost strength, I contrived to draw off the cover. Some white substance filled the whole interior* when I looked in. I put in my hand, and found it to be linen. (*Moonstone* 357–58; emphasis added)

This well could stand as the sequel to Basil's dream. Hutter rightly comments of this scene that here "the combination of sexual excitement and sexual fear seems to permeate Collins's language" ("Dreams" 205). It is significant that Blake's discovery of this linen nightgown should be figuratively represented as the spilling of his seed, that is, that we should have here a figurative ejaculation on the beach. The sexual aspects of Franklin's struggles with the case serve to confirm the impression that what is taking place here is an act of "dissemination"—in both the textual and sexual sense. These spillages from "between [his] knees" of linen and also of a long letter from Rosanna posthumously attesting to her love for Blake allow for an overlapping of both the sexual and textual sides of dissemination. Here Blake is figuratively disseminating at the meeting place of two figurative "legs" of land, the two oppositely-directed spits that are described as "run[ning]" out into the sea (55).[9] Through its emphasis on sexual dissemination, the beach scene serves, then, as an excellent counterpoint to Collins's story's earlier paradigmatic instance of textual dissemination: that moment when the irrepressible Miss

---

9. This topographical body analogy will be called into service again late in the story when Collins has Blake—as though working himself up to the crucial point through bodily vacillation—finally disseminates the story of his infamy to Ezra Jennings—publishes it, so to speak: "I told [Jennings] the truth, as unreservedly as I have told it in these pages" (430)—similarly at a pubic region of the landscape, at a fork in the road.

Clack had characterized her having tossed another of her innumerable religious tracts in at the window of a cab as once more an instance in which she was "sow[ing] the good seed" (259).[10]

There is of course also an undeniable textual element to the scene on the beach. Not only does Blake find in the box a long white substance—as though it were a large sheet of paper—bearing significant writing (a name) and a blot (the all important implicating seminal paint stain), but he also finds Rosanna's letter to him in which, adding one more turnabout to the sexual/textual dynamic, she suggests that initially she had thought Blake had had a sexual motive for being in Rachel's sitting-room after midnight (note that Collins has Blake leave her cabinet "drawer[s]" open). Of course, Blake, like the rest of us, is at that moment much less interested in the letter than in the testimony of the nightgown. When Betteredge approaches him, Blake, as though passing on—disseminating again—an amusingly perplexing Collins novel, laughs and hands him the gown (as he will later the letter) telling him to "read the riddle for himself" (359).

However, before Blake has himself apprised himself of the startling testimony on the gown, that is, before he has had his complacent self-certainty so thoroughly "overthrown" by the shock of recognizing "on the unanswerable evidence of the paint-stain" (359) the name of the thief, he will for a time have entered into a type of trance brought on by his discovery of that article of clothing that had been the primary focus of so much of Sergeant Cuff's unsuccessful initial investigation. This trance causes him to forget to look for the principal piece of evidence at that moment: the name on the gown. At this crucial point in the plot, the all-important disclosure is held in abeyance, withheld from the readers, by certain of Cuff's words having imprinted themselves, quite literally, on Blake's mind:

> "Find out whether there is any article of dress in this house with the stain of paint on it. Find out who that dress belongs to. Find out how the person can account for having been in the room, and smeared the paint, between midnight and three in the morning. If the person can't satisfy you, you haven't far to look for the hand that took the Diamond."
>
> One after another those words travelled over my memory, repeating themselves again and again with *a wearisome, mechanical reiteration.* (358; emphasis added)

---

10. Another example of Clack's dissemination of figurative seeds occurs when, instead of taking a flower from among those kept by Lady Verinder in the box at her window, she "add[s] one, in the shape of another book from [her] bag" (269). Also see Clack commenting that "[w]e must sow the good seed somehow" (237).

Blake's memory here would seem to be pre-establishing the case to be made later by a citation from Dr. William Carpenter, one of the two real-world authorities cited by Ezra Jennings as theoretical support for his controversial experiment of opium-induced re-enactment. Here Blake's memory has been rendered subject to that same iterability to which Derrida finds writing to be subject. While Derrida argues for allowing proper weight to the fact that *writing* must be repeatable in different contexts (recall: "a written sign carries with it a force that breaks with its context, that is, with the collectivity of presences organizing the moment of its inscription" ["Signature Event Context" 9]), the citation from Carpenter argues for a reproducibility of *sensations:*

> There seems much ground for the belief, that *every* sensory impression which has once been recognised by the perceptive consciousness, is registered (so to speak) in the brain, *and may be reproduced at some subsequent time,* although there may be no consciousness of its existence in the mind during the whole intermediate period. (*Moonstone* 440; second emphasis added)

The printing-press-like, "wearisome, mechanical reiteration" to which Cuff's words are subjected by Blake's mind implies that Blake's *psyche* has come to operate according to the iterability grounding the system of language. This basis in iterability implies that Blake continually faces the potential of being disarticulated from himself. His personality having gone over to the realm of what Derrida calls the "structural unconsciousness" of language ("Signature Event Context" 18), Blake is vulnerable to the corruptions inherent in iterability. Those corruptions have been pithily encapsulated by Derrida in a comment that I have cited more than once, that "Insofar as I make use of an instrument that bears within itself its repeatability, I am absented from what I use" (Derrida and Ricoeur 154).

During the experiment of re-enactment a few pages later, at the point when it looks like things are well on the way toward failure, we are told that Blake "rose again restlessly, and reiterated his first words. 'How do I know? The Indians may be hidden in the house'" (477). It is fitting that the concept of iterability should have been introduced in this context in *The Moonstone,* this so very Other-obsessed story, as there would seem to be for Derrida an inherent tie between the repetition of language and alterity:

> Through the possibility of repeating every mark as the same [iterability] makes way for an idealization that seems to deliver the full presence of

ideal objects . . . but this repeatability itself ensures that the full presence of a singularity thus repeated comports in itself *the reference to something else,* thus rending the full presence that it nevertheless announces. This is why iteration is not simply repetition. (*Limited* 129; emphasis added)

That "something else" to which iterability allows one access and toward which it carries one back might as well have been termed a something Other, for, as we had learned—in a passage cited also in the previous chapter— when Derrida had first introduced "iterability" he had emphasized its etymological connection to alterity (appropriately for our purpose of reading *The Moonstone,* this is a subcontinental alterity): "*iter,* again, [*sic*] probably comes from *itara, other* in Sanskrit, and everything that follows can be read as the working out of the logic that ties repetition to alterity ("Signature Event Context" 7). Derrida's qualifying "probably" aside, here the Sanskrit term for Other is being used to designate the repeated mark. Collins himself represents iterability in terms of Otherness. The Indians pursuing the Moonstone are an expression of the feared foreignness that dissemination represents. They are a tangible expression of Collins's unconscious understanding of the Otherness inherent in authorship, inherent, that is, not only in textual dissemination but also in the initial step of thinking in reciteable traces, and indeed perhaps in feeling in repeatable sensations. In this sense, "the Indians" are indeed in the house; they have always already been there. They will always be, for "the house" it will turn out was never to have been constituted without them. The intimate invasion carried out by iterability stands out most clearly when it is represented, as it is here, as Others coming to invade what had seemed to be a zone of singularity, a zone of sameness. Betteredge's "dogs" will be coming far too late and far too ineffectively and inefficiently to protect against this type of self-constitutive "invasion." Thus the sensationalistic, and timely, political dimensions of Collins's having represented the workings of language through a colonial metaphor should not be allowed to obscure the quite far-reaching literary-theoretical dynamics at play in the manifesto for authors that has come to be his most widely-disseminated work.

The Alienation of the Self

Returning to the beach scene in the narrative, Gabriel Betteredge's call in the distance brings Blake out of his musing on Cuff's words, prompting him to rush back, like an ebbing wave, to himself. Before Betteredge has reached him, Blake will have found the name on the gown and it will have turned out to be "MY OWN NAME."[11] At this moment, when the narrative of detection, of empire and figurative colonization through the collection of knowledge,[12] has met up with its counter-narrative, the narrative of dissemination—that narrative that recounts the unraveling of the self and the fracturing of the subject—the story has reached an important (and quite "sensational") milestone. The fact that it had all along been made evident that the paint stain would, were it ever to be found, incriminate the wearer as the thief of the diamond, coupled with the disclosure that Franklin Blake, our most dedicated detective character and our narrator of the moment as well, *is* that wearer, effectively brings the schizophrenia in him—in the figurative, etymological sense of "split mind"—out and up to the level of the narrative itself. Indeed, through a burgeoning chain-reaction, that schizophrenia seems also to be "caught" by the entities circumscribing Blake, the narrative and the book, stopping perhaps only at the person of the author himself. (Indeed, the only disclosure more shocking than the one we actually encounter in this story might have been Blake's having found the name to be "WILKIE COLLINS.") Here on this beach Blake is caught in a contradiction, the conflict being represented by way of an act of *detection* being figuratively presented as an act of *dissemination*. The single name here would be trying to contain both Franklin Blake the detective and Franklin Blake the thief, appropriately, as one might recall Betteredge's comment that Blake "seemed to pass his life in a state of perpetual contradiction with himself" (77). This self-contradictoriness Blake exemplifies is, I would argue, merely a fictional representation of the self-contradictoriness of the proprietary author (author-as-creator) caught in the act of disseminating, of publishing, as here Wilkie Collins the would-be *owner* of the text meets up with Wilkie Collins the active, alienated *disseminator* of it, here caught "red-handed," so to speak, as he writes from a certain real-world narrative frame of the discovery of the name of the thief while writing the potentially self-referential words "MY OWN NAME."

However, signs of the open-palmed/closed-fisted schizophrenia of the narrative, when we stop to consider, had been evident all along, appearing first perhaps at that moment when Betteredge—perhaps echoing that inaugurative pronouncement by that famous author/publisher launching his journal *All the Year Round*,[13] "It was the best of times, it was the worst

---

11. Meckier describes this scene as Blake's encounter with "a secret self" (134).

12. *The Moonstone* bears out Thomas Richards's contention in his remarkable *The Imperial Archive* that "the control of Empire hinges on a British monopoly over knowledge" (7).

13. *The Moonstone* was initially serialized in Dickens's *All the Year Round*. It was with good reason that Dickens decided to embark on the task of publishing his own journal, as he must have realized

of times"—had described his marital relations with the Orientally-named Selina Goby[14] as "six of one and half-a-dozen of the other" (44). Unwittingly giving that standard phrase a new twist, Betteredge had thus unconsciously signaled to us a fundamental lesson of the narrative: never to forget the other side, or perhaps that should be Other side, of the story. A significant manifestation of the "Otherness" inherent in language is the startling number of instances of necessary reinterpretation that take place in the narrative, instances, that is, where other interpretations turn out to be the right ones. For instance, Rosanna Spearman, having initially considered Blake to have had a sexual motive for visiting with Rachel at night, later comes to the conclusion that instead his being in the bedroom had had "a meaning *entirely different* to the meaning which I had given to it up to that time" (368; emphasis added). We also find Sergeant Cuff concluding in the end that he "*completely mistook* [his] case" (491; emphasis added). (One of Cuff's major missteps was of course to have assumed that the plain long cloth Rosanna had bought at Frizinghall was to be used to make a substitute nightgown for herself, and not, as it turned out, one for Franklin Blake. Under the delusion that initial interpretations are reliable—a complacency that was a perennial Collinsian target—Cuff confidently remarks, "Plain long cloth *means* a plain servant's nightgown. No, no, Mr Betteredge—all that is clear enough" [189; emphasis added]). And finally, Godfrey Ablewhite's pious personality turns out to have been screening a very different identity: "The side kept hidden from the general notice, exhibited this same gentleman in the *totally different* character of a man of pleasure" (506; emphasis added). In this narrative of other interpretations bringing about "totally" different, or "entirely" different, or "completely" different, viewings of the world, we see language's iterability respected through the duplicity, or more properly multiplicity, of meanings it makes possible. This need to take account of the multiform sign, of a potential Otherness inherent in the wor(l)d (the Indians always in the house?), was a lesson that Collins, professional Victorian author as he was, that is, as someone always positioned at the border between pen tip and page—between the textual empires of creation and preservation, control and dissemination—could not have helped knowing.

---

that the split between the mechanics of dissemination and the mechanics of creation leads to an unequal situation in which, economically, publishers stay on one side of the fence while authors, with a very few, much-publicized exceptions, huddle in their garrets on the other. See Patten's excellent study *Charles Dickens and His Publishers*.

14. Her last name calls to mind the Chinese desert and an Indian vegetable. Her first of course resonates with another significant facet of the story, Selina being the Greek goddess of the moon.

A PARTICULARLY striking instance of the encounter with the Other occurs in the subplot of Ezra Jennings, our remarkably dualistic doctor's assistant, coming to disturb the "sameness" of the standard English character, a "character" that, not surprisingly, turns textual soon enough. When Jennings meets the family and friends come from London to the Verinder house to witness the experiment of re-drugging Blake, he encounters several shocked gasps of surprise and a series of distrusting looks in response to his strange appearance. While his "gipsy-complexion, his fleshless cheeks, his gaunt facial bones, [and] his dreamy eyes" (417) undoubtedly contribute to the effect he has on the visitors, it is his parti-colored hair, black on top and white on the sides, that is the most remarkable thing about him. Rachel, commenting on the visitors' cool reception of him, remarks, "They seem to be in a conspiracy to persecute you. . . . What does it mean?" He responds, "Only the protest of the world, Miss Verinder—on a very small scale—against anything that is new" (469). The newness represented by Jennings's unusual appearance and by his "scientific" experiment of re-enactment is a newness that is meant to spill over into the author's world also, for it seems that Collins is having Jennings's experiment stand for the more general experiment that has been the former's writing and publishing of this relatively new type of suspense story. When Jennings comes to wish Blake good night on the evening of the re-enactment he reamrks on the latter's careless perusal of the room's reading matter:

> Mr Blake idly turned over the books on his bedroom table . . . *The Guardian; the Tatler;* Richardson's *Pamela;* Mackenzie's *Man of Feeling;* Roscoe's *Lorenzo de' Medici;* and Robertson's *Charles the Fifth*—all classical works: all (of course) immeasurably superior to anything produced in later times; and all (from my present point of view) possessing the one great merit of enchaining nobody's interest, and exciting nobody's brain. I left Mr Blake to the *composing* influence of Standard Literature, and occupied myself in *making* this entry in my journal. (470; emphasis added)

The phrasing in the last sentence implies that the journal entries that Jennings (and beyond him Collins) is occupied in "making" are not instances in which he is "composing" but rather ones in which he is paradoxically "dis-composing," for here Jennings (and indeed Collins also, that writer producing in "later times") juxtaposes what he undoubtedly knows to be the so-very-discomposing interest elicited by his journal entries with the "composing" interest offered by the insularity of Standard British Literature. (We are of course implicitly called on to remember here Betteredge's repeated turns to composing draughts of *Robinson Crusoe* earlier in the story whenever circumstances had threatened to get the better of him.) In this passage Collins implies that *The Moonstone,* especially that part contributed by Jennings, is a type of fiction that is different, that is new, in comparison to the old, solid, Standard Literature.

Jennings's composition will come to comprise part of what we know today as the book *The Moonstone.* By having the Other write a text that enters into the "sameness" of English fiction, that is, a solely settling func-tion–valuing style of fiction, Collins will open a path through which the breaking function has the chance of disclosing itself in his (and this larger) text. It is perhaps appropriate that that book's namesake, the Indian dia-mond, should be credited with bringing about an effect similar to that elic-ited by Jennings's diary "entries." Early on Betteredge remarks:

> [H]ere was our quiet English house suddenly invaded by a devilish Indian Diamond—bringing after it a conspiracy of living rogues, set loose on us by the vengeance of a dead man. . . . Who ever heard the like of it—in the nineteenth century, mind; in an age of progress, and in a country which rejoices in the blessings of the British constitution? Nobody ever heard the like of it, and, consequently, nobody can be expected to believe it. I shall go on with my story, however, in spite of that. (67)

Here we have an example of a type of reverse colonization occurring. The colony would seem to be a threat to the home country, to the equanimity of the British constitution. Not used to stories of Otherish rogues and Indian Diamonds pursued by the vengeance of dead men, the British Everyman is here bemoaning being assaulted by Otherness *coming from the outside.* However, the actual goal of Collins's narrative is to show that Otherness to have been inside all along. Early in the scene of the experiment Jennings pointedly remarks that "[t]here is a wonderful sameness in the solid side of the English character—just as there is a wonderful sameness in the solid expression of the English face" (469). That sameness, however, will soon enough be shaken apart—as is so often Betteredge's equanimity of mind by the "detective-fever" and the brown face of the Shivering Sand by, well, its shivering—when it is confronted with the realization that it has been merely one option among several "others." Jennings's narrative account of the consequences of his experiment with Franklin Blake's split identity thus testifies to the seemingly never-assimilable and therefore always shocking (to literary critics and Victorian readers alike) fact that the "Indians" are always already inside the house.

Passing through the Door of Communication

While the mystery novel must inevitably be interested in the question of the structure of its composition and the pace of its disclosures, *The Moonstone* is a mystery novel even more interested than usual in the composition of narratives.[15] It is perhaps the most overtly textually-oriented of all Collins's many textually-oriented fictions. Gabriel Betteredge and Drusilla Clack both begin their narratives with narratorial "hemmings-and-hawings" that are figurative repetitions of *Basil*'s opening question: "What am I now about to write?" (*Basil,* ed. Goldman 1). For Betteredge it is the stressful matter of how he is possibly to rival his hero, the author of *Robinson Crusoe,* in their now-common profession. For Miss Clack, more important even than the question of what she is to write are the fact that she is to be paid for it and the question of how much the not very sympathetically rendered Rachel Verinder intends to interfere with those writings through the intercessions of the editor of the manuscript, Franklin Blake. Indeed, Miss Clack continually remarks how tragic it is that she as the undoubtedly-cherished niece of the late Lady Verinder should have been reduced to the situation of being reliant on the payments accorded by Blake for her textual installments.

The textuality of the narrative is further highlighted in the gradual process of the solution of the mystery. That solution is of course centrally bound up with acts of writing, being based not only on a telling paint stain and the startling characters written on the nightgown that Franklin Blake dredges up from the Shivering Sands but also on Ezra Jennings's self-described "manuscript-experiments" (425) with Mr. Candy's delirious maunderings, that is, on his replacement—or manufacture, we are never sure which—of the missing characters not supplied by Candy. Indeed, many critics connect Jennings's manuscript reconstruction with the activity of the reader of *The Moonstone,* specifically with the reader's task of putting together the pieces of the mystery: our doctor's assistant's puzzle-solving thus becoming a dramatization of the readerly situation.[16] The search for the Moonstone here implies the reading of *The Moonstone.*

As if the narrative's serious stress on textuality were not enough, the self-reflexivity of the book's title additionally causes that topic to be brought to the fore, since we have, with each new adventure undergone by the

---

15. Laidlaw writes, "One of the things which *The Moonstone* is quite explicitly about is the process of its own writing" (220).

16. See for example Philip O'Neill, who writes, "*The Moonstone* asks to be read as a detective story, but a detective story which acts as a metaphor for the activity of reading itself. There is a passage in the novel which is a miniature of the work as a whole. This is Ezra Jennings' transcription of Candy's disjointed mutterings" (10).

diamond, the potential for seeing an analogous adventure being undergone by the text of the same name. This self-reflexivity takes perhaps its most overt form in the story's last lines, when we are presented with a direct conflation between the fictional and physical entities sharing the name "The Moonstone." Mr. Murthwaite tells us, "So the years pass, and repeat each other; so the same events revolve in the cycles of time. What will be the next adventures of the Moonstone? Who can tell!" (526). The book and the diamond are collapsed in this significantly non-italicized name, as Collins's role as author is stressed here. The answer to Murthwaite's diegetic discipline–defying question as to "who can tell"—but who as we will see, chooses not to—is none other than Wilkie Collins himself, the writer who has just finished "tell[ing]" the *previous* "adventures of the Moonstone." Here at the end of Collins's project the spotlight is turned where it should be, on the author.

Naturally, then, the scene of the "theft" of the Moonstone has significant implications for the question of the author's control over his mystery. In this context the precarious nature of publication and the ambiguous nature of the "guilt" that might attach to the passing of the book from author to reader is acknowledged. This situation being so very much akin to that one described in the Introduction, found in the discussions in *Millar v. Taylor* in which Justice Joseph Yates was able to see white where Chief Justice Lord Mansfield saw black, it is not surprising that the solution to the mystery should remain unclear even after things have ostensibly been cleared up. That is, even after the exposure of Blake's interactions with Ablewhite on the night of Rachel's birthday we are still unsure as to who is truly guilty of that theft. That all-important scene offers us one of the story's more disconcerting equivocations, for it has to be admitted that we readers face a fairly difficult task of it sustaining the high degree of indignation that the narrative would seem to be demanding be marshaled against Godfrey Ablewhite, our faithless trustee. One could well imagine the broad-minded reader bemusedly wondering what exactly it is that Ablewhite has done wrong. Pocketed the Moonstone? But, when you come right down to it, was it not *given* to him in the first place? Did not the character most intent on upholding societal values and undoing the mystery freely—albeit in an opium-induced waking dream—pass it along to Ablewhite?[17] Ablewhite's

---

17. Indeed Ross Murfin comments, "[Blake] put the gem into the hands of man who had not intended to steal anything that night but who must have been ready to seize a most felicitous opportunity. We sense that the real secret of the novel, then, is that Godfrey Abelwhite [*sic*], thief, was not really the primary agent of the theft . . . [but rather] Blake's unconscious. . . . Collins symbolically dramatizes his belief . . . that the line between innocence and guilt, legitimacy and illegitimacy, is about as fine as the one . . . that separates the active but unconscious taking of the gem and the passive

thinking could not have been clearer when he decided the next day simply to remain silent about his knowledge of the whereabouts of the diamond. He might appropriately have asked himself, "Am *I* the one who stole it, or is Franklin Blake the thief?"[18] The only factor on which the reader can base his or her disapproval of Ablewhite—a disapproval that the narrative is so very intent on instilling and sustaining that it goes out of its way to describe to us the various other interesting, if fundamentally beside-the-point, crimes committed by Ablewhite—would be the fact that Blake, even as he hands it over—and despite being under the influence of opium in which case he could hardly be expected to have any particular intentions of his own at all—*does not intend* for Godfrey Ablewhite to have it. (One recalls here Mansfield's statement that "the author does not *mean* to make [his property] common" [98 ER 253; emphasis added].)

The letter written by Sergeant Cuff—our most authoritative representative of policing officialdom—to Blake at the conclusion of the tale would seem, apparently, to make clear who should and should not be found to be guilty under these circumstances:

> "You saw [Ablewhite] (as he supposes) just as he was passing through the door of communication. At any rate, you called to him in a strange, drowsy voice.
>
> He came back to you. You looked at him in a dull sleepy way. You put the Diamond into his hand. You said to him 'Take it back, Godfrey, to your father's bank. It's safe there—it's not safe here.' You turned away unsteadily, and put on your dressing-gown. You sat down in the large arm-chair in your room. You said, 'I can't take it back to the bank. My head's like lead—and I can't feel my feet under me.' Your head sank on the back of the chair—you heaved a heavy sigh—and you fell asleep.

---

but conscious acceptance of it" (660). What Murfin views as an emphasis on the fine line between innocence and guilt or legitimacy and illegitimacy, I would reinflect as an emphasis on the line between author-as-creator and author-as-disseminator, as the move from "the active but unconscious taking of the gem and the passive but conscious acceptance of it" mirrors the fundamental transformation occurring in the situation, and legal status, of the author.

18. Ian Ousby writes, "[t]hough Ablewhite was the real villain, Franklin was the original thief of the diamond, if only in a technical sense" (119). Elisabeth Rose Gruner comments that "we establish that Godfrey is both a philandering debtor and a thief, but we never really establish that Franklin is neither" (138). And Rycroft touches on Godfrey's less than solid guilt when he describes him as a "scapegoat." But, of course, Rycroft's use of that term is motivated by other concerns than an interest in the inconclusive nature of that guilt, per se, as he is intent on proving that the real crime has taken place (symbolically) in Rachel's bedroom: "The theft of the Moonstone is a symbolic representation of the yet prohibited intercourse between Franklin Blake and Rachel and the loss of Rachel's virginity" ("Detective Story" 235).

> Mr Godfrey Ablewhite went back, with the Diamond, into his own room. His statement is, that he came to no conclusion, at that time—except that he would wait, and see what happened in the morning.
>
> When the morning came, your language and conduct showed that you were absolutely ignorant of what you had said and done overnight. At the same time, Miss Verinder's language and conduct showed that she was resolved to say nothing (in mercy to you) on her side. If Mr Godfrey Able-white chose to keep the Diamond, he might do so with perfect impunity. The Moonstone stood between him and ruin. He put the Moonstone into his pocket." (510–11)

One man calls back another just as the latter is traversing the threshold of "the door of communication." Here we are situated on the textual border, at the point where the potential alienation inherent in authorship becomes fully manifest. Blake's assertion that he would take the Moonstone back to the bank himself if he were only able, effectively casts the aptly-named Able-white as his trustee. It is as if the latter were one of Justice Yates's hypothetical friends enjoined to only peruse the manuscript. Godfrey, we are invited to conclude, true to his character, betrays that trust. However, it is hard to conclusively fault Ablewhite, since, in betraying the communicating author, he does only what language has always already been doing, what it itself is *required* to do in order to remain language. Because language has a breaking side as well as a settling one, it is necessarily going to "betray" any "con-clusive intentions"—if the coming into being of these is even possible—on the author's part. Here we have a text failing to be protected by the settling function—"Take it back, Godfrey, to your father's bank. It's safe there—it's not safe here"—and being recontextualized. Through that recontextualiza-tion—"he would wait, and see what happened in the morning"—the break-ing function of iterability effectively enters the picture. Collins has moved on from an investigation of the implications of a clear textual theft in the material domain such as that of Marian's diary by Fosco to an exploration of what occurs when a textual entity (The Moonstone/*The Moonstone*) relocates and thus ends up moving beyond its author's (perhaps addled) intention(s).

Taking It with You

Coupling the ambiguity surrounding Ablewhite's "theft" with the fact that the diamond that is exchanged could possibly be standing in, by means of the shared name, for the book that the writer is in the process of composing

and the reader is in the process of reading, one is confronted with a situation in which the problems of publishing a literary work—in any time
period, in any place—are brought forth in all their self-contradictory glory.
The fact that Blake, going further, is under the influence of opium during
this scene of the crossing of thresholds of "communication" is significant, at
both a narrative and authorial level. Adding a further twist, by having the
opium addict Ezra Jennings compose the narrative about Blake's drugging,
the narrative suggests to us, twice over, that the writer's recourse to language
is a recourse to a potentially very self-alienating medium. This is a lesson
that Collins could not himself have helped knowing as he was at this stage
of his life a professional author heavily addicted to opium.[19] Blake, while
under the influence of opium, tries to loan Ablewhite the stone only to find
the conditions that he would be setting violated, his intentions ignored or
radically misinterpreted. I would suggest that Blake's own unwilled "theft"
and passing on of the diamond is not, as it might have at first seemed, an
instance of insanity or amnesia, but rather an instance of dissemination
bringing with it an alienation of authorial proprietary control (and authorial intention), the self-reflexivity of the diamond's name suggesting that
the entity that Blake and Ablewhite exchange on the fateful night is in fact
The Moonstone. Blake at that crucial moment is, quite literally, as alienated
from himself as would be any writer who publishes a book. Indeed, he
would seem here to be the consummate "victim" of publication. This victim-
ization was not, however, one that Collins—true to character[20]—was willing
to accept in his own life. It was in the possible linguistic alienations always
menacing his real-world existence that Collins would find a model, one also
constantly being suggested to him by his daily alienation at the hands of
opium, that would eventually be allowing him to *overcome* the divestments
awaiting him at the hands of publication.

Over the course of the narrative's initial serialization Collins's authority
was contained within a finely-balanced chamber, a chamber created by the
stark contrast between dissemination and mystery. *The Moonstone*'s repeated
championing of an obstructionist privacy on the one hand and its repeated
menacing of that privacy on the other disclose its author's—and story's—
dual nature. The author-as-creator/author-as-disseminator distinction is one
that is usually effectively obscured by the ambiguous label "the author."[21]

---

19. See Peters 313. Alethea Hayter describes the scene well: "[T]he actions of an opium-dosed
man are described by an opium addict who is the invention of a writer dosed with opium" (259).

20. See Chapter 3 above for an analysis of his counter-attack on the American literary pirates.

21. Francis Kase does a thorough job of setting out "the various legal theories of copyright,"
arguing that there are ten different schools of thought regarding that right's basic premises: (1) the
reflection theory (that copyright is "a mere reflection of legal provisions prohibiting unauthorized
copying"); (2) the monopoly theory (that copyright is "a monopoly which has developed from the

However, the mystery form was and is a genre particularly adapted to allowing this distinction to be brought forward. The withholding and dispersal typical of this style of writing has always been evident in its somewhat oxymoronic name: the "mystery story." The act of composing a story that would be *telling* a *mystery*, that would be disclosing and not disclosing at the same time, naturally opens up a space that is safe from the knowledge of the readers, if only for a short while—that space in which is lodged the solution to the mystery. The answer as to "who done it" represents the author's safe zone, his integral self in the writing process, his autonomy from the insatiable demands of the readership in particular and of the system of dissemination in general.[22] It is our author's protection from the "curse" of dissemination.

And Collins's narrative would indeed seem to view dissemination as a curse. One of the most memorable aspects of the story is the fact that the diamond bears an Indian curse. And that curse would appear to have wrought certain dispersive effects on the Verinder household. At one point Franklin Blake comments to Betteredge:

> When I came here from London with that horrible Diamond . . . I don't believe there was a happier household in England than this. Look at the

---

printers' and publishers' privileges"); (3) the publishers' rights theory (that copyright is "the rights which the author assigns to his publisher for the purpose of a commercial exploitation of his work"); (4) the theory of intellectual property (that authors have a natural right to the products of their intellectual labor and that it is fitting that their rights in their "intellectual product" be "equated with the property in corporeal things"); (5) the theories of incorporeal property (that "copyright is a dominion over an incorporeal, intangible thing"); (6) the personality rights theory (that copyright is "a right of personality"); (7) the dualistic theories of copyright (that copyright "consists of two kinds of rights which are entirely different one from another," the pecuniary rights and the moral rights); (8) the sui generis right theory (that copyright is a "unitary right with different facets"); (9) the labor theory of copyright (that copyright is "a result of the author's labor, and . . . the author should be compensated for the expenditure of his labor"); and (10) the pragmatic school (that copyright "should be defined from the point of view of the author's interests and his claims, in terms of the protection recognized and secured by legislation") (1–15). I believe these ten views can be broken down into three different categories: publishers' rights schools or author-as-disseminator schools (schools 1–3), author-as-creator schools (schools 4–6 and 9), and schools that mix the two former categories (schools 7, 8, and 10). In this book I have not dealt with the issue of publishers' rights per se, seeing it as more imperative to deal with the rights of the author-as-disseminator—on which those publishers' rights are based in the modern age—in contrast to the rights of the author-as-creator.

22. Michel Foucault's "What is an Author?" is useful on this issue up to a point. However, as that essay is a defense of his earlier denigration of the concept of epoch-altering individual "genius" in *The Order of Things*, it is not surprising to find it essentially evading—despite its title—the substantive issue of what Foucault calls "the-man-and-his-work criticism" in order to "deal solely with the relationship between text and author and with the manner in which the text points to this 'figure' that, at least in appearance, is outside it and antecedes it" (*Foucault Reader* 101). That is, I believe that Foucault overdoes—given the nature of things, as opposed to simply their ordering—the deemphasizing of the author–work (essentially author-as-creator) dynamic in both *The Order of Things* and in "What is an Author?"

household now! *Scattered, disunited*—the very air of the place poisoned with
mystery and suspicion! Do you remember that morning at the Shivering
Sand, when we talked about my uncle Herncastle, and his birthday gift?
The Moonstone has served the Colonel's vengeance, Betteredge, by means
which the Colonel himself never dreamt of! (223; emphasis added)

Here, in the apparent realization of the god Vishnu's proclamation of certain
disaster to the "house and name" (34) of the mortal who lays hands on the
diamond, there would seem to have been a contagion among disseminal
registers as one effect of the "dissemination" of the diamond has been the
dispersal of the Verinder household (as well as of Blake's trust in his "own
name"). Here we encounter, in the "poisoning of the house" with mystery
and suspicion, the curse of the author's situation compelling a turn toward
the recompensatory genres of mystery and suspense rather than allowing a
remaining with the uncontrollably dispersive genres of, say, domestic and
realist fiction as the author endeavors to protect himself from the assaults
and divestments of publication. In this sense *The Moonstone* is bringing
the curse of mystery and suspicion into "the house" of nineteenth-century
English fiction.

THE VOLITIONAL ACT of publication had been claimed by Justice Yates
to be an undoing of the author's right: "If the author will voluntarily let
the bird fly, his property is gone; and it will be in vain for him to say 'he
meant to retain' what is absolutely flown and gone" (*Millar v. Taylor* 234).
Thus, it would seem that as soon as our author has finally agreed to tell his
"story," to its full extent, he has in effect given up, in Yates's view, his proprietary right over it. However, in the case of Collins's deployment of the
mystery genre the paradox of publication is most manifestly brought forth
throughout the narrative and, quite remarkably, overcome at its end: in *The
Moonstone* our author is finally able to be both disseminator and creator at
the same time. In a manner analogous to Franklin Blake's establishment of
his "innocence," Collins's solution to this problem is to disseminate, but to
have done so *without having willed that act.*

   Late in life Collins recounted to a friend the troubles he had had in writing *The Moonstone*. The actress Mary Anderson tells us,

   A great sufferer from gout in the eyes, he was forced to seek relief in opium.
   It was under its potent influence, he told me, that he invented the *dénoue-
   ment* of "The Moonstone." . . . "I dictated much of the book: the last part

largely under the effects of opium. When it was finished, I was not only pleased and astonished at the *finale,* but did not recognize it as my own." (142–43)

An explicit connection is made here between Blake's opium-beclouded hand-ing over of the diamond in the narrative and Collins's own act of publishing it, as Collins notes that he passed on the solution to *The Moonstone* to his amanuensis, and beyond her to his readers, while under the influence of that same drug. Thus, Thomas is more correct than he supposes when he says of Collins's alienation from the conclusion of his story, "[i]t would seem that Collins experienced in the writing of his own text, *the 'displacement' of indi-vidual authority* over the unconscious that is enacted and thematized in *The Moonstone*" (*Dreams* 211*n*26; emphasis added). In writing this tale Collins did indeed experience an alienation but it was not so much an alienation of "authority over the unconscious" as an alienation over authoriality.

Indeed, near the end of his story Collins takes his focus to its inner-most extreme, past publication, past the unpublished trace (the amanuensis stage), to the level of consciousness where, through a self-induced divest-ment by way of opium, that is, through a self-imposed divestment of con-sciousness, he renders harmless the effects of the publication of the crucial final phase of his mystery. It is important that Collins should not recog-nize the conclusion of *The Moonstone* as his own. As Collins's story nears its end, it is approaching the point of conclusive relinquishment-through-publication faced eventually by all mysteries. Before he reaches that point, however, Collins reverses in his own situation the author-as-creator/author-as-disseminator split inherent in mystery writing—the former manifesting itself most forcefully early in such a tale, the latter late—in order to give himself the space in which to "disappear" as disseminator before the end. Thus—escaping "silently into the night," so to speak—he enjoys all the benefits of publication while not having to undergo its pitfalls.

Collins indeed represents his situation as author through Blake. But in his own situation—instead of offering the reader a limited lending as had Blake and watching it go awry as any giving in to publication must—Col-lins succeeds where Blake failed. Collins publishes but refuses to be pres-ent at the divestment of that presence, at the moment when publication would want to bring about his alienation. Given the contemporary legal state of affairs for the Victorian author, Collins in *The Moonstone* mimics the present-absence imposed on the author by the law through having a character steal a diamond (bearing the same name as his book) while under the influence of opium. Here Blake is completely disseminator without an ounce of creator-ship about him. Collins then writes the solution to his mystery novel while himself under the influence of opium, thus maintaining both presence at the moment of creation and absence at the significant moment of the dissemination of that creation, thereby countering the legal discourse that had taken away perpetual ownership and replaced it with a limited monopoly called copyright. By paradoxically undoing what would have seemed his strongest defense against the threat posed by the dispersive side of publication, the integral authorial identity, Collins renders himself safe from publication. (Here publication must be content with feeding on itself, must be content to remain without source, so to speak.)[23] Collins thus overcomes publication's would-be divestment of him.

In *The Moonstone* Collins revises the Fosco–Marian diary reading scene, all the way up to the point of having Blake undergo a similar instance of usurpation, in his case a self-usurpation. However, Blake and Collins diverge in character, and destiny. One remains the victim of the breaking function, while the other successfully neutralizes it through a jump to the outside of the tension-filled system. Rather than simply allowing the breaking function to institute its usual schizophrenia in the personality, Collins pre-induces a different schizophrenia that then successfully counteracts the breaking function's proposed impositions. Generic manipulation coupled with drug manipulation finally becomes a way for Collins to control that function. Collins the creator, like a successful Fosco might have at the end of *The Woman in White,* lives on, flies on, in the reflected sky of his own particular "parody" of fully willed dissemination.

Having pre-emptively "Othered" himself, "pre-empted" himself, Collins creates a situation in which publication has no one and nothing to divest. We see the extent of this removal, or Colonial transportation, of himself in Ezra Jennings's characterization of the effect had by the opium on Franklin Blake on the night of Rachel's birthday party: "When the morning came, and the effect of the opium had been all slept off, you would wake up as absolutely ignorant of what you had done in the night as if you had been living at the Antipodes" (443). Collins is the disseminator not guilty of his own act. Having innocently committed himself to the publication of the solution of his mystery, he retains his proprietary right, as well as his privacy, on into perpetuity. By letting the Indians into the house beforehand, so to speak, Collins counters the divestment that had been awaiting him at the hands of a house full of eighteenth-century English Lords—and staid Victorian fictions—on final publication day.

---

23. One is put in mind of that paradox written of by Donne: "And death shall be no more; death, thou shalt die" (85).

IN CLOSING this chapter I would like to remark that it was especially appropriate, if solely perhaps a matter of chance, that Dickens's only explicitly titled mystery novel, *The Mystery of Edwin Drood* (1870), a work heavily influenced by *The Moonstone*,[24] should have been left incomplete at his death. The two authors having been close friends for many years prior to 1870, Collins's dependency on opium would have been known to Dickens, and perhaps this aspect of his story had its influence on the writer of *Drood*, that novel that begins in the manner that for Collins *The Moonstone* had ended, in an opium haze. In Dickens's case, the answer as to who killed Drood, no one?, himself?, Jasper?, Neville Landless?, the wind?, was kept by the author on into perpetuity. Indeed, in the context of the discourse of authorship, Dickens fulfilled quite well the requirements set forth by *The Moonstone* by publishing the first half of his mystery novel and no more.

Unfortunately, this particular type of evasion is only possible once in a lifetime. When his own time came, Collins was able to put himself also in this situation. He was able to become creator without muddying his hands as disseminator. His last novel, *Blind Love* (1890), was completed after his death from his notes by Sir Walter Besant.[25] Besant, in writing of the circumstances of the passing over of the composition, comments:

> The plot of the novel, every scene, every situation, from beginning to end, is the work of Wilkie Collins. The actual writing is entirely his up to a certain point: from that point to the end it is partly his, but mainly mine. . . .
>
> I have . . . carried out the author's wishes to the best of my ability. I would that he were living still, if only to regret that he had not been allowed to finish his last work with his own hand! (Collins, *Blind Love* 12)

Besant obviously did not understand the significant and far-reaching interests that were at stake in Collins's not finishing his last novel with "his own hand."

While these last two are admittedly rather extreme possible reactions, the situation in which the author was placed by the legal discourse of the nineteenth century was not a comfortable one and has remained just as uncomfortable since. One should not be surprised to find that legal situation having had its effects. Having been given a right but at the same time having been divested of it in the exercising of his vocation, the author was

---

24. See Forsyte 42–50, and Lonoff 150–70.

25. Besant had been the founder in 1884 of the Society of Authors, an organization defending authors' rights against pirates and publishers. Collins was "one of its charter members, and for a time served as vice-president of this group committed to fighting literary piracy" (Collins, *Blind Love* 46).

at pains to restructure the bargain. This is what he or she did and continues to do through the writing of mysteries, if only symbolically. Certainly in the nineteenth century the significant rift created between the author-as-creator and the author-as-disseminator was wide enough and the task of bridging that gap difficult enough to have significantly affected not only some of the modes of discourse of the period's fiction but also perhaps the modes of exit of some of the century's more prominent authors. One wonders when, if ever, that gap will close and cease to have its effects. It does not promise to be any time soon and thus this present century, like the one before it, promises to be a time when the writing of mysteries (an inherently paradoxical industry), with respect to authors rather than readers, will remain the opium of the masses.

Real Absences

Collins's Waiting Shadows

There . . . stands the living Woman in the Shadow's place!

    —Ozias Midwinter, in *Armadale* 266

What [I. A.] Richards reckoned to be a mistaken line of criticism, Empson took with full seriousness.

    —Haffenden, *William Empson* 1:208

A STUDY as devoted as is this one to the topic of iterability should not be shy about committing that writerly indiscretion of repeating itself, that is, of re-citing passages. Here I will be doing so not in the attempt to reinforce a particular "lesson"—as teachers of the various traditions know well, repetition is not without its inherent usefulness—but rather in an attempt to note how a new context might have altered our understanding and appreciation of the passage in question. Thus we might look here, as we did earlier in the Introduction, at the Cambridge critic George Steiner's declaration in his book *Errata* that he has throughout his career approached interpretation from a particular philosophical perspective—the defense of which perspective, apparently, also necessitates our critic's taking a swipe at deconstruction:

> It is this provisional subjectivity, this persistent need for reconsideration and amendment, which does give a certain legitimacy to the deconstructionist project. No external ruling, be it the trope of divine revelation, be it the

author's express dictum, can guarantee interpretation. Nor can consensus, itself always partial or temporary, across "canonic" and general literacy. . . . It is logically conceivable that the text before us signifies *nothing*, that it purposes or enacts non-sense. It is just possible that the author seeks to ironize his work into playful ghostliness. But the assumptions underlying this non-reading, this dissemination into the void, are themselves arbitrary and rooted substantively in the language in which they are expressed (deconstructionists and post-modernists pour out prolix treatises). I have, throughout my work, most explicitly in *Real Presences* (1989), proposed the contrary wager: on the relations, however opaque, of word to world, on intentionalities, however difficult to unravel, in texts, in works of art, soliciting recognition. Here, as so often in our muddled being, the vital grain, the life-pattern is that of common sense. (23)

Rather than noting Steiner's allegiance to "progress" in his formulation of this breaking-subduing "common sense," I wish here to highlight his contrast between the deconstructive outlook and his own "real presence"–based one, that last phrase having been brought into particular prominence by its new context, the light thrown on it by the foregoing analyses of Collins's major works and those works' interest in ideational silhouettes.

I would agree with Steiner's having placed these two standpoints, that of the deconstructionists and his own, in conflict. His perspective is consonant with that one that I have been describing in this study as "the settling world view," while deconstruction in its practice often manifests similarities to what I have been labeling the breaking function–based outlook. Steiner has a grand tradition standing behind him. At a certain point the Enlightenment went wholly over—despite the testimony of Yates's "constitution of things"—to the side of what he describes as "real presences." Perhaps this move was one of the Enlightenment's founding propositions, an effect of that turn away from paradox I discussed in the Introduction. Steiner's comment reemphasizes that this tradition continues alive and well today—and that it is still fighting fiercely (though, why it should feel the need to, remains unasked) against its opponents. I have attempted to show in this study that far from being a type of "non-reading" or "dissemination into the void," as Steiner's exceedingly-high high rhetoric would have it, the acknowledgment of the breaking function of iterability is a significant critical step toward properly perceiving the *whole* of the "life-pattern" of linguistic workings. Those workings are not at all "common-sensical"—in Steiner's current understanding, or usurpation, of that term—but that unsanctioned status does nothing to reduce their legitimacy, or effects.

Our Enlightenment-influenced "common sense"—based as it is, as is Steiner's commentary here, on the valorization of only one half of the workings of language—has to be improved upon, I would argue, by a post-Enlightenment "newly-common common sense," one that acknowledges also the workings of the ethereal side of language and the breaking function of iterability, that is, one that makes provision for "real absences."

This was the fundamental lesson that Collins long–novel project was teaching. In fashioning his major fictions Collins came to settle upon an excellent metaphor for representing those real absences: shadows in dumb show waiting to be filled up. The best example of this situation might be Magdalen's early portrayal in *No Name* of Lucy the maid in the Marrables' production of *The Rivals*. Later in that same novel she will take up in "the real world"—filling in the earlier stage-shadow—the role of the parlor-maid Louisa ("I shall call you Lucy, if you don't mind" [*No Name,* ed. Ford 512]) in Admiral Bartram's mansion. This move is an analog for Collins's parody of realism with which that novel had opened. It emphasizes that the real presences of the "real"-ist novel are always already screening real absences, screening the possibility of their proleptically becoming or subsequently being disclosed to have been modeled on (stage-)acting.

This could have been a strategy Collins learned from the practice of his painter father, that is, from the visual artist's procedure of making early on-site sketches, or shadows, to be filled in at a later point in time during the creation of the actual painting in the studio. In this context, there comes an interesting moment in Collins's *Memoirs of the Life of William Collins* in which his father's boyhood friend John Kirton is reported as commenting that when the two were young "His father, himself, his brother Frank and I, made long peregrinations in the fields between Highgate and Wilsden. He always had his sketch-book with him, and generally came home well stored. He was then very quick with his pencil" (1:25). The quick-penned Victorian serial novelist son, in this respect at least—at both the levels of practice and theory—would most definitely seem to have come to resemble the father.

We see this device of shadow-filling also in the three other masterpieces (perhaps this was what provided them with the depth necessary to be classed as masterpieces). In *The Woman in White,* Walter Hartright apologizes to the reader for his poor initial description of Laura Fairlie, commenting, "The woman who first gives life, light, and form to our shadowy conceptions of beauty, fills a void in our spiritual nature that has remained unknown to us till she appeared" (*Woman in White,* ed. Sutherland 50). Here a pre-existent shadow is disclosed to have been "haunting" us all along at the very moment that it comes to be filled up by a living, breathing human being. Similarly,

Hartright will remark that to be associating Anne with Laura is potentially to be setting underway some sort of curse: "To associate that forlorn,
friendless, lost woman, even by accidental likeness only, with Miss Fairlie,
seems like casting a shadow on the future of the bright creature who stands
looking at us now" (61). This prophecy will come to pass: "The sorrow and
suffering which I had once blamed myself for associating even by passing
thought with the future of Laura Fairlie, *had* set their profaning marks on
the youth and beauty of her face; and the fatal resemblance which I had
once seen and shuddered at seeing, in idea only, was now a real and living
resemblance which asserted itself before my own eyes"[1] (442–43; emphasis
in original). In *Armadale* the whole sense of suspense throughout the story
is generated for us, and for the characters as well, by the interval standing
between the presentation of the "shadows" in Allan Armadale 4's dream and
their eventually being filled up. This situation results in Ozias Midwinter's
wonder-filled pronouncement in the first epigraph above. Shadow-filling,
per se, does not at first seem a significant issue in *The Moonstone,* but this
all changes when we begin to consider Franklin Blake's movements on the
night of Rachel's birthday as a sort of "dream" that he has forgotten. Thus,
at the climax of the story he will be coming to fill in his own "shadow"—the
existence of which had been disclosed by his name on the nightgown—on
the night of the experiment of redrugging. We find a foreshadowing of this
process in the narrative: at one point when Blake sneaks up on a dozing Betteredge we read, "In the position in which I stood, *my shadow was projected
in front of me* by the slanting rays of the sun. Either the dogs saw it, or their
keen scent informed them of my approach: they started up with a growl"
(*Moonstone* 343; emphasis added). This is a harbinger of Blake's movement
into the position of his dream-shadow later in the story.

    This study has been an attempt to explore Collins's dealings with those
"real absences" always "present," so to speak, in the world, absences—Collins
was gradually coming to understand, indeed to teach himself—that must
be acknowledged. His beloved metaphor of the (sometimes unseen) shadow
waiting to be filled up disturbs the complacency of any sort of Enlightenment perspective finding the world to be composed solely of "real presences."
Collins's project makes the same critique, only in different language, as is
made by Derrida's having noted that "the 'we' of [Hegel's] *Phenomenology*

---

1. The doppelganger will continually be called "a shadow." For example, after Sir Percival's
death, Hartright will also say goodbye to the memory of Anne Catherick, commenting, "So the
ghostly figure which has haunted these pages as it haunted my life, goes down into the impenetrable
Gloom. Like a Shadow she first came to me, in the loneliness of the night. Like a Shadow she passes
away, in the loneliness of the dead" (*Woman in White,* ed. Sutherland 569).

of the Mind . . . does not *see* the nonbasis of play upon which (the) history (of meaning) is launched" (*Writing and Difference* 275–76).[2] The solidity of those presences is—as we saw with Franklin Blake's eventually-exploded early self-complacency in the belief that he was *not* the thief—always already menaced beforehand by that shadow-self (one's ironic or parodic doppelganger) always waiting in the wings to disclose itself. The realist novel is "real" or "serious," as we saw in our consideration of *No Name*'s parodic opening, only because it is constantly repressing its own fictionality and the always available possibility of its having been (or actually being) an ironic novel. It was with good reason that Paul de Man praised in "The Rhetoric of Temporality" the usefulness of "ironic" texts:

> Allegory and irony are . . . linked in their common demystification of an organic world postulated in a symbolic mode of analogical correspondences or in a mimetic mode of representation in which fiction and reality could coincide. It is especially against the latter mystification that irony is directed: the regression in critical insight found in the transition from an allegorical to a symbolic theory of poetry would find its historical equivalent in the regression from the eighteenth-century ironic novel . . . to nineteenth-century realism. (*Blindness and Insight* 222)

The ironic mode is just one of the myriad possibilities neglected by a "real presence" world-view. The progression in Collins's long–novel project demonstrates the poverty of such a view. I agree with De Man that losing the possibility of the ironic viewing of literature is a type of "regression." Collins himself—in his long–novel project's movement from the serious *Basil* to the ironic opening of *No Name*—seems to have understood it as such.

---

2. Or by Derrida's having noted that J. L. Austin's "negativities" (his Collinsian "shadow"-possibilities?) are always at work and irrepressible: "For, ultimately, isn't it true that what Austin excludes as anomaly, exception, 'non-serious,' *citation* (on stage, in a poem, or a soliloquy) is the determined modification of a general citationality—or, rather, a general iterability—without which there would not even be a 'successful' performative? So that—a paradoxical but unavoidable conclusion—a successful performative is necessarily an 'impure' performative . . . " ("Signature Event Context" 17). Similarly, he writes elsewhere, "I try in fact to respond point by point, in the most honest and rational way possible, to [Austin's student, John] Searle's arguments, the text of which is cited almost in its entirety. On the other hand, in so doing I multiply statements, discursive gestures, forms of writing, the structure of which reinforces my demonstration in something like a practical manner: that is, by providing instances of 'speech acts' which by themselves render impracticable and theoretically insufficient the conceptual oppositions upon which speech act theory in general, and Searle's version of it in particular, relies (serious/nonserious; literal/metaphoric or ironic; normal forms/parasitical forms; use/mention; intentional/nonintentional; etc.). This dual writing seemed to me to be consistent with the propositions I wanted simultaneously to demonstrate on the theoretical level and to exemplify in the practice of speech acts" (*Limited* 114).

He perceived that something had been lost in the "going unconscious" of the possibility of irony, that is, in the advent of the common Enlightenment practice of suppressing the breaking function. The goal of Collins's project was to undo that process.

The primary desire of the best narratives written by this remarkable author was the bringing back into the light the knowledge of that function perpetually cast by our culture into the "shadows," a knowledge that had been not so much lost as improperly, and thereafter always uncomfortably, repressed. The search for the breaking function having been continually characterized by Tradition as a philosophical "trifling," it was perhaps only going to have been traceable in the work of an author who found trifles to have been not without their significances, which is not to go so far as to say their "uses." In many ways Collins resembled his character Sergeant Cuff, who, as the opening epigraph to this book of mine makes clear, categorically did not believe in them. The creator's and his creation's experiences "along the dirtiest ways of this dirty little world" having apparently been similar, it should come as no surprise that Collins should have taken on board the rest of Cuff's thinking in the epigraph as well, that is, that he *also* should have come to believe in the always open possibility for a type of "murder" to be associating itself with—indeed perhaps even pointing directly back towards—an all too commonly ignored "spot of ink."

BIBLIOGRAPHY

Table of Cases

(Many of the following cases are taken from the English Reports, ed. A. Wood Renton, 178 vols., [London: Stevens, 1900–1932]. These are, as is conventional, cited by volume number, ER, page reference for first page, [year]. Cases cited as "US" are Supreme Court cases.)

A&M Records, Inc. v. Napster, Inc. 239 F.3d 1004 (9th Cir. 2001).
Abernethy v. Hutchinson 3 LJ Ch 209 (OS) (1825).
Boosey v. Jeffereys 155 ER 675 (1850).
Boosey v. Purday 154 ER 1159 (1849).
Carey v. Collier 5 F. Cas. 58, No. 2400. CCSDNY (1837).
Chappell v. Purday 153 ER 491 (1845).
Dickens v. Lee 8 *The Jurist* 183 (1844).
Donaldson v. Becket 98 ER 257; 1 ER 837. (1774).
Eldred v. Ashcroft 537 US 186 (2003).
Feist Publications, Inc. v. Rural Telephone Service Co. 499 US 340 (1991).
Jeffereys v. Boosey 10 ER 681 (1845).
Metro-Goldwyn-Mayer Studios, Inc. v. Grokster, Ltd. 545 US 913 (2005).
Millar v. Taylor 98 ER 201 (1769).
Prince Albert v. Strange 64 ER 293 (1849).
Routledge v. Low LR 3 HL 100 (1868).
Sheldon v. Metro-Goldwyn Pictures Corp. 81 F.2d 49 (2nd Cir. 1936).
Tonson v. Collins 96 ER 169 (1761); 96 ER 180 (1762).
Universal Music Australia Pty Ltd. v. Sharman License Holdings Ltd. 220 ALR 1 (2005) (Fed Ct (Aus)(Full Ct)).

Books and Articles

Ablow, Rachel. "Good Vibrations: The Sensationalization of Masculinity in *The Woman in White*." *Novel* 37:1/2 (2003–2004): 158–80.

Alexander, Isabella. *Copyright Law and the Public Interest in the Nineteenth Century.* Oxford: Hart Publishing, 2010.

Alford, William. *To Steal a Book Is an Elegant Offense: Intellectual Property Law in Chinese Civilization.* Stanford, CA: Stanford UP, 1995.

Alison, A[rchibald]. "Copyright." *Blackwood's* 51 (May 1842): 634–36.

Altick, Richard. *The Presence of the Present: Topics of the Day in the Victorian Novel.* Columbus: Ohio State UP, 1991.

———. *The Shows of London.* Cambridge, MA: Belknap Press, 1978.

Amidon, Stephen. "Wilkie Collins." *British Writers: Supplement VI.* Ed. Jay Parini. New York: Scribners, 2001. 91–104.

Anderson, John. "The Detective Story." *Art and Reality.* Ed. Janet Anderson et al. Sydney: Hale & Iremonger, 1982. 233–40.

Anderson, Mary. *A Few Memories.* London: Osgood, McIlvaine & Co., 1896.

Andrews, Alexander. *The History of British Journalism: From the Foundation of the Newspaper Press in England, to the Repeal of the Stamp Act in 1855, with Sketches of Press Celebrities.* 2 vols. London: Bentley, 1859.

Antill, Justine, and Peter Coles. "Copyright Duration: The European Community Adopts 'Three Score and Ten.'" *European Intellectual Property Review* 18.7 (July 1996): 379–83.

Arata, Stephen. "The Occidental Tourist: *Dracula* and the Anxiety of Reverse Colonization." *Victorian Studies* (Summer 1990): 621–45.

"Arguments of Counsel and Opinions of Judges Concerning Literary Property: Alexander and John Donaldsons, Booksellers in Edinburgh and London, Appellants from a Decree of the Court of Chancery; Thomas Becket, and Fourteen other Booksellers of London, Respondents." *Scots Magazine* 36 (March 1774): 121–26.

Armstrong, Nancy. *Desire and Domestic Fiction.* Oxford: Oxford UP, 1989.

Ashley, Robert. *Wilkie Collins.* London: Arthur Barker, 1952.

Auden, W. H. "The Guilty Vicarage." *The Dyer's Hand and Other Essays.* London: Faber and Faber, 1962. 146–58.

Austin, J. L. *How to Do Things with Words.* Ed. J. O. Urmson and Marina Sbisà. 2nd ed. Cambridge, MA: Harvard UP, 1975.

———. *Sense and Sensibilia.* Reconstructed from the manuscript notes by G. J. Warnock. Oxford: Oxford UP, 1964.

Bachman, Maria K., and Don Richard Cox, eds. *Reality's Dark Light: The Sensational Wilkie Collins.* Knoxville: U of Tennessee P, 2003.

Bagehot, Walter. "Economic Studies" (1879). *The Works and Life of Walter Bagehot.* Ed. Mrs. Russell Barrington. Vol 7. London: Longmans, Green, 1915. 91–285.

Baker, William, Andrew Gasson, Graham Law, and Paul Lewis. Introduction. *The Public Face of Wilkie Collins: The Collected Letters.* London: Pickering and Chatto, 2005. 1:xix–xliv.

Balzac, Honoré de. "Letter to Authors" (1834). *Revue de Paris* n.s. 11 (1834): 62–82. Trans. Luis Sundkvist. *Primary Sources on Copyright (1450–1900).* Ed. L. Bently and M. Kretschmer. www.copyrighthistory.org.

Barickman, Richard, Susan MacDonald, and Myra Stark. *Corrupt Relations: Dickens, Thackeray, Trollope, Collins, and the Victorian Sexual System.* New York: Columbia UP, 1982.

Barnes, James J. *Authors, Publishers, and Politicians: The Quest for an Anglo-American Copyright Agreement, 1815–1854.* London: Routledge and Kegan Paul, 1974.

Barthes, Roland. "The Death of the Author." Trans. Richard Howard. *The Rustle of Language.* New York: Hill & Wang, 1986. 49–55.

Bataille, Georges. *The Unfinished System of Nonknowledge.* Ed. Stuart Kendall. Trans. Michelle Kendall and Stuart Kendall. Minneapolis: U of Minnesota P, 2001.

Baudrillard, Jean. "The Precession of Simulacra." *Simulacra and Simulation.* Trans. Sheila Faria Glaser. Ann Arbor: U of Michigan P, 1994. 1–42.

———. *Selected Writings.* Ed. Mark Poster. Stanford, CA: Stanford UP, 1988.

———. *Simulacra et Simulation.* Paris: Galilee, 1987.

———. "Simulacra and Simulations." Trans. Paul Foss, Paul Patton, and Philip Beitchman. *Selected Writings.* By Baudrillard. 166–84.

———. *Simulations.* Trans. Philip Beitchman. New York: Semiotext(e), 1983.

———. "Symbolic Exchange and Death." Trans. Jacques Mourrain and Charles Levin. *Selected Writings.* By Baudrillard. 119–48.

Bearn, Gordon C. F. "Derrida Dry: Iterating Iterability Analytically." *Diacritics* 25.3 (Autumn 1995): 2–25.

Beasley, Edward. *Empire as the Triumph of Theory.* New York: Routledge, 2005.

Bedell, Jeanne F. "Wilkie Collins." *Twelve Englishmen of Mystery.* Ed. Earl F. Bargainnier. Bowling Green, OH: Popular Press, 1984. 8–33.

Benjamin, Walter. *Selected Writings. Vol. 4, 1938–1940.* Trans. Edmund Jephcott et al. Ed. Howard Eiland and Michael W. Jennings. Cambridge, MA: Belknap Press, 2003.

Bérubé, Michael. *The Employment of English: Theory, Jobs, and the Future of Literary Studies.* New York: New York UP, 1997.

Bhabha, Homi K. *The Location of Culture.* London: Routledge, 2006.

Birrell, Augustine. *Seven Lectures on the Law and History of Copyright in Books.* London: Cassell & Co., 1899.

Bisla, Sundeep. Rev. of *Patent Inventions: Intellectual Property and the Victorian Novel,* by Clare Pettitt. *Studies in the Novel* 39.1 (2007): 130–32.

Blackstone, William. *Commentaries on the Laws of England.* 4 vols. Oxford, 1765–69.

"Blackwood and Copyright in America." *Blackwood's Edinburgh Magazine* 63 (Jan. 1848): 127–28.

Booth, Bradford. "Wilkie Collins and the Art of Fiction." *Nineteenth-Century Fiction* 6.2 (September 1951): 131–43.

Borges, Jorge Luis. *Collected Fictions.* Trans. Andrew Hurley. New York: Penguin, 1999.

———. "Pierre Menard, Author of the *Quixote.*" Trans. James E. Irby. *Labyrinths.* Ed. Donald A. Yates and James E. Irby. New York: New Directions, 1964. 36–44.

Boswell, James. *Life of Johnson.* 6 vols. Ed. George Birkbeck Hill and L. F. Powell. Oxford: Clarendon Press, 1934.

Bové, Paul. *In the Wake of Theory.* Hanover, NH: Wesleyan UP, 1992.

Boyle, James. "Foreword: The Opposite of Property?" *Law & Contemporary Problems* 66 (Winter/Spring 2003): 1–33.

———. "A Politics of Intellectual Property: Environmentalism for the Net?" *Duke Law Journal* 47 (1997): 87–116.

————. *The Public Domain: Enclosing the Commons of the Mind.* New Haven, CT: Yale UP, 2010.

————. *Shamans, Software, and Spleens: Law and the Construction of the Information Society.* Cambridge, MA: Harvard UP, 1997.

————. "A Theory of Law and Information: Copyright, Spleens, Blackmail, and Insider Trading." *California Law Review* 80 (1992): 1413–1540.

Boyle, Thomas. *Black Swine in the Sewers of Hampstead: Beneath the Surface of Victorian Sensationalism.* New York: Viking, 1989.

Brantlinger, Patrick. *The Reading Lesson: The Threat of Mass Literacy in Nineteenth-Century British Fiction.* Bloomington: Indiana UP, 1998.

————. "What Is 'Sensational' about the 'Sensation Novel'?" *Nineteenth-Century Fiction* 37 (1982): 1–28.

Brooks, Peter. *Reading for the Plot.* New York: Knopf, 1984.

Brown, Gregory Stephen. *A Field of Honor: Writers, Court Culture, and Public Theater in French Literary Life from Racine to the Revolution.* New York: Columbia UP, 2005.

Burney, Ian A. *Poison, Detection, and the Victorian Imagination.* Manchester: Manchester UP, 2006.

Butler, Judith. "Imitation and Gender Insubordination." *The Judith Butler Reader.* Ed. Sarah Salih. London: Blackwell Publishing, 2004. 119–37.

Butterton, Glenn R. "Pirates, Dragons, and U. S. Intellectual Property Rights in China: Problems and Prospects of Chinese Enforcement." *Arizona Law Review* 38 (Winter 1996): 1081–123.

California Celebrities Rights Act 1985. California Civil Code Section 3344.

Caracciolo, Peter L. "Wilkie Collins and 'The God Almighty of Novelists': The Example of Scott in *No Name* and *Armadale*." *Wilkie Collins to the Forefront: Some Reassessments.* Ed. Nelson C. Smith and R. C. Terry. New York: AMS Press, 1995. 165–82.

Carey, Henry C. *Letters on International Copyright.* 1853. 2nd ed. New York: Kurd & Houghton, 1868.

Carrier, Michael A. "Cabining Intellectual Property through a Property Paradigm." *Duke Law Journal* 54.1 (October 2004): 1–143.

Carver, Peter John. "Millar v. Taylor (1769) *and the New Property of the Eighteenth Century*." LLM thesis UBC, 1990.

The Cases of the Appellants and Respondents in the Cause of Literary Property, Before the House of Lords. The Literary Property Debate: Six Tracts, 1764–1774. Ed. Stephen Parks. New York: Garland Press, 1975.

Cavallo, Guglielmo, and Roger Chartier, eds. *A History of Reading in the West.* Trans. Lydia G. Cochrane. Oxford: Polity Press, 1999.

Cervantes Saavedra, Miguel de. *The Adventures of Don Quixote.* Trans. J. M. Cohen. Harmondsworth, UK: Penguin, 1950.

————. *El Ingenioso Hidalgo Don Quixote De La Mancha: Parte Segunda.* Madrid: D. Miguel de Burgos, 1826.

Chartier, Roger. *The Cultural Origins of the French Revolution.* Trans. Lydia G. Cochrane. Durham, NC: Duke UP, 1991.

————. *The Order of Books: Readers, Authors, and Libraries in Europe between the Fourteenth and Eighteenth Centuries.* Cambridge: Polity Press, 1994.

Charvat, William. *The Profession of Authorship in America, 1800–1870.* Ed. Matthew J. Broccoli. Columbus: Ohio State UP, 1968.

Cheah, Pheng. "Nondialectical Materialism." *Diacritics* 38.1–2 (2008): 143–57.

Cheshire, Edward. "The Results of the Census of Great Britain in 1851, with a Description of the Machinery and Processes Employed to Obtain the Returns; Also an Appendix of Tables of Reference." *Journal of the Royal Statistical Society of London* 17 (1854): 45–72.

Clark, Aubert J. *The Movement for International Copyright in Nineteenth-Century America.* Westport, CT: Greenwood Press, 1960.

Clarke, William M. *The Secret Life of Wilkie Collins.* London: Allison & Busby, 1988.

Cohn, Dorrit. "Optics and Power in the Novel." *New Literary History* 26.1 (Winter 1995): 3–20.

———. "Reply to John Bender and Mark Seltzer." *New Literary History* 26.1 (Winter 1995): 35–37.

Coleman, William Rollin. "The University of Texas Collection of the Letters of Wilkie Collins, Victorian Novelist." Diss. University of Texas at Austin, 1975.

Coleridge, Samuel Taylor. *Biographia Literaria.* Ed. James Engell and W. Jackson Bate. Princeton, NJ: Princeton UP, 1983.

Colie, Rosalie L. *Paradoxia Epidemica: The Renaissance Tradition of Paradox.* Princeton, NJ: Princeton UP, 1966.

Collins, Wilkie. *After Dark.* Vol. 21 of *The Works of Wilkie Collins.* London: Chatto & Windus, 1885–93.

———. *Armadale.* Ed. John Sutherland. Harmondsworth, UK: Penguin, 1995.

———. *Basil.* Ed. Dorothy Goldman. Oxford: Oxford UP, 1990.

———. *Basil; A Story of Modern Life.* 3 vols. London: Bentley, 1852.

———. *Blind Love.* Ed. Maria K. Bachman and Don Richard Cox. Peterborough, ON: Broadview Press, 2003.

———. "Considerations on the Copyright Question Addressed to an American Friend." *International Review* 8 (1880): 609–18.

———. *The Dead Secret.* Vol. 4 of *The Works of Wilkie Collins.* London: Chatto & Windus, 1885–93.

———. *The Evil Genius: A Domestic Story.* New York: M. J. Ivers & Co., 1886.

———. *Hide and Seek.* Ed. Catherine Peters. Rev. ed., 1861 text. Oxford: Oxford UP, 1993.

———. *Iolani; or, Tahiti as It Was.* Ed. Ira B. Nadel. Princeton, NJ: Princeton UP, 1999.

———. *The Letters of Wilkie Collins.* Ed. William Baker and William M. Clarke. 2 vols. Basingstoke, UK: Macmillan, 1999.

———. *Mad Monkton and Other Stories.* Ed. Norman Page. Oxford: Oxford UP, 1998.

———. *Memoirs of the Life of William Collins, Esq., R. A.* 2 vols. London: Longman, Brown, Green, and Longmans, 1848.

———. *The Moonstone: A Romance.* Ed. J. I. M. Stewart. Harmondsworth, UK: Penguin, 1986.

———. *The New Magdalen.* Dover, NH: A. Sutton, 1995.

———. *No Name.* Ed. Virginia Blain. Oxford: Oxford UP, 1998.

———. *No Name.* Ed. Mark Ford. Harmondsworth, UK: Penguin, 1994.

———. "Portrait of an Author, Painted by His Publisher." *My Miscellanies.* By Collins. New York: Harper & Bros., 1874. 153–84.

———. "Preface to *La Femme en Blanc.*" Trans. into French E. D. Forgues. Trans. into English Paul Barrette. *The Woman in White.* By Collins. Ed. Maria Bachman and Don Richard Cox. Peterborough, ON: Broadview Press, 2006. 621–24.

———. *The Public Face of Wilkie Collins: The Collected Letters.* 4 vols. Ed. William Baker, Andrew Gasson, Graham Law, and Paul Lewis. London: Pickering and Chatto, 2005.

———. *Rambles beyond Railways: or, Notes in Cornwall Taken A-Foot.* 1851. London: Anthony Mott Ltd., 1982.

———. *A Rogue's Life: From His Birth to His Marriage.* Vol. 15 of *The Works of Wilkie Collins.* London: Chatto & Windus, 1885–93.

———. "The Unknown Public." *Household Words* 18 (21 August 1858): 217–22.

———. *The Woman in White.* Ed. Harvey Peter Sucksmith. 1980. Oxford: Oxford UP, 1992.

———. *The Woman in White.* Ed. John Sutherland. Oxford: Oxford UP, 1996.

———. *The Woman in White.* Ed. Matthew Sweet. Harmondsworth, UK: Penguin, 1999.

Collins, William. *Memoirs of a Picture.* London: C. Stower, 1805. 3 vols.

Conrad, Joseph. *Lord Jim.* Ed. Cedric Watts and Robert Hampson. Harmondsworth, UK: Penguin, 1989.

———. *The Secret Agent.* Ed. Martin Seymour-Smith. Harmondsworth, UK: Penguin, 1996.

Coombe, Rosemary J. "Author/izing the Celebrity: Publicity Rights, Postmodern Politics, and Unauthorized Genders." Woodmansee and Jaszi 101–31.

Crosby, Christina. Rev. of *The Material Interests of the Victorian Novel,* by Daniel Hack. *Victorian Studies* 18 (Spring 2006): 541–43.

Culler, Jonathan. *The Literary in Theory.* Stanford, CA: Stanford UP, 2007.

Cvetkovich, Ann. "Ghostlier Determinations: The Economy of Sensation and *The Woman in White.*" *Novel* 23.1 (1989): 24–43.

Dames, Nicholas. *Amnesiac Selves: Nostalgia, Forgetting, and British Fiction, 1810–1870.* Oxford: Oxford UP, 2001.

Darnton, Robert. "First Steps Toward a History of Reading." *Australian Journal of French Studies* 23 (1986): 5–30.

——— . "What Is the History of Books?" *Daedelus* (Summer 1982): 65–83.

David, Deirdre. "Rewriting the Male Plot in Wilkie Collins's *No Name:* Captain Wragge Orders an Omelette and Mrs. Wragge Goes into Custody." *Out of Bounds: Male Writers and Gender(ed) Criticism.* Ed. Laura Claridge and Elizabeth Langland. Amherst: U of Massachusetts P, 1990. 186–96.

Davis, Nuel Pharr. *The Life of Wilkie Collins.* Urbana: U of Illinois P, 1956.

De Certeau, Michel. "Micro-Techniques and Panoptic Discourse: A Quid pro Quo." *Heterologies: Dicourse on the Other.* Trans. Brian Massumi. Minneapolis: U of Minnesota P, 1986. 185–92.

Deleuze, Gilles. *The Logic of Sense.* Ed. Constantin V. Boundas. Trans. Mark Lester and Charles Stivale. New York: Columbia UP, 1990.

De Man, Paul. *Aesthetic Ideology.* Ed. Andrzej Warminski. Minneapolis: U of Minnesota P, 1996.

———. *Blindness and Insight.* 2nd ed. Rev. Minneapolis: U of Minnesota P, 1983.

———. *Allegories of Reading.* New Haven, CT: Yale UP, 1979.

———. "Roland Barthes and the Limits of Structuralism." *Romanticism and Contemporary Criticism.* Ed. E. S. Burt, Kevin Newmark, and Andrzej Warminski. Baltimore: Johns Hopkins UP, 1993. 164–77.

De Quincey, Thomas. *Confessions of an English Opium Eater and Other Writings.* Ed. Barry Milligan. London: Penguin, 2003.

Derrida, Jacques. *Archive Fever.* Trans. Eric Prenowitz. Baltimore: Johns Hopkins UP, 1998.

———. "Cogito and History of Madness." *Writing and Difference.* By Derrida. 31–63.

———. *Dissemination.* Trans. Barbara Johnson. Chicago: U of Chicago P, 1978.

———. *Edmund Husserl's* Origin of Geometry: *An Introduction.* Trans. John P. Leavey, Jr. Lincoln: U of Nebraska P, 1989.

———. "Following Theory." *Life. After. Theory.* Ed. Michael Payne and John Schad. London: Continuum, 2003. 1–51.

———. "*Fors:* The Anglish Words of Nicolas Abraham and Maria Torok." Trans. Barbara Johnson. *The Wolf Man's Magic Word: A Cryptonomy.* By Nicolas Abraham and Maria Torok. Trans. Nicholas Rand. Minneapolis: U of Minnesota P, 1986. xi–xlviii.

———. "Freud and the Scene of Writing." *Writing and Difference.* By Derrida. 196–231.

———. "From Restricted to General Economy: A Hegelianism without Reserve." *Writing and Difference.* By Derrida. 251–77.

———. "Justices." *Provocations to Reading: J. Hillis Miller and the Democracy to Come.* Ed. Barbara Cohen and Dragan Kujundzic. New York: Fordham UP, 2005. 228–61.

———. "The Law of Genre." Trans. Avital Ronell. *Critical Inquiry* 7.1 (1980): 55–81.

———. *Limited Inc.* Trans. Samuel Weber and Jeffrey Mehlman. Ed. Gerald Graff. Evanston, IL: Northwestern UP, 1988.

———. *Monolingualism of the Other; or, The Prosthesis of Origin.* Trans. Patrick Mensah. Stanford, CA: Stanford UP, 1998.

———. *Of Grammatology.* Corr. ed. Trans. Gayatri Chakravorty Spivak. 1974. Baltimore: Johns Hopkins UP, 1997.

———. *Paper Machine.* Trans. Rachel Bowlby. Stanford, CA: Stanford UP, 2005.

———. "*La parole soufflée.*" *Writing and Difference.* By Derrida. 167–95.

———. "Psyche: Inventions of the Other." Trans. Catherine Porter. *Psyche: Inventions of the Other.* Ed. Peggy Kamuf and Elizabeth Rottenberg. Stanford, CA: Stanford UP, 2007. 1:1–47.

———. "Signature Event Context." *Limited Inc.* By Derrida. 1–23.

———. "Some Statements and Truisms about Neologisms, Newisms, Postisms, Parasitisms, and Other Small Seismisms." Trans. Anne Tomiche. *The States of "Theory": History, Art, and Critical Discourse.* Ed. David Carroll. Stanford, CA: Stanford UP, 1990. 63–94.

———. *Specters of Marx.* Trans. Peggy Kamuf. New York: Routledge, 1994.

———. *Speech and Phenomena and Other Essays on Husserl's Theory of Signs.* Trans. David A. Allison. Evanston, IL: Northwestern UP, 1973.

———. "'To Do Justice to Freud': The History of Madness in the Age of Psychoanalysis." Trans. Pascale-Anne Brault and Michael Naas. *Critical Inquiry* 20.2 (Winter 1994): 227–66.

———. "Typewriter Ribbon: Limited Ink (2) ("within such limits")." *Material Events: Paul de Man and the Afterlife of Theory.* Ed. Tom Cohen et al. Minneapolis: U of Minnesota P, 2001. 277–360.

———. *Writing and Difference.* Trans. Alan Bass. Chicago: U of Chicago P, 1978.

Derrida, Jacques, and Paul Ricoeur. "Philosophy and Communication: Round-Table Discussion between Ricoeur and Derrida." Trans. Leonard Lawlor. *Imagination and Chance: The Difference between the Thought of Ricoeur and Derrida.* By Lawlor. Albany, NY: SUNY Press, 1992. 131–63.

Dever, Carolyn. "The Marriage Plot and Its Alternatives." Taylor, *Cambridge Companion* 112–24.

[Dickens, Charles.] "Insularities." *Household Words* 19 January 1856: 1.

———. "The Sensational Williams." *All the Year Round* 11 (1864): 14–17.

Dickens, Charles. *Bleak House.* Ed. Norman Page. Harmondsworth, UK: Penguin, 1985.

———. *David Copperfield.* Ed. Trevor Blount. Harmondsworth, UK: Penguin, 1985.

———. *Dombey and Son.* Ed. Peter Fairclough. Harmondsworth, UK: Penguin, 1985.

———. *Great Expectations.* Ed. Charlotte Mitchell. Harmondsworth, UK: Penguin, 1996.

———. *The Letters of Charles Dickens.* Ed. Madeline House, Graham Storey, Kathleen Tillotson, et al. 12 vols. Oxford: Clarendon Press, 1965–2002.

———. *Little Dorrit.* Ed. Stephen Wall and Helen Small. Harmondsworth, UK: Penguin, 1998.

———. *Martin Chuzzlewit.* Ed. P. N. Furbank. Harmondsworth, UK: Penguin, 1986.

———. *The Mystery of Edwin Drood.* Ed. David Paroissien. Harmondsworth, UK: Penguin, 2002.

———. *Oliver Twist.* Ed. Peter Fairclough. Harmondsworth, UK: Penguin, 1985.

———. *Our Mutual Friend.* Ed. Stephen Gill. Harmondsworth, UK: Penguin, 1971.

———. *The Pickwick Papers.* Ed. Robert L. Patten. Harmondsworth, UK: Penguin, 1986.

Disraeli, Benjamin. *Letters: 1848–1851.* Ed. M. G. Wiebe. Toronto: U of Toronto P, 1993.

Donne, John. *John Donne's Poetry.* Ed. A. L. Clements. New York: W. W. Norton, 1966.

Doody, Margaret Anne. Introduction to *Sense and Sensibility.* By Jane Austen. Ed. James Kinsley. Oxford: Oxford UP, 1990. vii–xlvi.

Dooley, Allen C. *Author and Printer in Victorian England.* Charlottesville: UP of Virginia, 1992.

Dougherty, Jay. "Not a Spike Lee Joint? Issues in the Authorship of Motion Pictures under U.S. Copyright Law." 49 *UCLA Law Review* 225 (2001).

Drew, John M. L. *Dickens the Journalist.* New York: Palgrave, 2003.

Drone, Eaton S. *A Treatise on the Law of Property in Intellectual Productions in Great Britain and the United States.* Boston: Little, Brown, and Co., 1879; South Hackensack, NJ: Rothman Reprints, 1972.

Eco, Umberto, with Richard Rorty, Jonathan Culler, and Christine Brooke-Rose. *Interpretation and Overinterpretation.* Ed. Stefan Collini. Cambridge: Cambridge UP, 1992.

Edelman, Bernard. *Ownership of the Image: Elements for a Marxist Theory of Law.* Trans. Elizabeth Kingdom. London: Routledge and Kegan Paul, 1979.

———. *Le sacre de l'auteur.* Seuil, 2004.

Eilenberg, Susan. "Copyright's Rhetoric and the Problem of Analogy in the British Eighteenth-Century Debates." *Romanticism and the Law.* Ed. Michael Macovski. Romantic Circles Electronic Editions (March 1999). http://www.rc.umd.edu/praxis/law/sebg.htm.

———. "Mortal Pages: Wordsworth and the Reform of Copyright." *ELH* 56 (1989): 351–74.

———. *Strange Power of Speech: Wordsworth, Coleridge, and Literary Possession.* New York: Oxford UP, 1992.

Eisenstein, Elizabeth L. "Some Conjectures about the Impact of Printing on Western Society and Thought: A Preliminary Report." *Journal of Modern History* 40.1 (1968): 1–56.

Elam, Diane. "White Narratology: Gender and Reference in Wilkie Collins's *The Woman* in White." *Virginal Sexuality and Textuality in Victorian Literature.* Ed. Lloyd Davis. Albany, NY: SUNY Press, 1993. 49–64.

Eliot, George. *Daniel Deronda.* Ed. Graham Handley. Oxford: Oxford UP, 1991.

Eliot, T. S. *Selected Essays,* 3rd ed. London: Faber and Faber, 1976.

———. *Selected Poems.* Orlando, FL: Harcourt Brace & Co., 1964.

Emerson, Ralph Waldo. *Selected Writings of Ralph Waldo Emerson.* Ed. William H. Gilman. New York: Signet Classics, 2003.

Emrys, A. B. *Wilkie Collins, Vera Caspary, and the Evolution of the Casebook.* Jefferson, NC: McFarland, 2011.

Erickson, Lee. "The Egoism of Authorship: Wordsworth's Poetic Career." *The Economy of Literary Form.* By Erickson. Baltimore: Johns Hopkins UP, 1996. 46–69.

Ezell, J. M., and Katherine O'Brien O'Keefe, eds. *Cultural Artifacts and the Production of Meaning: The Page, the Image, and the Body.* Ann Arbor: U of Michigan P, 1991.

Feather, John. "The Reform of the Law: 1800–1842." *Publishing, Piracy, and Politics: An Historical Study of Copyright in Britain.* By Feather. London: Mansell, 1994. 122–48.

Febvre, Lucien, and Henri-Jean Martin. *The Coming of the Book: The Impact of Printing, 1450–1800.* Trans. David Gerard. Ed. Geoffrey Nowell-Smith and David Wooton. London: NLB; Atlantic Highlands, NJ: Humanities Press, 1976. Reissued, London: Verso, 1997.

Felman, Shoshana. *The Scandal of the Speaking Body: Don Juan with J. L. Austin, or Seduction in Two Languages.* Trans. Catherine Porter. 1983. Stanford, CA: Stanford UP, 2003.

Fichte, Johann Gottlieb. "Proof of the Unlawfulness of Reprinting." Trans. Martha Woodmansee. Berlin: 1793. http://www.case.edu/affil/sce/authorship/Fichte,_Proof.doc.

Fineman, Joel. "The History of the Anecdote: Fiction and Fiction." *The New Historicism.* Ed. H. Aram Veeser. New York: Routledge, 1989. 49–76.

Flower, Desmond. "Authors and Copyright in the Nineteenth Century, with Unpublished Letters from Wilkie Collins." *Book-Collector's Quarterly* 7 (July–Sept 1932): 1–35.

"Foreign Invasion." *Household Words* 4.81 (11 Oct. 1851): 60–64.

Forster, John. *The Life of Charles Dickens.* 3 vols. Philadelphia: J. B. Lippincott, 1874.

Forsyte, Charles. *The Decoding of "Edwin Drood."* London: Gollancz, 1980.

Foucault, Michel. *Discipline and Punish: The Birth of the Prison.* Trans. Alan Sheridan. New York: Random House, 1979.

———. "My Body, This Paper, This Fire." Trans. Geoffrey Bennington. *Aesthetics, Method, and Epistemology.* Ed. James D. Faubion. New York: New Press, 1998. 393–417.

———. *The Order of Things: An Archeology of the Human Sciences.* New York: Vintage, 1994.

———. "What Is an Author?" Trans. Josué V. Harari. *The Foucault Reader.* Ed. Paul Rabinow. New York: Pantheon, 1984. 101–20.

———. "What Is an Author?" *Language, Counter-Memory, Practice: Selected Essays and Interviews.* Ed. Donald F. Bouchard. Trans. Donald F. Bouchard and Sherry Simon. Ithaca, NY: Cornell UP, 1977. 113–38.

Fox, Christopher. *Locke and the Scriblerians: Identity and Consciousness in Early Eighteenth-Century Britain.* Berkeley: U of California P, 1988.

Fox Bourne, Henry Richard. *English Newspapers: Chapters in the History of Journalism.* Vol. 2. London: Chatto & Windus, 1887. Reprint. London: Routledge, 2000.

Fox, Russell. *Justice in the Twenty-First Century.* London: Cavendish, 2000.

Freud, Sigmund. "Psychoanalytic Notes on an Autobiographical Account of a Case of Paranoia" [The Schreber Case]. *Standard Edition*. Ed. and trans. James Strachey. London: Hogarth Press, 1953–74. 12:12–79.

Gaines, Jane M. *Contested Culture: The Image, the Voice, and the Law*. Chapel Hill: U of North Carolina P, 1991.

Gallagher, Catherine. *Nobody's Story: The Vanishing Acts of Women Writers in the Marketplace, 1670–1820*. Berkeley: U of California P, 1994.

Gallagher, Catherine, Joel Fineman, and Neil Hertz. "More about 'Medusa's Head.'" *Representations* 4 (Autumn 1983): 55–72.

Gallagher, Catherine, and Stephen Greenblatt. *Practicing the New Historicism*. Chicago: U of Chicago P, 2000.

Gamer, Michael. *Romanticism and the Gothic: Reception and Canon Formation*. Cambridge: Cambridge UP, 2000.

Gaylin, Ann. *Eavesdropping in the Novel from Austen to Proust*. Cambridge: Cambridge UP, 2002.

Genette, Gerard. *Mimologics*. Trans. Thais E. Morgan. Lincoln: U of Nebraska P, 1995.

———. *Narrative Discourse: An Essay in Method*. Trans. Jane E. Lewin. Ithaca, NY: Cornell UP, 1980.

Geraldine, Sister M., CSJ. "Erasmus and the Tradition of Paradox." *Studies in Philology* 61.1 (1964): 41–63.

Gibbs-Smith, C. H., ed. "Extracts from Queen Victoria's Journal." *The Great Exhibition of 1851: A Commemorative Album*. London: His Majesty's Stationery Office, 1950. 15–25.

Gilbert, Sandra M., and Susan Gubar. *The Madwoman in the Attic: The Woman Writer and the Nineteenth-Century Literary Imagination*. New Haven, CT: Yale UP, 1979.

Gillespie, Tarleton. *Wired Shut: Copyright and the Shape of Digital Culture*. Cambridge, MA: MIT Press, 2007.

Ginsburg, Jane C. "'*Une Chose Publique*'? The Author's Domain and the Public Domain in Early British, French, and U.S. Copyright Law." *Cambridge Law Journal* 63.3 (November 2006): 636–70.

———. "Creation and Commercial Value: Copyright Protection of Works of Information." *Columbia Law Review* 90 (November 1990): 1865–1938.

Godkin, E. L. "Authors versus Readers." *The Nation* 6 (Jan.–June 1868): 147–48.

Goldstein, Paul. *Copyright's Highway: From Gutenberg to the Celestial Jukebox*. Rev. ed. Stanford, CA: Stanford UP, 2003.

González Echevarría, Roberto. *Love and the Law in Cervantes*. New Haven, CT: Yale UP, 2005.

Greetham, David. *Textual Scholarship: An Introduction*. New York: Garland, 1992.

———. *Theories of the Text*. Oxford: Oxford UP, 1999.

Gruner, Elisabeth Rose. "Family Secrets and the Mysteries of *The Moonstone*." *Victorian Literature and Culture* 21 (1993): 127–45.

Hack, Daniel. *The Material Interests of the Victorian Novel*. Charlottesville: UP of Virginia, 2005.

Haffenden, John. *William Empson*. 2 vols. Oxford: Oxford UP, 2005–2006.

Hall, David. *Cultures of Print: Essays in the History of the Book*. Amherst: U of Massachusetts P, 1996.

Hand, Learned. Decision in *Nichols v. Universal Pictures Corp*. 45 F.2nd Cir. 119 (1930). Rpt. in Kaplan and Brown 276–82.

Hansard Parliamentary Debates. 3rd series.

Harrison, Kimberly, and Richard Fantina, eds. *Victorian Sensations: Essays on a Scandalous Genre.* Columbus: Ohio State UP, 2006.

Hayter, Alethea. *Opium and the Romantic Imagination.* Berkeley: U of California P, 1970.

Heidegger, Martin. *Poetry, Language, Thought.* Trans. Albert Hofstadter. New York: Harper & Row, 1971.

Heller, Tamar. *Dead Secrets: Wilkie Collins and the Female Gothic.* New Haven, CT: Yale UP, 1992.

Hesse, Carla. "Englightenment Epistemology and the Laws of Authorship in Revolutionary France, 1777–1793." *Representations* 30 (1990): 109–37.

Hockett, Robert. "Whose Ownership? Which Society?" *Cardozo Law Review* 27 (Oct. 2005): 1–103.

Hogarth, Georgina. Letter to Anne Fields. 30 August 1873. MS. Huntington Library, California. Qtd. in Paul Lewis, "Contemporary Accounts [Version 1.2.51, 5 October 2006]," *The Wilkie Collins Pages,* 22 October 2006, http://www.wilkiecollins.com.

Horkheimer, Max, and Theodor W. Adorno. *The Dialectic of Enlightenment.* Trans. Edmund Jephcott. Stanford, CA: Stanford UP, 2002.

Horne, Lewis. "Magdalen's Peril." *Dickens Studies Annual* 20 (1991): 281–94.

Houtchens, Lawrence H. "Charles Dickens and International Copyright." *American Literature* 13 (1941–42): 18–28.

"How They Manage Matters in the Model Republic." *Blackwood's Edinburgh Magazine* 61 (April 1847): 492–500.

Hughes, Justin. "The Philosophy of Intellectual Property." *Georgetown Law Journal* 77 (December 1988): 287–366.

Hughes, Linda K., and Michael Lund. *Victorian Publishing and Mrs. Gaskell's Works.* Charlottesville: UP of Virginia, 1999.

Hughes, Winifred. *The Maniac in the Cellar: Sensation Novels of the 1860s.* Princeton, NJ: Princeton UP, 1980.

Hutchinson, Ross. *Locke in France, 1688–1734.* Oxford: Voltaire Foundation, 1991.

Hutter, A. D. "Dreams, Transformations, and Literature: The Implications of Detective Fiction." *Victorian Studies* 19 (1975): 181–209.

———. "Fosco Lives!" Bachman and Cox 195–238.

Hyde, Lewis. *Common as Air: Revolution, Art, and Ownership.* New York: Farrar, Straus, and Giroux, 2010.

Hyder, Clyde K. "Wilkie Collins and *The Woman in White.*" *PMLA* 54 (1939): 297–303.

"The International Copyright Congress: A Letter from a Member to a Literary Friend." *Blackwood's Edinburgh Magazine* 84 (Dec. 1858): 687–700.

Irwin, John T. *The Mystery to a Solution: Poe, Borges, and the Analytic Detective Story.* Baltimore: Johns Hopkins UP, 1996.

"Is Copyright Perpetual?" *American Law Review* 10 (1876): 16–38.

James, Henry. "Miss Braddon." *The Nation* 1 (1865): 593–94.

Jaszi, Peter. "Toward a Theory of Copyright: The Metamorphoses of 'Authorship.'" *Duke Law Journal* (1991): 455–502.

Johns, Adrian. *The Nature of the Book: Print Knowledge in the Making.* Chicago: U of Chicago P, 1998.

———. *Piracy: The Intellectual Property Wars from Gutenberg to Gates.* Chicago: U of Chicago P, 2009.

Johnson, Barbara. "The Frame of Reference: Poe, Lacan, Derrida." *Yale French Studies* 55/56 (1977): 457–505.

———. *A World of Difference*. Baltimore: Johns Hopkins UP, 1987.

Jones, Anna. "A Victim in Search of a Torturer: Reading Masochism in Wilkie Collins's *No Name*." *Novel* 33.2 (2000): 196–211.

Jones, Rowland. *The Origin of Language and Nations*. London: J. Hughs, 1764. Reprint. Menston, UK: Scolar Press, 1972.

Joseph, Gerhard. "Charles Dickens, International Copyright, and the Discretionary Silence of *Martin Chuzzlewit*." Woodmansee and Jaszi 259–70.

Kaestle, Carl F., Helen Damon-Moore, Lawrence C. Stedman, Katherine Tinsley, and William Vance Trollinger, Jr. *Literacy in the United States: Readers and Reading since 1880*. New Haven, CT: Yale UP, 1991.

Kant, Immanuel. *The Metaphysics of Morals*. Ed. and trans. Mary Gregor. Cambridge: Cambridge UP, 1996.

———. "On the Unlawfulness of Reprinting," Berlin, 1785. Trans. Luis Sundkvist, adapted from John Richardson's anonymous translation of 1799. *Primary Sources on Copyright (1450–1900)*. Ed. L. Bently and M. Kretschmer. www.copyrighthistory. org. 403–17.

Kaplan, Benjamin, and Ralph S. Brown, Jr., eds. *Cases on Copyright*. 2nd ed. Mineola, NY: Foundation Press, 1974.

Kaplan, Fred. *Dickens: A Biography*. New York: William Morrow & Co., 1988.

Kappel, Andrew J., and Robert L. Patten. "Dickens' Second American Tour and His 'Utterly Worthless and Profitless' American 'Rights.'" *Dickens Studies Annual* 7 (1978): 1–33.

Kase, Francis J. "Introduction: The Concept of Copyright." *Copyright Thought in Continental Europe: Its Development, Legal Theories, and Philosophy; A Selected and Annotated Bibliography*. South Hackensack, NJ: Rothman, 1967. 1–15.

Kawohl, Friedemann. "The Berlin Publisher Friedrich Nicolai and the Reprinting Sections of the Prussian Statute Book of 1794." *Privilege and Property: Essays on the History of Copyright*. Ed. Ronan Deazley, Martin Kretschmer, and Lionel Bently. Cambridge: Open Book Publishers, 2010. 207–40.

Kendrick, Walter. "The Sensationalism of *The Woman in White*." *Nineteenth-Century Fiction* 32.1 (June 1977): 18–35.

Kent, Christopher. "Probability, Reality, and Sensation in the Novels of Wilkie Collins." *Dickens Studies Annual* 20 (1991): 259–80.

Kilgour, Frederick G. *The Evolution of the Book*. Oxford: Oxford UP, 1998.

Klein, Ernest. *A Comprehensive Etymological Dictionary of the English Language*. Amsterdam: Elsevier, 1971.

Knapp, Steven, and Walter Benn Michaels. "Against Theory." *Critical Inquiry* 8.4 (Summer 1982): 723–42.

Knoepflmacher, U. C. "The Counterworld of Victorian Fiction and *The Woman in White*." *The Worlds of Victorian Fiction*. Ed. Jerome H. Buckley. Cambridge, MA: Harvard UP, 1975. 351–69.

Kreilkamp, Ivan. *Voice and the Victorian Storyteller*. Cambridge: Cambridge UP, 2005.

Kucich, John. "Collins and Victorian Masculinity." *Taylor, Cambridge Companion* 125–38.

———. *The Power of Lies: Transgression in Victorian Fiction*. Ithaca, NY: Cornell UP, 1994.

Laidlaw, R. P. "'Awful Images and Associations': A Study of Wilkie Collins's *The Moonstone*." *Southern Review: An Australian Review of Literary Studies* 9 (1976): 211–27.

Lambert, Gavin. *The Dangerous Edge.* London: Barrie & Jenkins, 1975.

Lansbury, Coral. *The Old Brown Dog: Women, Workers, and Vivisection in Edwardian England.* Madison: U of Wisconsin P, 1985.

Law, Graham. "The Professional Writer and the Literary Marketplace." Taylor, *Cambridge Companion* 97–111.

Lawson, Lewis. "Wilkie Collins and *The Moonstone*." *American Imago* 20 (1963): 61–79.

Lessig, Lawrence. *Code and Other Laws of Cyberspace.* New York: Basic Books, 1999.

———. *Free Culture: How Big Media Uses Technology and the Law to Lock Down Culture and Control Creativity.* New York: Penguin, 2004.

———. *The Future of Ideas: The Fate of the Commons in a Connected World.* New York: Vintage, 2001.

Levine, George. *The Realistic Imagination.* Chicago: U of Chicago P, 1981.

Lindenbaum, Peter. "Milton's Contract." Woodmansee and Jaszi 175–90.

"Literary Property." *New York Review* 8 (April 1839): 273–307.

"Literary Property." *United States Magazine and Democratic Review* 2.7 (1838): 289–311.

Litman, Jessica. *Digital Copyright.* Amherst, NY: Prometheus Books, 2001.

Locke, John. *Two Treatises of Government.* Ed. Peter Laslett. Cambridge: Cambridge UP, 1988.

Loesberg, Jonathan. "The Ideology of Narrative Form in Sensation Fiction." *Representations* 13 (1986): 115–38.

Lonoff, Sue. "Charles Dickens and Wilkie Collins." *Nineteenth-Century Fiction* 35 (1980): 150–70.

Lukács, Georg. "The Ideology of Modernism." *Marxism and Human Liberation.* Trans. John and Necke Mander. New York: Dell, 1973. 277–307.

Macaulay, Thomas Babington. *The Works of Lord Macaulay, Complete, Edited by His Sister Lady Trevelyan.* 8 vols. London: Longmans, Green, and Co., 1875.

Macfarlane, Robert. *Original Copy: Plagiarism and Originality in Nineteenth-Century Literature.* Oxford: Oxford UP, 2007.

Malloch, A. E. "The Technique and Function of the Renaissance Paradox." *Studies in Philology* 53.2 (1956): 191–203.

Mallon, Thomas. *Stolen Words.* New York: Harvest, 2001.

Man, John. *The Gutenberg Revolution: The Story of a Genius and the Invention That Changed the World.* London: Review Press, 2002.

Mangham, Andrew. *Violent Women and Sensation Fiction: Crime, Medicine, and Victorian Popular Culture.* London: Palgrave Macmillan, 2007.

———, ed. *Wilkie Collins: Interdisciplinary Essays.* Newcastle: Cambridge Scholars Press, 2007.

[Mansel, H. L.] "Sensation Novels." *Quarterly Review* 113 (1863): 481–514.

Martin, Henri-Jean. *The History and Power of Writing.* Trans. Lydia G. Cochrane. Chicago: U of Chicago P, 1994.

"Martin Chuzzlewit." *Brother Jonathan* 29 July 1843: 379–80.

Matthews, Brander. "American Authors and British Pirates." *New Princeton Review* 1 (Jan. 1888): 47–65.

Maynard, John. *Literary Intention, Literary Interpretations, and Readers.* Peterborough, ON: Broadview Press, 2009.

McGill, Meredith. *American Literature and the Culture of Reprinting, 1834–1853*. Philadelphia: U of Pennsylvania P, 2002.

Meckier, Jerome. *Hidden Rivalries in Victorian Fiction: Dickens, Realism, and Revaluation*. Lexington: UP of Kentucky, 1987.

Mejan, Maurice. "Affaire de Madame de Douhault," 3:5ff., and "Suite de l'affaire de Madame de Douhault," 6:5–92. *Receuil des causes célèbres*. 2nd ed. Paris, 1808–1814.

Mencken, H. L. *The American Language: An Inquiry into the Development of English in the United States*. New York: A. A. Knopf, 1936.

Michie, Helena. "'There is No Friend Like a Sister': Sisterhood as Sexual Difference." *Sororophobia: Differences among Women in Literature and Culture*. By Michie. London: Oxford UP, 1992. 15–50.

Miller, D. A. *The Novel and the Police*. Berkeley: U of California P, 1988.

Miller, Henry K. "The Paradoxical Encomium with Special Reference to Its Vogue in England, 1600–1800." *Modern Philology* 53.3 (1956): 145–78.

Miller, J. Hillis. *Literature as Conduct—Speech Acts in Henry James*. New York: Fordham UP, 2005.

———. *Speech Acts in Literature*. Stanford, CA: Stanford UP, 2001.

Milley, H. J. W. "*The Eustace Diamonds* and *The Moonstone*." *Studies in Philology* 36 (October 1939): 651–63.

Milton, John. *Paradise Lost*. Ed. Merritt Y. Hughes. New York: Odyssey Press, 1962.

Moretti, Franco. *Graphs, Maps, and Trees: Abstract Models for a Literary History*. New York: Verso, 2005.

———, ed. *The Novel. Vol. 1, History, Geography, and Culture*. Princeton, NJ: Princeton UP, 2006.

———, ed. *The Novel. Vol. 2, Forms and Themes*. Princeton, NJ: Princeton UP, 2006.

"The most hopeless subject." *The Times* 26 November 1851: p. 4, cols. C–D.

Mott, Frank Luther. *Golden Multitudes: The Story of Best Sellers in the United States*. New York: Macmillan Co., 1947.

———. *A History of American Magazines*. 5 vols. Cambridge, MA: Belknap, 1957–68.

Murfin, Ross. "The Art of Representation: Collins' *The Moonstone* and Dickens' Example." *English Literary History* 49 (1982): 653–72.

Nabokov, Vladimir. *Bend Sinister*. New York: Vintage, 1990.

———. *Pale Fire*. New York: Vintage, 1989.

Nayder, Lillian. *Unequal Partners: Charles Dickens, Wilkie Collins, and Victorian Authorship*. Ithaca, NY: Cornell UP, 2002.

———. *Wilkie Collins*. New York: Twayne, 1997.

Nelson, Cary, ed. *Will Teach for Food: Academic Labor in Crisis*. Minneapolis: U of Minnesota P, 1997.

Nemesvari, Richard. "'Judged by a Purely Literary Standard': Sensation Fiction, Horizons of Expectation, and the Generic Construction of Victorian Realism." Harrison and Fantina 15–28.

"Note" on "The International Copyright Question: Protest against the Doctrine of the *Democratic Review* Thereon." *United States Magazine and Democratic Review* 12 (1843): 614–16.

Novalis. *Sämmtliche Werke*. Vol. 1. Leipzig: Diederichs, 1901.

Nowell-Smith, Simon. *International Copyright in the Reign of Queen Victoria*. Oxford: Clarendon Press, 1968.

Noyes, Russell. "Wordsworth and the Copyright Act of 1842: Addendum." *PMLA* 76 (1961): 380–83.

Oliphant, Margaret. "Novels." *Blackwood's* 94 (1863): 168–83.

———. "Novels." *Blackwood's* 102 (1867): 257–80.

———. "Sensation Novels." *Blackwood's* 91 (1862): 564–84.

O'Neill, Philip. *Wilkie Collins: Women, Property, and Propriety.* London: Macmillan, 1988.

Ousby, Ian. *Bloodhounds of Heaven: The Detective in English Fiction from Godwin to Doyle.* Cambridge, MA: Harvard UP, 1976.

Page, Norman, ed. *Wilkie Collins: The Critical Heritage.* London: Routledge & Kegan Paul, 1974.

Paget, Francis Edward, Rev. *Lucretia or, The Heroine of the Nineteenth Century: A Correspondence, Sensational and Sentimental.* London: Joseph Masters, 1868.

Pal-Lapinski, Piya. *The Exotic Woman in Nineteenth-Century British Fiction and Culture: A Reconsideration.* Durham, NH: U of New Hampshire P, 2005.

Patry, William. *Copyright Law and Practice.* Vol. 3. N.p.: The Bureau of National Affairs, 1994.

———. *How to Fix Copyright.* Oxford: Oxford UP, 2012.

———. *Moral Panics and the Copyright Wars.* Oxford: Oxford UP, 2009.

Patten, Robert L. *Charles Dickens and His Publishers.* Oxford: Clarendon Press, 1978.

Patterson, Lyman Ray. *Copyright in Historical Perspective.* Nashville: Vanderbilt UP, 1968.

Paulson, Ronald. "Gothic Fiction and the French Revolution." *English Literary History* 48 (1981): 532–54.

Payn, James. "A National Wrong." *Chambers's Edinburgh Journal* 4th ser., 47 (1870): 107–10.

Pederson-Krag, Geraldine. "Detective Stories and the Primal Scene." *Psychoanalytic Quarterly* 18 (1949): 207–14.

Perkins, Pamela, and Mary Donaghy. "A Man's Resolution: Narrative Strategies in Wilkie Collins' *The Woman in White.*" *Studies in the Novel* 22.4 (Winter 1990): 392–402.

Peters, Catherine. *The King of Inventors: A Life of Wilkie Collins.* London: Secker & Warburg, 1991.

Peterson, Audrey. *Victorian Masters of Mystery: From Wilkie Collins to Conan Doyle.* New York: Ungar, 1984.

Pettitt, Clare. *Patent Inventions—Intellectual Property and the Victorian Novel.* Oxford: Oxford UP, 2004.

Pfau, Thomas. "The Philosophy of Shipwreck: Gnosticism, Skepticism, and Coleridge's Catastrophic Modernity." *MLN* 122 (2007): 949–1004.

Phillips, Walter C. *Dickens, Reade, and Collins, Sensation Novelists: A Study in the Conditions and Theories of Novel Writing in Victorian England.* New York: Columbia UP, 1919; New York: Russell & Russell, 1962.

Phillips, Watts. *The Woman in Mauve: A Sensation Drama, in Three Acts.* London: Thomas Hailes Lacy, 1856.

Poe, Edgar Allan. *The Complete Works of Edgar Allan Poe.* Vol. 17. Ed. James A. Harrison. New York: Thomas Crowell, 1902.

———. *Poetry, Tales, and Selected Essays.* New York: Library of America, 1996.

———. "Reviews." *Broadway Journal* 1.1 (4 January 1845): 2–3.

———. "Some Secrets of the Magazine Prison-House." *Broadway Journal* 1.7 (15 February 1845): 103–4.

———. *The Works of the Late Edgar Allan Poe.* Ed. Rufus Griswold. 4 vols. New York: Redfield, 1857.

Poovey, Mary. "The Man-of-Letters Hero: *David Copperfield* and the Professional Writer." *Uneven Developments: The Ideological Work of Gender in Mid-Victorian England.* By Poovey. London: Virago, 1989. 89–125.

———. "Recent Studies of Gender" (review). *Modern Philology* 88.4 (May 1991): 415–20.

Post, Robert C. "Rereading Warren and Brandeis: Privacy, Property, and Appropriation." *Case Western Law Review* 41 (1991): 647–80.

Poulet, Georges. "Criticism and the Experience of Interiority." Trans. Catherine Macksey and Richard Macksey. *Reader-Response Criticism: From Formalism to Post-Structuralism.* Ed. Jane P. Tompkins. Baltimore: Johns Hopkins UP, 1980. 41–49.

Pratt, Mary Louise. "The Ideology of Speech-Act Theory." *Centrum* n.s. 1 (1981): 5–18.

Price, Leah. *The Anthology and the Rise of the Novel: From Richardson to George Eliot.* Cambridge: Cambridge UP, 2003.

Proudhon, Pierre-Joseph. *What Is Property?* Ed. and trans. Donald R. Kelley and Bonnie G. Smith. Cambridge: Cambridge UP, 1994.

Pykett, Lyn. "Collins and the Sensation Novel." Taylor, *Cambridge Companion* 50–64.

———. *The Sensation Novel: From* The Woman in White *to* The Moonstone. Plymouth, UK: Northcote House, 1994.

———. *Wilkie Collins.* Oxford: Oxford UP, 2005. Authors in Context Series.

Radin, Margaret Jane. "Property and Personhood." *Stanford Law Review* 34.5 (1982): 957–1015.

Rance, Nicholas. *Wilkie Collins and Other Sensation Novelists: Walking the Moral Hospital.* Basingstoke, UK: Macmillan, 1991.

Reade, Charles. *The Eighth Commandment.* Boston: Ticknor and Fields, 1860.

———. "The Rights and the Wrongs of Authors: To the Editor of the 'Pall Mall Gazette.'" *Readiana: Comments on Current Events.* London: Chatto and Windus, 1896. 111–205.

Reed, John R. "English Imperialism and the Unacknowledged Crime of *The Moonstone.*" *Clio* 2 (1973): 281–90.

Reitz, Caroline. "Colonial 'Gwilt': In and around Wilkie Collins's *Armadale.*" *Victorian Periodicals Review* 33.1 (Spring 2000): 92–103.

Reuters. "China, Russia Top U.S. Worst Pirates List Again." 2 May 2011. http://www.reuters.com/article/2011/05/02/oukwd-uk-usa-trade-piracy-idAFTRE74177S20110502.

Rev. of *On International Copyright; in a Letter to the Hon. William C. Preston, Senator of the United States,* by Francis Lieber. *North American Review* 51.2 (1840): 513–15.

Rev. of *Projet de loi relatif à une Convention littéraire entre la France et la Grande-Bretagne, précédé de l'exposé des motifs présenté par M. Turgot, Ministre des Affaires Etrangères, 11 Nov., 1851,* by Assemblée Nationale Legislative. *Edinburgh Review* 95 (Jan 1852): 145–52.

Rice, Grantland. *The Transformation of Authorship in America.* Chicago: U of Chicago P, 1997.

Richards, I. A. *Practical Criticism: A Study of Literary Judgment.* San Diego: Harcourt Brace & Co., 1929.

———. *Principles of Literary Criticism.* 2nd ed. 1926. London: Routledge, 2001.

Richards, Thomas. *The Imperial Archive: Knowledge and the Fantasy of Empire.* London: Verso, 1993.

Richardson, Maurice. "Introduction." *Novels of Mystery from the Victorian Age*. By Richardson. New York: Pilot Omnibus, 1946. vii–xvi.

Richetti, John, John Bender, Deirdre David, and Michael Seidel. *The Columbia History of the British Novel*. New York: Columbia UP, 1994.

Rose, Mark. "The Author as Proprietor: *Donaldson v. Becket* and the Genealogy of Modern Authorship." *Representations* 23 (Summer 1988): 51–85.

———. "The Author in Court: *Pope v. Curll* (1741)." Woodmansee and Jaszi 211–29.

———. *Authors and Owners: The Invention of Copyright*. Cambridge, MA: Harvard UP, 1993.

———. "Copyright and Its Metaphors." *UCLA Law Review* 50.1 (Oct. 2002): 1–15.

———. "Mothers and Authors: *Johnson v. Calvert* and the New Children of Our Imaginations." *Critical Inquiry* 22 (Summer 1996): 613–33.

Rotman, Brian. *Signifying Nothing: The Semiotics of Zero*. Stanford, CA: Stanford UP, 1993.

Roy, Ashish. "The Fabulous Imperialist Semiotic of Wilkie Collins's *The Moonstone*." *New Literary History* 24 (1993): 657–81.

Ryan, Alan. *Property and Political Theory*. Oxford: Blackwell, 1984.

Rycroft, Charles. "A Detective Story: Psychoanalytic Observations." *Psychoanalytic Quarterly* 26 (1957): 229–45.

Said, Edward. "Invention, Memory, and Place." *Critical Inquiry* 26.2 (Winter 2000): 175–92.

Saint-Amour, Paul K. *The Copywrights: Intellectual Property and the Literary Imagination*. Ithaca, NY: Cornell UP, 2003.

[Sala, G. A.] "The Foreign Invasion." *Household Words* 4.81 (11 Oct. 1851): 60–64.

Saunders, David. *Authorship and Copyright*. London: Routledge, 1992.

Saussure, Ferdinand de. *Cours de linguistique générale*. Ed. Charles Bally and Albert Sechehaye. Paris: Payot, 1985.

———. *Course in General Linguistics*. Trans. Roy Harris. London: Duckworth, 1983.

Sayers, Dorothy. *The Omnibus of Crime*. New York: Harcourt, Brace, 1929.

———. *Wilkie Collins: A Critical and Bibliographical Study*. Ed. E. R. Gregory. Toledo, OH: The Friends of the University of Toledo Libraries, 1977.

Schmitt, Cannon. "Alien Nation: Gender, Genre, and English Nationality in Wilkie Collins's *The Woman in White*." *Genre* 26 (1993): 283–310.

Sedgwick, Eve Kosofsky. *Between Men: English Literature and Male Homosocial Desire*. New York: Columbia UP, 1985.

Sessional Papers of the House of Commons. 1837.

Seville, Catherine. *The Internationalisation of Copyright Law: Books, Buccaneers, and the Black Flag in the Nineteenth Century*. Cambridge: Cambridge UP, 2006.

———. *Literary Copyright Reform in Early Victorian England: The Framing of the 1842 Copyright Act*. Cambridge: Cambridge UP, 1999.

Shakespeare, William. *The Riverside Shakespeare*. Ed. G. Blakemore Evans et al. Boston: Houghton Mifflin, 1974.

Shell, Marc. *Money, Language, and Thought*. Baltimore: Johns Hopkins UP, 1982.

Shelley, Mary Wollstonecraft. *Frankenstein, or The Modern Prometheus*. The 1818 text. Ed. James Rieger. Chicago: U of Chicago P, 1982.

Sheridan, Richard Brinsley. *The School for Scandal and Other Plays*. Ed. Michael Cordner. Oxford: Oxford UP, 1998.

Shillingsburg, Peter L. *Pegasus in Harness: Victorian Publishing and W. M. Thackeray.* Charlottesville: UP of Virginia, 1992.

Showalter, Elaine. *A Literature of Their Own.* Princeton, NJ: Princeton UP, 1977.

Smith, Nelson C., and R. C. Terry, eds. *Wilkie Collins to the Forefront: Some Reassessments.* New York: AMS Press, 1995.

Society for Promoting Christian Knowledge. *Industry of Nations, as Exemplified in the Great Exhibition of 1851.* London: The Society, 1852.

Solberg, T. "The Bibliography of International Copyright in the Congress of the United States, 1837–1891." *Publisher's Weekly* 39 (6 June 1891): 788–93.

———. "Copyright Law Reform." *Yale Law Journal* 35 (Nov. 1925): 48–75.

Spivak, Gayatri Chakravorty. *The Post-Colonial Critic: Interviews, Strategies, Dialogues.* Ed. Sarah Harasym. New York: Routledge, 1990.

———. "Three Women's Texts and a Critique of Imperialism." *"Race," Writing, and Difference.* Ed. Henry Louis Gates, Jr. Chicago: U of Chicago P, 1986. 262–80.

St. Clair, William. *The Reading Nation in the Romantic Period.* Cambridge: Cambridge UP, 2004.

Stange, G. Robert. Rev. of *No Name,* by Wilkie Collins. *Nineteenth-Century Fiction* 34.1 (June 1979): 96–100.

Steinberg, Sigfrid Henry. *Five Hundred Years of Printing.* Rev. John Trevitt. 4th ed. New Castle, DE: Oak Knoll Press, 1996.

Steiner, George. *Errata: An Examined Life.* New Haven, CT: Yale UP, 1997.

Steinlight, Emily. "Why Novels Are Redundant: Sensation Fiction and the Overpopulation of Literature." *ELH* 79.2 (Summer 2012): 501–35.

Stewart, Susan. *Crimes of Writing.* Durham, NC: Duke UP, 1994.

Stone, Brad. "Amazon Erases Orwell Books from Kindle." *New York Times* 18 July 2009: B1.

[Stylus]. *American Publishers and English Authors.* Baltimore: Eugene L. Didier, 1879.

Sutherland, John. "The Great Copyright Disaster." *London Review of Books* 17.1 (12 January 1995): 3–4.

———. *Is Heathcliff a Murderer?: Great Puzzles in Nineteenth-Century Fiction.* Oxford: Oxford UP, 2002.

———. "Publishing History: A Hole in the Centre of Literary Sociology." *Critical Inquiry* 14 (1988): 574–89.

———. *Victorian Fiction: Writers, Publishers, Readers.* Basingstoke, UK: Palgrave Press, 1995.

———. *Victorian Novelists and Publishers.* London: Athlone Press, 1976.

———. "What Sells Best, and Why." Rev. of *The Economy of Literary Form: English Literature and the Industrialization of Publishing, 1800–1850,* by Lee Erickson. *Times Literary Supplement* 31 May 1996: 27.

———. "Wilkie Collins and the Origins of the Sensation Novel." *Dickens Studies Annual* 20 (1991): 243–58.

Swartz, Richard. "Patrimony and the Figuration of Authorship in the Eighteenth-Century Literary Property Debates." *Works and Days* 7.2 (1989): 29–54.

———. "Wordsworth, Copyright, and the Commodities of Genius." *Modern Philology* 89 (May 1992): 482–509.

Talairach-Vielmas, Laurence. *Wilkie Collins, Medicine, and the Gothic.* Cardiff: U of Wales P, 2009.

Talfourd, Thomas Noon. *A Speech Delivered by Thomas Noon Talfourd, Sergeant at Law, in the House of Commons, on Thursday, 18th May, 1837, on moving for leave to bring in a bill to consolidate the law relating to copyright and to extend the term of its duration*. London: Moxon, 1837.

Taylor, Jenny Bourne. *In the Secret Theatre of Home: Wilkie Collins, Sensation Narrative, and Nineteenth-Century Psychology*. London: Routledge, 1988.

Taylor, Jenny Bourne, ed. *The Cambridge Companion to Wilkie Collins*. Cambridge: Cambridge UP, 2006.

Thomas, Ronald R. *Dreams of Authority: Freud and the Fictions of the Unconscious*. Ithaca, NY: Cornell UP, 1990.

———. "Wilkie Collins and the Sensation Novel." *The Columbia History of the British Novel*. Ed. John Richetti. New York: Columbia UP, 1994. 479–507.

Thoms, Peter. *The Windings of the Labyrinth: Quest and Structure in the Major Novels of Wilkie Collins*. Athens: Ohio UP, 1992.

Ticknor, Caroline. *Hawthorne and His Publisher*. Boston: Houghton Mifflin Company, 1913.

Tondre, Michael. "'The Interval of Expectation': Delay, Delusion, and the Psychology of Suspense in *Armadale*." *ELH* 78.3 (Fall 2011): 585–608.

Trodd, Anthea. *Domestic Crime in the Victorian Novel*. Basingstoke, UK: Macmillan, 1989.

Trollope, Anthony. *An Autobiography*. Ed. Michael Sadleir and Frederick Page. Oxford: Oxford UP, 1992.

Tromp, Marlene. *The Private Rod: Marital Violence, Sensation, and the Law in Victorian Britain*. Charlottesville: UP of Virginia, 2000.

Twain, Mark. Letter, *Springfield* (Mass.) *Republican*. *Publisher's Weekly* 20 (July–December 1881): 884–85.

Vaidhyanathan, Siva. *The Anarchists in the Library: How the Clash between Freedom and Control Is Hacking the Real World and Crashing the System*. New York: Basic Books, 2004.

———. *Copyrights and Copywrongs: The Rise of Intellectual Property and How It Threatens Creativity*. New York: New York UP, 2001.

Vanden Bossche, Chris R. "The Value of Literature: Representations of Print Culture in the Copyright Debate of 1837–1842." *Victorian Studies* (Autumn 1994): 41–68.

Veeser, H. Aram. Introduction. *The New Historicism*. Ed. H. Aram Veeser. New York: Routledge, 1989. ix–xvi.

Ward, William S. "An Early Champion of Wordsworth: Thomas Noon Talfourd." *PMLA* 68 (1953): 992–1000.

Warren, Samuel D., and Louis D. Brandeis. "The Right to Privacy." *Harvard Law Review* 4 (1890): 193–220.

Weber, Samuel. *Theatricality as Medium*. New York: Fordham UP, 2004.

Welsh, Alexander. *From Copyright to Copperfield: The Identity of Dickens*. Cambridge, MA: Harvard UP, 1987.

Whalen, Terence. *Edgar Allan Poe and the Masses: The Political Economy of Literature in Antebellum America*. Princeton, NJ: Princeton UP, 1999.

[Whately, Richard]. "Modern Novels." Rev. of *Northanger Abbey, and Persuasion*, by the author of *Sense and Sensibility, Pride and Prejudice, Mansfield Park*, and *Emma*, 4 vols., new edition. *Quarterly Review* 24 (January 1821): 352–76.

"Who Owns an Author's Ideas?" *The Nation* 4.104 (27 June 1867): 520–22.

Wiley, Margaret. *The Subtle Knot.* Cambridge, MA: Harvard UP, 1952.

Wiley, Vicki Corkran. "Wilkie Collins's 'Secret Dictate': *The Moonstone* as a Response to Imperialist Panic." Harrison and Fantina 225–33.

Wilson, Edmund. *Classics and Commercials.* New York: Noonday Press, 1950.

———. "Who Cares Who Killed Roger Ackroyd?" *Classics and Commercials.* By Wilson. 257–65.

———. "Why Do People Read Detective Stories?" *Classics and Commercials.* By Wilson. 231–37.

Wood, Ellen. *East Lynne.* Ed. Andrew Maunder. Peterborough, ON: Broadview Press, 2000.

Woodmansee, Martha. "The Cultural Work of Copyright: Legislating Authorship in Britain, 1837–1842." *Law in the Domains of Culture.* Ed. Austin Sarat and Thomas R. Kearns. Ann Arbor: U of Michigan P, 2000. 65–96.

———. "The Genius and the Copyright: Economic and Legal Conditions of the Emergence of the 'Author.'" *Eighteenth-Century Studies* 17.4 (Summer 1984): 425–48.

Woodmansee, Martha, and Peter Jaszi, eds. *The Construction of Authorship: Textual Appropriation in Law and Literature.* Durham, NC: Duke UP, 1994.

Wordsworth, William. *The Letters of William and Dorothy Wordsworth.* Ed. Ernest De Selincourt. Rev. and ed. Alan G. Hill, Mary Moorman, and Chester L. Shaver. 2nd ed. 8 vols. Oxford: Clarendon Press, 1967–1993.

Wynne, Deborah. *The Sensation Novel and the Victorian Family Magazine.* New York: Palgrave, 2001.

Yates, Edmund. "Mr. Wilkie Collins in Gloucester Place." *Celebrities at Home.* 3rd ser. London: Office of the World, 1879. 145–56. Rpt. in Wilkie Collins, *The Woman in White,* ed. Sucksmith, appendix C: 588–94.

Young-Zook, Monica M. "Wilkie Collins's Gwilt-y Conscience: Gender and Colonialism in *Armadale.*" Harrison and Fantina, 234–45.

Zall, Paul M. "Wordsworth and the Copyright Act of 1842." *PMLA* 70 (1955): 132–44.

Zigarovich, Jolene. "Wilkie Collins, Narrativity, and Epitaph." *Dickens Studies Annual* 36 (2005): 229–64.

⊹ INDEX ⊹